THE LADY'S OWN COOKERY BOOK, AND NEW DINNER-TABLE DIRECTORY

LECTOR HOUSE PUBLIC DOMAIN WORKS

THE LADY'S OWN COOKERY BOOK, AND NEW DINNER-TABLE DIRECTORY

CHARLOTTE CAMPBELL BURY

ISBN: 978-93-89614-45-9

Published: 1844

LECTOR HOUSE LLP
E-MAIL: lectorpublishing@gmail.com

THE LADY'S OWN COOKERY BOOK, AND NEW DINNER-TABLE DIRECTORY;

BY

CHARLOTTE CAMPBELL BURY

IN WHICH WILL BE FOUND A LARGE COLLECTION OF ORIGINAL RECEIPTS,

INCLUDING NOT ONLY
THE RESULT OF THE AUTHORESS'S MANY YEARS OBSERVATION,
EXPERIENCE, AND RESEARCH,
BUT ALSO THE

CONTRIBUTIONS

OF AN EXTENSIVE CIRCLE OF ACQUAINTANCE:
ADAPTED TO THE USE OF

PERSONS LIVING IN THE HIGHEST STYLE,

AS WELL AS THOSE OF
MODERATE FORTUNE.

THIRD EDITION.

1844.

PREFACE.

The Receipts composing the Volume here submitted to the Public have been collected under peculiarly favourable circumstances by a Lady of distinction, whose productions in the lighter department of literature entitle her to a place among the most successful writers of the present day. Moving in the first circles of rank and fashion, her associations have qualified her to furnish directions adapted to the manners and taste of the most refined Luxury; whilst long and attentive observation, and the communications of an extensive acquaintance, have enabled her equally to accommodate them to the use of persons of less ample means and of simpler and more economical habits.

When the task of arranging the mass of materials thus accumulated devolved upon the Editor, it became his study to give to them such a form as should be most convenient for constant reference. A glance at the "Contents," which might with equal propriety be denominated an Index, will, he flatters himself, convince the reader that this object has been accomplished. It will there be seen that the Receipts, upwards of Sixteen Hundred in number, are classed under Eleven distinct Heads, each of which is arranged in alphabetical order—a method which confers on this Volume a decided advantage over every other work of the kind, inasmuch as it affords all the facilities of a Dictionary, without being liable to the unpleasant intermixture of heterogeneous matters which cannot be avoided in that form of arrangement.

The intimate connexion between the Science of Cookery and the Science of Health, the sympathies subsisting between every part of the system and the stomach, and the absolute necessity of strict attention not less to the manner of preparing the alimentary substances offered to that organ than to their quality and quantity, have been of late years so repeatedly and so forcibly urged by professional pens, that there needs no argument here to prove the utility of a safe Guide and Director in so important a department of domestic economy as that which is the subject of this Volume. In many more cases, indeed, than the uninitiated would imagine, is the healthy tone of the stomach dependent on the proper preparation of the food, the healthy tone of the body in general on that of the stomach, and the healthy tone of the mind on that of the body: consequently the first of these conditions ought to command the vigilance and solicitude of all who are desirous of securing the true enjoyment of life—the *mens sana in corpore sano.*

The professed Cook may perhaps be disposed to form a mean estimate of these pages, because few, or no learned, or technical, terms are employed in them; but this circumstance, so far from operating to the disparagement of the work, must prove a strong recommendation to the Public in general. The chief aim, in fact, of the noble Authoress has been to furnish such plain directions, in every branch of the culinary art, as shall be really useful to English masters and English servants, and to the humble but earnest practitioner. Let those who may desire to put this collection of receipts to the test only give them a fair trial, neither trusting to conceited servants, who, despising all other methods, obstinately adhere to their own, and then lay the blame of failure upon the directions; nor committing their execution to careless ones, who neglect the means prescribed for success, either in regard to time, quantities, or cleanliness; and the result will not fail to afford satisfactory evidence of their pleasant qualities and practical utility.

CONTENTS

BROTHS.

FISH.

MADE DISHES.

THE LADY'S OWN COOKERY BOOK

MEATS AND VEGETABLES.

CONTENTS

xix

POULTRY.

GAME.

SAUCES.

CONFECTIONARY.

WINES, CORDIALS, LIQUEURS, &C.

CONTENTS

lv

THE LADY'S OWN COOKERY BOOK.

GENERAL DIRECTIONS.

THE following directions may appear trite and common, but it is of the greatest consequence that they be strictly observed:

Attend to minute cleanliness. Never wipe a dish, bowl, or pan, with a half dirty napkin, or give the vessel a mere rinse in water and think that it is then fit for use. See that it be dried and pure from all smell before you put in any ingredient.

Never use the hands when it is possible to avoid it; and, when you do, have a clean basin of water to dip them in, and wipe them thoroughly several times while at work, as in mixing dough, &c.

Use silver or wooden spoons; the latter are best for all confectionery and puddings. Take care that the various spoons, skewers, and knives, be not used promiscuously for cookery and confectionery, or even for different dishes of the same sort.

If an onion is cut with any knife, or lies near any article of kitchen use, that article is not fit for service till it has been duly scoured and laid in the open air. The same remark applies to very many strong kitchen herbs. This point is scarcely ever enough attended to.

In measuring quantities, be extremely exact, having always some particular vessel set apart for each ingredient (best of earthenware, because such cannot retain any smell) wherewith to ascertain your quantities. Do nothing by guess, how practised soever you may deem yourself in the art: nor say "Oh! I want none of your measures for such a thing as a little seasoning," taking a pinch here and there. Be assured you will never in that way make a dish, or a sauce, twice in the same manner; it may be good by *chance*, but it will always be a *chance*, and the chances are very much against it; at all events it will not be precisely the *same* thing, and precision is the very essence of good cookery.

The French say *Il faut que rien ne domine*—No one ingredient must predominate. This is a good rule to please general taste and great judges; but, to secure the favour of a particular palate it is not infallible: as, in a good herb soup, for instance, it may better delight the master or mistress that some one herb or savoury meat *should* predominate. Consult, therefore, the peculiarities of the tastes of your employer; for, though a dish may be a good dish of its kind, if it is not suited to the taste of the eater of what avail is it?

Let not the vanity of the cook induce you to forget the duty of a servant, which is, in the first place, to please his master: be particular, therefore, in enquiring what things please your employer. Many capital cooks will be found for great feasts and festivals, but very few for every-day service, because this is not "eye-service," but the service of principle and duty. Few, indeed, there are who will take equal pains to make one delicate dish, one small exquisite dinner, for the three hundred and sixty-five days in the year; yet this is by far the most valuable attainment of the two.

The great secret of all cookery consists in making fine meat jellies; this is done at less expence than may be imagined by a *careful, honest* cook. For this purpose let all parings of meats of every kind, all bones, however dry they may appear, be carefully collected, and put over a very slow fire in a small quantity of water, always adding a little more as the water boils down. Skim this juice when cool: and, having melted it a second time, pass it through a sieve till thoroughly pure: put no salt or pepper; use this fine jelly for any sauce, adding herbs, or whatever savoury condiments you think proper, at the time it is used.

Be careful all summer long to dry vegetables and herbs. Almost every herb and vegetable may be dried and preserved for winter use; for on these must chiefly depend all the varied flavours of your dishes. Mushrooms and artichokes strung on a string, with a bit of wood knotted in between each to prevent their touching, and hung in a dry place, will be excellent; and every species of culinary herb may be preserved either in bottles or paper bags.

A CATALOGUE OF THINGS IN SEASON.

JANUARY.

Fish.

Cod, skate, thornback, salmon, soles, eels, perch, carp, tench, flounders, prawns, lobsters, crabs, shrimps, cockles, muscles, oysters, smelts, whiting.

Game and Poultry.

Hares, pheasants, partridges, wild ducks, widgeon, teal, capons, pullets, fowls, chickens, squab-pigeons, tame rabbits, woodcocks, snipes, larks, blackbirds, and wood-pigeons.

Fruit.

Portugal grapes, the Kentish russet, golden French kirton, Dutch pippins, non-pareils, pearmains, russetting apples, and all sorts of winter pears.

Roots and Vegetables.

Many sorts of cabbages, savoys, sprouts, and greens, parsnips, carrots, turnips, potatoes, celery, endive, cabbage-lettuces, leeks, onions, horseradish, small salad under glasses, sweet herbs, and parsley, green and white brocoli, beet-root, beet-leaves and tops, forced asparagus, cucumbers in hotbeds, French beans and peas in the hothouse.

FEBRUARY.

Fish.

Cod, skate, thornback, salmon, sturgeon, soles, flounders, whitings, smelts, crabs, lobsters, prawns, shrimps, oysters, eels, crawfish, carp, tench, and perch.

Game and Poultry.

Hares and partridges till the 14th. Turkeys, capons, pullets with eggs, fowls, chickens, tame rabbits, woodcocks, snipes, all sorts of wild-fowl, which begin to decline in this month.

Fruit.

Nearly the same as last month.

Roots and Vegetables.

The same as last month.

MARCH.

Fish.

Cod and codlings, turbot, salmon, skate, thornback, smelts, soles, crabs, lobsters, prawns, flounders, plaice, oysters, perch, carp, tench, eels, gudgeons, mullet, and sometimes mackerel, comes in.

Poultry.

Turkeys, pullets, fowls, chickens, ducklings, tame rabbits, pigeons, guinea-fowl.

Fruit.

Pineapples, the golden ducket, Dorset pippins, rennetings, Loan's pearmain, nonpareils, John apples, the later bonchretien and double-blossom pears.

Roots and Vegetables.

Carrots, parsnips, turnips, potatoes, beet, leeks, onions, green and white brocoli, brocoli sprouts, brown and green cole, cabbage sprouts, greens, spinach, small salad, parsley, sorrel, corn salad, green fennel, sweet herbs of all sorts, cabbage lettuces, forced mushrooms, asparagus forced, cucumbers in hotbeds, French beans and peas in hothouses, and young radishes and onions.

APRIL.

Fish.

Salmon, turbot, mackerel, skate, thornback, red and grey mullet, gurnets, pipers, soles, lobsters, oysters, prawns, crawfish, smelts, carp, perch, pike, gudgeons, eels, and plaice.

Game and Poultry.

Pullets, fowls, chickens, ducklings, pigeons, tame rabbits, and sometimes young leverets, guinea-fowl.

Fruit.

A few apples and pears, pineapples, hothouse grapes, strawberries, cherries, apricots for tarts, and green gooseberries.

Roots and Vegetables.

Carrots, potatoes, horseradish, onions, leeks, celery, brocoli sprouts, cabbage plants, cabbage lettuce, asparagus, spinach, parsley, thyme, all sorts of small salads, young radishes and onions, cucumbers in hotbeds, French beans and peas in the hothouse, green fennel, sorrel, chervil, and, if the weather is fine, all sorts of sweet herbs begin to grow.

MAY.

Fish.

Turbot, salmon, soles, smelts, trout, whiting, mackerel, herrings, eels, plaice, flounders, crabs, lobsters, prawns, shrimps, crawfish.

Game and Poultry.

Pullets, fowls, chickens, guinea-fowl, green geese, ducklings, pigeons, tame rabbits, leverets, and sometimes turkey poults.

Fruit.

Strawberries, green apricots, cherries, gooseberries, and currants, for tarts, hothouse pineapples, grapes, apricots, peaches, and fine cherries.

Roots and Vegetables.

Spring carrots, horseradish, beet-root, early cauliflower, spring cabbage, sprouts, spinach, coss, cabbage, and Silesia lettuces, all sorts of small salads, asparagus, hotspur beans, peas, fennel, mint, balm, parsley, all sorts of sweet herbs, cucumbers and French beans forced, radishes, and young onions, mushrooms in the cucumber beds.

JUNE.

Fish.

Turbot, trout, mackerel, mullet, salmon, salmon trout, soles, smelts, eels, lobsters, crabs, crawfish, prawns, and shrimps.

Game and Poultry.

Spring fowls, and chickens, geese, ducks, turkey poults, young wild and tame rabbits, pigeons, leverets, and wheatears.

Fruit.

Pineapples, currants, gooseberries, scarlet strawberries, hautboys, several sorts of cherries, apricots, and green codlings.

Roots and Vegetables.

Young carrots, early potatoes, young turnips, peas, garden beans, cauliflowers, summer cabbages, spinach, coss, cabbage, and Silesia lettuces, French beans, cucumbers, asparagus, mushrooms, purslain, radishes, turnip-radishes, horseradish, and onions.

JULY.

Fish.

Turbot, salmon, salmon trout, Berwick and fresh water trout, red and grey mullet, Johndories, skate, thornback, maids, soles, flounders, eels, lobsters, crawfish, prawns, and shrimps.

Game and Poultry.

Leverets, geese, ducks and ducklings, fowls, chickens, turkey poults, quails, wild rabbits, wheatears, and young wild ducks.

Fruit.

Pineapples, peaches, apricots, scarlet and wood strawberries, hautboys, summer apples, codlings, summer pears, green-gage and Orleans plums, melons, currants, gooseberries, raspberries, cherries of all kinds, and green walnuts to pickle.

Roots and Vegetables.

Carrots, potatoes, turnips, onions, cauliflowers, marrowfat and other peas, Windsor beans, French beans, mushrooms, sorrel, artichokes, spinach, cabbages, cucumbers, coss and cabbage lettuces, parsley, all sorts of sweet and potherbs, mint, balm, salsify, and field mushrooms.

AUGUST.

Fish.

Codlings, some turbot, which goes out this month, skate, thornback, maids, haddock, flounders, red and grey mullet, Johndories, pike, perch, gudgeons, roach, eels, oysters, crawfish, some salmon, salmon trout, Berwick and fresh water trout.

Game and Poultry.

Leverets, geese, turkey poults, ducks, fowls, chickens, wild rabbits, quails, wheatears, young wild ducks, and some pigeons.

Fruit.

Pineapples, melons, cherries, apricots, peaches, nectarines, apples, pears, all sorts of plums, morella cherries, filberts and other nuts, currants, raspberries, late gooseberries, figs, early grapes, mulberries, and ripe codlings.

Roots and Vegetables.

Carrots, parsnips, turnips, potatoes, onions, horseradish, beet-root, shalots, garlic, cauliflower, French beans, later peas, cucumbers, cabbages, sprouts, coss lettuce, endive, celery, parsley, sweet herbs, artichokes, artichoke suckers, chardoons, mushrooms, and all sorts of small salads.

SEPTEMBER.

Fish.

Cod, codlings, skate, thornback, haddocks, soles, whitings, herrings come in full season, salmon, smelts, flounders, pike, perch, carp, tench, eels, lampreys, oysters, cockles, muscles, crawfish, prawns, and shrimps.

Game and Poultry.

Hares, leverets, partridges, quails, young turkeys, geese, ducks, capons, pullets, fowls, chickens, pigeons, wild and tame rabbits, wild ducks, widgeon, teal, plover, larks, and pippets.

Fruit.

Pineapples, melons, grapes, peaches, plums, nectarines, pears, apples, quinces, medlars, filberts, hazel nuts, walnuts, morella cherries, damsons, white and black bullace.

Roots and Vegetables.

Carrots, parsnips, potatoes, turnips, leeks, horseradish, beet-root, onions, shalots, garlic, celery, endive, coss and cabbage lettuces, artichokes, French beans, latter peas, mushrooms, cucumbers, red and other cabbages, cabbage plants, Jerusalem artichokes, parsley, sorrel, chervil, thyme, all sorts of sweet herbs, mint, balm, all sorts of small salad.

OCTOBER.

Fish.

Cod, codlings, brill, haddocks, whiting, soles, herrings, cole-fish, halibut, smelts, eels, flounders, perch, pike, carp, tench, oysters, cockles, muscles, lobsters, crabs, crawfish, prawns, and shrimps.

Game and Poultry.

Hares, leverets, pheasants, partridges, moor-game, grouse, turkeys, geese, ducks, capons, pullets, fowls, chickens, pigeons, wild and tame rabbits, all sorts of wild-fowl, larks, plovers, woodcocks, snipes, wood-pigeons, pippets.

Fruit.

Pineapples, peaches, grapes, figs, medlars, all sorts of fine apples and pears, white plums, damsons, white and black bullace, quinces, filberts, walnuts, and chesnuts.

Roots and Vegetables.

Carrots, parsnips, potatoes, turnips, leeks, horseradish, onions, shalots, garlic, beet-root, artichokes, latter cauliflowers, red and white cabbages, savoys, cabbage plants, green and white brocoli, chardoons, green and brown cole, celery, endive, spinach, sorrel, chervil, parsley, purslain, all sorts of sweet herbs, coss and cabbage lettuces, rocambole, and all sorts of small salads.

NOVEMBER.

Fish.

Cod, salmon, herrings, barbel, halibut, smelts, flounders, whiting, haddock, pipers, gurnets, pike, perch, carp, tench, eels, lobsters, crabs, oysters, muscles, cockles, crawfish, prawns, and shrimps.

Game and Poultry.

The same as last month.

Fruit.

Pineapples, all sorts of winter pears, golden pippins, nonpareils, all sorts of winter apples, medlars, white and black bullace, and walnuts kept in sand.

Roots and Vegetables.

Turnips, potatoes, carrots, parsnips, beets, chardoons, onions, shalots, garlic, rocambole, cauliflowers in the greenhouse, red and other cabbages, savoys, cabbage plants, winter spinach, forced asparagus, late cucumbers, forced mushrooms, parsley, sorrel, chervil, thyme, all sorts of sweet herbs, celery, endive, cabbage lettuces, brown and green cole, and all sorts of small salads under glasses.

DECEMBER.

Fish.

Cod, codlings, halibut, skate, sturgeon, soles, salmon, gurnets, haddock, whiting, sometimes turbots come with the soles, herrings, perch, pike, carp, tench, eels, lobsters, crabs, crawfish, muscles, cockles, prawns, shrimps, Thames flounders, and smelts.

Game and Poultry.

Hares, pheasants, partridges, moor or heath game, grouse, turkeys, geese, capons, pullets, fowls, chickens, all sorts of wild-fowl, wood cocks, snipes, larks, wild and tame rabbits, dottrels, wood-pigeons, blackbirds, thrushes, plover both green and grey.

Fruit.

All sorts of winter pears and apples, medlars, chesnuts, Portugal grapes and grapes hung in the room, and walnuts kept in sand.

Roots and Vegetables.

Same as the last month.

Beef, mutton, and veal, are in season all the year; house lamb in January, February, March, April, May, October, November, and December. Grass lamb comes in at Easter and lasts till April or May; pork from September till April or May; roasting pigs all the year; buck venison in June, July, August, and September; doe and heifer venison in October, November, December, and January.

GENERAL RULES FOR A GOOD DINNER.

THERE should be always two soups, white and brown, two fish, dressed and undressed; a bouilli and petits-patés; and on the sideboard a plain roast joint, besides many savoury articles, such as hung beef, Bologna sausages, pickles, cold ham, cold pie, &c. some or all of these according to the number of guests, the names of which the head-servant ought to whisper about to the company, occasionally offering them. He should likewise carry about all the side-dishes or *entrées*, after the soups are taken away in rotation. A silver lamp should be kept burning, to put any dish upon that may grow cold.

It is indispensable to have candles, or plateau, or epergne, in the middle of the table.

Beware of letting the table appear loaded; neither should it be too bare. The soups and fish should be dispatched before the rest of the dinner is set on; but, lest any of the guests eat of neither, two small dishes of patés should be on the table. Of course, the meats and vegetables and fruits which compose these dinners must be varied according to the season, the number of guests, and the tastes of the host and hostess. It is also needless to add that without iced champagne and Roman punch a dinner is not called a dinner.

These observations and the following directions for dinners are suitable to persons who chuse to live *fashionably*; but the receipts contained in this book will suit any mode of living, and the persons consulting it will find matter for all tastes and all establishments. There is many an excellent dish not considered adapted to a fashionable table, which, nevertheless, is given in these pages.

A DINNER FOR FOURTEEN OR SIXTEEN PERSONS.

N.B. It is the fashion to lay two table-cloths, and never to leave the table uncovered. Of course, the individual things must be varied according to the season.

FIRST COURSE.

Queen Soup, white,
removed by
Plain boiled Turbot.
Petits Patés of Oysters.

Plateau, or Epergne, or Candles.

Petits Patés of Chickens.
Herb Soup, brown,
removed by
Dressed fish (Salmon.)

Remove the whole and set on as follows:—

FIRST COURSE (CONTINUED).

Sweetbreads, larded.

Reindeer Tongues, highly dressed in sauce.

Macaroni, with Parmesan cheese.

Mutton Cutlets glazed in onion sauce.

Stewed Beef, with Vegetables.

Dressed Peas.

Plateau.

Stuffed Cabbage.

Small Beef Pies.

Rissoles of Veal and Ham, served in sauce.

Dressed Eggs.

Supreme of Fowls.

Vol-au-vent.

Roasted Turkey,
with truffles,
morels, chesnuts, &c.

Small breast
of Veal
glazed brown,
with
Peas under.

On the sideboard, fish sauces, cold pie, hot ham, saddle of mutton roasted; pickles, cucumbers, salad, mashed potatoes, greens, and cauliflowers, crumbs of bread, and grated Parmesan cheese. These should be handed round, to eat with soup, or game, or fowl, if liked.

SECOND COURSE.

Cauliflower,
with cheese.

Larded Hare,
removed by
Souffle[1].

Apples
in compote.

Orange
Jelly.

Puffs and
Tartlets.

Stewed
Partridges.

Plateau.

Dressed
Pigeons.

Creams
in
Glasses.

Italian
Cream.

Small Pud-
dings,
with sauce.

Two roasted Pheasants,
one larded,
one plain,
removed by
Fondu[2].

Jerusalem
Artichokes.

Remove the whole.

---

[1] Light sweet Pudding.
[2] Melted Cheese.

THIRD COURSE.

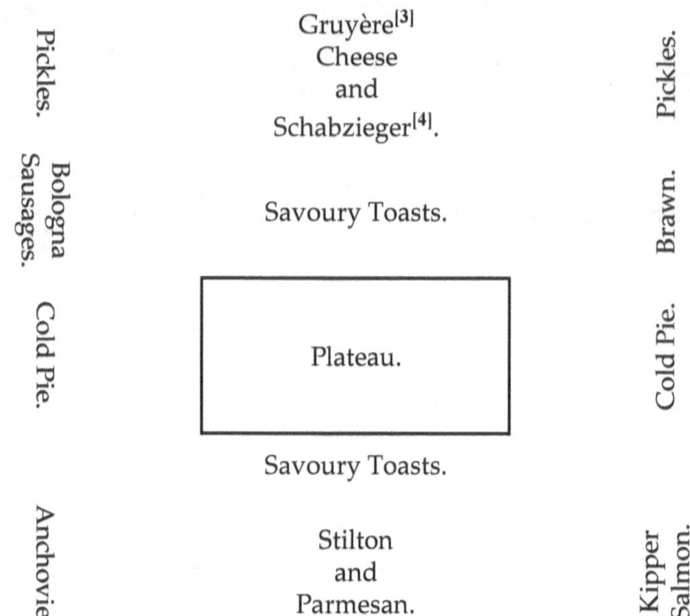

Gruyère[3]
Cheese
and
Schabzieger[4].

Savoury Toasts.

Plateau.

Savoury Toasts.

Stilton
and
Parmesan.

Pickles.

Bologna Sausages.

Cold Pie.

Anchovies.

Pickles.

Brawn.

Cold Pie.

Kipper Salmon.

Radishes, cucumbers, salad, butter, &c. to be handed from the side table.

DESSERT.

Cream Ice,
removed by
a Preserved
Pineapple.

Cake.

Plateau.

Cake.

Pistachio Nuts and Orange chips.

Dried Sweet-meats.

Chantilly Basket.

Almonds and Rai-sins.

Figs.

Pre-served Plums.

Pyramid with various Sweetmeats.

Preserves of Apricots.

---

[3] Swiss cheeses.
[4] Swiss cheeses.

Brandy
Cherries.

Water Ice
à la Macedoine,
removed by
Grapes.

Sugared
Walnuts.

DINNER FOR TWELVE OR FOURTEEN PERSONS.

FIRST COURSE.

White Soups,
removed by plain Fish:
removed by Bouilli,
dressed according to
any
of the various receipts.

Patés.

Lamb Cutlets and Asparagus sauce.

Stewed Chicken.

Dressed Vegetable
in a mould.

Fricandeau, or Sorrel sauce.

Beef Olives.

Plateau.

Small savoury Pies.

Small Ham, glazed.

Macaroni
in a mould.

Patés.

Breast of Veal, stewed
white, as per receipt.

Dressed Eggs.

Small Ragout of Mutton.

Any of the Brown
Soups,
removed by any of the
dressed Fish.

Sideboard furnished with plain joint and vegetables of all sorts, pickles, &c.

SECOND COURSE.

Grouse.

Tart.

Plateau.

Trifle.

Leveret.

Charlotte.

Jelly.

Par-tridges.

Fried Arti-chokes.

Plover's Eggs.

Cus-tards.

Wood-cocks.

Dressed Sea Kale.

THIRD COURSE.

Various Cheeses,
with
Red Herring.

Savoury Toasts.

Plateau.

Savoury Toasts.

Potted Game.

Radishes,
Cucumbers,
&c.

Sausages, &c.

DESSERT.

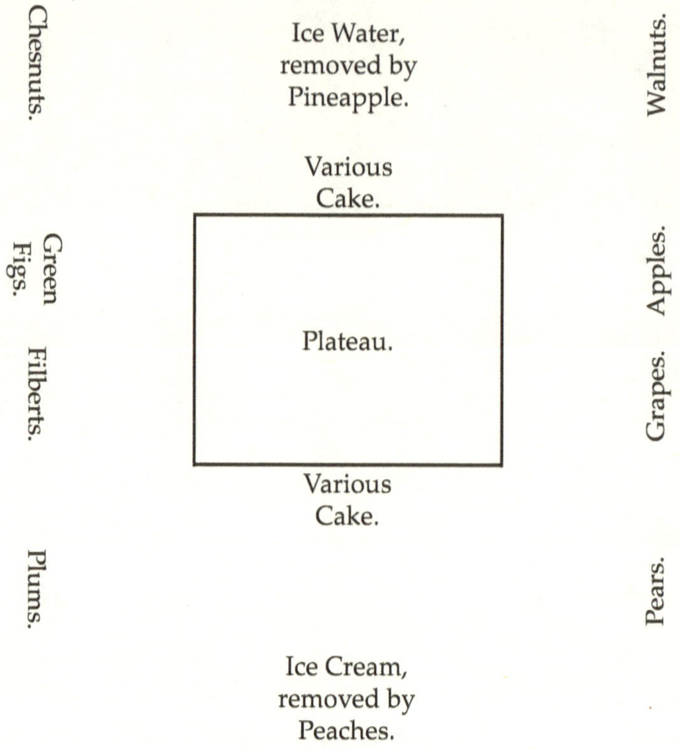

Ice Water,
removed by
Pineapple.

Various
Cake.

Chesnuts.

Walnuts.

Green Figs.

Filberts.

Plums.

Plateau.

Apples.

Grapes.

Pears.

Various
Cake.

Ice Cream,
removed by
Peaches.

DINNER FOR TEN OR TWELVE PERSONS.

FIRST COURSE.

Brown Soup,
removed by
Fish,
removed by
Boiled Turkey,
white sauce.

Scotch Collops, brown. — Vol-au-vent of Chicken. — Cutlets with Tomata sauce. — Macaroni in paste.

Ragout of Ham. — Fricandeau, with Spinach. — Rissoles of Fowl. — Patés of Veal.

Plateau.

White Soup,
removed by
Dressed Fish,
removed by
Roast Mutton.

Sideboard — salad, brocoli, mashed potatoes, cold pie, potted meats.

SECOND COURSE.

Peahen,
larded.

Orange Jelly. — Stewed Truffles. — Tart, Sponge Cake, with Custard.

Plum Puddings. — Blanc-mange. — Eggs, with white sauce, cheesecakes.

Plateau.

Two
Wild Fowls.

Sideboard, Sea Kale, Pickles, Greens, Potatoes.

THIRD COURSE.

Gruyère—Schabzieger.

Butter.

Celery.

Grated Parmesan.

Rad-ishes.

Cheese in square pieces.

Plateau.

Salad.

DESSERT.

Ice.

Biscuits.

Cur-rants.

Apricots.

Various Cakes.

Straw-berries.

Pre-served Orange.

Preserved Pine.

Plateau.

Cherries.

Cakes.

Peaches.

Gooseber-ries.

Wafers.

Ice.

DINNER FOR EIGHT PERSONS.

FIRST COURSE.

Dressed Asparagus.

Patés of Veal and Ham.

Fish,
removed by
Loin of Mutton,
rolled with
Tomata sauce.

Dressed Tongues.

Beef Olives. Stewed Spinach.

Plateau.

Soup,
removed by
Roast Neck of Veal,
with rich white sauce
and Mushrooms.

Macaroni.

Stewed Spinach.

Sideboard, a bouilli, a joint, pickles, plain boiled vegetables, &c.

SECOND COURSE.

Dressed Eggs.

Dressed French beans.

Stewed Pigeons,
removed by
a Fondu.

Apple Tart.

Four small Plum Puddings.

Plateau.

<table>
<tr><td>Fried Artichokes.</td><td>Roast Fowl,
with
Water Cresses,
removed by
Souffle.</td><td>Dressed Ham.</td></tr>
</table>

When a plain roast fowl, there should be on the sideboard egg sauce or bread sauce; if a plain duck, wine sauce or onion sauce.

CHEESE COURSE.

Various Cheeses,
Bologna Sausages,
Pickles.
Savoury Toasts,
&c. &c.

DESSERT.

Ice Cream,
removed by
a large Cake
stuck with
Sweetmeats.

<table>
<tr><td>Oranges.</td><td></td><td>Brandy
Cherries.</td><td></td><td>Dry Pre-
serves.</td></tr>
<tr><td></td><td>Wet Pre-
serves.</td><td>Plateau.</td><td>Apples.</td><td></td></tr>
<tr><td></td><td></td><td>Brandy
Peaches.
Strawberries.</td><td></td><td></td></tr>
</table>

DINNER FOR SIX PERSONS.

FIRST COURSE.

Asparagus Soup,
removed by
Fish,
removed by
Roast Veal
bechamelled.

Small Ham.

Sea Kale,
white sauce.

Plateau.

Stewed Turnips, browned.

Mutton Cutlets, Sauce piquante.

Alamode
Beef.

SECOND COURSE.

Turkey Poult stuffed,
glazed brown,
fine rich brown sauce
under.

Blancmange.

Croquets
of Potatoes.

Plateau.

Dressed Peas.

Stewed Duck,
with Truffles, Morells,
&c.

Tart.

THIRD COURSE.

Two or three sorts of cheeses (plain), a small fondu, relishes, &c.

DESSERT.

Brandy Peaches.

Ice,
removed by
Preserved Citron.

Apples.

<table>
<tr><td rowspan="2">Oranges.</td><td style="text-align:center; border:1px solid;">Plateau.</td><td rowspan="2">Dry Pre-
serves.</td></tr>
<tr><td style="text-align:center;">Large Cake
like a hedgehog,
stuck with Almonds.</td></tr>
</table>

DINNER FOR FOUR PERSONS.

FIRST COURSE.

Hare Soup,
removed by
Fish,
removed by
Bouilli Beef.

Tendrons de veau. | Plateau. | Dressed Ham. Brocoli.

Chicken Pie

SECOND COURSE.

Widgeon.

Raspberry Cream. Croquettes of Potatoes. | Plateau. | Stewed French Beans.   Tart.

Partridge.

Cheese as usual.

DESSERT.

Orange Chips.   Dry Preserves.
Wet Preserves.   Wafers.

SOUPS.

Almond Soup.

TAKE lean beef or veal, about eight or nine pounds, and a scrag of mutton; boil them gently in water that will cover them, till the gravy be very strong and the meat very tender; then strain off the gravy and set it on the fire with two ounces of vermicelli, eight blades of mace, twelve cloves, to a gallon. Let it boil till it has the flavour of the spices. Have ready one pound of the best almonds, blanched and pounded very fine; pound them with the yolks of twelve eggs, boiled hard, mixing as you pound them with a little of the soup, lest the almonds should grow oily. Pound them till they are a mere pulp: add a little soup by degrees to the almonds and eggs until mixed together. Let the soup be cool when you mix it, and do it perfectly smooth. Strain it through a sieve; set it on the fire; stir it frequently; and serve it hot. Just before you take it up add a gill of thick cream.

Asparagus Soup.

Put five or six pounds of lean beef, cut in pieces and rolled in flour, into your stewpan, with two or three slices of bacon at the bottom: set it on a slow fire and cover it close, stirring it now and then, till your gravy is drawn; then put in two quarts of water and half a pint of pale ale; cover it close and let it stew gently for an hour. Put in some whole pepper and salt to your taste. Then strain out the liquor and take off the fat; put in the leaves of white beet, some spinach, some cabbage lettuce, a little mint, sorrel, and sweet marjoram, pounded; let these boil up in your liquor. Then put in your green tops of asparagus, cut small, and let them boil till all is tender. Serve hot, with the crust of a French roll in the dish.

Another.

Boil three half pints of winter split peas; rub them through a sieve; add a little gravy; then stew by themselves the following herbs:—celery, a few young onions, a lettuce, cut small, and about half a pint of asparagus, cut small, like peas, and stewed with the rest; colour the soup of a pea green with spinach juice; add half a pint of cream or good milk, and serve up.

Calf's Head Soup.

Take a knuckle of veal, and put as much water to it as will make a good soup; let it boil, skimming it very well. Add two carrots, three anchovies, a little mace, pepper, celery, two onions, and some sweetherbs. Let it boil to a good soup, and strain it off. Put to it a full half pint of Madeira wine; take a good many mushrooms, stew them in their own liquor; add this sauce to your soup. Scald the calf's head as for a hash; cut it in the same manner, but smaller; flour it a little, and fry it of a fine brown. Then put the soup and fried head together into a stewpan, with some oysters and mushrooms, and let them stew gently for an hour.

Carrot Soup.

Take about two pounds of veal and the same of lean beef; make it into a broth or gravy, and put it by until wanted. Take a quarter of a pound of butter, four large fine carrots, two turnips, two parsnips, two heads of celery, and four onions; stew these together about two hours, and shake it often that they may not burn to the stewpan; then add the broth made as above, boiling hot, in quantity to your own judgment, and as you like it for thickness. It should be of about the consistency of pea-soup. Pass it through a tamis. Season to your taste.

Another.

Take four pounds of beef, a scrag of mutton, about a dozen large carrots, four onions, some pepper and salt; put them into a gallon of water, and boil very gently for four hours. Strain the meat, and take the carrots and rub them very smooth through a hair sieve, adding the gravy by degrees till about as thick as cream. The gravy must have all the fat taken off before it is added to the carrots. Turnip soup is made in the same way.

Clear Soup.

Take six pounds of gravy beef; cut it small, put it into a large stewpan, with onions, carrots, turnips, celery, a small bunch of herbs, and one cup of water. Stew these on the fire for an hour, then add nine pints of boiling water; let it boil for six hours, strain it through a fine sieve, and let it stand till next day; take off the fat; put it into a clean stewpan, set it on the fire till it is quite hot; then break three eggs into a basin, leaving the shells with them. Add this to the soup by degrees; cover close till it boils; then strain it into a pan through a fine cloth. When the eggs are well beaten, a little hot soup must be added by degrees, and beaten up before it is put into the stewpan with the whole of the soup.

Clear Herb Soup.

Put celery, leeks, carrots, turnips, cabbage lettuce, young onions, all cut fine, with a handful of young peas: give them a scald in boiling water; put them on a sieve to drain, and then put them into a clear consommé, and let them boil slowly till the roots are quite tender. Season with a little salt. When going to table put a little crust of French roll in it.

Cod's Head Soup.

Take six large onions, cut them in slices, and put them in a stewpan, with a quarter of a pound of the freshest butter. Set it in a stove to simmer for an hour, covered up close; take the head, and with a knife and fork pick all the fins you can get off the fish. Put this in a dish, dredge it well with flour, and let it stand. Take all the bones of the head and the remainder, and boil them on the fire for an hour, with an English pint of water. Strain off the liquor through a sieve, and put it to your onions; take a good large handful of parsley, well washed and picked clean; chop it as fine as possible; put it in the soup; let it just boil, otherwise it will make it yellow. Add a little cayenne pepper, two spoonfuls of anchovy, a little soy, a little of any sort of ketchup, and a table-spoonful of vinegar. Then put the fish that has been set aside on the plate into the stewpan to the soup, and let it simmer for ten minutes. If not thick enough add a small piece of butter rolled in flour.

Crawfish Soup.

Boil off your crawfish; take the tails out of the shells; roast a couple of lobsters; beat these with your crawfish shells; put this into your fish stock, with some crusts of French rolls. Rub the whole through a tamis, and put your tails into it. You may farce a carp and put in the middle, if you please, or farce some of the shells and stick on a French roll.

Crawfish, or Lobster Soup.

Take some middling and small fishes, and put them in a gallon of water, with pepper, salt, cloves, mace, sweetherbs, and onions; boil them to pieces, and strain them out of the liquor. Then take a large fish, cut the flesh off one side, make force-meat of it, and lay it on the fish; dredge grated bread in it, and butter a dish well; put it in the oven and bake it. Then take one hundred crawfish, break the shells of the tails and claws, take out the meat as whole as you can; pound the shells and add the spawn of a lobster pounded; put them into the soup, and, if you like, a little veal gravy; give them a boil or two together. Strain the liquor off into another saucepan, with the tops of French bread, dried, beat fine, and sifted. Give it a boil to thicken; then brown some butter, and put in the tails and claws of the crawfish, and some of the forcemeat made into balls. Lay the baked fish in the middle of the dish, pour the soup boiling hot on it; if you like, add yolks of eggs, boiled hard, pounded, and mixed by degrees with the soup.

Curry or Mulligatawny Soup.

Boil a large chicken or fowl in a pint of water till half done; add a table-spoonful of curry powder, with the juice of one lemon and a half; boil it again gently till the meat is done.

For a large party you must double the quantity of all the articles, and always proportion the water to the quantity of gravy you think the meat will yield.

Eel Soup.

Take two pounds of eels; put to them two quarts of water, a crust of bread, two or three blades of mace, some whole pepper, one onion, and a bunch of sweet herbs. Cover them close, and let them stew till the liquor is reduced to one half, and if the soup is not rich enough it must boil till it is stronger.—Then strain it, toast some bread, and cut it in small.

This soup will be as good as if meat were put into it. A pound of eels makes a pint of soup.

Fish Soup.

Stew the heads, tails, and fins, of any sort of flat fish or haddock. Strain and thicken with a little flour and butter; add pepper, salt, anchovy, and ketchup, to taste. Cut the fish in thick pieces, and let them stew gently till done.

French Soup.

Take the scrag end of a neck of mutton, or two pounds of any meat, and make it into very strong broth; then take one large cabbage, three lettuces, three carrots, one root of celery, and two onions; cut them all small, and fry them with butter. Pour your broth upon your vegetables a little at a time, cover it up close, and let it stew three hours or more. Serve with the vegetables.

Friar's Chicken.

Stew a knuckle of veal, a neck of mutton, a large fowl, two pounds of giblets, two large onions, two bunches of turnips, one bunch of carrots, a bunch of thyme, and another of sage, eight hours over a very slow stove, till every particle of juice is extracted from the meat and vegetables. Take it off the stove, pass it through a hair tamis; have ready a pound of grated veal, or, what is better, of grated chicken, with a large bunch of parsley, chopped very fine and mingled with it. Put this into the broth; set it on the stove again, and while there break four raw eggs into it. Stir the whole for about a quarter of an hour and serve up hot.

Giblet Soup. No. 1.

Take the desired quantity of strong beef gravy; add to it a few slices of veal fried in butter; take a piece of butter rolled in flour, and with it fry some sliced onion and thyme; when made brown, add it to the soup. When sufficiently stewed, strain and put to it two spoonfuls of ketchup, a few spoonfuls of Madeira, and a little lemon juice. The giblets being separately stewed in a pint of water, add their gravy to the soup.

Giblet Soup. No. 2.

Parboil the giblets, and pour the water from them; put them into fresh water or thin gravy, with a large onion stuck with cloves; season it to your taste; boil them till the flesh comes from the bones. Mix the yolk of an egg with flour into a paste; roll it two or three times over with a rollingpin; cut it in pieces, and thicken the soup with it.

Giblet Soup. No. 3.

Take three pair of goose giblets; scald and cut them as for stewing; set them on the fire in three quarts of water, and when the scum rises skim them well: put in a bundle of sweet herbs, some cloves, mace, and allspice, tied in a bag, with some pepper and salt. Stew them very gently till nearly tender: mix a quarter of a pound of butter with flour, and put it in, with half a pint of white wine, and a little cayenne pepper. Stew them till thick and smooth; take out the herbs and spices; skim well; boil the livers in a quart of water till tender, and put in. Serve up in a terrine or dish.

Gravy Soup. No. 1.

Put two pounds of gravy beef, cut in small pieces, with pepper, salt, some whole pepper, and a piece of butter, the size of a walnut, into a stewpan. When drawn to a good gravy, pour in three quarts of boiling water; add some mace, four heads of celery, one carrot, and three or four onions. Let them stew gently about an hour and a half; then strain; add an ounce and half of vermicelli, and let it stew about ten minutes longer.

Gravy Soup. No. 2.

Take two ox melts, cut them in pieces, season them with pepper and salt, and dredge them with flour. Shred two large onions, fry them of a nice brown colour, put them at the bottom of the saucepan with a piece of butter. Take one ox rump, stew it with carrots and celery and twelve allspice. Then put all together and strain well. This quantity will make three quarts. You may send the ox rump to table in the soup, if approved. Two carrots and two heads of celery will be sufficient.

Gravy Soup. No. 3.

Cut the lean part of a shin of beef, the same of a knuckle of veal, and set the bones of both on the fire, in two gallons of water, to make broth. Put the meat in a stewpan; add some lean bacon or ham, one carrot, two turnips, two heads of celery, two large onions, a bunch of sweet herbs, some whole pepper, two race of ginger, six cloves. Set these over the fire, let it draw till all the gravy is dried up to a nice brown; then add the broth that is made with the bones. Let it boil slowly four or five hours. Make the soup the day before you want to use it, that you may take the fat clean from the top, also the sediment from the bottom. Have ready some turnips, carrots, and cabbage lettuces, cut small, and one pint of young peas; add these to your soup; let it boil one hour, and it will be ready, with salt to your taste.

Hare Soup.

Skin the hare, and wash the inside well. Separate the limbs, legs, shoulders, and back; put them into a stewpan, with two glasses of port wine, an onion stuck with four cloves, a bundle of parsley, a little thyme, some sweet basil and marjoram, a pinch of salt, and cayenne pepper. Set the whole over a slow fire, and let it simmer for an hour; then add a quart of beef gravy and a quart of veal gravy; let the whole simmer gently till the hare is done. Strain the meat; then pass the soup through a sieve, and put a penny roll to soak in the broth. Take all the flesh of the hare from the bones, and pound it in a mortar, till fine enough to be rubbed through a sieve, taking care that none of the bread remains in it. Thicken the broth with the meat of the hare; rub it all together till perfectly fine, like melted butter, not thicker; heat it, and serve it up very hot. Be careful not to let it boil, as that will spoil it.

Another.

Half roast a good-sized hare; cut the back and legs in square pieces; stew the remaining part with five pints of good broth, a bunch of sweet herbs, three blades of mace, three large shalots, shred fine, two large onions, one head of celery, one dozen white pepper, eight cloves, and a slice of ham. Simmer the whole together three hours; then strain and rub it through a hair sieve with a wooden spoon; return the gravy into a stewpan; throw in the back and legs, and let it simmer three quarters of an hour before you send it to table.

Hessian Soup.

Take seven pints of water, one pint of split peas, one pound of lean beef, cut into small slices, three quarters of a pound of potatoes, three ounces of ground rice, two heads of celery, two onions, or leeks. Season with pepper and salt, and dried mint, according to your taste. Let it all boil slowly together till reduced to five pints.

Another.

One pound of beef, one pint of split peas, three turnips, four ounces ground rice, three potatoes, three onions, one head of celery, seven pints of water. Boil till reduced to six pints; then strain it through a hair sieve, with a little whole pepper.

Mock Turtle Soup. No. 1.

Take a calf's head, very white and very fresh, bone the nose part of it; put the head into some warm water to discharge the blood; squeeze the flesh with your hand to ascertain that it is all thoroughly out; blanch the head in boiling water. When firm, put it into cold water, which water must be prepared as follows: cut half a pound of fat bacon, a pound of beef suet, an onion stuck with two cloves, two thick slices of lemon; put these into a vessel, with water enough to contain the head; boil the head in this, and take it off when boiled, leaving it to cool. Then make your sauce in the following manner: put into a stewpan a pound of ham cut into slices; put over the ham two knuckles of veal, two large onions, and two carrots; moisten with some of the broth in which you have boiled the head to half the depth of the meat only; cover the stewpan, and set it on a slow fire to sweat through; let the broth reduce to a good rich colour; turn up the meat for fear of burning. When you have a very good colour, moisten with the whole remaining broth from the head; season with a very large bundle of sweet herbs, sweet basil, sweet marjoram, lemon-thyme, common thyme, two cloves, and a bay leaf, a few allspice, parsley, and green onions and mushrooms. Let the whole boil together for one hour; then drain it. Put into a stewpan a quarter of a pound of very fresh butter, let it melt over a very slow fire; put to this butter as much flour as it can receive till the flour has acquired a very good brown colour; moisten this gradually with the broth till you have employed it all; add half a bottle of good white wine;

let the sauce boil that the flour may be well done; take off all the scum and fat; pass it through a sieve. Cut the meat off the calf's head in pieces of about an inch square; put them to boil in the sauce; season with salt, a little cayenne pepper, and lemon juice. Throw in some forcemeat balls, made according to direction, and a few hard yolks of eggs, and serve up hot.

Mock Turtle. No. 2.

Take a calf's head with the skin on; let it be perfectly well cleaned and scalded, if it is sent otherwise from the butcher's. You should examine and see that it is carefully done, and that it looks white and clean, by raising the skin from the bone with a knife. Boil it about twenty minutes; put it in cold water for about ten minutes; take the skin clean from the flesh, and cut it in square pieces. Cut the tongue out, and boil it until it will peel; then cut it in small pieces, and put it all together. Line the bottom of a soup-pot with slices of ham, a bay-leaf, a bunch of thyme, some other herbs, and an onion stuck with six cloves. Cover all this with a slice of fat bacon, to keep the meat from burning, dry it in a clean cloth, and lay it in the pot with salt, cayenne pepper, and as much mace as will lie on a shilling: and cover the meat over with the parings of the head, and some slices of veal. Add to it a pint of good strong broth; put the cover over the pot as close as possible, and let it simmer two hours. When the head is tender, make the browning as follows: put into a stewpan a good quarter of a pound of butter; as it boils, dredge in a very little flour, keeping it stirring, and throw in by degrees an onion chopped very fine, a little thyme, parsley, &c. picked, also chopped very fine. Put them in by degrees, stirring all the time; then add a pint of good strong broth, a pint of good Madeira wine, and all the liquor with your meat in the stewpot. Let them boil all together, till the spirit of the wine is evaporated, for that should not predominate. Add the juice of two or three large.lemons; then put in the head, tongue, &c.; skim the fat off as it rises. Dish it very hot; add forcemeat balls and hard eggs, made thus: take six or eight and boil them hard; then take the yolks, and pound them in a mortar with a dust of flour, and half or more of a raw egg, (beaten up) as you may judge sufficient. Rub it all to a paste; add a little salt; then roll them into little eggs, and add them, with the forcemeat balls, to the turtle when you dish it.

Mock Turtle. No. 3.

Neat's feet instead of calf's head; that is, two calf's feet and two neat's feet.

Mock Turtle. No. 4.

Two neat's and two calf's feet cut into pieces an inch long, and put into two quarts of strong mutton gravy, with a pint of Madeira. Take three dozen oysters, four anchovies, two onions, some lemon-peel, and mace, with a few sweet herbs; shred all very fine, with half a tea-spoonful of cayenne pepper, and add them to the feet. Let all stew together two hours and a quarter. Just before you send it to table, add the juice of two small lemons, and put forcemeat balls and hard eggs to it.

Mulligatawny Soup. No. 1.

Cut in pieces three fowls; reserve the best pieces of one of them for the terrine; cut the remainder very small: add to them a pound of lean ham, some garlic, bay-leaves, spices, whole mace, peppercorns, onions, pickles of any kind that are of a hot nature, and about four table-spoonfuls of good curry-powder. Cover the ingredients with four quarts of strong veal stock, and boil them till the soup is well flavoured: then strain that to the fowl you have reserved, which must be fried with onions. Simmer the whole till quite tender, and serve it up with plain boiled rice.

Mulligatawny Soup. No. 2.

Boil a knuckle of veal of about five pounds weight; let it stand till cold; then strain, and fry it in a little butter. Strain the liquor, and leave it till cold; take the fat off. Fry four onions brown in butter, add four dessert spoonfuls of curry-powder, a little turmeric, a little cayenne; put all these together in the soup. Let it simmer for two hours, and if not then thick enough, add a little suet and flour, and plain boiled rice to eat with it; and there should be a chicken or fowl, half roasted, and cut up in small pieces, then fried in butter of a light brown colour, and put into the soup instead of the veal, as that is generally too much boiled.

Mulligatawny Soup. No. 3.

Have some good broth made, chiefly of the knuckle of veal: when cold skim the fat off well, and pass the broth when in a liquid state through the sieve. Cut a chicken or rabbit into joints, (chicken or turkey is preferable to rabbit,) fry it well, with four or five middle-sized onions shred fine; shake a table-spoonful of curry-powder over it, and put it into the broth. Let it simmer three hours, and serve it up with a seasoning of cayenne pepper.

Onion Soup. No. 1.

Take twelve large Spanish onions, slice and fry them in good butter. Let them be done very brown, but not to burn, which they are apt to do when they are fried. Put to them two quarts of boiling water, or weak veal broth; pepper and salt to your taste. Let them stew till they are quite tender and almost dissolved; then add crumbs of bread made crisp, sufficient to make it of a proper thickness. Serve hot.

Onion Soup. No. 2.

Boil three pounds of veal with a handful of sweet herbs, and a little mace; when well boiled strain it through a sieve, skim off all the fat. Pare twenty-five onions; boil them soft, rub them through a sieve, and mix them with the veal gravy and a pint of cream, salt, and cayenne pepper, to your taste. Give it a boil and serve up; but do not put in the cream till it comes off the fire.

Onion Soup. No. 3.

Take two quarts of strong broth made of beef; twelve onions; cut these in four quarters, lay them in water an hour to soak. Brown four ounces of butter, put the onions into it, with some pepper and salt, cover them close, and let them stew till tender: cut a French loaf into slices, or sippets, and fry them in fresh butter; put them into your dish, and boil your onions and butter in your soup. When done enough, squeeze in the juice of a lemon, and pour it into your dish with the fried sippets. You may add poached eggs, if it pleases your palate.

Ox Head Soup.

Bone the head and cut it in pieces; wash it extremely clean from the blood; set it on the fire in three gallons of water. Put in a dozen onions, eight turnips, six anchovies, and a bundle of sweet herbs. Let all stew together very gently, till it is quite tender. Carefully skim off all the fat as it boils, but do not stir it. Take cabbage lettuce, celery, chervil, and turnips, all boiled tender and cut small; put them into the soup, and let them boil all together half an hour.

Another.

To half an ox's head put three gallons of water, and boil it three hours. Clean and cut it small and fine; let it stew for an hour with one pint of water, which must be put to it boiling; then add the three gallons boiling.

Green Pea Soup. No. 1.

Take a knuckle of veal of about four pounds, chop it in pieces, and set it on the fire in about six quarts of water, with a small piece of lean ham, three or four blades of mace, the same of cloves, about two dozen peppercorns, white and black, a small bundle of sweet herbs and parsley, and a crust of French roll toasted crisp. Cover close, and let it boil very gently over a slow fire till reduced to one half; then strain it off, and add a full pint of young green peas, a fine lettuce, cut small, four heads of celery, washed and cut small, about a quarter of a pound of fresh butter made hot, with a very little flour dredged into it, and some more lettuce cut small and thrown in. Just fry it a little; put it into the soup; cover it close, and let it stew gently over a slow fire two hours. Have a pint of old peas boiled in a pint of water till they are very tender, then pulp them through a sieve; add it to the soup, and let it all boil together, putting in a very little salt. There should be two quarts. Toast or fry some crust of French roll in dice.

Green Pea Soup. No. 2.

Put one quart of old green peas into a gallon of water, with a bunch of mint, a crust of bread, and two pounds of fresh meat of any sort. When these have boiled gently for three hours, strain the pulp through a colander; then fry spinach, lettuce, beet, and green onions, of each a handful, not too small, in butter, and one pint of green peas, boiled; pepper and salt. Mix all together, and let them just boil. The spinach must not be fried brown, but kept green.

Green Pea Soup. No. 3.

Boil the shells of your youngest peas in water till all the sweetness is extracted from them; then strain, and in that liquor boil your peas for the soup, with whole pepper and salt. When boiled, put them through a colander; have ready the young peas boiled by themselves; put a good piece of butter in a frying-pan with some flour, and into that some lettuce and spinach; fry it till it looks green, and put it into the soup with the young peas. When the greens are tender, it is done enough.

Green Pea Soup. No. 4.

Boil a quart of old peas in five quarts of water, with one onion, till they are soft; then work them through a sieve.—Put the pulp in the water in which the peas were boiled, with half a pint of young peas, and two cabbage lettuces, cut in slices; then let it boil half an hour; pepper and salt, to your taste.—Add a small piece of butter, mixed with flour, and one tea-spoonful of loaf sugar.

Green Pea Soup. No. 5.

Make a good stock for your soup of beef, mutton, and veal; season to your palate; let it stand till cold, then take off all the fat. Take some old peas, boil them in water, with a sprig of mint and a large lettuce, strain them through a sieve; mix them with your soup till of proper thickness. Then add three quarters of a pint of cream; simmer it up together, and have ready half a pint of young peas, or asparagus, ready boiled to throw in. If the soup is not of a fine green, pound some spinach, and put in a little of the juice, but not too much.

Green Pea Soup. No. 6.

Take a quart of old peas, three or four cabbage lettuces, two heads of celery, two leeks, one carrot, two or three turnips, two or three old onions, and a little spinach that has been boiled; put them over the fire with some good consommé, and let them do gently, till all are very tender. Rub the whole through a tamis, or hair-sieve; put it in the pot. Have about half a pint of very young peas, and the hearts of two cabbage lettuces, cut fine and stewed down in a little broth. Put all together, with a small faggot of mint, and let it boil gently, skimming it well. When going to table, put into it fried bread, in dice, or crust of French roll. This quantity will be sufficient for a terrine.

Winter Pea Soup.

Take two quarts of old peas, a lettuce, a small bit of savoury, a handful of spinach, a little parsley, a cucumber, a bit of hock of bacon; stew all together till tender. Rub the whole through a colander; add to it some good gravy, and a little cayenne or common pepper. These quantities will be sufficient for a large terrine. Send it up hot with fried bread.

Pea Soup. No. 1.

Take two pints of peas, one pound of bacon, two bunches of carrots and onions, two bunches of parsley and thyme; moisten the whole with cold water, and let them boil for four hours, adding more water to them if necessary. When quite done, pound them in a mortar, and then rub them through a sieve with the liquor in which they have been boiling. Add a quart of the mixed jelly soup, boil it all together, and leave it on a corner of the fire till served. It must be thick and smooth as melted butter, and care taken throughout that it does not burn.

Pea Soup. No. 2.

Take about three or four pounds of lean beef; cut it in pieces and set it on the fire in three gallons of water, with nearly one pound of ham, a small bundle of sweet herbs, another of mint, and forty peppercorns. Wash a bunch of celery clean, put in the green tops; then add a quart of split peas. Cover it close, and let the whole boil gently till two parts out of three are wasted. Strain it off, and work it through a colander; put it into a clean saucepan with five or six heads of celery, washed and cut very small; cover it close, and let it stew till reduced to about three quarts: then cut some fat and lean bacon in dice, fry them just crisp; do the same by some bread, and put both into the soup. Season it with salt to your taste. When it is in the terrine, rub a little dried mint over it. If you chuse it, boil an ox's palate tender, cut it in dice, and put in, also forcemeat balls.

Pea Soup. No. 3.

To a quart of split peas put three quarts of water, two good turnips, one large head of celery, four onions, one blade of ginger, one spoonful of flour of mustard, and a small quantity of cayenne, black pepper, and salt. Let it boil over a slow fire till it is reduced to two quarts; then work it through a colander with a wooden spoon. Set it on the fire, and let it boil up; add a quarter of a pound of butter mixed with flour; beat up the yolks of three eggs, and stir it well in the soup. Gut a slice of bread into small dice; fry them of a light brown; put them into your soup-dish, and pour the soup over them.

Pea Soup. No. 4.

Boil one onion and one quart of peas in three quarts of water till they are soft; then work them through a hair sieve. Mix the pulp with the water in which the peas were boiled; set it over the fire and let it boil; add two cabbage lettuces, cut in slices, half a pint of young peas, and a little salt. Let it boil quickly half an hour; mix a little butter and flour, and boil in the soup.

Portable Soup.

Strip all the skin and fat off a leg of veal; then cut all the fleshy parts from the bone, and add a shin of beef, which treat in the same way; boil it slowly in three gallons of water or more according to the quantity of the meat; let the pot be closely covered: when you find it, in a spoon, very strong and clammy, like a rich jelly, take it off and strain it through a hair sieve into an earthen pan. After it is thoroughly cold, take off any fat that may remain, and divide your jelly clear of the bottom into small flatfish cakes in chinaware cups covered. Then place these cups in a large deep stewpan of boiling water over a stove fire, where let it boil gently till the jelly becomes a perfect glue; but take care the water does not get into the cups, for that will spoil it all. These cups of glue must be taken out, and, when cold, turn out the glue into a piece of new coarse flannel, and in about six hours turn it upon more fresh flannel, and keep doing this till it is perfectly dry—if you then lay it by in a dry warm place, it will presently become like a dry piece of glue. When you use it in travelling, take a piece the size of a large walnut, seasoning it with fresh herbs, and if you can have an old fowl, or a very little bit of fresh meat, it will be excellent.

Potato Soup.

Five large carrots, two turnips, three large mealy potatoes, seven onions, three heads of celery; slice them all thin, with a handful of sweet herbs; put them into one gallon of water, with bones of beef, or a piece of mutton; let them simmer gently till the vegetables will pulp through a sieve. Add cayenne pepper, salt, a pint of milk, or half a pint of cream, with a small piece of butter beaten up with flour.

Rabbit Soup.

One large rabbit, one pound of lean ham, one onion, one turnip, and some celery, two quarts of water; let them boil till the rabbit is tender. Strain off the liquor; boil a pint of cream, and add it to the best part of the rabbit pounded; if not of the thickness you wish, add some flour and butter, and rub it through a sieve. It must not be boiled after the cream is added.

Root Soup.

Potatoes, French turnips, English turnips, carrots, celery, of each six roots; pare and wash them; add three or four onions; set them on the fire with the bones of a rump of beef, or, if you have no such thing, about two pounds of beef, or any other beef bones. Chop them up, and put them on the fire with water enough to cover them; let them stew very gently till the roots are all tender enough to rub through a sieve. This done, cut a few roots of celery small, and put it to the strained soup. Season it with pepper and salt, and stew it gently till the celery is tender; then serve it with toast or fried bread. A bundle of herbs may be boiled in it, just to flavour it, and then taken out.

Scotch Leek Soup.

You make this soup to most advantage the day after a leg of mutton has been boiled, into the liquor from which put four large leeks, cut in pieces. Season with pepper and salt, and let it boil gently for a quarter of an hour. Mix half a pint of oatmeal with cold water till quite smooth; pour this into the soup; let it simmer gently half an hour longer; and serve it up.

To brown or colour Soup.

To brown soup, take two lumps of loaf-sugar in an iron spoon; let it stand on the stove till it is quite black, and put it into soup.

Seasoning for Soups and Brown Sauces.

Salt a bullock's liver, pressing it thoroughly with a great weight for four days. Take ginger and every sort of spice that is used to meat, and half a pound of brown sugar, a good quantity of saltpetre, and a pound of juniper-berries. Rub the whole in thoroughly, and let it lie six weeks in the liquor, boiling and skimming every three days, for an hour or two, till the liver becomes as hard as a board. Then steep it in the smoke liquor that is used for hams, and afterwards hang it up to smoke for a considerable time. When used, cut slices as thin as a wafer, and stew them down with the jelly of which you make your sauce or soup, and it will give a delightful flavour.

Soup. No. 1.

A quarter of a pound of portable soup, that is, one cake, in two quarts of boiling water; vegetables to be stewed separately, and added after the soup is dissolved.

Soup. No. 2.

Take a piece of beef about a stone weight, and a knuckle of veal, eight or ten onions, a bunch of thyme and parsley, an ounce of allspice, ten cloves, some whole pepper and salt; boil all these till the meat is all to pieces. Strain and take off the fat. Make about a quart of brown beef gravy with some of your broth; then take half a pound of butter and a good handful of flour mixed together, put it into a stewpan, set it over a slow fire, keeping it stirring till very brown; have ready what herbs you design for your soup, either endive or celery; chop them, but not too small; if you wish for a fine soup add a palate and sweetbreads, the palate boiled tender, and the sweetbreads fried, and both cut into small pieces. Put these, with herbs, into brown butter; put in as much of your broth as you intend for your soup, which must be according to the size of your dish. Give them a boil or two, then put in a quart of your gravy, and put all in a pot, with a fowl, or what you intend to put in your dish. Cover it close, and, let it boil an hour or more on a slow fire. Should it not be seasoned enough, add more salt, or what you think may be necessary: a fowl, or partridge, or squab pigeons, are best boiled in soup and to lie in the dish with it.

Soup. No. 3.

Cut three pounds of beef and one pound of veal in slices and beat it. Put half a pound of butter and a piece of bacon in your pan, brown it, and sprinkle in half a spoonful of flour. Cut two onions in; add pepper and salt, a bit of mace, and some herbs, then put in your meat, and fry it till it is brown on both sides. Have in readiness four quarts of boiling water, and a saucepan that will hold both water and what is in your frying-pan. Cover it close; set it over a slow fire and stew it down, till it is wasted to about five pints; then strain it off, and add to it what soup-herbs you like, according to your palate. Celery and endive must be first stewed in butter; and peas and asparagus first boiled, and well drained from the butter, before you put it to the soup. Stew it some time longer, and skim off all the fat; then take a French roll, which put in your soup-dish; pour in your soup, and serve it up. Just before you take it off the fire, squeeze in the juice of a lemon.

If veal alone is used, and fowl or chicken boiled in it and taken out when enough done, and the liquor strained, and the fowl or chicken put to the clear liquor, with vermicelli, you will have a fine white soup; and the addition of the juice of a lemon is a great improvement.

The French cooks put in chervil and French turnips, lettuce, sorrel, parsley, beets, a little bit of carrot, a little of parsnips, this last must not boil too long—all to be strained off: to be sent up with celery, endive (or peas) or asparagus, and stuffed cucumbers.

Soup without Meat.

Take two quarts of water, a little pepper, salt, and Jamaica pepper, a blade of mace, ten or twelve cloves, three or four onions, a crust of bread, and a bunch of sweet herbs; boil all these well. Take the white of two or three heads of endive, chopped, but not too small. Put three quarters of a pound of butter in a stewpan that will be large enough to hold all your liquor. Set it on a quick fire till it becomes very brown; then put a little of your liquor to prevent its turning, or oiling; shake in as much flour as will make it rather thick; then put in the endive and an onion shred small, stirring it well. Strain all your liquor, and put it to the butter and herbs; let it stew over a slow fire almost an hour. Dry a French roll, and let it remain in it till it is soaked through, and lay it in your dish with the soup. You may make this soup with asparagus, celery, or green peas, but they must be boiled before you put them to the burnt butter.

Soup for the Poor.

Eight pails of water, two quarts of barley, four quarts of split peas, one bushel of potatoes, half a bushel of turnips, half a bushel of carrots, half a peck of onions, one ounce of pepper, two pounds of salt, an ox's head, parsley, herbs, boiled six hours, produce one hundred and thirty pints. Boil the meat and take off the first scum before the other ingredients are put in.

Another.

To feed one hundred and thirty persons, take five quarts of Scotch barley, one quart of Scotch oatmeal, one bushel of potatoes, a bullock's head, onions, &c., one pound and half of salt.

Soup and Bouilli

may be made of ox-cheek, stewed gently for some hours, and well skimmed from the fat, and again when cold. Small suet dumplings are added when heated for table as soup.

Soupe à la Reine, or Queen's Soup.

Soak a knuckle of veal and part of a neck of mutton in water; put them in a pot with liquor, carrots, turnips, thyme, parsley, and onions. Boil and scum it; then season with a head or two of celery; boil this down; take half a pound of blanched almonds, and beat them; take two fowls, half roasted, two sweetbreads set off; beat these in a mortar, put them in your stock, with the crumbs of two French rolls; then rub them through a tamis and serve up.

Another.

For a small terrine take about three quarters of a pound of almonds; blanch, and pound them very fine. Cut up a fowl, leaving the breast whole, and stew in consommé. When the breast is tender, take it out, (leaving the other parts to stew with the consommé) pound it well with the almonds and three hard-boiled yolks of eggs, and take it out of the mortar. Strain the consommé, and put it, when the fat is skimmed off, to the almonds, &c. Have about a quarter of a pint of Scotch barley boiled very tender, add it to the other ingredients, put them into a pot with the consommé, and stir it over the fire till it is boiling hot and well mixed. Rub it through a tamis, and season it with a little salt; it must not boil after being rubbed through.

Soupe Maigre. No. 1.

Take the white part of eight loaved lettuces, cut them as small as dice, wash them and strain them through a sieve. Pick a handful of purslain and half a handful of parsley, wash and drain them. Cut up six large cucumbers in slices about the thickness of a crown-piece. Peel and mince four large onions, and have in readiness three pints of young green peas. Put half a pound of fresh butter into your stewpan; brown it of a high colour, something like that of beef gravy. Put in two ounces of lean bacon cut clean from the rind, add all your herbs, peas, and cucumbers, and thirty corns of whole pepper; let these stew together for ten minutes; keep stirring to prevent burning. Put one gallon of boiling water to a gallon of small broth, and a French roll cut into four pieces toasted of a fine yellow brown. Cover your stewpan, and let it again stew for two hours. Add half a drachm of beaten mace, one clove beaten, and half a grated nutmeg, and salt to your taste. Let it boil up, and squeeze in the juice of a lemon. Send it to table with all the bread and the herbs that were stewed in it.

Soupe Maigre. No. 2.

Take of every vegetable you can get, excepting cabbage, in such quantity as not to allow any one to predominate; cut them small and fry them brown in butter; add a little water, and thicken with flour and butter. Let this stew three hours very gently; and season to your taste. The French add French rolls.

Soupe Maigre. No. 3.

Half a pound of butter, put in a stewpan over the fire, and let it brown. Cut two or three onions in slices, two or three heads of celery, two handfuls of spinach, a cabbage, two turnips, a little parsley, three cabbage lettuces, a little spice, pepper and salt. Stew all these about half an hour; then add about two quarts of water, and let it simmer till all the roots are tender. Put in the crust of a French roll, and send it to table.

Soupe Maigre. No. 4.

Cut three carrots, three turnips, three heads of celery, three leeks, six onions, and two cabbage lettuces in small pieces; put them in your stewpan with a piece of butter, the size of an egg, a pint of dried or green peas, and two quarts of water, with a little pepper and salt. Simmer the whole over the fire till tender; then rub it through a sieve or tamis; add some rice, and let it simmer an hour before you serve it up.

Soupe Maigre. No. 5.

Take three carrots, three turnips, three heads of celery, three leeks, six onions, two cabbage lettuces; cut them all in small pieces, and put them in your stewpan, with a piece of butter about the size of an egg, and a pint of dried or green peas, and two quarts of water. Simmer them over the fire till tender, then rub through a sieve or tamis. Add some rice, and let it simmer an hour before you serve it up.

Soupe Santé, or Wholesome Soup.

Take beef and veal cut in thin slices; put sliced turnips, carrots, onions, bacon, in the bottom of your stewpan; lay your meat upon these, and over it some thin thyme, parsley, a head or two of celery. Cover the whole down; set it over a charcoal fire; draw it down till it sticks to the bottom; then fill up with the above stock. Let it boil slowly till the goodness is extracted from your meat; then strain it off. Cut and wash some celery, endive, sorrel, a little chervil, spinach, and a piece of leek; put these in a stewpan, with a bit of butter. Stew till tender, then put this in your soup; give it a boil up together, and skim the fat off. Cut off the crust of French rolls; dry and soak them in some of your soup; put them into it, and serve your soup.

Spanish Soup.

Put the scrag end of a neck of veal, two calves' feet, two pounds of fresh beef, one old fowl, into a pot well tinned, with six quarts of water, and a little salt, to raise the scum, which must be very carefully taken off. Let these boil very gently two hours and a half, till the water is reduced to four quarts; then take out all the meat, strain the broth, and put to it a small quantity of pepper, mace, cloves, and cinnamon, finely pounded, with four or five cloves of garlic. A quarter of an hour afterwards add eight or ten ounces of rice, with six ounces of ham or bacon, and a drachm of saffron put into a muslin bag. Observe to keep it often stirred after the rice is in, till served up. It will be ready an hour and a half after the saffron is in. You should put a fowl into it an hour before it is ready, and serve it up whole in the soup.

This soup will keep two or three days.

Turnip Soup.

Make a good strong gravy of beef or mutton; let it stand till cold; take off all the fat; pare some turnips and slice them thin; stew them till tender, then strain them through a sieve; mix the pulp with the gravy, till of a proper thickness:—then add three quarters of a pint of cream; boil it up, and send it to table.

Veal Soup.

Take a knuckle of veal, and chop it into small pieces; set it on the fire with four quarts of water, pepper, mace, a few herbs, and one large onion. Stew it five or six hours; then strain off the spice, and put in a pint of green peas until tender. Take out the small bones, and send the rest up with the soup.

Vegetable Soup. No. 1.

Take a quart of beef jelly and the same quantity of veal jelly: boil it, have some carrots and turnips, cut small, previously boiled in a little of the jelly; throw them in, and serve it up hot.

Vegetable Soup. No. 2.

Take two cabbage and two coss lettuces, one hard cabbage, six onions, one large carrot, two turnips, three heads of celery, a little tarragon, chervil, parsley, and thyme, chopped fine, and a little flour fried in a quarter of a pound of butter (or less will do). Then add three quarts of boiling water; boil it for two hours, stir it well, and add, before sending it to table, some crumbs of stale bread: the upper part of the loaf is best.

Vegetable Soup. No. 3.

Let a quantity of dried peas (split peas), or haricots, (lentils) be boiled in common water till they are quite tender; let them then be gradually passed through a sieve with distilled water, working the mixture with a wooden spoon, to make what the French call a *puré*: and let it be made sufficiently liquid with distilled water to bear boiling down. Then let a good quantity of fresh vegetables, of any or all kinds in their season, especially carrots, lettuces, turnips, celery, spinach, with always a few onions, be cut into fine shreds, and put it into common boiling water for three or four minutes to blanch; let them then be taken out with a strainer, added to and mixed with the *puré*, and the whole set to boil gently at the fire for at least two hours. A few minutes before taking the soup from the fire, let it be seasoned to the taste with pepper and salt.

The soup, when boiling gently at the fire, should be very frequently stirred, to prevent its sticking to the side of the pan, and acquiring a burnt taste.

Vegetable Soup. No. 4.

Cut two potatoes, one turnip, two heads of celery, two onions, one carrot, a bunch of sweet herbs; put them all into a stewpan; cover close; draw them gently for twenty minutes, then put two quarts of good broth, let it boil gently, and afterwards simmer for two hours. Strain through a fine sieve; put it into your pan again; season with pepper and salt, and let it boil up.

Vegetable Soup. No. 5.

Take four turnips, two potatoes, three onions, three heads of celery, two carrots, four cabbage lettuces, a bunch of sweet herbs, and parsley. The vegetables must be cut in slices; put them into a stewpan, with half a pint of water; cover them close; set them over the fire for twenty minutes to draw; add three pints of broth or water, and let it boil quickly. When the vegetables are tender rub them through a sieve. If you make the soup with water, add butter, flour, pepper, and salt. Let it be of the thickness of good cream, and add some fine crumbs of bread with small dumplings.

Vermicelli Soup.

Break the vermicelli a little, throw it into boiling water, and let it boil about two minutes. Strain it in a sieve, and throw it into cold water: then strain and put it into a good clear consommé, and let it boil very slowly about a quarter of an hour. When it is going to table, season with a little salt, and put into it a little crust of French roll.

West India Soup, called Pepper Pot.

A small knuckle of veal and a piece of beef of about three pounds, seven or eight pounds of meat in all; potherbs as for any other soup. When the soup is skimmed and made, strain it off. The first ingredient you add to the soup must be some dried ocre (a West India vegetable), the quantity according to your judgment. It is hard and dry, and therefore requires a great deal of soaking and boiling. Then put in the spawn of the lobsters you intend for your soup, first pounding it very fine, and mixing it by degrees with a little of your soup cooled, or it will be lumpy, and not so smooth as it should be. Put it into the soup-pot, and continue to stir some time after it is in. Take about two middling handfuls of spinach and about six hearts of the inside of very nice greens; scald both greens and spinach before you put them to the soup, to take off the rawness; the greens require most scalding. Squeeze them quite dry, chop and put them into the soup; then add all the fat and inside egg and spawn you can get from the lobsters, also the meat out of the tails and claws. Add the green tops only of a large bundle of asparagus, of the sort which they call sprew-grass, previously scalded; a few green peas also are very good. After these ingredients are in, the soup should no more than simmer; and when the herbs are sufficiently tender it is done enough. This soup is not to be clear, on the contrary thick with the lobster, and a perfect mash with the lobster and greens. You are to put in lobster to your liking; I generally put in five or six, at least of that part of them which is called fat, egg, and inside spawn, sufficient to make it rich and good. It should look quite yellow with this. Put plenty of the white part also, and in order that none of the goodness of the lobsters should be lost, take the shells of those which you have used, bruise them in a mortar, and boil them in some of the broth, to extract what goodness remains; then strain off the liquor and add it to the rest. Scoop some potatoes round, half boiling them first, and put into it. Season with red pepper. Put in a piece of nice pickled pork, which must be first scalded, for fear of its being too salt; stew it with the rest and serve it.

White Soup. No. 1.

Take two chickens; skin them; take out the lungs and wash them thoroughly; put them in a stewpan with some parsley. Add a quart of veal jelly, and stew them in this for one hour over a very slow fire. Then take out the chickens, and put a penny roll to soak in the liquor; take all the flesh of the chickens from the bones, and pound it in a mortar, with the yolk of three eggs boiled hard. Add the bread (when soaked enough) and pound it also with them; then rub the whole finely through a sieve. Add a quart more jelly to the soup, and strain it through a sieve; then put the chicken to the soup. Set a quart of cream on the fire till it boils, stirring it all the time; when ready to serve, pour that into the soup and mix it well together. Have ready a little vermicelli, boiled in a little weak broth, to throw into the soup, when put into the terrine.

White Soup. No. 2.

Have good stock made of veal and beef; then take about a pound of veal, and the like quantity of ham, cut both into thin slices, and put them into a stewpan, with a pint of water and two onions cut small. Set it on the fire and stew it down gently, till it is quite dry, and of a rather light brown colour; then add the stock, and let it all stew till the veal and ham are quite tender. Strain it off into the stewpot; add a gill or more of cream, some blanched rice boiled tender, the quantity to your own judgment, the yolks of six eggs beaten up well with a little new milk: let the soup be boiling hot before the eggs are added, which put to it by degrees, keeping it stirring over a slow fire. Serve it very hot: to prevent curdling, put the soup-pot into a large pot of boiling water, taking care that not the least drop of water gets in, and so make it boiling hot.

White Soup. No. 3.

Cut one pound of veal, or half a fowl, into small pieces; put to it a few sweet herbs, a crust of bread, an ounce of pearl barley well washed. Set it over a slow fire, closely covered; let it boil till half is consumed; then strain it and take off the fat. Have ready an ounce of sweet almonds blanched, pound them in a marble mortar, adding a little soup to prevent their oiling. Mix all together. When you send it up, add one third of new milk or cream, salt and pepper to taste.

White Soup. No. 4.

Take a knuckle of veal, and put water according to the quantity of soup you require; let it boil up and skim it; then put in three ounces of lean bacon or ham, with two heads of celery, one carrot, one turnip, two onions, and three or four blades of mace, and boil for three or four hours. When properly boiled, strain it off, taking care to skim off all the fat; then put into it two ounces of rice, well boiled, half a pint of cream beaten up, and five or six yolks of eggs. When ready to serve, pour the soup to the eggs backward and forward to prevent it from curdling, and send it to table. You must boil the soup once after you add the cream, and before you put it to the eggs. Three laurel leaves put into it in summer and six in winter make a pleasant addition, instead of sweet almonds.

White Soup. No. 5.

Make your stock with veal and chicken, and beat half a pound of almonds in a mortar very fine, with the breast of a fowl. Put in some white broth, and strain off. Stove it gently, and poach eight eggs, and lay in your soup, with a French roll in the middle, filled with minced chicken or veal, and serve very hot.

White Soup. No. 6.

Take a knuckle of veal; stew it with celery, herbs, slices of ham, and a little cayenne and white pepper; season it to your taste. When it is cleared off, add one pound of sweet almonds, a pint of cream, and the yolks of eight eggs, boiled hard and finely bruised. Mix these all together in your soup; let it just boil, and send it up hot. You may add a French roll; let it be nicely browned.

The ingredients here mentioned will make four quarts.

White Soup. No. 7.

Stock from a boiled knuckle of veal, thickened with about two ounces of sweet almonds, beaten to a paste, with a spoonful of water to prevent their oiling; a large slice of dressed veal, and a piece of crumb of bread, soaked in good milk, pounded and rubbed through a sieve; a bit of fresh lemon-peel and a blade of mace in the finest powder. Boil all together about half an hour, and stir in about a pint of cream without boiling.

BROTHS.

Broth for the Poor.

A good wholesome broth may be made at a very reasonable rate to feed the poor in the country. The following quantities would furnish a good meal for upwards of fifty persons.

Take twenty pounds of the very coarse parts of beef, five pounds of whole rice, thirteen gallons of water; boil the meat in the water first, and skim it very well; then put in the rice, some turnips, carrots, leeks, celery, thyme, parsley, and a good quantity of potatoes; add a good handful of salt, and boil them all together till tender.

Another.

Four hundred quarts of good broth for the poor may be made as follows:— Good beef, fifty pounds weight; beeves' cheeks, and legs of beef, five; rice, thirty pounds; peas, twenty-three quarts; black pepper, five ounces and a half; cayenne pepper, half an ounce; ground ginger, two ounces; onions, thirteen pounds; salt, seven pounds and a half; with celery, leeks, carrots, dried mint, and any other vegetable.

Broth for the Sick. No. 1.

Boil one ounce of very lean veal, fifteen minutes in a little butter, and then add half a pint of water; set it over a very slow fire, with a spoonful of barley and a piece of gum arabic about the size of a nut.

Broth for the Sick. No. 2.

Put a leg of beef and a scrag of mutton cut in pieces into three or four gallons of water, and let them boil twelve hours, occasionally stirring them well; and cover close. Strain the broth, and let it stand till it will form a jelly; then take the fat from the top and the dross from the bottom.

Broth for the sick. No. 3.

Take twelve quarts of water, two knuckles of veal, a leg of beef, or two shins, four calves' feet, a chicken, a rabbit, two onions, cloves, pepper, salt, a bunch of sweet herbs. Cover close, and let the whole boil till reduced to six quarts. Strain and keep it for use.

Barley Broth.

Take four or five pounds of the lean end of a neck of mutton, soak it well in cold water for some time, then put it in a saucepan with about four quarts of water and a tea-cupful of fine barley. Just before it boils take it off the fire and skim it extremely well; put in salt and pepper to your taste, and a small bundle of sweet herbs, which take out before the broth is sent up. Then let it boil very gently for some hours afterwards; add turnips, carrots, and onions, cut in small pieces, and continue to boil the broth till the vegetables are quite done and very tender. When nearly done it requires to be stirred frequently lest the barley should adhere.

Another.

Put on whatever bones you have; stew them down well with a little whole pepper, onions, and herbs. When done, strain it off, and next day take off all the fat. Take a little pearl barley, boil it a little and strain it off; put it to the broth, add a coss lettuce, carrot, and turnip, cut small. Boil all together some time, and serve it up.

Chervil Broth for Cough.

Boil a calf's liver and two large handfuls of chervil in four quarts of spring water till reduced to one quart. Strain it, and take a coffee-cupful night and morning.

Hodge-Podge.

Stew a scrag of mutton: put in a peck of peas, a bunch of turnips cut small, a few carrots, onions, lettuce, and some parsley. When sufficiently boiled add a few mutton chops, which must stew gently till done.

Leek Porridge.

Peel twelve leeks; boil them in water till tender; take them out and put them into a quart of new milk; boil them well; thicken up with oatmeal, and add salt according to the taste.

Madame de Maillet's Broth.

Two ounces of veal, six carrots, two turnips, one table-spoonful of gum arabic, one table-spoonful of rice, two quarts of water; simmer for about two hours.

Mutton Broth.

The bone of a leg of mutton to be chopped small, and put into the stewpan with vegetables and herbs, together with a little drop of water, and drawn as gravy soup; add boiling water.

Pork Broth.

Take a leg of pork fresh cut up; beat it and break the bone; put it into three gallons of soft water, with half an ounce of mace and the same quantity of nutmeg. Let it boil very gently over a slow fire, until two thirds of the water are consumed.

Strain the broth through a fine sieve, and when it is cold take off the fat. Drink a large cupful in the morning fasting, and between meals, and just before going to bed, warmed. Season it with a little salt. This is a fine restorative.

Potage.

Boil a leg of beef, and a knuckle of veal, with a bunch of sweet herbs, a little mace and whole pepper, and a handful of salt. When the meat is boiled to rags or to a very strong broth, strain it through a hair sieve, and when it is cold, take off the fat. With raw beef make a gravy thus: cut your beef in pieces, put them in a frying-pan with a piece of butter or a slice of bacon, fry it very brown, then put it to some of your strong broth, and when it grows browner and thick till it becomes reduced to three pints of gravy, fill up your strong broth to boil with a piece of butter and a handful of sweet herbs. Afterwards a chicken must be boiled and blanched and cut in slices; and two or three sweetbreads fried very brown; a turnip also sliced and fried. Boil all these half an hour, and put them in the dish in which you intend to serve up, with three French rolls (cut in halves) and set it over a fire with a quart of your gravy, and some of your broth, covered with a dish, till it boils very fast, and as it reduces fill up with your broth till your bread is quite soaked. You may put into the dish either a duck, pigeon, or any bird you please; but whichever you choose, roast it first, and then let it boil in the dish with your bread. This may be made a pea soup, by only rubbing peas through a sieve.

Scotch Pottage.

Place a tin saucepan on the fire with some boiling water; stir in Scotch oatmeal till it is of the desired consistence: when done, pour it in a basin and add milk or cream to it. It is more nutritious to make it of milk instead of water, if the stomach will bear it. The Scotch peasantry live entirely on this strengthening food. The best Scotch oatmeal is to be bought at Dudgeon's, in the Strand.

Scotch Broth.

Boil very tender a piece of thin brisket of beef, with trimmings of any other meat, or a piece of gravy beef; cut it into square pieces; strain off the broth and put it in a soup-pot; add the beef, cut in squares, with plenty of carrots, turnips, celery, and onions, cut in shapes and well boiled before put to the broth, and, if liked, some very small suet dumplings first boiled. Season it to your palate.

Turnip Broth.

Have a sufficient quantity of good strong broth as for any other soup, taking care that it is not too strongly flavoured by any of the roots introduced into it. Peel a good quantity of the best turnips, selecting such as are not bitter. Sweat them in butter and a little water till they are quite tender. Rub them through a tamis, mix them with the broth; boil it for about half an hour. Add half a pint of very good cream, and be careful not to have too fierce a fire, as it is apt to burn.

Another.

Put one pound of lean veal, pulled into small pieces in a pipkin, with two large or three middling turnips. Cover the pipkin very close, to prevent water from getting into it; set it in a pot of water, and let it boil for two or three hours. A tea-cupful of the broth produced in the pipkin may be taken twice or thrice a day.

Veal Broth. No. 1.

Take ten or twelve knuckles, such as are cut off from legs and shoulders of mutton, at the very shank; rub them with a little salt, put them in a pan of water for two or three hours, and wash them very clean; boil them in a gallon of spring water for an hour. Strain them very clean, then put in two ounces of hartshorn shavings, and the bottom crust of a penny loaf; let it boil till the water is reduced to about three pints; strain it off, and when cold skim off the fat. Take half a pint warm before you rise, and the same in bed at night. Make it fresh three times a week in summer, and twice a week in winter: do not put in any lamb bones. This is an excellent thing.

Veal Broth. No. 2.

Soak a knuckle of veal for an hour in cold water; put it into fresh water over the fire, and, as the scum rises, take it off; let it stew gently for two hours, with a little salt to make the scum rise. When it is sufficiently stewed, strain the broth from the meat. Put in some vermicelli; keep the meat hot; and as you are going to put the soup into the terrine add half a pint of cream.

Veal Broth. No. 3.

Take one pound of lean veal, one blade of mace, two table-spoonfuls of rice, one quart of water; let it boil slowly two hours; add a little salt.

Veal Broth. No. 4.—Excellent for a Consumption.

Boil a knuckle of veal in a gallon of water; skim and put to it half a pound of raisins of the sun, stoned, and the bottoms of two manchets, with a nutmeg and a half sliced, and a little hartshorn. Let it boil till reduced to half the quantity; then pound it all together and strain. Add some brown sugar-candy, some rose-water, and also the juice of a lemon, if the patient has no cough.

FISH.

Carp and Tench.

Scale the fish, take out the gut and gall; save all the blood. Split the carp if large; cut it in large pieces, and salt it. Boil some sliced parsley roots and onions tender in half a pint of water, adding a little cayenne pepper, ginger, cloves, and allspice, a lemon sliced, a little vinegar, and moist sugar, one glass of red wine, and some butter rolled in flour. Then put in the fish, and let it boil very fast for half an hour in a stewpan. The blood is to be put in the sauce.

Carp, to stew.

Scale, gut, and cleanse them; save the roes and milts; stew them in some good broth: season, to your taste, with a bundle of herbs, onions, anchovies, and white wine; and, when they are stewed enough, thicken the sauce with the yolks of five eggs. Pass off the roes, dip them in yolk of egg and flour, and fry them with some sippets of French bread; then fry a little parsley, and, when you serve up, garnish the dish with the roes, parsley, and sippets.

Another way.

Have your carp fresh out of the water; scale and gut them, washing the blood out of each fish with a little claret; and save that after so doing. Cut your carp in pieces, and stew in a little fresh butter, a few blades of mace, winter savory, a little thyme, and three or four onions; after stewing awhile, take them out, put them by, and fold them up in linen, till the liquor is ready to receive them again, as the fish would otherwise be boiled to pieces before the liquor was reduced to a proper thickness. When you have taken out your fish, put in the claret that you washed out the blood with, and a pint of beef or mutton gravy, according to the quantity of your fish, with some salt and the butter in which you stewed the carp; and when this butter is almost boiled to a proper thickness put in your fish again; stew all together, and serve it up. Two spoonfuls of elder vinegar to the liquor when taken up will give a very agreeable taste.

Cod, to stew.

Cut a cod into thin pieces or slices; lay them in rows at the bottom of a dish; put in a pint of white wine, half a pound of butter, a few oysters, with their liquor, a little pepper and salt, with some crumbs of bread. Stew them all till they are done enough. Garnish the dish with lemon.

Cod, Ragout of.

Wash the cod clean, and boil it in warm water, with vinegar, pepper, salt, a bay-leaf, and lemon. Make a sauce of burnt butter, fried flour, capers, and oysters. When you serve it up put in some black pepper and lemon-juice.

Cod's Head, to boil.

Take vinegar and salt, a bunch of sweet herbs, and an onion; set them on the fire in a kettle of water; boil them and put in the head; and, while it is boiling, put in cold water and vinegar. When boiled, take it up, put it into a dish, and make sauce as follows:—Take gravy and claret, boiled with a bundle of sweet herbs and an onion, two or three anchovies, drawn with two pounds of butter, a pint of shrimps, oysters, the meat of a lobster shred fine. You may stick little toasts on the head, and lay on and about the roe, milt, and liver. Garnish the dish with fried parsley, lemon, barberries, horseradish, and fried fish.

Crab, to dress.

Take all the body and the meat of the legs, and put them together in a dish to heat, with a little broth or gravy, just to make them moist. When hot, have ready some good broth or gravy, with an anchovy dissolved in it, and the juice of a small lemon, heated; afterwards thicken it up with butter, and stir it in the crab, as it is, hot: then serve all up in the shell.

Crab or Lobster, to butter.

The crabs or lobsters being boiled and cold, take all the meat out of the shells and body; break the claws and take out the meat. Shred it small; add a spoonful or two of claret, a little vinegar, and a grated nutmeg. Let it boil up till it is thoroughly hot; then put in some melted butter, with anchovies and white gravy; thicken with the yolk of an egg or two, and when very hot put it into the large shell. Put crumbs of bread over it, and brown it with a salamander.

Crab, or Lobster, to stew. No. 1.

A little cayenne, vinegar, butter, flour, and salt. Cover it with water and let it stew gently.

Crab, or Lobster, to stew. No. 2.

When the lobsters are boiled, take out the tail and claws, and dip them in white wine; strew over them nutmeg, cloves, mace, salt, and pepper, mixed together. Then pour over them some melted butter with a little white wine in it; send them to the bakehouse, and let them stand in a slow oven about half an hour. Pour out the butter and wine, and pour on some fresh butter; when cold, cover them, and keep them in a cold place.

Crab, or Lobster, to stew. No. 3.

Boil the lobsters; when cold take out all the meat; season it well with pepper, salt, nutmeg and mace pounded. Put it into an earthen pot with as much clarified butter as will cover it; bake it well. While warm, take it out of the pot, and let the butter drain from it. Break it as fine as you can with a spoon or knife; add more seasoning if required; put it as close as possible in the pot, and cover with clarified butter. The hen lobsters are best for this purpose, as the eggs impart a good colour. It may be pounded in a marble mortar, but, if baked enough, will do as well without it.

Crawfish, to make red.

Rub the fish with aqua vitæ, which will produce the desired effect most completely.

Eels broiled whole.

Skin, wash, and dry your eels, and score them with the knife, seasoning them with pepper, salt, thyme, parsley, and crumbs of bread, turning them round and skewering them across; you may either roast or broil them as you like best: the sauce to be melted butter with lemon juice.

Eels, to collar.

Scour large silver eels with salt; slit them, and take out the back-bones; wash and dry them; season with shred parsley, sage, an onion, and thyme. Then roll each into collars, in a cloth; tie them close with the heads, bones, and a bundle of herbs, and boil them in salt and water. When tender, take them up, and again tie them close; drain the pickle, and put them into it.

Eels, to fry.

Cut every eel into eight pieces; mix them with a proper quantity of yolks of eggs, and well season with pepper, and salt, and bread rubbed fine, with parsley and thyme; then flour them, and fry them. You may cook them as plain as you like, with only salt and flour, and serve them up with melted butter and fried parsley.

Eels, to pot.

Into an earthen pan put Jamaica and common pepper, pounded fine, and salt; mix them and strew some at the bottom of the pan; cut your eels and lay them over it, and strew a little more seasoning over them. Then put in another layer of eels, repeating this process till all the eels are in. Lay a few bay leaves upon them, and pour as much vinegar as you may think requisite; cover the pan with brown paper and bake them. Pour off the liquor, cover them with clarified butter, and lay them by for use.

Eels, to pickle.

Drain, wash, and well cleanse your eels, and cut off the heads. Cut them in lengths of four or five inches, with their skins on; stew in them some pepper and salt, and broil them on a gridiron a fine colour: then put them in layers in a jar, with bay-leaf, pepper, salt, a few slices of lemon, and a few cloves. Pour some good vinegar on them; tie strong paper over, and prick a few holes in it. It is better to boil the seasoning with some sweet herbs in the vinegar, and let it stand to be cold before it is put over the eels. Two yolks of eggs boiled hard should be put in the vinegar with a tea-spoonful of flour of mustard. Two yolks are sufficient for twelve pounds of eels.

Eels, to roast.

Skin your eels; turn, scotch, and wash them with melted butter; skewer them crosswise; fix them on the spit, and put over them a little pepper, salt, parsley, and thyme; roast them quick. Fry some parsley, and lay it round the dish; make your sauce of butter and gravy.

Eels, to spitchcock.

Leave the skin on the eels; scour them with salt; wash them; cut off their heads and slit them on the belly side; take out the bone and guts. Wash and wipe them well; cut them in pieces three inches long, and wipe them quite dry. Put two ounces of butter, with a little minced parsley, thyme, sage, pepper and salt, and a little chopped shalot, in a stewpan; when the butter is melted, stir the ingredients together, and take the pan off the fire; mix the yolks of two eggs with them and dip the eels in, a piece at a time; then roll them in bread crumbs, making as much stick on as you can. Rub the gridiron with a bit of suet; set it over a clear fire, and broil your eels of a fine crisp brown; dust them with crisp parsley. Sauce, anchovy and butter, or plain butter in a boat.

Another way.

Wash your eels well in their skins with salt and water; dry and slit them; take out the back-bone, and slash them: season them with chopped parsley, thyme, salt, and pepper. Clean the inside with melted butter; cut them into pieces about three inches long and broil them; make the sauce with butter and orange juice.

Eels, to stew.

Take five pounds of middling shafflings, cut off their heads, skin, and cut them in pieces as long as your finger. Wash them in several waters; dry them well with a cloth, lay them in a pan, sprinkle over them half an ounce of white salt, and let them lie an hour. Lay them in a stewpan, and add half a pint of French white wine, a quarter of a pint of water, two cloves beaten, a blade of mace, a large onion peeled, and the rind of a lemon; stew all these gently half an hour: then take the eels out of the liquor, skim off all the fat, and flour the eels all over; put to the liquor in which they were stewed an anchovy, washed and boned, and mix sorrel and parsley, half a handful of each, and half a pound of fresh butter. Let it just boil up; put in the eels; when they boil, lay them on sippets in your dish, and send them up hot to table.

Another way.

Cover the fish close in a stewpan with a piece of butter as big as a walnut rolled in flour, and let it stew till done enough, which you will know by the eels being very tender. Take them up and lay them on a dish; strain your sauce, and give it a quick boil and pour it over the fish. Garnish with lemon.

Fish, to recover when tainted.

When fish of any kind is tainted plunge it in cold milk, which will render it sweet again.

Fish, in general, to dress.

Take water, salt, half a pint of vinegar, a sprig of thyme, a small onion, and a little lemon peel; boil them all together, then put in your fish, and when done enough take them out, drain them well, and lay them over a stove to keep hot.

If you fry fish, strew some crumbs of grated bread very fine over them, and fry them in sweet oil; then drain them well and keep them hot.

Fish, to dress in Sauce.

Cut off the heads, tails, and fins, of two or three haddocks or other small fish; stew them in a quart of water, with a little spice and anchovy, and a bunch of sweet herbs, for a quarter of an hour; and then skim. Roll a bit of butter in flour, and thicken the liquor; put down the fish, and stew them with a little chopped parsley, and cloves, or onions.

Fish hashed in Paste.

Cut the fish into dice about three quarters of an inch square; prepare white sauce the same as for fowls, leaving out the mushrooms and truffles; add a little anchovy sauce to give it a good colour, and a pinch of cayenne pepper and salt. When the sauce is done, throw in the dice of fish, and when thoroughly hot serve it.

There should be a little more butter in the sauce than is commonly used in the white sauce for fowls.

Fish, to Cavietch.

Cut the fish into slices, season them with pepper and salt, and let them lie for an hour; dry them well with a cloth, flour and fry them brown in oil: boil a quantity of vinegar proportionate to that of the fish to be prepared: cover the fish with slices of garlic and some whole pepper and mace; add the same quantity of oil as vinegar, mix them well together, and salt to your taste. When the fish and liquor are quite cold, slice onions and lay at the bottom of the pan; then put a layer of fish, and so on, till the whole is in. The liquor must be cold before it is poured on the fish.

Gudgeon.

Dress as you would smelts.

Haddocks, to bake.

Bone two or three haddocks, and lay them in a deep pan with pepper, salt, butter and flour, and two or three anchovies, and sufficient water to cover them. Cover the pan close for an hour, which is required to bake them, and serve them in the saucepan.

Haddock baked.

Let the inside of the gills be drawn out and washed clean; fill with bread crumbs, parsley, sweet herbs chopped, nutmeg, salt, pepper, a bit of butter, and grated lemon-peel; skewer the tail into the mouth, and rub it well with yolk of egg. Strew over bread crumbs, and stick on bits of butter. Bake the fish in a common oven, putting into the dish a little white wine and water, a bit of mace, and lemon-peel. Serve up with oyster sauce, white fish sauce, or anchovy sauce; but put to the sauce what gravy is in the dish, first skimming it.

Haddock Pudding.

Skin the fish; take out all the bones, and cut it in thin slices. Butter the mould well, and throw round it the spawn of a lobster, before it is boiled. Put alternate slices of haddock and lobster in the mould, and season to your taste. Beat up half a pint of cream or more, according to the size of the mould, with three eggs, and pour on it: tie a cloth over, and boil it an hour. Stew oysters to go in the dish. Garnish with pastry.

Herring.

The following is a Swedish dish: Take salted herring, some cold veal, an apple, and an onion, mince them all fine, and mix them well together with oil and vinegar.

Lampreys, to pot.

Well cleanse your lampreys in the following manner: the intestines and the pipe which nature has given them instead of a bone must be taken clear away, by opening them down the belly from head to tail. They must then be rubbed with wood-ashes, to remove the slime. Then rub with salt, and wash them in three or four waters. Let them be quite free from water before you proceed to season them thus:—take, according to the quantity you intend to pot, allspice ground with an equal quantity of black pepper, a little mace, cayenne pepper, salt, about the same quantity as that of all the other seasoning; mix these well together, and rub your lampreys inside and out. Put them into an earthen pan or a well-tinned copper stewpan, with some good butter under and over, sufficient to cover them, when dissolved. Put in with them a few bay-leaves and the peel of a lemon. Let them bake slowly till they are quite done; then strain off the butter, and let them lie on the back of a sieve till nearly cold. Then place them in pots of suitable size, taking great care to rub the seasoning well over them as you lay them in; because the seasoning is apt to get from the fish when you drain them. Carefully separate the butter which you have strained from the gravy; clarify it, and, when almost cold, pour it into your pots so as to cover your fish completely. If you have not sufficient butter for this purpose you must clarify more, as the fish must be entirely hid from sight. They are fit for use the next day.

Great care must be taken to put them into the pots quite free from the gravy or moisture which they produce.

Another way.

Skin your fish, cleanse them with salt, and wipe them dry. Beat some black pepper, mace, and cloves; mix them with salt, and season your fish with it. Put them in a pan; cover with clarified butter; bake them an hour and season them well; remove the butter after they are baked; take them out of their gravy, and lay them on a coarse cloth to drain. When quite cold, season them again with the same seasoning. Lay them close in the pot; cover them completely with clarified butter; and if your butter is good, they will keep a long time.

Lobsters, to butter.

Put by the tails whole, to be laid in the middle of the dish; cut the meat into large pieces; put in a large piece of butter, and two spoonfuls of Rhenish wine; squeeze in the juice of a lemon, and serve it up.

Lobster Fricassee.

Cut the meat of a lobster into dice; put it in a stewpan with a little veal gravy; let it stew for ten minutes. A little before you send it to table beat up the yolk of an egg in cream: put it to your lobster, stirring it till it simmers. Pepper and salt to your taste. Dish it up very hot, and garnish with lemon.

Lobsters, to hash.

Take the meat out of a boiled lobster as whole as you can. Break all the shells; to these and the remains of the body, the large claws excepted, as they have no goodness in them, put some water, cayenne pepper, salt, and common pepper. Let them stew together till the liquor has a good flavour of the lobster, but observe that there must be very little water, and add two teaspoonfuls of anchovy pickle. Strain through a common sieve; put the meat of the lobster to the gravy; add some good rich melted butter, and send to table. Lobster sauce is made in the same way, only the meat should be cut smaller than for hashing. Hen lobsters are best.

Lobsters, to pot.

Boil four moderate-sized lobsters, take off the tails, and split them. Take out the flesh as whole as possible; pick the meat out of the body and chine; beat it fine, and season with pepper, salt, nutmeg, and mace, and season separately, in the same manner, the tails and claws, which must also be taken out as whole as you can. Clarify a pound of the very finest butter; skim it clean; put in the tails and claws, with what you have beaten, and let it boil a very short time, stirring it all the while lest it should turn. Let it drain through a sieve, but not too much; put it down close in a pot, and, when it is a little cooled, pour over the butter which you drained from it. When quite cold, tie it down. The butter should be the very best, as it mixes with the lobster spawn, &c., and is excellent to eat with the rest or spread upon bread.

Lobsters, to stew.

Half boil two fine lobsters; break the claws and take out the meat as whole as you can; cut the tails in two, and take out the meat; put them in a stewpan, with half a pint of gravy, a gill of white wine, a little beaten mace, cayenne pepper, salt, a spoonful of ketchup, a little anchovy liquor, and a little butter rolled in flour. Cover and stew them gently for twenty minutes. Shake the pan round frequently to prevent the contents from sticking; squeeze in a little lemon. Cut the chines in four; pepper, salt, and broil them. Put the meat and sauce in a dish, and the chines round for garnish.

Lobster Curry Powder.

Eleven ounces of coriander seed, six drachms of cayenne pepper, one ounce of cummin, one ounce and a half of black pepper, one ounce and a half of turmeric, three drachms of cloves, two drachms of cardamoms.

Lobster Patés.

Rub two ounces of butter well into half a pound of flour; add one yolk of an egg and a little water, and make it into a stiff paste. Sheet your paté moulds very thin, fill them with crumbs of bread, and bake lightly. Turn out the crumbs and save them. Cut your lobster small; add to it a little white sauce, and season with pepper and salt. Take care that it is not too thin. Fill your moulds; cover with the crumbs which you saved, and a quarter of an hour before dinner put them into the oven to give them a light colour.

Oyster patés are done the same way.

Lobster Salad.

Boil a cauliflower, pull it in pieces, and put it in a dish with a little pepper, salt, and vinegar. Have four or five hard-boiled eggs, boiled beet-root, small salad, and some anchovies, nicely cleaned and cut in lengths. Put a layer of small salad at the bottom of the dish, then a layer of the cauliflower, then the eggs cut in slices, then the beet, and so on. Take the claws and tail of the lobster, cut as whole as possible, and trim, to be laid on the top. The trimmings and what you can get out may be put in at the time you are laying the cauliflower, &c. in the dish. Make a rich salad sauce with a little elder vinegar in it, and pour it over. Lay the tails and claws on the top, and cross the shreds of the anchovies over them.

Mackarel à la maitre d'hotel.

Boil the fish, and then put it in a stewpan, with a piece of butter and sweet herbs. Set it on the fire till the butter becomes oil.

Mackarel, to boil.

Boil them in salt and water with a little vinegar. Fennel sauce is good to eat with them, and also coddled gooseberries.

Mackarel, to broil.

You may split them or broil them whole; pepper and salt them well. For sauce, scald some mint and fennel, chop them small; then melt some butter and put your herbs in. You may scald some gooseberries and lay over your mackarel.

Mackarel, to collar.

Collar them as eels, only omit the sage, and add sweet herbs, a little lemon-peel, and seasoning to your taste.

Mackarel, to fry.

For frying you may stuff the fish with crumbs of bread, parsley well chopped, lemon-peel grated, pepper and salt, mixed with yolk of egg. Serve up with anchovy or fennel sauce.

Mackarel, to pickle.

Cut the mackarel into four or five pieces; season them very high; make slits with a penknife, put in the seasoning, and fry them in oil to a good brown colour. Drain them very dry; put them into vinegar, if they are to be kept for any time; pour oil on the top.

Mackarel, to pot.

Proceed in the same manner as with eels.

Mackarel, to souse.

Wash and clean your fish: take out the roes, and boil them in salt and water; when enough, take them out and lay them in the dish; pour away half the liquor they were boiled in, and add to the rest of the liquor as much vinegar as will cover them and two or three bay leaves. Let them lie three days before they are eaten.

Mackarel Pie.

Cut the fish into four pieces; season them to your taste with pepper, salt, and a little mace, mixed with a quarter of a pound of beef suet, chopped fine. Put at the bottom and top, and between the layers of fish, a good deal of young parsley, and instead of water a little new milk in the dish for gravy. If you like it rich, warm about a quarter of a pint of cream, which pour in the pie when baked; if not, have boiled a little gravy with the heads. It will take the same time to bake as a veal pie.

Mullet, to boil.

Let them be boiled in salt and water, and, when you think them done enough, pour part of the water from them, and put a pint of red wine, two onions sliced, some nutmeg, salt, and vinegar, beaten mace, a bunch of sweet herbs, and the juice of a lemon. Boil all these well together, with two or three anchovies; put in your fish; and, when they have simmered some time, put them into a dish and strain the sauce over. If you like, shrimps or oysters may be added.

Mullet, to broil.

Let the mullet be scaled and gutted, and cut gashes in their sides; dip them in melted butter, and broil them at a great distance from the fire. Sauce—anchovy, with capers, and a lemon squeezed into it.

Mullet, to fry.

Carefully scale and gut the fish, score them across the back, and then dip them into melted butter. Melt some butter in a stewpan; let it clarify. Fry your mullet in it; when done, lay them on a warm dish. Sauce—anchovy and butter.

Oysters, to stew.

Take a quart of large oysters; strain the liquor from them through a sieve; wash them well, and take off the beards. Put them in a stewpan, and drain the liquor from the settlings. Add to the oysters a quarter of a pound of butter mixed with flour and a gill of white wine, and grate in a little nutmeg with a gill of cream. Keep them stirred till they are quite thick and smooth. Lay sippets at the bottom of the dish; pour in your oysters, and lay fried sippets all round.

Another way.

Put a quarter of a pound of butter into a clean stewpan, and let it boil. Strain a pint of oysters from their liquor; put them into the butter; and let them stew with some parsley minced small, a little shalot shred small, and the yolks of three eggs well beaten up with the liquor strained from the oysters. Put all these together into the stewpan with half a pound more butter; shake it and stew them a little; if too much, you make the oysters hard.

Oysters, ragout of.

Twenty-five oysters, half a table-spoonful of soy, double the quantity of vinegar, a piece of butter, and a little pepper, salt, and flour.

Oysters, to pickle.

Blanch the oysters, and strain off the liquor; wash the oysters in three or four waters; put them into a stewpan, with their liquor and half a pint of white wine vinegar, two onions sliced thin, a little parsley and thyme, a blade of mace, six cloves, Jamaica pepper, a dozen corns of white pepper, and salt according to your taste. Boil up two or three minutes; let them stand till cold; then put them into a dish, and pour the liquor over them.

Oyster Patés. No. 1.

Stew the oysters in their own liquor, but do not let them be too much done; beard them; take a table-spoonful of pickled mushrooms, wash them in two or three cold waters to get out the vinegar; then cut each mushroom into four, and fry them in a little butter dusted over with flour. Take three table-spoonfuls of veal jelly, and two spoonfuls of cream; let it boil, stirring all the while; add a small bit of butter. Season with a pinch of salt, and one of cayenne pepper. Throw the oysters, which you have kept warm in a cloth near the fire, into the sauce; see that it is all hot; then have the patés ready, fill them with the oysters and sauce, and put a top on each. When the paste of oyster patés is done, remove the tops gently and cleanly with a knife; take out the flaky part of the paste inside and from the inside of the top; cut six little pieces of bread square so as to fill the inside; lay on the top of the paste. Then place them on a sheet of paper in a dish, and put them before the fire, covering them with a cloth to keep them hot. When you are going to serve them take out the piece of bread, and fill the patés with the oysters and sauce.

Oyster Patés. No. 2.

Spread some puff-paste about half an inch thick. Cut out six pieces with a small tea-cup. Rub a baking sheet over with a brush dipped in water, and put the patés on it at a little distance from each other. Glaze them thoroughly with the yolk and white of egg mixed up; open a hole at the top of each with a small knife; cut six tops of the size of a crown-piece, and place them lightly on the patés. Let them be baked, and when done remove the tops, and place the crust on paper till ready to serve up; then fill them with oysters (as described in the preceding recipe) put the tops over them, and dish them upon a folded napkin.

Oyster Patés. No. 3.

Parboil your oysters, and strain them from their liquor, wash the beard, and cut them in flour. Put them in a stewpan, with an ounce of butter rolled in flour, half a gill of cream, and a little grated lemon-peel, if liked. Free the oyster liquor from sediment, reduce it by boiling to one half; add cayenne pepper and salt. Stir it over the fire, and fill your patés.

Oyster Loaves.

Cut out the crumb of three French rolls; lay them before the fire till they are hot through, turning them often. Melt half a pound of butter; put some into the loaves; put on their tops, and boil them till they are buttered quite through. Then take a pint of oysters, stewed with half a pint of water, one anchovy, a little pepper and salt, a quarter of a pound of butter, and as much sauce as will make your sauce thick. Give it a boil. Put as many oysters into your loaves as will go in; pour the rest of the sauce all over the loaves in the dish in which they are served up.

Oyster Pie.

Beard the oysters; scald and strain them from their liquor, and season the liquor with pepper, salt, and anchovy, a lump of butter, and bread crumbs. Boil up to melt the anchovies; then just heat your oysters in it; put them all together into your pie-dish, and cover them with a puff-paste.

If you put your oysters into a fresh pie, you must cover them at the top with crisped crumbs of bread; add more to the savouring if you like it.

Perch, to fricassee.

Boil the perch, and strip them of the bones; half cover them with white wine; put in two or three anchovies, a little pepper and salt, and warm it over the fire. Put in a little parsley and onions, with yolks of eggs well beaten. Toss it together; put in a little thick butter; and serve it up.

Pike, to dress.

If you would serve it as a first dish, do not scale it; take off the gills, and, having gutted it, boil it in court bouillon, as a side-dish, or *entrée*. It may be served in many ways. Cut it into pieces, and put it into a stewpan, with a bit of butter, a bunch of all sorts of sweet herbs, and some mushrooms; turn it a few times over the fire, and shake in a little flour; moisten it with some good broth and a pint of white wine, and set it over a brisk fire. When it is done, add a trifle of salt and cayenne pepper, the yolk of three eggs, and half a pint of cream, stirring it till well mixed. Serve up hot.

Pike stuffed, to boil.

Clean a large pike; take out the gills; prepare a stuffing with finely grated bread, all sorts of sweet-herbs, particularly thyme, some onions, grated lemon-peel, oysters chopped small, a piece of butter, the boiled yolk of two eggs, and a sufficient quantity of suet to hold the ingredients together. Put them into the fish, and sew it up. Turn the tail into the mouth, and boil it in pump water, with two spoonfuls of vinegar and a handful of salt. It will take forty minutes to boil, if a large fish.

Pike, to boil, à-la-Française.

Wash well, clean, and scale a large pike, and cut it into three pieces; boil an equal quantity of white wine and water with lemon-peel, and when the liquor boils put your pike in, with a handful of salt. When done, lay it on sippets, and stick it with bits of fried bread. Sauce—melted butter, with slices of lemon in it, the yolks of three eggs, and some grated nutmeg. Pour your sauce over the pike, and serve it up.

Pike, to broil.

Split it, and scotch it with a knife on the outside; season it with salt; put the gridiron on a clear fire, make it very hot, then lay on the pike; baste it with butter, turn it often, and, when broiled crisp and stiff put it into a dish, and serve it up with butter and the juice of lemons, or white wine vinegar. Garnish with slices of oranges or lemons.

Pike in Court Bouillon.

Scale and well wash your pike; lay it in a pan; pour vinegar and salt over it; let it lie for an hour, then take it out, season with pepper, a little salt, sweet herbs, cloves, and a bay leaf, with a piece of butter. Wrap it up in a napkin, and put it into a stewpan, with some white wine, a lemon sliced, a little verjuice, nutmeg, cloves, and a bay leaf. Let this liquor boil very fast; put in the pike, and when done lay it on a warm dish, and strain the liquor into a saucepan; add to it an anchovy washed and boned, a few capers, a little water, and a piece of butter rolled in flour: let these simmer till of proper thickness, and pour them over the fish.

Pike Fricandeau.

Cut a pike in several pieces, according to its size, after having scaled, gutted, and washed, it. Lard all the upper part with bacon cut small, and put it into a stew-pan with a glass of red wine (or white wine if for white sauce) some good broth, a bunch of sweet-herbs, and some lean veal cut into dice. When it is stewed and the sauce strained off, complete it in the manner of any other fricandeau; putting a good sauce under it, either brown or white, as you chuse.

Pike, German way of dressing—delicious!

Take a pike of moderate size; when well washed and cleansed, split it down the back, close to the bone, in two flat pieces. Set it over the fire in a stewpan with salt and water; half boil it. Take it out; scale it; put it into the stewpan again, with a very little water, and some mushrooms, truffles, and morels, an equal quantity, cut small; add a bunch of sweet herbs. Let it stew very gently, closely covered, over a very slow fire, or the fish will break; when it is almost done, take out the herbs, put in a cupful of capers, chopped small, three anchovies split and shred fine, a piece of butter rolled in flour, and a table-spoonful of grated Parmesan cheese. Pour in a pint of white wine, and cover the stewpan quite close. When the ingredients are mixed, and the fish quite done, lay it in a warm dish, and pour the sauce over it.

Pike, to pot.

After scaling the fish, cut off the head, split it, take out the back-bone, and strew it over with bay salt and pepper. Cover and bake it; lay it on a coarse cloth to drain, and when cold put it in a pot that will just hold it, and cover with clarified butter.

If not well drained from the gravy it will not keep.

Pike, to roast.

Scale and slash the fish from head to tail; lard it with the flesh of eels rolled up in sweet-herbs and seasoning; fill it with fish and forced meat. Roast it at length; baste and bread it; make the sauce of drawn butter, anchovies, the roe and liver, with mushrooms, capers, and oysters. Ornament with sliced lemon.

Pike au Souvenir.

Wash a large pike; gut and dry it; make a forcemeat with eel, anchovy, whiting, pepper, salt, suet, thyme, bread crumbs, parsley, and a bit of shalot, mixed with the yolks of eggs; fill the inside of the fish with this meat; sew it up; after which draw with your packing-needle a piece of packthread through the eyes of the pike, through the middle and the tail also in the form of S; wash it over with the yolk of an egg, and strew it with the crumbs of bread. Roast or bake it with a caul over it. Sauce—melted butter and capers.

Pike à la Tatare, or in the Tartar fashion.

Clean your pike; gut and scale it; cut it into bits, and lay it in oil, with salt, cayenne pepper, parsley, scallions, mushrooms, two shalots, the whole shred very fine; grate bread over it and lay it upon the gridiron, basting it, while broiling, with the rest of the oil. When it is done of a good colour, serve it in a dry dish, with sauce *à la remoulade* [see Sauces] in a sauce-boat.

Fresh Salmon, to dress.

Cut it in slices, steep it in a little sweet butter, salt and pepper, and broil it, basting it with butter while doing. When done, serve over it any of the fish sauces, as described (see the Sauces), or you may serve it with court bouillon, which will do for all kinds of fish whatever.

Salmon, to dress en caisses, that is, in small paper cases.

Take two slices of fresh salmon, about the thickness of half a finger; steep it an hour in sweet butter with mushrooms, a clove of garlic, and a shalot, all shred fine, half a laurel-leaf, thyme, and basil, reduced to a fine powder, salt, and whole pepper. Then make a neat paper box to contain your salmon; rub the outside of it with butter, and put the salmon with all its seasoning and covered with grated bread into it; do it in an oven, or put the dish upon a stove, and, when the salmon is done, brown it with a salamander. When you serve it, squeeze in the juice of a large lemon. If you serve it with Spanish sauce, the fat must be taken off the salmon before you put in the sauce.

Salmon à la Poële, or done on the Stove.

Put three or four slices of fillet of veal, and two or three of ham, having carefully cut off the fat of both, at the bottom of a stewpan, just the size of the salmon you would serve. Lay the salmon upon it, and cover it with thin slices of bacon, adding a bunch of parsley, scallions, two cloves of garlic, and three shalots. Boil it gently over a moderate stove fire, a quarter of an hour; moisten it with a glass of champagne, or fine white wine; let it continue to stew slowly till thoroughly done; and the moment before you serve it strain off the sauce, laying the salmon in a hot dish. Add to the sauce five or six spoonfuls of cullis; let it boil up two or three times, and then pour it over the salmon, and serve up.

Scallops.

Pick the scallops, and wash them extremely clean; make them very dry. Flour them a very little. Fry them of a fine light brown. Make a nice, strong, light sauce of veal and a little ham; thicken a very little, and gently stew the scallops in it for half an hour.

Shrimps, to pot.

Pick the finest shrimps you can procure; season them with a little mace beaten fine, and pepper and salt to your taste. Add a little cold butter. Pound all together in a mortar till it becomes a paste. Put it into small pots, and pour over it clarified butter.

Another way.

To a quart of pickled shrimps put two ounces of fresh butter, and stew them over a moderate fire, stirring them about. Add to them while on the fire twelve white peppercorns and two blades of mace, beaten very fine, and a very little salt.—Let them stew a quarter of an hour: when done, put them down close in pots, and pour clarified butter over them when cold.

Smelts, to fry.

Dry and rub them with yolk of egg; flour or strew some fine bread crumbs on them; when fried, lay them in the dish with their tails in the middle of it. Anchovy sauce.

Smelts, to pickle.

Take a quarter of a peck of smelts, and put them into a jar, and beat very fine half an ounce of nutmegs, and the same quantity of saltpetre and of pepper, a quarter of an ounce of mace, and a quarter of a pound of common salt. Wash the fish; clean gut them, after which lay them in rows in a jar or pan; over every layer of smelts strew your seasoning, with some bay-leaves, and pour on boiled red wine sufficient to cover them. Put a plate or a cover over, and when cold tie them down close.

Smelts, to pot.

Clean the inside of the fish, and season them with salt, pounded mace, and pepper. Bake them, and when nearly cold lay them upon a cloth; then put them into pots, taking off the butter from the gravy; clarify it with more butter, and pour it on them.

Soles, to boil.

The soles should be boiled in salt and water. Anchovy sauce.

Soles, to boil, à-la-Française.

Put a quart of water and half a pint of vinegar into an earthen dish; skin and clean a pair of soles; put them into vinegar and water, let them remain there for two hours. Dry them with a cloth, and put them into a stewpan, with a pint of wine, a quarter of a pint of water, a little sweet marjoram, a very little thyme, an onion stuck with four cloves, and winter savory. Sprinkle a very little bay salt, covering them close. Let them simmer gently till they are done; then take them out, and lay them in a warm dish before the fire. Put into the liquor, after it is strained, a piece of butter rolled in flour; let it boil till of a proper thickness; lay your soles in the dish, and pour the sauce over them.

A small turbot or any flat fish may be done the same way.

Soles, to stew.

Cut and skin the soles, and half fry them; have ready the quantity you like of half white wine and half water, mixed with some gravy, one whole onion, and a little whole pepper. Stew them all together, with a little shred lemon, and a few mushrooms. When they are done enough, thicken the sauce with good butter, and serve it up.

Water Souchi.

Put on a kettle of water with a good deal of salt in it, and a good many parsley roots; keep it skimmed very clean, and when it boils up throw in your perch or whatever fish you use for the purpose. When sufficiently boiled, take them up and serve them hot. Have ready a pint or more of water, in which parsley roots have been boiled, till it has acquired a very strong flavour, and when the fish are dished throw some of this liquor over them. The Dutch sauce for them is made thus:—To a pint of white wine vinegar add a blade or two of mace; let it stew gently by the fire, and, when the vinegar is sufficiently flavoured by the mace, put into it about a pound of butter. Shake the saucepan now and then, and, when the butter is quite melted, make all exceedingly hot; have ready the yolks of four good eggs beaten up. You must continue beating them while another person gently pours to them the boiling vinegar by degrees, lest they should curdle; and continue stirring them all the while. Set it over a gentle fire, still continuing to stir until it is very hot and of the thickness you desire; then serve it.

Sprats, to bake.

Wipe your sprats with a clean cloth; rub them with pepper and salt, and lay them in a pan. Bruise a pennyworth of cochineal; put it into the vinegar, and pour it over the sprats with some bay-leaves. Tie them down close with coarse paper in a deep brown pan, and set them in the oven all night. They eat very fine cold.

You may put to them a pint of vinegar, half a pint of red wine, and spices if you like it; but they eat very well without.

Sturgeon, to roast.

Put a walnut-sized bit of butter (or more if it is a large fish), rolled in flour, in a stewpan, with sweet-herbs, cloves, a gill of water, and a spoonful of vinegar; stir it over the fire, and when it is lukewarm take it off, and put in your sturgeon to steep. When it has been a sufficient time to take the flavour of the herbs, roast it, and when done, serve it with court bouillon, or any other fish sauce.

Turbot, to dress.

Wipe your turbot very dry, then take a deep stewpan, put in the fish, with two bay-leaves, a handful of parsley, a large onion stuck with cloves, some salt, and cayenne; heat a pint of white wine boiling hot, and pour it upon the turbot; then strain in some very strong veal gravy, (made from your stock jelly,) more than will cover it; set it over a stove, and let it simmer very gently, that the full strength of the ingredients may be infused into it. When it is quite done, put it on a hot dish; strain the gravy into a saucepan, with some butter and flour to thicken it.

Plaice, dabs, and flounders, may be dressed in the same way.

Turbot, plain boiled.

Make a brine with two handfuls of salt in a gallon of water, let the turbot lie in it two hours before it is to be boiled; then set on a fish-kettle, with water enough to cover it, and about half a pint of vinegar, or less if the turbot is small; put in a piece of horseradish; when the water boils put in the turbot, the white side upper-most, on a fish-plate; let it be done enough, but not too much, which will be easily known by the look. A small one will take twenty minutes, a large one half an hour. Then take it up, and set it on a fish-plate to drain, before it is laid in the dish. See that it is served quite dry. Sauce—lobster and white sauce.

Turbot, to boil.

Put the turbot into a kettle, with white wine vinegar and lemon; season with salt and onions; add to these water. Boil it over a gentle fire, skimming it very clean. Garnish with slices of lemon on the top.

Turbot, to boil in Gravy.

Wash and well dry a middling sized turbot; put it with two bay-leaves into a deep stew-dish, with some cloves, a handful of parsley, a large onion, and some salt and pepper, add a pint of boiling hot white wine, strain in some strong veal gravy that will more than cover the fish, and remove it on one side that the in-gredients may be well mixed together. Lay it on a hot dish, strain the gravy into a saucepan with some butter and flour, pour a little over the fish, and put the re-mainder in a sauce terrine.

Turbot, to boil in Court Bouillon, with Capers.

Be very particular in washing and drying your turbot. Take thyme, parsley, sweet-herbs of all sorts, minced very fine, and one large onion sliced; put them into a stewpan, then lay in the turbot—the stewpan should be just large enough to hold the fish—strew over the fish the same herbs that are under it, with some chives and a little sweet basil; pour in an equal quantity of white wine and white wine vinegar, till the fish is completely covered; strew in a little bay salt with some pepper. Set the stewpan over a stove, with a very gentle fire, increasing the heat by degrees, till it is done sufficiently. Take it off the fire, but do not take the turbot out: let it stand on the side of the stove. Set a saucepan on the fire, with a pound of butter and two anchovies, split, boned, and carefully cleansed, two large spoonfuls of capers cut small, some chives whole, and a little cayenne, nutmeg grated, a little flour, a spoonful of vinegar, and a little broth. Set the saucepan over the stove, keep shaking it round for some time, and then leave it at the side of the stove. Take up the stewpan in which is the turbot, and set it on the stove to make it quite hot; then put it in a deep dish; and, having warmed the sauce, pour it over it, and serve up.

Soles, flounders, plaice, &c. are all excellent dressed in the same way.

Turbot, to fry.

It must be a small turbot. Cut it across, as if it were ribbed; when it is quite dry, flour it, and put it into a large frying-pan with boiling butter enough to cover it; fry it brown, then drain it. Put in enough claret to cover it, two anchovies, salt, a scruple of nutmeg and ginger, and let it stew slowly till half the liquor is wasted; then take it out, and put in a piece of butter, of the size of a walnut, rolled in flour, and a lemon minced, juice and all. Let these ingredients simmer till of a proper thickness. Rub a hot dish with an eschalot or onion; pour the sauce in, and lay the turbot carefully in the midst.

Turbot or Barbel, glazed.

Lard the upper part of your turbot or barbel with fine bacon. Let it simmer slowly between slices of ham, with a little champagne, or fine white, and a bunch of sweet-herbs. Put into another stewpan part of a fillet of veal, cut into dice, with one slice of ham; stew them with some fine cullis, till the sauce is reduced to a thick gravy. When thoroughly done, strain it off before you serve it, and, with a feather, put it over your turbot to glaze it. Then pour some good cullis into the stewpan, and toss it up as a sauce to serve in the dish, adding the juice of a lemon.

Turbot, to dress en gras, or in a rich fashion.

Put into a stewpan a small quantity of broth, several slices of veal, and an equal quantity of ham, a little cayenne, and a bunch of sweet-herbs. Let it stew over a very slow stove, and add a glass of champagne. When this is completely done, serve it with any of the sauces, named in the article Sauces, added to its own.

Turbot or Barbel, to dress en maigre, or in a lean fashion.

Put into a stewpan a large handful of salt, a pint of water, a clove of garlic, onions, and all sorts of sweet kitchen herbs, the greater variety the better, only an equal quantity of each. Boil the whole half an hour over a slow fire; let it settle. Pour off the clear part of the sauce, and strain it through a sieve; then put twice as much rich milk as there is of the brine, and put the fish in it over a very slow fire, letting it simmer only. When your turbot is done, pour over it any of the sauces named as being proper for fish in the article Sauces.

Turtle, to dress.

After having killed the turtle, divide the back and belly, cleaning it well from the blood in four or five waters, with some salt; take away the fins from the back, and scrape and scald them well from the scales; then put the meat into the saucepan, with a little salt and water just to cover it; stew it, and keep skimming it very clean all the while it is stewing. Should the turtle be a large one, put a bottle of white wine; if a small one, half that quantity. It must be stewed an hour and a half before you put in the wine, and the scum have done rising; for the wine being put in before turns it hard; and, while it is stewing, put an onion or two shred fine, with a little parsley, thyme, salt, and black pepper. After it has stewed tender, take it out of the saucepan, and cut it into small pieces; let the back shell be well washed clean from the blood, and rub it with salt, pepper, thyme, parsley, and onions, shred fine, mixed well together; put a layer of seasoning into the shell, and lay on your meat, and so continue till the shell is filled, covering it with seasoning. If a large turtle, two pounds of butter must be cut into bits, and laid between the seasoning and the meat. You must thicken the soup with butter rolled in flour. An hour and a half is requisite for a large turtle.

Whiting, to dry.

Take the whiting when they come fresh in, and lay them in salt and water about four hours, the water not being too salt. Hang them up by the tails two days near a fire, after which, skin and broil them.

MADE DISHES.

Asparagus forced in French Rolls.

Take out the crumb of three French rolls, by first cutting off a piece of the top crust; but be careful to cut it so neatly that the crust fits the place again. Fry the rolls brown in fresh butter. Take a pint of cream, the yolks of six eggs beaten fine, a little salt and nutmeg; stir them well together over a slow fire until the mixture begins to be thick. Have ready a hundred of small asparagus boiled; save tops enough to stick in the rolls; the rest cut small and put into the cream; fill the rolls with it. Before you fry the rolls, make holes thick in the top crust to stick the asparagus in; then lay on the piece of crust, and stick it with asparagus as if it was growing.

Eggs, to dress.

Boil or poach them in the common way. Serve them on a piece of buttered toast, or on stewed spinach.

Eggs buttered. No. 1.

Take the yolks and whites; set them over the fire with a bit of butter, and a little pepper and salt; stir them a minute or two. When they become rather thick and a little turned in small lumps, pour them on a buttered toast.

Eggs buttered. No. 2.

Put a lump of butter, of the size of a walnut; beat up two eggs; add a little cream, and put in the stewpan, stirring them till they are hot. Add pepper and salt, and lay them on toast.

Eggs buttered. No. 3.

Beat the eggs well together with about three spoonfuls of cream and a little salt; set the mass over a slow fire, stirring till it becomes thick, without boiling, and have a toast ready buttered to pour it upon.

Milk with a little butter, about the size of a walnut, may be used instead of the cream.

Eggs, Scotch.

Take half a pound of the flesh of a fowl, or of veal, or any white meat (dressed meat will do), mince it very small with half a pound of suet and the crumb of a

French roll soaked in cream, a little parsley, plenty of lemon-peel shred very small, a little pepper, salt, and nutmeg; pound all these together, adding a raw egg, till they become a paste. Boil as many eggs as you want very hard; take out the yolks, roll them up in the forcemeat, and make them the size and shape of an egg. Fry them till they are of a light brown, and toss them up in a good brown sauce. Quarter some hard-boiled eggs, and spread them over your dish.

Eggs for second Course.

Boil five eggs quite hard; clear away the shells, cut them in half, take out the yolks, and put the whites into warm water. Pound the yolks in a mortar till they become very fine. Have ready some parsley and a little onion chopped as fine as possible; add these to the yolks, with a pinch of salt and cayenne pepper. Add a sufficient quantity of hot cream to make it into a thick even paste; fill the halves of the whites with this, and keep the whole in hot water. Prepare white sauce; place the eggs on a dish in two rows, the broad part downward; pour the sauce over them, and serve up hot.

Eggs to fry as round as Balls.

Put three pints of clarified butter into a deep stewpan; heat it as hot as for fritters, and stir the butter with a stick till it turns round like a whirlpool. Break an egg into the middle, and turn it round with the stick till it is as hard as a poached egg. The whirling round of the butter makes it as round as a ball. Take it up with a slice; put it in a dish before the fire. Do as many as you want; they will be soft, and keep hot half an hour. Serve on stewed spinach.

Eggs, fricassee of.

Boil the eggs pretty hard; cut them in round slices; make white sauce and pour it over them; lay sippets round your dish, and put a whole yolk in the middle.

Eggs à la Crême.

Boil the eggs, which must be quite fresh, twelve minutes; and throw them into cold water. When cold, take off the shell without breaking the white. Have a little shalot and parsley minced fine and mixed; pass it with a little fresh butter. When done enough, set it to cool. Cut the eggs through the middle; put the whites into warm water; pound the yolks very fine; put them into your stewpan, with a little cream, pepper, and salt. Make the whole very hot, and dish. Two gills of cream will be sufficient for ten eggs.

Ham, essence of.

Take six pounds of ham; cut off all the skin and fat, and cut the lean into slices about an inch thick; lay them in the bottom of a stewpan, with slices of carrots, parsnips, six onions sliced; cover down very close, and set it over a stove. Pour on a pint of veal cullis by degrees, some fresh mushrooms cut in pieces, if to be had, if not, mushroom powder, truffles, morels, two cloves, a basil leaf, parsley, a crust of bread, and a leek. Cover down close, and let it simmer till the meat is quite dissolved. A little of this sauce will flavour any lighter sauce with great zest and delicacy.

Maccaroni in a mould of Pie Crust.

Prepare a paste, as generally made for apple-pies, of an oval shape; put a stout bottom to it and no top; let it bake by the fire till served. Prepare a quarter of a pound of maccaroni, boil it with a little salt and half an ounce of butter; when done, put it in another stewpan with an ounce more of butter, a little grated cheese, and a spoonful of cream. Drain the maccaroni, and toss it till the cheese be well mixed; pour it into a dish; sprinkle some more grated cheese over it, and baste it with a little butter. When ready to be served, put the maccaroni into the paste, and dish it up hot without browning the cheese.

Maccaroni, to dress. No. 1.

Stew one pound of gravy beef to a rich gravy, with turnips and onions, but no carrots; season it high with cayenne, and fine it with whites of eggs. When the gravy is cold, put in the maccaroni; set it on a gentle fire; stir it often that it may not burn, and let it stew an hour and a half. When you serve it up add of Cheshire cheese grated as much as will make the maccaroni relishing.

Maccaroni. No. 2.

Boil two ounces of maccaroni in plenty of water an hour and a half, and drain it through a sieve. Put it into a saucepan, and beat a little bit of butter, some pepper and salt, and as much grated cheese as will give a proper flavour. Put it into the saucepan with the maccaroni, and add two spoonfuls of cream. Set it on the fire, and stew it up. Put it on your dish; strew a little grated cheese over it, and brown with a salamander.

Maccaroni. No. 3.

Boil the maccaroni till tender; cut it in pieces about two inches long; put it into either white or brown sauce, and let it stew gently for half an hour. Either stir in some grated cheese, or send it in plain. Pepper and salt to your taste.

Maccaroni. No. 4.

Soak a quarter of a pound of maccaroni in milk for two hours; put it into a stewpan, boil it well, and thicken with a little flour and butter. Season it with pepper and salt to your taste; and add three table-spoonfuls of cream. Put it in a dish; add bread crumbs and sliced cheese, and brown with a salamander.

Maccaroni. No. 5.

Set on the fire half a gallon of water; when it boils put into it one pound of maccaroni, with a quarter of a pound of salt; let it boil a quarter of an hour, then strain very dry, put it in a stewpan with a quarter of a pound of fresh butter; let it fry a quarter of an hour longer. Add pepper and grated cheese; stew them together; then put the maccaroni into a terrine, and shake some grated cheese on it. It is very good with a-la-mode beef gravy instead of butter.

Maccaroni. No. 6.

Boil a quarter of a pound of maccaroni till it is quite tender; lay it on a sieve to drain; then put it into a tossing-pan with about a gill of cream and a piece of butter rolled in flour. Boil five minutes, pour it on a plate, and lay Parmesan cheese toasted all over it.

Maccaroni. No. 7.

Break a quarter of a pound of pipe maccaroni into pieces about an inch long, put it into a quart of boiling broth; boil it for three hours; then strain it off from the broth, and make a sauce with a bit of butter, a little flour, some good broth, and a little cream; when it boils add a little Parmesan cheese. Put your maccaroni into the sauce, and just stir it together. Put it on the dish for table, with grated Parmesan cheese over it, and give it a good brown colour with a hot shovel or salamander.

Maccaroni. No. 8.

Boil three ounces of maccaroni in water till quite tender; lay it on a sieve to drain; when dry, put it into a stewpan, over a charcoal fire, with three or four spoonfuls of fresh cream, one ounce of butter, and a little grated Parmesan cheese. Set it over a slow fire till quite hot, but it must not boil; pour it into your hot dish; shake a little of the cheese over the top, and brown with a salamander.

Omelets.

should be fried in a small frying-pan, made for the purpose; with a small quantity of butter. Their great merit is to be thick; therefore use only half the number of whites that you do of yolks of eggs. The following ingredients are the basis of all omelets: parsley, shalot, a portion of sweet-herbs, ham, tongue, anchovy, grated cheese, shrimps, oysters, &c.

Omelet. No. 1.

Slice very thin two onions, about two ounces each; put them in a stewpan with three ounces of butter; keep the pan covered till done, stirring now and then, and, when of a nice brown, stir in as much flour as will produce a stiff paste. Add by degrees as much water or milk as will make it the thickness of good cream, and stew it with pepper and salt; have ready hard-boiled eggs (four or five); you may either shred or cut them in halves or quarters.

Omelet. No. 2.

Beat five eggs lightly together, a small quantity of shalot, shred quite fine; parsley, and a few mushrooms. Fry, and be careful not to let it burn. When done add a little sauce.

Omelet. No. 3.

Break five eggs into a basin; add half a pint of cream, a table-spoonful of flour, a little pounded loaf-sugar, and a little salt. Beat it up with a whisk for five minutes; add candied citron and orange peel; fry it in two ounces of butter.

Omelet. No. 4.

Take six or seven eggs, a gill of good cream, chopped parsley, thyme, a very small quantity, shalot, pepper, salt, and a little grated nutmeg. Put a little butter in your frying-pan, which must be very clean or the omelet will not turn out. When your butter is melted, and your omelet well beat, pour it in, put it on a gentle fire, and as it sets keep moving and mixing it with a spoon. Add a little more butter if required. When it is quite loose from the bottom, turn it over on the dish in which it is to be served.

Omelet. No. 5.

Break eight eggs into an earthen pan, with a little pepper and salt, and water sufficient to dissolve the salt; beat the eggs well. Throw an ounce and a half of fresh butter into a frying-pan; melt it over the fire; pour the eggs into the pan; keep turning them continually, but never let the middle part be over the fire. Gather all the border, and roll it before it is too much done; the middle must be kept hollow. Roll it together before it is served. A little chopped parsley and onions may be mixed with the butter and eggs, and a little shalot or pounded ham.

Omelet. No. 6.

Four eggs, a little scraped beef, cayenne pepper, nutmeg, lemon peel, parsley, burnet, chervil, and onion, all fried in lard or butter.

Asparagus Omelet.

Beat up six eggs, put some cream to them. Boil some asparagus, cut off the green heads, and mix with the eggs; add pepper and salt. Make the pan hot; put in some butter; fry the omelet, and serve it hot.

A French Omelet.

Beat up six eggs; put to them a quarter of a pint of cream, some pepper, salt, and nutmeg; beat them well together. Put a quarter of a pound of butter, made hot, into your omelet-pan, and fry it of a light brown. Double it once, and serve it up plain, or with a white sauce under it. If herbs are preferred, there should be a little parsley shred, and green onion cut very fine, and serve up fried.

Ragout for made dishes.

Boil and blanch some cocks' combs, with sweetbreads sliced and lambs' stones; mix them up in gravy, with sweet-herbs, truffles, mushrooms, oysters, and savoury spice, and use it when you have occasion.

Trouhindella.

Chop fine two pounds of veal, fat and lean together; slice crumb of bread into some warm milk: squeeze it out of the milk and put it to the veal; season with pepper, salt, and nutmeg; make it up in three balls, and fry it in butter half an hour. Put a quart of mutton or veal broth into the pan, and let it stew three quarters of an hour, or till it is reduced to a quarter of a pint of strong gravy.

MEATS AND VEGETABLES.

Artichokes, to fricassee.

Scrape the bottom clean; cut them into large dice, and boil them, but not too soft. Stove them in a little cream, seasoned with pepper and salt; thicken with the yolks of four eggs and melted butter, and serve up.

Bacon, to cure. No. 1.

Use two pounds of common salt; one pound of bay salt; one pound of brown sugar; two ounces of saltpetre; two ounces of ground black pepper.

Bacon, to cure. No. 2.

Take half a pound of saltpetre, or let part of it be petre salt, half a pound of bay salt, and one pound of coarse sugar; pound and mix them well together. Rub this mixture well into the bacon, and cover it completely with common salt. Dry it thoroughly, and keep it well packed in malt dust.

Bacon, to cure. No. 3.

For sixty pounds' weight of pork take three pounds of common salt, half a pound of saltpetre, and half a pound of brown sugar. The sugar must be put on first and well rubbed in, and last of all the common salt. Let the meat lie in salt only a week, and then hang it at a good distance from the fire, but in a place where a fire is constantly kept. When thoroughly dry, remove it into a garret, and there let it remain till wanted for use.

Barbicue.

Cut either the fore quarter or leg of a small pork pig in the shape of a ham; roast it well, and a quarter of an hour before it is enough done, baste it with Madeira wine; then strain the Madeira and gravy in the dripping-pan through a sieve; mix to your taste with cayenne pepper and lemon-juice; and serve it in the dish.

Alamode Beef. No. 1.

Take a piece of the round of beef, fresh and tender; beat it well, and to six pounds of beef put one pound of bacon, cut into large pieces for larding, and season it with pepper, cloves, and salt. Lard your beef, and put it into your stewpan, with a bay-leaf or two, and two or three onions, a bunch of parsley, a little lemon-peel, three spoonfuls of vinegar, and the same quantity of beer. Cover it close, and set it over a gentle charcoal fire; stew it very gently that your liquor may come out; and shake it often to prevent its sticking. As the liquor increases, make your fire a little stronger, and, when enough done, skim off all the fat, and put in a glass of claret. Stew it half an hour longer, and when you take it off your fire squeeze in the juice of a lemon, and serve up. It must stew five hours; and is as good cold as hot.

Alamode Beef. No. 2.

Lard the mouse-buttock with fat bacon, sprinkled with parsley, scallions, mushrooms, truffles, morels, one clove of garlic shred fine, salt, and pepper. Let it stew five or six hours in its own gravy, to which add, when it is about half done, a large spoonful of brandy. It should be done in an earthen vessel just large enough to contain it, and may be served hot or cold.

Alamode Beef. No. 3.

Lard a piece of beef with fat bacon, dipped in pepper, vinegar, allspice, and salt; flour it all over; cut two or three large onions in thin slices; lay them at the bottom of the stewpan with as much butter as will fry your beef; lay it in and brown it all over; turn it frequently. Pour to it as much boiling water as will cover it; add a little lemon-peel, and a bunch of herbs, which must be taken out before done enough; when it has stewed about two hours turn it. When finished, put in some mushrooms or ketchup, and serve up.

Alamode Beef, in the French manner.

Take the best part of the mouse-buttock, between four and seven pounds, larded well with fat bacon, and cut in square pieces the length and thickness of your beef. Before you lard it, take a little mace, six cloves, some pepper and salt, ground all together, and mix it with some parsley, shalot, and a few sweet-herbs; chop them small, roll your bacon in this mixture, and lard your beef. Skewer it well, and tie it close with a string; put two or three slices of fat bacon at the bottom of your stewpan, with three slices of carrot, two onions cut in two, and half a pint of water; put your beef in, and set your stewpan on the fire. After the beef has stewed about ten minutes, add more hot water, till it half covers the meat; let it boil till you feel with your finger that your beef is warm or hot through. Lay two or three slices of fat bacon upon your beef, add a little mace, cloves, pepper, and salt, a few slices of carrot, a small bunch of sweet-herbs, and celery tied together, a little garlic if you like it. Cut a piece of paper, of the size of your cover; well grease it with butter or lard; put it over your pan, cover it close, and let it stew over a very slow fire seven or eight hours. If you like to eat the beef cold, do not uncover the pan till it is so, for it will be the better for it. If you choose to stew a knuckle of veal with the beef, it will add greatly to the flavour.

Rump of Beef, with onions.

Having extracted the bones, tie it compactly in a good shape, and stew it in a pan that will allow for fire at the top. Put in a pint of white wine, some good broth, a slice of veal, two of bacon, or ham, which is better, a large bunch of kitchen herbs, pepper and salt. When the beef is nearly half done, add a good quantity of onions. The beef being thoroughly done, take it out and wipe off the grease; place it in the dish in which it is to be served at table, put the onions round it, and pour over it a good sauce, any that suits your taste.

Rump of Beef, to bake.

Bone a rump of beef; beat it thoroughly with a rolling-pin, till it is very tender; cut off the sinew, and lard it with large pieces of bacon; roll your larding seasoning first—of pepper, salt, and cloves. Lard athwart the meat that it may cut handsomely; then season the meat all over with pepper and salt, and a little brown sugar. Tie it neatly up with packthread across and across, put the top undermost, and place it in an earthen pan. Take all the bones that came out of it, and put them in round and round the beef, so that it cannot stir; then put in half a pound of butter, two bay-leaves, two shalots, and all sorts of seasoning herbs, chopped fine. Cover the top of the pot with coarse paste; put it in a slow oven; let it stand eight hours; take it out, and serve it in the dish in which it is to go to table, with its own juice, and some have additional broth or gravy ready to add to it if it is too dry.

Rump of Beef, cardinal fashion.

Choose a rump of beef of moderate size, say ten or twelve pounds; take out the bones; beat it, and lard it with a pound of the best bacon, mingled with salt and spices, without touching the upper parts. Rub half a quarter of a pound of saltpetre in powder into the meat that it may look red; and put it into a pan with an ounce of juniper-berries a little bruised, a tea-spoonful of brown sugar, a little thyme, basil, and a pound of salt; and there let it remain, the pan being covered close, for eight days. When the meat has taken the salt, wash it in warm water, and put some slices of bacon upon the upper part on that side which is covered with fat, and tie a linen cloth over it with packthread. Let it stew gently five hours, with a pint and a half of red wine, a pint of water, six onions, two cloves of garlic, five carrots, two parsnips, a laurel leaf, thyme, basil, four or five cloves, parsley, and scallions. When it is done, it may be either served up hot, or left to cool in its own liquor, and eaten cold.

Beef, sausage fashion.

Take a slice of beef, about half an inch thick and four or five wide; cut it in two equal parts; beat them well to make them flat, and pare the edges neatly. Mince your parings with beef suet, parsley, onions, mushroom, a shalot, two leaves of basil, and mix them into a forcemeat with the yolks of four eggs. A little minced ham is a great addition. Spread this forcemeat upon the slices of beef, and roll them up in the form of sausages. Tie them with packthread, and stew them in a little broth, a glass of white wine, salt, pepper, an onion stuck with cloves, a carrot, and a parsnip. When they are done, strain off the liquor, and, having skimmed off the fat, reduce it over the fire to the consistence of a sauce; take care that it be not too highly flavoured, and serve it over your sausages, or they may be served on sorrel, spinach, or any other sauce you prefer.

Ribs and Sirloin of Beef.

When the ribs and sirloin are tender, they are commonly roasted, and eaten with their own gravy. To make the sirloin still better, take out the fillet: cut it into thin slices, and put it into a stewpan, with a sauce made with capers, anchovies, mushrooms, a little garlic, truffles, and morels, the whole shred fine, turned a few times over the fire, with a little butter, and moistened with some good cullis. When the sauce is skimmed and seasoned to your taste, put in the fillet with the gravy of the meat, and heat and serve it over the ribs or sirloin.

Rib of Beef, en papillotes, (in paper.)

Cut a rib of beef neatly, and stew it with some broth and a little pepper and salt. When the meat is done enough, reduce the sauce till it sticks to the rib, and then steep the rib in butter, with parsley, scallions, shalots, and mushrooms, shred fine, and a little basil in powder. Wrap the rib, together with its seasoning, in a sheet of white paper, folding the paper round in the form of a curling paper or papillote; grease the outside, and lay it upon the gridiron, on another sheet of greased paper, over a slow fire. When it is done, serve it in the paper.

Brisket of Beef, stewed German Fashion.

Cut three or four pounds of brisket of beef in three or four pieces of equal size, and boil it a few minutes in water; in another pan boil the half of a large cabbage for a full quarter of an hour; stew the meat with a little broth, a bunch of parsley, scallions, a little garlic, thyme, basil, and a laurel-leaf; and an hour afterwards put in the cabbage, cut into three pieces, well squeezed, and tied with packthread, and three large onions. When the whole is nearly done, add four sausages, with a little salt and whole pepper, and let it stew till the sauce is nearly consumed; then take out the meat and vegetables, wipe off the grease, and dish them, putting the beef in the middle, the onions and cabbage round, and the sausages upon it. Strain the sauce through a sieve, and, having skimmed off the fat, serve it over the ragout. The beef will take five hours and a quarter at the least to stew.

Beef, to bake.

Take a buttock of beef; beat it in a mortar; put to it three pounds of bacon cut in small pieces; season with pepper and salt, and mix in the bacon with your hands. Put it into a pot, with some butter and a bunch of sweet-herbs, covering it very close, and let it bake six hours. When enough done, put it into a cloth to strain; then put it again into your pot, and fill it up with butter.

Beef bouilli.

Take the thick part of the brisket of beef, and let it lie in water all night; tie it up well, and put it to boil slowly, with a small faggot of parsley and thyme, a bag of peppercorns and allspice, three or four onions, and roots of different sorts: it will take five or six hours, as it should be very tender. Take it out, cut the string from it, and either glaze it or sprinkle some dry parsley that has been chopped very fine over it; sprinkle a little flour on the top of it, with gherkin and carrot. The chief sauce for it is *sauce hachée*, which is made thus: a little dressed ham, gherkin, boiled carrot, and the yolk of egg boiled, all chopped fine and put into brown sauce.

Another way.

Take about eight or nine pounds of the middle part of the brisket; put it into your stew-kettle (first letting it hang up for four or five days) with a little whole pepper, salt, and a blade or two of mace, a turnip or two, and an onion, adding about three pints or two quarts of water. Cover it up close, and when it begins to boil skim it; let it stand on a very slow fire, just to keep it simmering. It will take five hours or more before it is done, and during that time you must take the meat out, in order to skim off the fat. When it is quite tender take your stewpan, and brown a little butter and flour, enough to thicken the gravy, which you must put through a colander, first adding sliced carrots and turnips, previously boiled in another pot. You may also, if you choose, put in an anchovy, a little ketchup, and juice of lemon; but these are omitted according to taste. When the gravy is thus prepared, put the meat in again; give it a boil, and dish it up.

Relishing Beef.

Take a round of the best piece of beef and lard it with bacon; half roast it; put it in a stewpan, with some gravy, an onion stuck with cloves, half a pint of white wine, a gill of vinegar, a bunch of sweet-herbs, pepper, cloves, mace, and salt; cover it down very close, and let it only simmer till it is quite tender. Take two ox-palates, two sweetbreads, truffles, morels, artichoke-bottoms, and stew them all together in some good gravy, which pour over the beef. Have ready forcemeat balls fried, made in different shapes; dip some sippets into butter, fry and cut them three-corner-ways, stick them into the meat; lay the balls round the dish.

Beef, to stew.

Take a pound and a half of the fat part of a brisket, with four pounds of stewing beef, cut into pieces; put these into a stewpan, with a little salt, pepper, a bunch of sweet-herbs and onions, stuck with cloves, two or three pieces of carrots, two quarts of water, and half a pint of good small beer. Let the whole stew for four hours; then take some turnips and carrots cut into pieces, a small leek, two or three heads of celery, cut small, and a piece of bread toasted hard. Let these stew all together one hour longer; then put the whole into a terrine, and serve up.

Another way.

Put three pounds of the thin part of the brisket of beef and half a pound of gravy beef in a stewpan, with two quarts of water, a little thyme, marjoram, parsley, whole pepper and salt, a sufficient quantity, and an onion; let it stew six hours or more; then add carrots, turnips, (cut with a machine) and celery cut small, which have all been previously boiled; let the vegetables be stewed with the beef one hour. Just before you take it off the fire, put in some boiled cabbage chopped small, some pickled cucumbers and walnuts sliced, some cucumber liquor, and a little walnut liquor. Thicken the sauce with a lump of butter rolled in flour. Strew the cut vegetables over the top of the meat.

Cold Beef, to dress.

Slice it as thin as possible; slice, also, an onion or shalot; squeeze on it the juice of a lemon or two; then beat it between two plates, as you do cucumbers. When it is very well beaten, and tastes sharp of the lemon, put it into the dish, in which it is to be served; pick out the onion, and strew over it some fine shred parsley and fine bread crumbs; then pour on it oil and mustard well mixed; garnish with sliced lemon.

Cold Boiled Beef, to dress.

When your rump or brisket of beef has been well boiled in plain water, about an hour before you serve it up take it out of the water, and put it in a pot just large enough to contain it. There let it stew, with a little of its own liquor, salt, basil, and laurel; and, having drained, put it into the dish on which it is to be served for table, and pour over it a sauce, which you must have previously ready, made with gravy, salt, whole pepper, and a dash of vinegar, thickened over the stove with the yolks of three eggs or more, according to the size of the beef and the quantity of sauce wanted. Then cover beef and all with finely grated bread; baste it with butter, and brown it with a salamander.

Cold Beef, to pot.

Cut the beef small; add to it some melted butter, two anchovies well washed and boned, a little Jamaica pepper beat very fine. Beat them well together in a marble mortar till the meat is yellow; then put it into pots, and cover it with clarified butter.

Beef Steaks to broil.

When your steak is nearly broiled, chop some large onions, as fine as possible, and cover the steak thickly with it, the last time you turn it, letting it broil till fit to send to table, when the onion should quite cover the steak. Pour good gravy in the dish to moisten it.

Beef Steaks and Oysters.

Put two dozen oysters into a stewpan with their own liquor; when it boils add a spoonful of water; when the oysters are done drain them in a sieve, and let the liquor settle; then pour it off clear into another vessel; beard them, and add a pint of jelly gravy to the liquor; add a piece of butter and two spoonfuls of flour to thicken it. Let this boil fifteen minutes; then throw in the oysters, and let it stand. Take a beef-steak, pare it neatly round, and dress it as usual; when done, lay it on a hot dish, and pour the sauce and oysters over it.

Rump Steaks broiled, with Onion Gravy.

Peel and slice two large onions; put them into a stewpan with two table-spoon-fuls of water; set it on a slow fire till the water is boiled away and the onions have become a little brown. Add half a pint of good broth; boil the onions till tender; strain the broth from them, and chop them fine; thicken with flour and butter, and season with mushroom ketchup, pepper, and salt; put the onions in, and boil it gently for five minutes: pour the gravy over a broiled rump-steak.

Beef Steaks, to stew.

Pepper and salt two fine rump steaks; lay them in a stewpan with a few cloves, some mace, an onion, one anchovy, a bundle of sweet herbs, a gill of white wine, and a little butter mixed with flour; cover them close, stew them very gently till they are tender, and shake the pan round often to keep them from sticking. Take them carefully out, flour and fry them of a nice brown in fresh butter, and put them in a dish. In the mean time strain off the gravy from the fat out of the fry-ing-pan, and put it in the sauce, with a dozen oysters blanched, and a little of the oyster liquor; give it a boil up, pour it over the steaks, and garnish with horserad-ish. You may fry them first and then stew them; put them in a dish, and strain the sauce over them without any oysters, as a common dish.

Another way.

Beat three pounds of rump steaks; put them in a stewpan, with a pint of water, the same quantity of small beer, six cloves, a large onion, a bunch of sweet-herbs, a carrot, a turnip, pepper, and salt. Stew this very gently, closely covered, for four or five hours; but take care the meat does not go to rags, by being done too fast. Take up the meat, and strain the gravy over it. Have turnips cut into balls, and carrots into shapes, and put them over the meat.

Beef Olives.

Take a rump of beef, cut into steaks, about five inches long and not half an inch thick. Lay on some good forcemeat, made with veal; roll them, and tie them round once or twice, to keep them in a neat shape. Mix some crumbs of bread, egg, a little grated nutmeg, pepper and salt; fry them brown; have ready some good gravy, with a few truffles, morels, and mushrooms, boiled together. Pour it into the dish and send them to table, after taking off the string that tied them in shape.

Another way.

Cut steaks from the inside of the sirloin, about an inch thick, six inches long, and four or five broad: beat and rub them over with yolk of egg; strew on bread crumbs, parsley chopped, lemon-peel shred, pepper and salt, and chopped suet. Roll them up tight, skewer them; fry or brown them in a Dutch oven; stew them in some beef broth or gravy until tender. Thicken the gravy with a little flour; add ketchup, and a little lemon juice, and, to enrich it, add pickled mushrooms, hard yolks of eggs, and forcemeat balls.

Pickle for Beef.

To four gallons of water put a sufficient quantity of common salt; when quite dissolved, to bear an egg, four ounces of saltpetre, two ounces of bay salt, and half a pound of coarse sugar. Boil this pickle for twenty minutes, skim it well, and strain it. When quite cold, put in your beef, which should be quite covered with the pickle, and in nine days it will be fit for use; or you may keep it three months, and it will not be too salt. The pickle must be boiled and well skimmed at the end of six weeks, and every month afterwards; it will then keep three months in summer and much longer in winter.

Beef, to salt.

Into four gallons of water put one pound and a half of coarse brown sugar, two ounces of saltpetre, and six pounds of bay salt; boil and skim as long as any scum rises. When cold, put in the meat, which must be quite covered with pickle: once in two months boil up the pickle again, skimming carefully. Add in the boiling two ounces of coarse sugar, half a pound of bay salt, and the same pickle will be good for twelve months. It is incomparable for hung beef, hams, or neats' tongues. When you take them out of this pickle, clean, dry, and put them in a paper bag, and hang them up in a dry place.

Pork may be pickled in the same manner.

Beef, to salt.

Eight pounds of salt, six ounces of saltpetre, one pound and a half of brown sugar, four gallons of water; boil all together, skim and put on the beef when cold; the beef to be kept under the pickle with a weight.

Beef, to dry.

Salt it in the same way as your hams; keep it in your pickle a fortnight or three weeks, according to its size; hang it up to dry for a few days; then have it smoked the same as hams.

Hung Beef. No. 1.

Take a round, ribs, rump, or sirloin; let it lie in common salt for a month, and well cover it with the brine. Rub a little saltpetre over it two or three days before it is hung up; observing, before it is put up to dry, to strew it over with bran or oatmeal, to keep it from the dust; or, which will answer the same purpose, wrap it up in strong coarse paper. It is not to be smoked; only hang it up in the kitchen, and not too near the fire. The time of hanging to dry must be regulated by the quantity of air in which it is suspended, or left to the discretion of the person who has the care of it. The time which it must lie in water before dressing depends upon the driness of the meat. Half boil it in simmering water, and afterwards roast. It must not be cut till cold.

Hung Beef. No. 2.

Take the under-cliff of a small buttock of beef, two ounces of common salt, and one ounce of saltpetre, well beaten together: put to it half a pint of vinegar with a sprig of thyme. Rub the beef with this pickle every morning for six days, and let it lie in it. Then dry it well with a cloth, and hang it up in the chimney for a fortnight. It must be made perfectly dry before it will be fit for eating; it should also be kept in a dry place.

Hung Beef. No. 3.

Take the tenderest part of beef, and let it hang in the cellar as long as you can, taking care that it is not in the least tainted. Take it down, wash it well in sugar and water. Dry six-pennyworth of saltpetre and two pounds of bay salt, and pound them fine; mix with it three large spoonfuls of brown sugar; rub your beef thoroughly with it. Take common salt, sufficient according to the size of the beef to salt it; let it lie closely covered up until the salts are entirely dissolved, which will be in seven or eight days. Turn it every day, the under part uppermost, and so on for a fortnight; then hang it where it may have a little warmth of the fire. It may hang in the kitchen a fortnight. When you use it, boil it in hay and pump water very tender: it will keep boiled two or three months, rubbing it with a greasy cloth, or putting it for two or three minutes into boiling water to take off any mouldiness.

Beef for scraping.

To four pounds of lean buttock of beef take one ounce of saltpetre and some common salt, in which let the meat lie for a month; then hang it to dry for three weeks. Boil it for grating when wanted.

Italian Beef.

Take a round of beef, about fifteen or eighteen pounds; rub it well with three ounces of saltpetre, and let it lie for four hours in it. Then season it very well with beaten mace, pepper, cloves, and salt sufficient; let it then lie in that seasoning for twelve days; wash it well, and put it in the pot in which you intend to bake it, with one pound of suet shred fine, and thrown under and over it. Cover your pot and paste it down: let it stew six hours in its own liquor, and eat it cold.

Red Beef.

Twelve pounds of ribs of beef boned, four ounces of bay salt, three ounces of saltpetre; beat them fine, and mix with half a pound of coarse sugar, two pounds of common salt, and a handful of juniper berries bruised. Rub the beef well with this mixture, and turn it every day about three weeks or a month; bake it in a coarse paste.

Another way.

Take a piece of brisket of beef, about sixteen or eighteen pounds; make the pickle for it as follows:—saltpetre and bay salt, one pound and a half of each, one pound of coarse brown sugar, and six pounds of common salt; add to these three gallons of water. Set it on the fire and keep it stirring, lest the salts should burn; as it boils skim it well till clear: boil it about an hour and a half. When it is quite cold, put in the beef, and let it lie in a pan that will hold it properly; turn it every day, and let it remain in about a fortnight. Take it out, and just wash it in clean water, and put it into the pot in which you stew it with some weak broth; then add slices of fat bacon, fat of veal, any pieces of fat meat, the more fat the better, especially of veal, also a pint of brandy, a full pint of wine, a handful of bay-leaves, a few cloves, and some blades of mace, about two large carrots, one dozen of large on-ions, a good bundle of sweet-herbs, some parsley, and two or three turnips. Stew it exceedingly gently for eight hours. The broth should cover the meat while it is stewing, and keep the slices of fat as much over it as you can; the seldomer you uncover the pot the better. When you think it sufficiently tender, which try with your finger, take it off, and, though it may appear tender enough to fall to pieces, it will harden sufficiently when it grows cold. It should remain in the pot just as it is taken off the fire till it is very nearly if not quite cold. It will eat much better for being so left, and you will also not run the risk of breaking the beef in pieces, as you would by removing it whilst hot.

Collar of Beef.

Bone the navel and navel round; make sufficient pickle to cover it, as strong as to bear an egg, with bay salt; beat two ounces of saltpetre very fine, and strew half of it on your beef before you lay it in your pickle. Then lay it in an earthen pan, and press it down in the liquor with a weight, as it must be all covered. Let it remain thus for four or five days, stirring it however once every day. Take it out, let the brine drain from it, lay it on a table, and season it with nutmeg, pepper, cloves, and mace, some parsley, thyme, and sweet marjoram, of each a little, and eight anchovies sliced; roll it up with these like brawn, and bind it quite fast with strong tape. Then put it into a pan, deep enough for it to stand upright; fill the pan with water, and cover it with paste. Make your oven very hot, put it in, and let it remain there five or six hours; then take it out, and, having removed the tape, roll it in a cloth; hang it up till cold. If you think it not salt enough, before you bake it, put a little salt with your spice and herbs, for baking in water abates much of its saltness.

Another.

Salt a flank of beef with white salt, and let it lie for forty-eight hours. Wash it, and hang it in the wind to dry for twenty-four hours. Then take pepper, salt, cloves, saltpetre, all beaten fine, and mix them together; rub the beef all over; roll it up hard, and tie it fast with tape. Put it in a pan, with a few bay-leaves, and four pounds of butter. Cover the pot with rye paste, and bake it with household bread.

Bisquet, to make.

Cut some slips of white paper; butter and place them at the bottom and sides of the pan you make your bisquet in; then cut thin collops of veal, or whatever meat you make it of; lay them on the paper, and cover them with forcemeat. Put in anything else you like, carrots, &c.; close the top with forcemeat and veal, and pa-per again; put it in the oven or stove, and, when done, and you want to dish it, turn the pan upside down from the dish; take the paper off, and pour good gravy on it.

Boar's Head, to dress whole.

When the head is cut off, the neck part must be boned, and the tongue taken out. The brains also must be taken out on the inside, so as not to break the bone and skin on the outside. When boned, singe the hair off, and clean it; then put it for four or five days into a red pickle made of saltpetre, bay salt, common salt, and coarse brown sugar, rubbing the pickle in every day. When taken out of the pickle, lay the tongue in the centre of the neck or collar; close the meat together as close as you can, and bind it with strong tape up to the ears, the same as you would do brawn; then put it into a pot or kettle, the neck downward, and fill the pot with good broth and Rhenish wine, in the proportion of one bottle of wine to three pints of broth, till it is covered a little above the ears. Season the wine and broth with small bunches of sweet-herbs, such as basil, winter savory, and marjoram, bay-leaves, shalots, celery, carrots, turnips, parsley-roots, with different kinds of spices. Set it over the fire to boil; when it boils, put it on one side to boil gently, till the head is tender. Take it out of the liquor, and put it into an earthen pan; skim all the fat off the liquor; strain it through a sieve into the head; put it by until it is quite cold, and then it will be fit for use.

Brawn, to keep.

Put some bran and three handfuls of salt into a kettle of water; boil and strain it through a sieve, and, when cold, put your brawn into it.

Hog's head like Brawn.

Wash it well; boil it till the bones will come out; when cold, put the inside of the cheek together with salt between; put the ears round the sides. Put the cheeks into a cloth, press them into a sieve, or anything round; lay on a weight for two days. Have ready a pickle of salt and water, with about a pint of malt, boiled together; when cold, put in the head.

Mock Brawn.

Take two pair of neats' feet; boil them very tender, and take the flesh clean from the bones. Boil the belly piece of pork till nearly done, then bone it, and roll the meat of the feet up very tight in the pork. Take a strong cloth, with some coarse tape; roll it round very tight; tie it up in the cloth; boil it till it is so tender that a skewer may go through it; let it be hung in a cloth till it is quite cold; after which put it into some sousing liquor, and keep it for use.

Cabbage, farced.

Take a fine white-heart cabbage, about as big as a quarter of a peck, lay it in water two or three hours, half boil it, put it in a colander to drain, then cut out the heart, but take very great care not to break off any of the outside leaves. Fill it with forcemeat made thus:—take a pound of veal, half a pound of bacon, fat and lean together; cut them small, and beat them fine in a mortar, with the yolks of four eggs boiled hard; season with pepper and salt, a little beaten mace, a very little lemon-peel, some parsley chopped fine, a very little thyme, and three anchovies.

When these are beat fine, take the crumb of a stale roll, some mushrooms, either fresh or pickled, and the heart of the cabbage which you cut out. Chop it very fine; mix all together with the yolk of an egg; fill the hollow of the cabbage, and tie it round with thread. Lay some slices of bacon in the bottom of a stewpan, and upon these some thin slices of coarse beef, about one pound: put in the cabbage, cover it close, and let it stew gently over a slow fire, until the bacon begins to stick to the bottom of the pan. Shake in a little flour; then put in a quart of good broth, an onion stuck with cloves, two blades of mace, some whole pepper, a little bundle of sweet-herbs; cover close, and let it stew gently an hour and a half. Put in a glass of red wine, give it a boil, and take it up; lay it in a dish, and strain the gravy over it, untying the packthread first. This is a very good dish, and makes the next day an excellent hash, with a veal steak nicely boiled and laid on it.

Calf's Head.

Scald the hair off; trim and pare it, and make it look as neat as possible. Take out the bones, and have ready palates boiled tender, hard-boiled yolks of eggs, oysters just scalded, and very good forcemeat: stuff all this into the head, and sew it close in a cloth. Boil it gently for full three hours. Make a strong good gravy for sauce. Garnish with fried bacon.

Calf's Head, to dress like Turtle.

The wool must be scalded off in the same manner as the hair is taken off a little pig, which may be done at the butcher's; then wash and parboil it; cut the meat from the bones, and put it in a saucepan, with as much of the broth as will just cover it. Put in half a tea-spoonful of cayenne pepper, and some common pepper and salt, a large onion, and a faggot of sweet-herbs; take out the herbs and the onion before it breaks. About half an hour before it is done, put three quarters of a pint of white or raisin wine; have ready the yolks of six or eight eggs boiled hard, which you must make into small balls, and put in just before you serve it up. It will take two hours and a half, or perhaps three hours doing, over a slow fire.

Calf's Head, to hash. No. 1.

Let the calf's head be washed dean, and boiled tender; then cut the meat off one half of the head in small slices. To make the sauce, take some parsley, thyme, and a very little onion, let them be chopped fine; then pass them in a stewpan over the fire, with some butter, till tender. Add some flour, a very little pepper and salt, and some good strong broth, according to your quantity of meat; let it boil, then skim it, put the meat into it, and add a little lemon-juice and a little white wine; let all boil together about ten minutes. There may be some force-meat balls added, if liked. The other half of the head must be scored like diamonds, cross and across; then rub it with some oiled butter and yolk of egg; mix some chopped parsley and thyme, pepper, salt, a little nutmeg, and some bread crumbs; strew the head all over with this; broil it a nice light brown, and put it on the hash when dished. Scald the brains, and cut them in four pieces; rub them with yolk of egg, then let them be crumbed, with the same crumbs and herbs as the head was done with, and fried a light brown; lay them round the dish with a few slices of bacon or ham fried. The brains may be done, to be sent up alone on a plate, as follows:—Let the brains be washed and skinned; let them be boiled in broth, about twenty-five minutes; make a little white sauce of some butter, flour, salt, a little cream, and a little good broth; let it just boil; then pick a little green sage, a little parsley picked very small, and scalded till tender; the brains, parsley, and sage, must be strained off, and put into the white sauce, and let it come to a boil, just before you put them on the dish to send up.

Calf's Head, to hash. No. 2.

Take half a calf's head, cover it with water in a large saucepan, and boil it till the meat comes from the bone. Cut it into pieces; put it into some of the liquor in which the head was boiled, and let it stew till it becomes thick. Add a little salt and mace, and put it into a mould.

Calf's Head, to hash. No. 3.

Your calf's head being half boiled and cooled, cut it in thin slices, and fry it in a pan of brown butter; put it into your tossing pan with gravy; stew it till tender; toss it up with burnt butter, or butter rolled in flour. Garnish with forcemeat balls, and fritters, made of the brains, mixed up with eggs, a little cream, a dust of flour, nutmeg, and a little parsley, boiled and chopped fine. Mix them all well together, and fry them in little cakes; put a few bits of bacon and lemon round the dish.

Calf's Head, to hash. No. 4.

Half boil the head; cut it into round pieces; season with nutmeg, salt, pepper, and a large onion. Save all the gravy, put in a pint of white wine, a quarter of a pound of butter, and four spoonfuls of oyster liquor: let it stew with the meat, not too fast: thicken it with a little butter and a dozen of oysters, and, when dished, add some rolled bacon, forcemeat balls, and the brains fried in thin cakes, very brown, and the size of a crown-piece, laid round the dish. Garnish with lemon and pickled mushrooms; lemon pickle is an addition.

Calf's Head, to hash. No. 5.

Have the head well cleaned; boil it well, cut in slices half of the head, and have some good ragout of forcemeat, truffles, mushrooms, morels, and artichoke bottoms, also some veal sweet-herbs. Season your ragout, and throw in your slices, a bit of garlic and parsley, with some thyme, and squeeze a lemon in it, but be cautious to have it skimmed well. Take the other part of the head, and score it like diamonds; season with salt and pepper, and rub it over with an egg and some crumbs of bread. Then broil it, pour the hash into the dish; let the half head lie in the middle, and cut and set off the brains afterwards in slices. Fry bacon, and lay slices round the dish with sliced lemon.

Calf's Head fricassee.

Clean well a calf's head, boil it and cut in square pieces of about an inch; put half a pint of its own liquor, and mix it well with some mushrooms, sweetbreads, yolks of eggs, artichoke bottoms, and cream. Season with nutmeg and mace, and squeeze in a lemon: but serve it up hot.

Calf's Head, to pickle.

Take out the bones and clean the head carefully: wash it well with eggs, seasoning it with pepper, salt, nutmeg, thyme, and parsley. Put some forcemeat on it, and roll it up. Boil it tender; take it up, lay it in sturgeon-pickle for four days; and if you please you may cut it in pieces as you would sturgeon.

Calf's Liver.

Lay it for a few hours in milk, then dry and fry it in butter.

Cauliflowers, with White Sauce.

Boil the cauliflowers in small pieces till tender; drain them in a sieve; when quite dry lay them in a dish; season the sauce with a little pepper and salt, and pour it pretty thick over them.

Celery, to stew.

Cut and trim a dozen heads of celery; put them in cold water to blanch; stew them in a little butter, salt, and water. When done enough they should be quite soft, but not broken. Drain them, and have ready a rich white sauce, the same that is used for boiled chickens, only without truffles or mushrooms; pour this sauce over the celery, and serve hot.

Another way.

Take a dozen white heads of celery, cut about two inches long, wash them clean, and put them in a stewpan, with a pint of gravy, a glass of white wine, a bundle of sweet-herbs, pepper, and salt: cover close, and stew them till they are tender. Then take out the sweet-herbs; put in a piece of butter mixed with flour; let it stew till it is thick, and dish it up.

Celery à la Crême.

Take a dozen white heads of celery, cut about two inches long; wash them very clean, and boil them in water till they are very tender; have ready half a pint of cream, a little butter mixed with flour, a little nutmeg, and salt; boil it up till thick and smooth; put in the celery, give it a toss or two, and dish it up.

Scotch Collops.

Take a piece of the fillet of veal, as much as will cut into fifteen pieces, of the size and thickness of a crown-piece; shake a little flour over it; put a little butter into a frying-pan, and melt it; fry the slices of veal quick till they are brown, and lay them in a dish near the fire. Then prepare a sauce thus: take a little butter in a stewpan and melt it; add a table-spoonful of flour; stir it about till it is as smooth as cream; put in half a pint each of beef and veal jelly, cayenne pepper and salt, a pinch of each, and one glass of white wine, twenty-four pieces of truffles the size of a shilling, and a table-spoonful of mushrooms: wash them thoroughly from vinegar; squeeze the juice of half a lemon; stew the sauce gently for one hour; then throw in the veal, and stew it all together for five minutes. Serve quite hot, laying the veal regularly in the dish.

Another way.

Cut the lean part of a leg of veal into thin collops; beat them with the back of a knife; season with pepper and salt, shred thyme and parsley, and flour them well. Reserve some of the meat to make balls. Taking as much suet as meat, shred it small; then beat it in a mortar; season with pepper, salt, shred herbs, a little shred onion, and a little allspice. Put in an egg or two, according to the quantity. Make balls, and fry them in good dripping; keep them warm. Then fry your collops with clarified butter, till they are brown enough; and, while they are warming in the pan, put in your sauce, which must be made thus:—have some good glaze, a little white wine, a good piece of butter, and two yolks of eggs. Put your balls to the collops; flour and make them very hot in the pan; put in your sauce, shake them well, and let them boil. If you would have them white, put strong broth instead of glaze and half a pint of cream.

Scotch Collops, brown.

Cut your collops thin and from the fillet. Season them with salt and pepper, and fry them off quick and brown. Brown a piece of butter thickened with flour, and put in some good gravy, mushrooms, morels, truffles, and forcemeat balls, with sweetbread dried. Squeeze in a lemon, and let the whole boil till of a proper thickness. Then put in your collops, but do not let them boil; toss them up quick, and serve up.

Collops, White. No. 1.

Take a small slice of veal, cut thin slices from it, and beat them out very thin: butter a frying-pan very lightly, place them in it, and pass them on the fire, but not to get any colour. Trim them round, and put them into white sauce.

Collops, White. No. 2.

Cut the veal very thin; put it into a stewpan with a piece of butter and one clove of shalot; toss it in a pan for a few minutes. Have ready to put to it some cream, more or less according to the quantity of veal, a piece of butter mixed with flour, the yolk of an egg, a little nutmeg, and a tea-spoonful of lemon-pickle. Stir it over the fire till it is thick enough, but do not let it boil. If you choose forcemeat balls, have them ready boiled in water, and take out the shalot before you dish up: ten minutes will do them.

Collops, White. No. 3.

Hack and cut your collops well; season with pepper and salt, and fry them quick of a pale colour in a little bit of butter. Squeeze in a lemon: put in half a pint of cream and the yolks of four eggs. Toss them up quick, and serve them hot.

Collops, to mince.

Chop some beef as fine as possible; the under part of roasted beef without any fat is best. Put some onions, pepper, and salt to it. Then put a little butter in the frying-pan; when it is melted, put in the meat, and stew it well. Add a cupful of gravy; if you have none, water will do. Just before it is done put in a little vinegar.

Collops of cold beef.

Take off all the fat from the inside of a sirloin of beef; cut it neatly into thin collops, about the size of a crown or half-crown piece, as you like for size, and cut them round. Slice an onion very small; boil the gravy that came from the beef when roasted, first clearing it of all the fat, with a little water; season it with pepper, and, instead of salt, anchovies dissolved in walnut ketchup, or the liquor from pickled walnuts, and a bundle of sweet-herbs. Let this boil before you put in the collops; put them in with a good piece of butter rolled in a little flour; shake it round to thicken it, and let it do no longer than till the collops are thoroughly heated, lest they be hard. This does better than fresh meat. Serve it hot with pickles, or slices of stewed cucumbers, cut round, like the meat, and placed alternately with it round the dish.

Cucumbers, to stew.

Pare twelve cucumbers, and slice them rather thicker than for eating; put them to drain, and lay them in a coarse cloth till dry. Flour and fry them brown in butter; then put to them some gravy, a little claret, some pepper, cloves, and mace; let them stew a little; then roll a bit of butter in flour, and toss them up. A sufficient quantity of onion should be sliced thin, and done like the cucumbers.

Curry Powder, from a Resident in India. No. 1.

Half a pound of coriander seed, two ounces of black pepper, two ounces of cummin seed, one ounce of turmeric, one ounce and half of ground rice: all the above must be finely pounded; add cayenne to your taste. Mix all well together; put it into a dish close before the fire; roast it well for three or four hours; and, when quite cold, put it into a bottle for use.

Curry Powder. No. 2.

Thirteen ounces of coriander seed,* two ounces of fenugreek seed,* (if not liked this may be omitted,) one ounce of cayenne pepper, or powdered capsicums, six ounces of pale-coloured turmeric,* five ounces of black pepper. Pound the whole very fine; set it in a Dutch oven before the fire to dry, turning it often; when cold put it into a dry bottle; cork, and keep it in a dry place. So prepared, curry-powder will keep for many years.

The ingredients marked thus * may be procured at Apothecaries' Hall, or at any wholesale chemist's.

Curry Powder. No. 3.

One pound of turmeric, one pound of coriander seed, one pound of ginger, six ounces of cardamom, four ounces of cummin, one ounce of long pepper, pounded and mixed together. Cayenne pepper may also be added.

Curry, Indian. No. 1.

Curry may be made of chicken, rabbits, lobster, or of any species of fish, flesh, or fowl. Fry the material with onions, as for mulligatawny, a small piece of garlic, eight almonds, and eight sweet chesnuts. Put it all into a stewpan, with a spoonful or two of curry-powder, a large tea-cupful of strong good gravy, and a large piece of butter. Let the whole stew gently till the gravy becomes very thick and is nearly evaporated.

Particular attention should be paid in sending this dish up hot, and always with plenty of rice in a separate dish; most people like pickle with it.

Curry. No. 2.

Chop one or two onions very fine; put them into a stewpan with some butter, and let them remain on a slow fire till they are well done, taking care not to let them burn. Pour off the butter: put in one dessert spoonful of powder and a little gravy; stir it about till it is well mixed; set it on a slow fire till it is all sufficiently done. Put in a little lemon-juice; when nearly done, thicken the gravy with flour. Let the rice be very well picked and afterwards cleansed; it ought to be washed in several waters, and kept in water till it is going to be boiled. Have the meat or fish ready, pat it into the stewpan, and stir it about till it is well mixed. The rice must be boiled twenty minutes quickly, and the scum taken off; the water to be thrown off and the saucepan uncovered till it is dry enough. Meat used for this curry must be previously fried.

Curry. No. 3.

Fry onions, ginger, garlic, and meat, in one ounce of butter, of a light brown; stew it with a table-spoonful of curry-powder and three pints of water, till it comes to a pint and a half. A good half hour before dinner, put in greens, such as brocoli, cauliflower, sliced apple, and mango, the juice of one lemon, grated ginger, and cayenne, with two spoonfuls of cream, and a little flour to thicken it.

Curry. No. 4.

Skin and prepare two chickens as for a fricassee; wash them very clean, and stew them in a pint and a half of water for about five minutes. Strain off the liquor, and put the chickens in a clean dish. Slice three large onions, and fry them in about two ounces of butter. Put in the chickens, and fry them together till they are brown. Take a quarter of an ounce of curry-powder, and salt to your palate, and strew over the chickens while they are frying; then pour in the liquor in which they were first stewed, and let them stew again for half an hour. Add a quarter of a pint of cream and the juice of two lemons. Have rice boiled dry to eat with it. Rabbits do as well as chickens.

Curry. No. 5.

Take two chickens, or in the same proportion of any other kind of flesh, fish, or fowl; cut the meat small; strew a little salt and pepper over it; add a small quantity of onion fried in butter; put one table-spoonful of curry-powder to your meat and onions; mix them well together with about three quarters of a pint of water. Put the whole in a stewpan covered close; let it stew half an hour before you open the pan; then add the juice of two lemons, or an equal quantity of any other souring. Let it stew again till the gravy appears very thick and adheres to the meat. If the meat floats in the gravy, the curry will not be considered as well made. Salt to your palate.

Curry. No. 6.

Mix together a quart of good gravy, two spoonfuls of curry-powder, two of soy, a gill of red wine, a little cayenne pepper, and the juice of a lemon. Cut a breast of veal in square pieces, and put it in a stewpan with a pint of gravy; stew slowly for a quarter of an hour; add the rest of the gravy with the ingredients, and stew till done.

Curry. No. 7.

Take a fowl, fish, or any meat you like; cut it in slices; cut up two good sized onions very fine; half fry your fowl, or meat, with the onions, in a quarter of a pound of butter. Add two table-spoonfuls of curry-powder, fry it a little longer, and stew it well; then add any acid you like, a little salt, and half a pint of water. Let all stew together until the meat is done.

Farcie, to make.

Take the tender part of a fillet of veal, free from sinew, and mince it fine, with a piece of the fat of ham, some chopped thyme, basil, and marjoram, dried, and a little seasoning according to the palate. Put the whole in a stewpan, and keep stirring it till it is warm through; then put it on a sieve to drain. When the liquor has run from it, pound the farcie, while warm, in a mortar, adding the drained liquor, by degrees, till the whole is again absorbed in the meat, which must be pounded very fine. Put it in an earthen pot, and steam it for half an hour with a slice of fat ham; cover over the pot to prevent the steam from getting to it; when cold, pour on some good jelly made of the lean of ham and veal, and take care to pour it on cold (that is, when the jelly is just dissolved,) otherwise it will raise the farcie. When livers are to be had, put a third of them with the ham and veal, as above directed, and the farcie will be better.

Forcemeat, to make. No. 1.

Chop small a pound of veal, parsley, thyme, a small onion, and a pound of beef; grate the inside of three French rolls, and put all these together, with pepper, salt, soup, and nutmeg, seasoning it to your taste; add as many eggs as will make it of a proper stiffness, and roll them into balls.

Forcemeat. No. 2.

Take half a pound of the lean of a leg of veal, with the skin picked off, cut it into small pieces, and mince it very small; shred very fine a pound of beef-suet and grate a nutmeg into both; beat half as much mace into it with cloves, pepper, and salt, a little rosemary, thyme, sweet marjoram, and winter savory. Put all these to the meat in a mortar, and beat all together, till it is smooth and will work easily with your hands, like paste. Break two new laid eggs to some white bread crumbs, and make them into a paste with your hands, frying it in butter. If you choose, leave out the herbs.

Forcemeat. No. 3.

A pound of veal, full its weight in beef suet, and a bit of bacon, shred all together; beat it in a mortar very fine; season with sweet-herbs, pepper, and salt. When you roll it up to fry, add the yolks of two or three eggs to bind it; you may add oysters or marrow.

Fricandeau.

Take a piece of veal next to the udder; separate the skin, and flatten the meat on a clean cloth; make slits in the bottom part, that it may soak up seasoning, and lard the top very thick and even. Take a stewpan that will receive the veal without confining it; put at the bottom three carrots cut in slices, two large onions sliced, a bunch of parsley, the roots cut small, a little mace, pepper, thyme, and a bay-leaf; then lay some slices of very fat bacon, so as entirely to cover the vegetables, and make a pile of bacon in the shape of a tea-cup. Lay the veal over this bacon; powder a little salt over it; then put sufficient broth, and some beef jelly, lowered with warm water, to cover the bottom of the stewpan without reaching the veal. Lay a quantity of fine charcoal hot on the cover of the pan, keeping a very little fire beneath; as soon as it begins to boil, remove the stewpan, and place it over a very slow and equal fire for three hours and a half, removing the fire from the top; baste it frequently with liquor. When it has stewed the proper time, try if it is done by putting in a skewer, which will then go, in and out easily. Put a great quantity of fire again on the top of the stewpan till the bacon of the larding becomes quite firm; next remove the veal, and keep it near the fire; reduce the liquor to deep rich gravy to glaze it, which pour over the top only where it is larded; and, when it is served, put the fricandeau in a dish, and the puré of spinach, which is to be ready according to the receipt given in the proper place, (See Spinach to stew,) to lay round the dish.

Ham, to cure. No. 1.

Take a ham of young pork; sprinkle it with salt, and let it lie twenty-four hours. Having wiped it very dry, rub it well with a pound of coarse brown sugar, a pound of juniper berries, a quarter of a pound of saltpetre, half a pint of bay salt, and three pints of common salt, mixed together, and dried in an iron pot over the fire, stirring them the whole time. After this, take it off the fire, when boiled, and let it lie in an earthen glazed pan three weeks, but it must be often turned in the time, and basted with the brine in which it lies. Then hang it up till it has done dripping; and dry it in a chimney with deal saw-dust and juniper berries.

Ham, to cure. No. 2.

For two hams, take half a pound of bay salt, two ounces of saltpetre, two ounces of sal prunella, half a pound of brown sugar, half a pound of juniper berries, half a pound of common salt; beat them all, and boil them in two quarts of strong beer for half an hour very gently. Leave out one ounce of saltpetre to rub the hams over-night. Put them into the pickle, and let them lie a month or five weeks, basting them every day. Pickle in the winter, and dry in wood smoke; let them hang up the chimney a fortnight.

Ham, to cure. No. 3.

Hang up a ham two days; beat it well on the fleshy side with a rollingpin; rub in an ounce of saltpetre, finely powdered, and let it lie a day. Then mix together an ounce of sal prunella with two large handfuls of common salt, one handful of bay salt, and a pound of coarse sugar, and make them hot in a stewpan. While hot, rub it well in with two handfuls more of common salt; then let it lie till it melts to brine. Turn the meat twice every day for three weeks, and dry it like bacon.

Ham, to cure — the Thorpe way. No. 4.

The following are the proportions for two hams, or pigs' faces: Boil one pound of common salt, three ounces of bay salt, two ounces and a half of saltpetre, and one pound of the coarsest brown sugar, in a quart of strong old beer. When this pickle is cold, well rub the hams or faces with it every day for a fortnight. Smoke them with horse litter for two hours; then hang them to dry in a chimney where wood is burned for a fortnight, after which, hang them in a dry place till wanted for use. They are not so good if used under eight months or after a year old.

Ham, to cure. No. 5.

For one large ham take one pound of coarse sugar, one pound common salt, a quarter of a pound of saltpetre, and two ounces of bay salt, boiled in a quart of strong ale, or porter. When cold put it to your ham; and let it lie in the pickle three weeks, turning the ham every day.

Ham, to cure. No. 6.

Put two ounces of sal prunella, a pound of bay salt, four pounds of white salt, a pound of brown sugar, half a pound of saltpetre, to one gallon of water; boil it a quarter of an hour, keeping, it well skimmed, and, when cold, pour it from the sediment into the vessel in which you steep, and let the hams remain in the pickle about a month; the tongues a fortnight. In the same manner Dutch beef may be

made by letting it lie in the pickle for a month, and eight or ten days for collared beef; dry them in a stove or chimney. Tongues may be cured in the same manner.

Ham, to cure. No 7.

Four gallons of spring water, two pounds of bay salt, half a pound of common salt, two pounds of treacle, to be boiled a quarter of an hour, skimmed well, and poured hot on the hams. Let them be turned in the pickle every day, and remain three weeks or a month; tongues may be cured in the same way.

Ham, to cure. No. 8.

One ounce of pepper, two of saltpetre, one pound of bay salt, one ounce of sal prunella, one pound of common salt. Rub these in well, and let the ham lie a week after rubbing; then rub over it one pound of treacle or coarse sugar. Let it lie three weeks longer; take it up, steep it twenty-four hours in cold water, and then hang it up.

Ham, to cure. No. 9.

One pound of common salt, half a pound of bay salt, four ounces of saltpetre, two ounces of black pepper; mix them together, and rub the ham very well for four days, until the whole is dissolved. Then take one pound and a half of treacle and rub on, and let it lie in the pickle one month; turning it once a day. When you dress it, let the water boil before you put it in.

Ham, to cure. No. 10.

Into four gallons of water put one pound and a half of the coarsest sugar, two ounces of saltpetre, and six pounds of common salt; boil it, carefully taking off the scum till it has done rising; then let it stand till cold. Having put the meat into the vessel in which you intend to keep it, pour on the liquor till it is quite covered. If you wish to keep the meat for a long time, it will be necessary once in two or three months to boil the pickle over again, clearing off the scum as it rises, and adding, when boiling, a quarter of a pound of sugar, half a pound of salt, and half an ounce of saltpetre; in this way the pickle will keep good for a year. When you take the meat out of the pickle, dry it well before it is smoked. Hams from fifteen to twenty pounds should lie in pickle twenty-four days; small hams and tongues, fifteen days; a small piece of beef about the same time. Hams and beef will not do in the same pickle together. After the hams are taken out, the pickle must be boiled again before the beef is put in.

The same process may be used for beef and tongues.

Ham, to cure. No. 11.

Mix one pound and a half of salt, one pound and a half of coarse sugar, and one ounce of saltpetre, in one quart of water; set it on the fire, and keep stirring the liquor till it boils. Skim it. When boiled about five minutes take it off, and pour it boiling hot on the leg of pork, which, if not quite covered, must be turned every day. Let it remain in the pickle one month; then hang it in the chimney for six weeks. These proportions will cure a ham of sixteen pounds. When the ham is taken out of the pickle, the liquor may be boiled up again and poured boiling hot upon pigs' faces. After that boil again, and pour it cold upon a piece of beef, which will be excellent. It will then serve cold for pigs' or sheep's tongues, which must be well washed and rubbed in a little of the liquor and left in the remainder.

Ham, to cure. No. 12.

Take a ham of fifteen pounds, and wash it well with a quarter of a pint of vinegar, mixed with a quarter of a pound of the coarsest sugar. Next morning rub it well with three quarters of a pound of bay salt rolled, on the lean part; baste it often every day for fourteen days, and hang it up to dry.

Ham, to cure. No. 13.

Three ounces of saltpetre, bay salt and brown sugar two ounces of each, a small quantity of cochineal; mix them all together, and warm them over the fire. Rub the hams well with it, and cover them over with common salt.

Ham, to cure. No. 14.

Take a quantity of spring water sufficient to cover the meat you design to cure; make the pickle with an equal quantity of bay salt and common salt; add to a pound of each one pound of coarse brown sugar, one ounce of saltpetre, and one ounce of petre-salt; let the pickle be strong enough to bear an egg. If you design to eat the pork in a month or six weeks, it is best not to boil the pickle; if you intend it for the year, the pickle must be boiled and skimmed well until it is perfectly clear; let it be quite cold before you use it. Rub the meat that is to be preserved with some common salt, and let it lie upon a table sloping, to drain out all the blood; wipe it very dry with a coarse cloth before you put it into the pickle. The proportion of the pickle may be this: four pounds of common salt, four pounds of bay salt, three pounds of coarse sugar, two ounces of saltpetre, and two ounces of petre-salt, with a sufficient quantity of spring water to cover what you do, boiled as directed above. Let the hams lie about six weeks in the pickle, and then send them to be smoked. Beef, pork, and tongues, may be cured in the same manner: ribs of beef done in this way are excellent.

Ham, to cure. No. 15.

Wash the ham clean; soak it in pump water for an hour; dry it well, and rub into it the following composition: saltpetre two ounces, bay salt nine ounces, common salt four ounces, lump sugar three ounces; but first beat them separately into a fine powder; mix them together, dry them before the fire, and then rub them into the ham, as hot as the hand can bear it. Then lay the ham sloping on a table; put on it a board with forty or fifty pounds weight; let it remain thus for five days; then turn it, and, if any of the salt is about it, rub it in, and let it remain with the board and weight on it for five days more; this done rub off the salt, &c. When you intend to smoke it, hang the ham in a sugar hogshead, over a chaffing-dish of wood embers; throw on it a handful of juniper-berries, and over that some horse-dung, and cover the cask with a blanket. This may be repeated two or three times the same day, and the ham may be taken out of the hogshead the next morning. The quantity of salt here specified is for a middle sized ham. There should not be a hole cut in the leg, as is customary, to hang it up by, nor should it be soaked in brine. Hams thus cured will keep for three months without smoking, so that the whole quantity for the year may be smoked at the same time. The ham need not be soaked in water before it is used, but only washed clean. Instead of a chaffing-dish of coals to smoke the hams, make a hole in the ground, and therein put the fire; it must not be fierce: be sure to keep the mouth of the hogshead covered with a blanket to retain the smoke.

Westphalia Ham, to cure. No. 1.

Cut a leg of pork to the shape of a Westphalia ham; salt it, and set it on the fire in a skillet till dry, and put to it two ounces of saltpetre finely beaten. The salt must be put on as hot as possible. Let it remain a week in the salt, and then hang it up in the chimney for three weeks or a month. Two ounces of saltpetre will be sufficient for the quantity of salt required for one ham.

Westphalia Ham, to cure. No. 2.

Let the hams be very well pricked with a skewer on the wrong side, hanging them in an airy place as long as they will keep sweet, and with a gallon of saltpetre make a pickle, and keep stirring it till it will bear an egg; boil and skim it and put three pounds of brown sugar to it. Let the hams lie about a month in this pickle, which must be cold when they are put in; turn them every day; dry them with saw-dust and charcoal. The above is the quantity that will do for six hams.

Westphalia Ham, to cure. No. 3.

Rub every ham with four ounces of saltpetre. Next day put bay salt, common salt, and coarse sugar, half a pound of each, into a quart of stale strong beer, adding a small quantity of each of these ingredients for every ham to be made at that time. Boil this pickle, and pour it boiling hot over every ham. Let them lie a fortnight in it, rubbing them well and turning them twice a day. Then smoke the ham for three days and three nights over a fire of saw-dust and horse-litter, fresh made from the stable every night; after which smoke them for a fortnight over a wood fire like other bacon.

Westphalia Ham, to cure. No. 4.

For two hams the following proportions may be observed: wash your hams all over with vinegar, and hang them up for two or three days. Take one pound and a half of the brownest sugar, two ounces of saltpetre, two ounces of bay salt, and a quart of common salt; mix them together; heat them before the fire as hot as you can bear your hand in, and rub it well into the hams before the fire, till they are very tender. Lay them in a tub made long for that purpose, or a butcher's tray, that will hold them both, one laid one way and the other the contrary way, and strew the remainder of the ingredients over them. When the salt begins to melt, add a pint of vinegar, and let them lie three weeks, washing them with the liquor and turning them every day. Dry them in saw-dust smoke; hang them in a cellar; and if they mould it will do them no harm, as these hams require damp and not extreme driness. Juniper-berries thrown into the fire at which they are smoked greatly improve their flavour.

Westphalia Ham, to cure. No. 5.

One pound of common salt, one pound of bay salt, four ounces of saltpetre, two ounces of black pepper; pound them separately, then mix them, and rub the ham very well until the whole is used. Rub one pound of treacle on them; lay them in the pickle one month, turning them every day. The quantity here specified will do for two hams. Before you hang them up, steep them in a pail of water for twelve hours.

Westphalia Ham, to cure. No. 6.

Make a good brine of salt and water, sufficiently strong to bear an egg; boil and skim it clean, and when quite cold rub the meat with sal prunella and saltpetre mixed together. Put it in a vessel, and pour your brine into it; and, when the ham has been in the brine about fourteen days, take it out, drain it, and boil the brine, putting in a little salt, and letting it boil till clear. Skim it, and when cold put in your ham, rubbing it over with saltpetre, &c. as you did at first. Then let your ham again lie in the brine for three weeks longer; afterwards rub it well with bran, and have it dried by a wood fire.

English Hams, to make like Westphalia. No. 1.

Cut your legs of pork like hams; beat them well with a wooden mallet, till they are tender, but great care must be taken not to crack or break the skin, or the hams will be spoiled. To three hams take half a peck of salt, four ounces of saltpetre, and five pounds of coarse brown sugar; break all the lumps, and mix them well together. Rub your hams well with this mixture, and cover them with the rest. Let them lie three days; then hang them up one night, and put as much water to the salt and sugar as you think will cover them; the pickle must be strong enough to bear an egg: boil and strain it, and, when it is cold, pack your hams close, and cover them with the pickle at least an inch and half above their tops. Let them lie for a fortnight; then hang them up one night; the next day rub them well with bran, and hang them in the chimney of a fire-place in which turf, wood, or sawdust is burned. If they are small they will be dry enough in a fortnight; if large, in two or three days more. Then hang them up against a wall near a fire, and not in a damp place. Tongues may be cured in the same manner, and ribs of beef may be put in at the same time with the hams. You must let the beef lie in the pickle three weeks, and take it out when you want to boil it without drying it.

English Hams, to make like Westphalia. No. 2.

Cut off with the legs of young well grown porkers part of the flesh of the hind loin; lay them on either side in cloths, and press out the remaining blood and moisture, laying planks on them with heavy weights, which bring them into form; then salt them well with common salt and sugar finely beaten, and lay them in troughs one upon another, pressed closely down and covered with hyssop. Let them remain thus for a fortnight; then pass through the common salt, and with saltpetre rub them well over, which may be continued three or four days, till they soak. Take them out, and hang them in a close barn or smoke-loft; make a moderate fire under them, if possible of juniper-wood, and let them hang to sweat and dry well. Afterwards hang them up in a dry and airy place to the wind for three or four days, which will remove the ill scent left by the smoke; and wrap them up in sweet hay. To dress them, put them into a kettle of water when it boils; keep them well covered till they are done, and very few can distinguish them from the true Westphalia.

English Hams, to make like Westphalia. No. 3.

Take a ham of fifteen or eighteen pounds weight, two ounces of saltpetre, one pound of coarse sugar, one ounce of petre-salt, one ounce of bay salt, and one ounce of sal prunella, mixed with common salt enough to cover the ham completely. Turn your ham every other day, and let it remain in salt for three weeks. Take it out, rub a little bran over it, and dry it in a wood fire chimney, where a constant fire is kept: it will be fit for eating in a month. The quantity of the above ingredients must be varied according to the size of your ham. Before you dress it soak it over-night in water.

Hams from bacon pigs are better than pork. An onion shred small gives it a good flavour.

Green Hams.

Salt a leg of pork as for boiling, with a little saltpetre to make it red. Let it lie three weeks in salt, and then hang for a month or six weeks; but if longer it is of no consequence. When boiled, stuff with young strawberry leaves and parsley, which must be particularly well washed or they will be gritty.

Ham, to prepare for dressing without soaking.

Put the ham into a coarse sack well tied up, or sew it up in a cloth. Bury it three feet under ground in good mould; there let it remain for three or four days at least. This is an admirable way. The ham eats much mellower and finer than when soaked.

Ham, to dress.

Boil the ham for two hours; take it out and trim it neatly all round; prepare in a stewpan some thin slices of veal, so as to cover the bottom; add to it two bunches of carrots sliced, six large onions, two cloves, two bunches of parsley, a tea-spoonful of cayenne pepper, a pint of beef jelly, a bottle of white wine, and three pints of boiling water. Place the ham in the stewpan, and let it boil an hour and three quarters; then serve it immediately without sauce, preserving the sauce for other use.

Ham, to roast.

Tie or sew up the ham in a coarse cloth, put it into a sack, and bury it three or four feet under ground, for three or four days before you dress it. Wash it in warm water, pare it, and scrape the rind. Spit and lay it down to roast. Into a broad stew-pan put a pint of white wine, a quart of good broth, half a pint of the best vinegar, two large onions sliced, a blade of mace, six cloves, some pepper, four bay-leaves, some sweet basil, and a sprig of thyme. Let all these have a boil; and set the liquor under the ham, and baste very frequently with it. When the ham is roasted, take up the pan; skim all the fat off; pour the liquor through a fine sieve; then take off the rind of the ham, and beat up the liquor with a bit of butter; put this sauce under, and serve it.

Ham, entrée of.

Cut a dozen slices of ham; take off the fat entirely; fry them gently in a little butter. Have a good brown rich sauce of gravy; and serve up hot, with pieces of fried bread, cut of a semicircular shape, of the same size as the pieces of ham, and laid between them.

Ham toasts.

Cut slices of dressed ham, and thin slices of bread, or French roll, of the same shape; fry it in clarified butter; make the ham hot in cullis, or good gravy, thickened with a little floured butter. Dish the slices of ham on the toast; squeeze the juice of a Seville orange into the sauce; add a little pepper and salt; and pour it over them.

Ham and Chicken, to pot. Mrs. Vanbrugh's receipt.

Put a layer of ham, then another of the white part of chicken, just as you would any other potted meat, into a pot. When it is cut out, it will shew a very pretty stripe. This is a delicate way of eating ham and chicken.

Another way.

Take as much lean of a boiled ham as you please, and half the quantity of fat; cut it as thin as possible; beat it very fine in a mortar, with a little good oiled butter, beaten mace, pepper, and salt; put part of it into a china pot. Then beat the white part of a fowl with a very little seasoning to qualify the ham. Put a layer of chicken, then one of ham, then another of chicken at the top; press it hard down, and, when it is cold, pour clarified butter over it. When you send it to table in the pot, cut out a thin slice in the form of half a diamond, and lay it round the edge of the pot.

Herb sandwiches.

Take twelve anchovies, washed and cleaned well, and chopped very fine; mix them with half a pound of butter; this must be run through a sieve, with a wooden spoon. With this, butter bread, and make a salad of tarragon and some chives, mustard and cress, chopped very small, and put them upon the bread and butter.

Add chicken in slices, if you please, or hard-boiled eggs.

Hog's Puddings, Black. No. 1.

Steep oatmeal in pork or mutton broth, of milk; put to it two handfuls of grated bread, a good quantity of shred herbs, and some pennyroyal: season with salt, pepper, and ginger, and other spices if you please; and to about three quarts of oatmeal put two pounds of beef suet shred small, and as much hog suet as you may think convenient. Add blood enough to make it black, and half a dozen eggs.

Hog's Puddings, Black. No. 2.

To three or four quarts of blood, strained through a sieve while warm, take the crumbs of twelve-pennyworth of bread, four pounds of beef suet not shred too fine, chopped parsley, leeks, and beet; add a little powdered marjoram and mint, half an ounce of black pepper, and salt to your taste. When you fill your skins, mix these ingredients to a proper thickness in the blood; boil them twenty minutes, pricking them as they rise with a needle to prevent their bursting.

Hog's Puddings, Black. No. 3.

Steep a pint of cracked oatmeal in a quart of milk till tender; add a pound of grated bread, pennyroyal, leeks, a little onion cut small, mace, pepper, and salt, to your judgment. Melt some of the leaf of the fat, and cut some of the fat small, according to the quantity made at once; and add blood to make the ingredients of a proper consistence.

Hog's Puddings, White. No. 1.

Take the pith of an ox, and lay it in water for two days, changing the water night and morning. Then dry the pith well in a cloth, and, having scraped off all the skin, beat it well; add a little rose-water till it is very fine and without lumps. Boil a quart or three pints of cream, according to the quantity of pith, with such spices as suit your taste: beat a quarter of a pound of almonds and put to the cream. When it is cold, rub it through a hair sieve; then put the pith to it, with the yolks of eight or nine eggs, some sack, and the marrow of four bones shred small; some sweetmeats if you like, and sugar to your taste: if marrow cannot be procured suet will do. The best spices to put into the cream are nutmeg, mace, and cinnamon; but very little of the last.

Hog's Puddings, White. No. 2.

Take a quart of cream and fourteen eggs, leaving out half the whites; beat them but a little, and when the cream boils up put in the eggs; keep them stirring on a gentle fire till the whole is a thick curd. When it is almost cold, put in a pound of grated bread, two pounds of suet shred small, having a little salt mixed with it, half a pound of almonds well beaten in orange-flower water, two nutmegs grated, some citron cut small, and sugar to your taste.

Hog's Puddings, White. No. 3.

Take two pounds of grated bread; one pint and a half of cream; two pounds of beef suet and marrow; half a pound of blanched almonds, beat fine with a gill of brandy; a little rose-water; mace, cloves, and nutmeg, pounded, a quarter of an ounce; half a pound of currants, well picked and dried; ten eggs, leaving out half the whites; mix all these together, and boil them half an hour.

Kabob, an India ragout.

This dish may be made of any meat, but mutton is the best. Take a slice from a tender piece, not sinewy, a slice of ginger, and a slice of onion, put them on a silver skewer alternately, and lay them in a stewpan, in a little plain gravy. This is the kabob. Take rice and split peas, twice as much rice as peas; boil them thoroughly together, coloured with a little turmeric, and serve them up separately or together. The ginger must be steeped over-night, that you may be able to cut it.

Another way.

To make the kabob which is usually served up with pilaw, take a lean piece of mutton, and leave not a grain of fat or skin upon it; pound it in a mortar as for forcemeat; add half a clove of garlic and a spoonful or more of curry-powder, according to the size of the piece of meat, and the yolk of an egg. Mix all well together; make it into small cakes; fry it of a light brown, and put it round the pilaw.

Leg of Lamb, to boil.

Divide the leg from the loin of a hind quarter of lamb; slit the skin off the leg, and cut out the flesh of one side of it, and chop this flesh very small; add an equal quantity of shred beef suet and some sweet-herbs shred small; season with nutmeg, pepper, and salt; break into it two eggs. Mix all well together, put it into the leg, sew it up, and boil it. Chop the loin into steaks, and fry them, and, when the leg is boiled enough, lay the steaks round it. Take some white wine, anchovies, nutmeg, and a quarter of a pound of butter; thicken with the yolks of two eggs; pour it upon the lamb, and so serve it up. Boil your lamb in a cloth.

Leg of Lamb, with forcemeat.

Slit a leg of lamb on the wrong side, and take out as much meat as possible, without cutting or cracking the outward skin. Pound this meat well with an equal weight of fresh suet: add to this the pulp of a dozen large oysters, and two anchovies boned and clean washed. Season the whole with salt, black-pepper, mace, a little thyme, parsley, and shalot, finely shred together; beat them all thoroughly with the yolks of three eggs, and, having filled the skin tight with this stuffing, sew it up very close. Tie it up to the spit and roast it. Serve it with any good sauce.

Shoulder of Lamb, grilled.

Half roast, then score, and season it with pepper, salt, and cayenne. Broil it; reserve the gravy carefully; pass it through a sieve to take off all fat. Mix with it mushroom and walnut ketchup, onion, the size of a nut, well bruised, a little chopped parsley, and some of the good jelly reserved for sauces. Put a good quantity of this sauce; make it boil, and pour it boiling hot on the lamb when sent to table.

Lamb, to ragout.

Roast a quarter of lamb, and when almost done dredge it well with grated bread, which must be put into the dish you serve it up in; take veal cullis, salt, pepper, anchovy, and lemon juice; warm it, lay the lamb in it, and serve it up.

Lamb, to fricassee.

Cut the hind quarter of lamb into thin slices, and season them with spice, sweet-herbs, and a shalot; fry and toss them up in some strong broth, with balls and palates, and a little brown gravy to thicken it.

Miscellaneous directions respecting Meat.

A leg of veal, the fillet without bone, the knuckle for steaks, and a pie; bone of fillet and knuckle for soup.—Shoulder of veal, knuckle cut off for soup.—Breast of veal, thin end stews, or re-heats as a stew.—Half a calf's head boils, then hashes, with gravy from the bones.—For mock turtle soup, neats' feet instead of calf's head, that is, two calves' feet and two neats' feet.—Giblets of all poultry make gravy.—Ox-cheek, for soup and kitchen.—Rump of beef cut in two, thin part roasted, thick boiled: or steaks and one joint, the bone for soup.—The trimmings of many joints will make gravy.—To boil the meat white, well flour the joint and the cloth it is boiled in, not letting any thing be boiled with it, and frequently skimming the grease.—Lamb chops fried dry and thin make a neat dish, with French beans in cream round them. A piece of veal larded in white celery sauce, to answer the chops.—Dressed meat, chopped fine, with a little forcemeat, and made into balls about the size of an egg, browned and fried dry, and sent up without any sauce.—Sweetbreads larded in white celery sauce.—To remove taint in meat, put the joint into a pot with water, and, when it begins to boil, throw in a few red clear cinders, let them boil together for two or three minutes, then take out the meat, and wipe it dry.—To keep hams, when they are cured for hanging up, tie them in brown paper bags tight round the hocks to exclude the flies, which omission occasions maggots.—Ginger, where spice is required, is very good in most things.

Meat, general rule for roasting and boiling.

The general rule for roasting and boiling meat is as follows: fifteen minutes to a pound in roasting, twenty minutes to a pound in boiling.

On no account whatever let the least drop of water be poured on any roast meat; it soddens it, and is a bad contrivance to make gravy, which is, after all, no gravy, and totally spoils the meat.

Meat, half-roasted or under-done.

Cut small pieces, of the size of a half-crown, of half-roasted mutton, and put them into a saucepan with half a pint of red wine, the same quantity of gravy, one anchovy, a little shalot, whole pepper, and salt; let them stew a little; then put in the meat with a few capers, and, when thoroughly hot, thicken with butter rolled in flour.

Mustard, to make.

Mix three table-spoonfuls of mustard, one of salt, and cold spring water sufficient to reduce it to a proper thickness.

Chine of Mutton, to roast.

Let the chine hang downward, and raise the skin from the bone. Take slices of lean gammon of bacon, and season it with chives, parsley, and white pepper; spread them over the chine, and lay the bacon upon them. Turn the skin over them, and tie it up; cover with paper, and roast. When nearly done, dredge with crumbs of bread, and serve up, garnishing with mutton cutlets.

Mutton chops, to stew.

Put them in a stewpan, with an onion, and enough cold water to cover them; when come to a boil, skim and set them over a very slow fire till tender; perhaps about three quarters of an hour.

Turnips may be boiled with them.

Mutton cutlets.

Cut a neck of mutton into cutlets; beat it till very tender; wash it with thick melted butter, and strew over the side which is buttered some sweet-herbs, chopped small, with grated bread, a little salt, and nutmeg. Lay it on a gridiron over a charcoal fire, and, turning it, do the same to that side as the other. Make sauce of gravy, anchovies, shalots, thick butter, a little nutmeg, and lemon.

Mutton cutlets, with onion sauce.

Cut the cutlets very small; trim all round, taking off all the fat; cut off the long part of the bone; put them into a stewpan, with all the trimmings that have been cut off, together with one onion cut in slices; add some parsley, a carrot or two, a pinch of salt, and six table-spoonfuls of mutton or veal jelly, and let them stew till the cutlets are of a brown colour all round, but do not let them burn. Take out the cutlets, drain them in a sieve, and let them cool; then strain the sauce till it becomes of a fine glaze, and re-warm them. Have ready some good onion sauce; put it in the middle of the dish; place the cutlets—eight, if they are small—round it, and serve the glaze with them; take care it does not touch the onion sauce, but pour it round the outside part.

Mutton hams, to make.

Cut a hind quarter of mutton like a ham. Take one ounce of saltpetre, one pound of coarse sugar, and one pound of common salt; mix them together, and rub the ham well with them. Lay it in a hollow tray with the skin downward; baste it every day for a fortnight; then roll it in sawdust, and hang it in wood smoke for a fortnight. Boil and hang it in a dry place; cut it out in rashers. It does not eat well boiled, but is delicious broiled.

Haricot Mutton.

Take a neck of mutton, and cut it in the same manner as for mutton chops. When done, lay them in your stewpan, with a blade of mace, some whole peppercorns, a bunch of sweet-herbs, two onions, one carrot, one turnip, all cut in slices, and lay them over your mutton. Set your stewpan over a slow fire, and let the chops stew till they are brown; turn them, that the other side may be the same. Have ready some good gravy, and pour on them, and let them stew till they are very tender. Your ragout must be turnips and carrots cut into dice, and small onions, all boiled very tender, and well stirred up in the liquor in which your mutton was stewed.

Another way.

Fry mutton chops in butter till they are brown, but not done through. Lay them flat in a stewpan, and just cover them with gravy. Put in small onions, whole carrots, and turnips, scooped or cut into shapes; let them stew very gently for two hours or more. Season the chops before you fry them with pepper and salt.

Leg of Mutton.

To give a leg of mutton the taste of mountain meat, hang it up as long as it will keep fresh; rub it every day with ginger and coarse brown sugar, leaving it on the meat.

Leg of Mutton in the French fashion.

A leg of mutton thus dressed is a very excellent dish. Pare off all the skin as neatly as possible; lard the leg with the best lard, and stick a few cloves here and there, with half a clove of garlic, laid in the shank. When half roasted, cut off three or four thin pieces, so as not to disfigure it, about the shank bone; mince these very fine with sage, thyme, mint, and any other sweet garden herbs; add a little beaten ginger, very little, three or four grains; as much cayenne pepper, two spoonfuls of lemon juice, two ladlefuls of claret wine, a few capers, the yolks of two hard-boiled eggs: stew these in some meat jelly, and, when thoroughly stewed, pour over your roast, and serve it up. Do not spare your meat jelly; let the sauce be in generous quantity.

Leg of Mutton or Beef, to hash.

Cut small flat pieces of the meat, taking care to pare the skin and sinews, but leaving as much fat as you can find in the inside of the leg; season with a little salt and cayenne pepper and a little soup jelly; put in two whole onions, two bunches of parsley, the same of thyme, and a table-spoonful of mushroom-powder. Take two or three little balls of flour and butter, of the size of a nut, to thicken the sauce; beat it well together; let this simmer a little while; take off the scum; put in the meat, and let it boil. Serve up hot, with fried bread round it.

Another way.

Take the mutton and cut it into slices, taking off the skin and fat; beat it well, and rub the dish with garlic; put in the mutton with water, and season with salt, an onion cut in half, and a bundle of savoury herbs; cover it, and set it over a stove and stew it. When half stewed, add a little white wine (say two glasses) three blades of mace, and an anchovy; stew it till enough done; then take out the onion and herbs, and put the hash into the dish, rubbing a piece of butter in flour to thicken it, and serve it up.

Loin of Mutton, to stew.

Cut your mutton in steaks, and put it into as much water as will cover it. When it is skimmed, add four onions sliced and four large turnips.

Neck of Mutton, to roast.

Draw the neck with parsley, and then roast it; and, when almost enough, dredge it with white pepper, salt, and crumbs; serve it with the juice of orange and gravy.

Neck of Mutton, to boil.

Lard a neck of mutton with lemon-peel, and then boil it in salt and water, with sweet-herbs. While boiling, stew a pint of oysters in their own liquor, half a pint of white wine, and the like quantity of broth; put in two or three whole onions and some anchovies, grated nutmeg, and a little thyme. Thicken the broth with the yolks of four eggs, and dish it up with sippets. Lay the oysters under the meat, and garnish with barberries and lemon.

Neck of Mutton, to fry.

Take the best end of a neck of mutton, cut it into steaks, beat them with a rolling-pin, strew some salt on them, and lay them in a frying-pan: hold the pan over a slow fire that may not burn them: turn them as they heat, and there will be gravy enough to fry them in, till they are half done. Then put to them some good gravy; let them fry together, till they are done; add a good bit of butter, shake it up, and serve it hot with pickles.

Saddle of Mutton and Kidneys.

Raise the skin of the fore-chine of mutton, and draw it with lemon and thyme; and with sausage-meat farce part of it. Take twelve kidneys, farce, skewer, and afterwards broil them; and lay round horseradish between, with the gravy under.

Shoulder of Mutton, to roast in blood.

Cut the shoulder as you would venison; take off the skin, and let it lie in blood all night. Take as much powder of sweet-herbs as will lie on a sixpence, a little grated bread, pepper, nutmeg, ginger, and lemon-peel, the yolks of two eggs boiled hard, about twenty oysters, and some salt; temper these all together with the blood; stuff the meat thickly with it, and lay some of it about the mutton; then wrap the caul of the sheep about the shoulder; roast it, and baste it with blood till it is nearly done. Take off the caul, dredge, baste it with butter, and serve it with venison sauce. If you do not cut it venison fashion, yet take off the skin, because it will eat tough; let the caul be spread while it is warm, and, when you are to dress it, wrap it up in a cloth dipped in hot water. For sauce, take some of the bones of the breast; chop and put to them a whole onion, a little lemon-peel, anchovies, and a little spice. Stew these; add some red wine, oysters, and mushrooms.

Shoulder, or Leg of Mutton, with Oysters.

Make six holes in either a shoulder or leg of mutton with a knife: roll in eggs with your oysters, with crumbs and nutmeg, and stuff three or four in every hole. If you roast, put a caul over it; if for boiling, a napkin. Make some good oyster sauce, which lay under, and serve up hot.

Roasted Mutton, with stewed Cucumbers.

Bone a neck and loin of mutton, leaving on only the top bones, about an inch long; draw the one with parsley, and lard the other with bacon very closely; and, after skewering, roast them. Fry and stew your cucumbers; lay them under the mutton, and season them with salt, pepper, vinegar, and minced shalot, and put the sauce under the mutton, garnishing with pickled cucumbers and horseradish.

Mutton to eat like Venison.

Boil and skin a loin of mutton; take the bones, two onions, two anchovies, a bunch of sweet-herbs, some pepper, mace, carrot, and crust of bread; stew these all together for gravy; strain it off, and put the mutton into a stewpan with the fat side downward; add half a pint of port wine. Stew it till thoroughly done.

Mutton in epigram.

Roast a shoulder of mutton till it is three parts done, and let it cool; raise the skin quite up to the knuckle, and cut off all to the knuckle. Sauce the blade-bone; broil it, and hash the rest, putting in some capers, with good gravy, pickled cucumbers, and shalots. Stir them well up, and lay the blade-bone on the skin.

Mushrooms, to stew brown.

Take some pepper and salt, with a little cayenne and a little cream; thicken with butter and flour. To do them white, cut out all the black inside.

Newmarket John.

Cut the lean part of a leg of mutton in little thin collops; beat them; butter a stewpan, and lay the collops all over. Have ready pepper, salt, shalot or garlic, and strew upon them. Set them over a very slow fire. As the gravy draws, turn over the collops, and dredge in a very little flour; have ready some good hot gravy. Shake it up all together, and serve with pickles.

Ox-cheek, to stew.

Choose one that is fat and young, which may be known by the teeth; pick out the eye-balls; cut away the snout and all superfluous bits. Wash and clean it perfectly; well dry it in a cloth, and, with the back of a cleaver, break all the bones in the inside of the cheek; then with a rollingpin beat the flesh of the outside. If it is intended for the next day's dinner, proceed in this manner:—quarter and lard it with marrow; then pour on it garlic or elder vinegar so gently that it may sink into the flesh; strew salt over it, and let it remain so till morning. Then put it into a stewpan, big enough, if you do both cheeks, to admit of their lying flat close to one another; but first rub the pan well with garlic, and with a spoon spread a pound of butter and upwards at the bottom and sides of the pan. Strew cloves and beaten mace on the cheeks, also thyme and sweet marjoram, finely chopped; then put in as much white wine as will cover them an inch or more above the meat, but wash not off the other things by pouring it on. Rub the lid of the pan with garlic, and cover it so close that no steam can escape. Make a brisk fire under it, and, when the cover is so hot that you cannot bear your hand on it, then a slack fire will stew it, but keep it so that the cover be of the same heat as long as it is stewing. It must not be uncovered the whole time it is doing: about three hours will be sufficient. When you take it up, be careful not to break it; take out the loose bones; pour the liquor on the cheek; clear from the fat and the dross, and put lemon-juice to it. Serve it hot.

Another way.

Soak it in water, and make it very clean; put it in a gallon of water, with some potherbs, salt, and whole pepper. When stewed, so that the bones will slip out easily, take it up and strain off the soup; put a bit of butter in the frying-pan with some flour, and fry the meat brown, taking care not to burn it. Put some of the soup to the flour and butter, with ketchup, mushrooms, anchovy, and walnut liquor. Lay the cheek in a deep dish, and pour the sauce over it.

Ox-tail ragout.

Some good gravy must first be made, and the tail chopped through every joint, and stewed a long time in it till quite tender, with an onion stuck with cloves, a table-spoonful of port or Madeira wine, a tea-spoonful of soy, and a little cayenne. Thicken the gravy with a little flour.

Another.

Take two or three ox-tails; put them in a saucepan, with turnips, carrots, onions, and some black peppercorns; stew them for four hours. Take them out; cut them in pieces at every joint; put them into a stewpan with some good gravy, and scraped turnip and carrot; or cut them into the shape of a ninepin; pepper and salt to your taste; add the juice of half a lemon; and send it to table very hot.

Peas, to stew.

Take a quart of fine peas, and two small or one large cabbage lettuce; boil the lettuce tender; take it out of the water, shake it well, and put it into the stewpan, with about two ounces of butter, three or four little onions cut small, and the peas. Set them on a very slow fire, and let them stew about two hours; season them to your taste with pepper and a tea-spoonful of sugar; and, instead of salt, stew in some bits of ham, which you may take out or leave in when you serve it. There should not be a drop of water, except what inevitably comes from the lettuce.

Another way.

To your peas, add cabbage lettuces cut small, a small faggot of mint, and one onion; pass them over the fire with a small bit of butter, and, when they are tender and the liquor from them reduced, take out the onion and mint, and add a little white sauce. Take care it be not too thin; season with a little pepper and salt.

Green Peas, to keep till Christmas.

Gather your peas, when neither very young nor old, on a fine dry day. Shell, and let two persons holding a cloth, one at each end, shake them backward and forward for a few minutes. Put them into clean quart bottles; fill the bottles, and cork tight. Melt some rosin in a pipkin, dip the necks of the bottles into it, and set them in a cool dry place.

Another way.

Shell the peas, and dry them in a gentle heat, not much greater than that of a hot summer's day. Put them when quite dry into linen bags, and hang them up in a dry place. Before they are boiled, at Christmas or later, steep them in half milk, half water, for twelve or fourteen hours; then boil them as if fresh gathered. Beans and French beans may be preserved in the same manner.

Red Pickle, for any meat.

A quarter of a pound of saltpetre, a large common basinful of coarse sugar, and coarse salt. A leg of pork to lie in it a fortnight.

Beef Steak Pie.

Rump steaks are preferable to beef; season them with the usual seasoning, puff-paste top and bottom, and good gravy to fill the dish.

Calf's Head Pie.

Parboil the head; cut it into thin slices; season with pepper and salt; lay them into a crust with some good gravy, forcemeat balls, and yolks of eggs boiled hard. Bake it about an hour and a half; cut off the lid; thicken some good gravy with a little flour; add some oysters; serve it with or without a lid.

Mutton or Grass Lamb Pie.

Take a loin of mutton or lamb, and clear it from fat and skin; cut it into steaks; season them well with pepper and salt; almost fill the dish with water; lay puff paste at top and bottom.

Veal Pie (common).

Make exactly as you would a beef-steak pie.

Veal Pie (rich).

Take a neck, a fillet, or a breast of veal, cut from it your steaks, seasoned with pepper, salt, nutmeg, and a few cloves, truffles, and morels; then slice two sweetbreads; season them in the same manner, and put a layer of paste round the dish; then lay the meat, yolks of eggs boiled hard, and oysters at the top: fill it with water. When taken out of the oven, pour in at the top through a funnel some good boiled gravy, thickened with cream and flour boiled up.

Veal and Ham Pie.

Take two pounds of veal cutlets, or the best end of the neck, cut them in pieces about half the size of your hand, seasoned with pepper and a very little salt, and some dressed ham in slices. Lay them alternately in the dish with forcemeat or sausage meat, the yolks of three eggs boiled hard, and a gill of water.

Veal Olive Pie.

Make your olives as directed in the receipt for making olives; put them into a crust; fill the pie with water: when baked, pour in some good gravy, boiled and thickened with a little good cream and flour boiled together. These ingredients make an excellent pie.

Beef Olive Pie.

Make your olives as you would common beef olives; put them into puff paste, top and bottom; fill the pie with water, when baked, pour in some good rich gravy.

Pig, to barbicue.

The best pig for this purpose is of the thick neck breed, about six weeks old. Season the barbicue very high with cayenne, black pepper, and sage, finely sifted; which must be rubbed well into the inside of the pig. It must then be sewed up and roasted, or, if an oven can be depended upon, it will be equally good baked. The sauce must be a very high beef gravy, with an equal quantity of Madeira wine in it. Send the pig to table whole. Be careful not to put any salt into the pig, as it will change its colour.

Pig, to collar.

Have your pig cut down the back, and bone and wash it clean from the blood; dry it well, and season it with spice, salt, parsley, and thyme, and roll it hard in a collar; tie it close in a dry cloth and boil it with the bones, in three pints of water, a quart of vinegar, a handful of salt, a faggot of sweet-herbs, and whole spice. When tender, let it cool and take it off; take it out of the cloth, and keep it in the pickle.

Pig, to collar in colours.

Boil and wash your pig well, and lay it on a dresser: chop parsley, thyme, and sage, and strew them over the inside of the pig. Beat some mace and cloves, mix with them some pepper and salt, and strew that over. Boil some eggs hard, chop the yolks, and put them in layers across your pig; boil some beet-root, and cut that into slices, and lay them across; then roll it up in a cloth and boil it. Before it is cold, press it with a weight, and it will be fit for use.

Pig, to pickle or souse.

Take a fair fat pig, cut off his head, and cut him through the middle. Take out the brains, lay them in warm water, and leave them all night. Roll the pig up like brawn, boil till tender, and then throw it into an earthen pan with salt and water. This will whiten and season the flesh; for no salt must be put into the boiling for fear of turning it black. Then take a quart of this broth and a quart of white wine, boil them together, and put in three or four bay-leaves: when cold, season your pig, and put it into this sauce. It will keep three months.

Pig, to roast.

Chop the liver small by itself: mince blanched bacon, capers, truffles, anchovy, mushrooms, sweet-herbs and garlic. Season and blanch the whole. Fill your pig with it; tie it up; sprinkle some good olive oil over it; roast and serve it up hot.

Another way.

Put a piece of bread, parsley, and sage, cut small, into the belly with a little salt; sew up the belly; spit the pig, and roast it; cut off the ears and the under-jaws, which you will lay round; making a sauce with the brains, thick butter and gravy, which lay underneath.

Pig, to dress lamb fashion.

After skinning the pig, but leaving the skin quite whole, with the head on, chine it down, as you would do mutton, larding it with thyme and lemon-peel; and roast it in quarters like lamb. Fill the other part with a plum-pudding; sew the belly up, and bake it.

Pigs' Feet and Ears, fricassee of.

Clean the feet and ears, and boil them very tender. Cut them in small shreds, the length of a finger and about a quarter of an inch in breadth; fry them in butter till they are brown but not hard; put them into a stewpan with a little brown gravy and a good piece of butter, two spoonfuls of vinegar, and a good deal of mustard—enough to flavour it strong. Salt to your taste; thicken with very little flour. Put in half an onion; then take the feet, which should likewise be boiled as tender as for eating; slit them quite through the middle; take out the large bones; dip them in eggs, and strew them over with bread crumbs, seasoned with pepper and salt; boil or fry them, and put them on the ragout, into which squeeze some lemon-juice.

Pigs' Feet and Ears, ragout of.

Split the feet, and take them out of souse; dip them in eggs, then in bread-crumbs and chopped parsley; fry them in lard. Drain them; cut the ears in long narrow slips; flour them; put them into some good gravy; add ketchup, morels, and pickled mushrooms; stew them into the dish, and lay on the feet.

Pig's Head, to roll.

Take the belly-piece and head of pork, rub it well with saltpetre and a very little salt; let it lie three or four days; wash it clean; then boil the head tender, and take off all the meat with the ears, which cut in pieces. Have ready four neats' feet, also well boiled; take out the bones, cut the meat in thin slices, mix it with the head, and lay it with the belly-piece: roll it up tight, and bind it up, and set it on one end, with a trencher upon it; set it within the tin, and place a heavy weight upon that, and let it stand all night. In the morning take it out, and bind it with a fillet; put it in some salt and water, which must be changed every four or five days. When sliced, it looks like brawn. It is also good dipped in butter and fried, and eaten with melted butter, mustard, and vinegar: for that purpose the slices should be only about three inches square.

Pilaw, an Indian dish.

Take six or eight ribs of a neck of mutton; separate and take off all the skin and fat, and put them into a stewpan with twelve cloves, a small piece of ginger, twelve grains of black pepper, and a little cinnamon and mace, with one clove of garlic. Add as much water as will serve to stew these ingredients thoroughly and make the meat tender. Then take out the mutton, and fry it in nice butter of a light brown, with some small onions chopped fine and fried very dry; put them to the mutton-gravy and spice in which it was stewed, adding a table-spoonful of curry-powder and half an ounce of butter. After mixing all the above ingredients well together, put them to the rice, which should be previously half boiled, and let the whole stew together, until the rice is done enough and the gravy completely absorbed. When the pilaw is dished for table, it should be thinly covered with plain boiled rice to make it look white, and served up very hot.

Pork, to collar.

Bone and season a breast of pork with savoury spice, parsley, sage, and thyme; roll it in a hard collar of cloth; tie it close, and boil it, and, when cold, keep it in souse.

Pork, to pickle.

Having boned your pork, cut it into such pieces as will lie most conveniently to be powdered. The tub used for this purpose must be sufficiently large and sound, so as to hold the brine; and the narrower and deeper it is the better it will keep the meat. Well rub the meat with saltpetre; then take one part of bay and two parts of common salt, and rub every piece well, covering it with salt, as you would a flitch of bacon. Strew salt in the bottom of the tub; lay the pieces in it as closely as possible, strewing salt round the sides of the tub, and if the salt should even melt at the top strew no more. Meat thus cured will keep a long time.

Another way.

Cut your pork into small pieces, of the size you would boil at one time; rub all the pieces very well with salt, and lay them on a dresser upon boards made to slope that the brine may run off. After remaining three or four days, wipe them with a dry cloth; have ready a quantity of salt mixed with a small portion of salt-petre: rub each piece well with this mixture, after which cover them all over with salt. Put them into an earthen jar, or large pan, placing the pieces as close together as possible, closing the top of the jar or pan, so as to prevent all external air from getting in; put the shoulder pieces in a pan by themselves. Pork prepared in this manner will keep good a year.

Chine of Pork, to stuff and roast.

Make your stuffing of parsley, sage, thyme, eggs, crumbs of bread, and season it with salt, pepper, nutmeg, and shalot; stuff the chine thick, and roast it gently. When about a quarter roasted, cut the skin in slips, making your sauce with lemon-peel, apples, sugar, butter, and mustard, just as you would for a roast leg.

Another way.

Take a chine of pork that has hung four or five days; make holes in the lean, and stuff it with a little of the fat leaf, chopped very small, some parsley, thyme, a little sage, and shalot, cut very fine, and seasoned with pepper and salt. It should be stuffed pretty thick. Have some good gravy in the dish. For sauce, use apple sauce.

Pork Cutlets.

Cut off the skin of a loin or neck of pork and make cutlets; season them with parsley, sage, and thyme, mixed together with crumbs of bread, pepper, and salt; broil them, and make sauce with mustard, butter, shalot, and gravy, and serve up hot.

Gammon, to roast.

Let the gammon soak for twenty-four hours in warm water. Boil it tender, but not too much. When hot, score it with your knife; put some pepper on it, and then put it into a dish to crisp in a hot oven; but be mindful to pull the skin off.

Leg of Pork, to broil.

After skinning part of the fillet, cut it into slices, and hack it with the back of your knife; season with pepper, salt, thyme, and sage, minced small. Broil the slices on the gridiron, and serve with sauce made with drawn butter, sugar, and mustard.

Spring of Pork, to roast.

Cut off the spring of a knuckle of pork, and leave as much skin on the spring as you can, parting it from the neck, and taking out the bones. Rub it well with salt, and strew it all over with thyme shred small, parsley, sage, a nutmeg, cloves, and mace, beaten small and well mixed together. Rub all well in, and roll the whole up tight, with the flesh inward. Sew it fast, spit it lengthwise, and roast it.

Potatoes, to boil. No. 1.

The following is the celebrated Lancashire receipt for cooking potatoes:— Cleanse them well, put them in cold water, and boil them with their skins on exceedingly slow. When the water bubbles, throw in a little cold water. When they are done, drain the water completely away through a colander; return them into a pot or saucepan without water; cover them up, and set them before the fire for a quarter of an hour longer. Do not pare the potatoes before they are boiled, which is a very unwholesome and wasteful practice.

Potatoes, to boil. No. 2.

Scrape off the rind; put them into an iron pot; simmer them till they begin to crack, and allow a fork to pierce easily; then pour off the water, and put aside the lid of the pot, and sprinkle over some salt. Place your pot at the edge of the fire, and there let it remain an hour or more, and during this time all the moisture of the potatoes will gradually exhale in steam, and you will find them white or flaky as snow. Take them out with a spoon or ladle.

Potatoes, to boil. No. 3.

Boil them as usual; half an hour before sending to table, throw away the water from them, and set the pot again on the fire; sufficient moisture will come from the potatoes to prevent the pot from burning; let them stand on the half stove, and not be peeled until sent to table.

Potatoes, to bake.

Wash nicely, make into balls, and bake in the Dutch oven a light brown. This forms a neat side or corner dish.

Potato balls.

Pound some boiled potatoes in a mortar, with the yolks of two eggs, a little pepper, and salt; make them in balls about the size of an egg; do them over with yolk of egg and crumbs of bread; then fry them of a light brown for table; five balls for a corner dish.

Croquets of Potatoes.

Boil some potatoes in water, strain them, and take sufficient milk to make them into a mash, rather thick; before you mix the potatoes put the peel of half a lemon, finely grated, one lump of sugar, and a pinch of salt; strain the milk after heating it, and add the potatoes; mash them well together; let the mash cool; roll it into balls of the shape and size of an egg; let there be ten or twelve of them; brush them over with the yolk of egg, and roll them in crumbs of bread and a pinch of salt. Do this twice over; then fry them of a fine brown colour, and serve them with fried parsley round.

Potatoes, to fry.

After your potatoes are nicely boiled and skinned, grate them, and to every large table-spoonful of potatoes add one egg well beat, and to each egg a small spoonful of cream, with some salt. Drop as many spoonfuls as are proper in a pan in which is clarified butter.

Potatoes, to mash.

After the potatoes are boiled and peeled, mash them in a mortar, or on a clean board, with a broad knife, and put them into a stewpan. To two pounds of potatoes put in half a pint of milk, a quarter of a pound of butter, and a little salt; set them over the fire, and keep them stirred till the butter is melted; but take care they do not burn to the bottom. Dish them up in what form you please.

Potatoes, French way of cooking.

Boil the potatoes in a weak white gravy till nearly done; stir in some cream and vermicelli, with three or four blades of mace, and let it boil till the potatoes are sufficiently done, without being broken.

Potatoes, à-la-Maitre d'hotel.

Cut boiled potatoes into slices, not too thin; simmer them in a little plain gravy, a bit of butter rubbed in a little flour, chopped parsley, pepper, and salt, and serve hot.

Rice, to boil.

To boil rice well, though a simple thing, is rarely well done. Have two quarts of water boiling, while you wash six ounces of rice, picked clean. Change the water three or four times. When the rice is clean, drain and put it into the boiling water. Boil twenty minutes; add three quarters of a table-spoonful of salt. Drain off the water well—this is the most essential point—set it before the fire, spread thin to dry. When dry, serve it up. If the rice is not dry, so that each grain separates easily from the others, it is not properly boiled.

Another way.

Put one pound of rice into three quarts of boiling water; let it remain twenty minutes. Skim the water, and add one ounce of hog's lard and a little salt and pepper. Let it simmer gently over the fire closely covered, for an hour and a quarter, when it will be fit for use. This will produce eight pounds of savoury rice.

Rissoles. No. 1.

Take a roasted fowl, turkey, or pullet; pull it into shreds; there must be neither bone nor skin. Cut some veal and ham into large dice; put it into a stewpan, with a little thyme, carrots, onions, cloves, and two or three mushrooms. Make these ingredients simmer over a slow fire for two hours, taking care they do not burn; put in a handful of flour, and stir well, with a pint of cream and as much good broth; let the whole then stew for a quarter of an hour; continue to stir with a wooden spoon to prevent its burning. When it is done enough, strain it through a woollen strainer; then put in the whole meat of the poultry you have cut, with which you must make little balls of the size of pigeons' eggs. Dip them twice in very fine crumbs of bread; wrap them in paste, rolled very thin; then fry them in lard, which should be very hot.

Rissoles. No. 2.

Take the fleshy parts and breasts of two fowls, which cut into small dice, all of an equal size; then throw them into some white sauce, and reduce it till it becomes very thick and stiff. When this is cold, cut it into several pieces, and roll them to the size and shape of a cork; then roll them in crumbs of bread very fine; dip them into some white and yolks of eggs put up together with a little salt, and roll them again in bread. If they are not stiff enough to keep their shape, this must be repeated; then fry them of a light brown colour, drain them, wipe off the grease, and serve them with fried parsley between them.

Rissoles. No. 3.

Take of the puré made as directed for pheasant, veal, or game, (see Pheasant under the head Game) a sufficient quantity for eight rissoles, then a little of the jelly of veal, say about half a pint; put in it a pinch of salt and of cayenne pepper, two table-spoonfuls of cream, the yolk of one egg, and a piece of butter of the size of a walnut; mix this sauce well together over the fire, strain it, and then add the puré. Let it cool, and prepare a little puff-paste sufficient to wrap the rissoles once over with it, taking care to roll the paste out thin. Fry them, and send them up with fried parsley, without sauce. The rissoles must be made stiff enough not to break in the frying.

Rice.

One pound of veal or fowl, chopped fine; have ready some good bechamel sauce mixed with parsley and lemon-juice; mix it of a good thickness. When cold, make it up into balls, or what shape you please; dip them in yolks of eggs and bread crumbs, and fry them a few minutes before they go to table. They should be of a light brown, and sent up with fried parsley.

A Robinson, to make.

Take about eight or ten pounds of the middle of a brisket of beef; let it hang a day; then salt it for three days hung up; afterwards put it in strong red pickle, in which let it remain three weeks. Take it out, put it into a pot with plenty of water, pepper, a little allspice, and onion; let it simmer for seven or eight hours, but never let it boil. When quite tender, take out all the bones, spread it out on a table to cool, well beat it out with a rollingpin, and sprinkle with cayenne, nutmeg, and very little cloves, pounded together. Put it in a coarse cloth after it is rolled; twist it at each end to get out the fat, and bind it well round with broad tape; in that state let it remain three days.

Salad, to dress.

Two or three eggs, two or three anchovies, pounded, a little tarragon chopped very fine, a little thick cream, mustard, salt, and cayenne pepper, mixed well together. After these are all well mixed, add oil, a little tarragon, elder, and garlic vinegar, so as to have the flavour of each, and then a little of the French vinegar, if there is not enough of the others to give the requisite taste.

Bologna Sausages.

Have the fillets of young, tender porkers, and out of the weight of twenty-five pounds three parts are to be lean and one fat; season them well in the small shredding with salt and pepper, a little grated nutmeg, and a pint of white wine, mixed with a pint of hog's blood; stirring and beating it well together, with a little of the sweet-herbs finely chopped; with a funnel open the mouths of the guts, and thrust the meat gently into it with a clean napkin, as by forcing it with your hands you may break the gut. Divide them into what lengths you please; tie them with fine thread, and let them dry in the air for two or three days, if the weather be clear and a brisk wind, hanging them in rows at a little distance from each other in the smoke-loft. When well dried, rub off the dust they contract with a clean cloth; pour over them sweet olive-oil, and cover them with a dry earthen vessel.

English Sausages.

Chop and bruise small the lean of a fillet of young pork; to every pound put a quarter of a pound of fat, well skinned, and season it with a little nutmeg, salt, and pepper, adding a little grated bread; mix all these well together, and put it into guts, seasoned with salt and water.

Another way.

Take six pounds of very fine well fed pork, quite free from gristle and fat; cut it very small, and beat it fine in a mortar; shred six pounds of suet, free from skin, as fine as possible. Take a good deal of sage, the leaves picked off and washed clean, and shred fine as possible; spread the meat on a clean table; then shake the sage, about three large spoonfuls, all over; shred the yellow part of the rind of a lemon very fine, and throw that over, with as much sweet-herbs, when shred fine, as will fill a large spoon; grate two nutmegs over it, with two tea-spoonfuls of bruised pepper, and a large spoonful of salt. Then throw over it the suet, and mix all well together, and put it down close in a pot. When you use it, roll it up with as much beaten egg as will make the sausages roll smooth; let what you fry them in be hot before you put them into the pan; roll them about, and when they are thoroughly hot, and of a fine light brown colour, they are done. By warming a little of the meat in a spoon when you are making it, you will then taste if it is seasoned enough.

Oxford Sausages.

Take the best part of a leg of veal and of a leg of pork, of each three pounds; skin it well, and cut it into small dice. Take three pounds of the best beef suet (the proportion of which you may increase or diminish according to your taste,) skin it well; add a little sage, and chop it all together as fine as forcemeat. When chopped, put in six or seven eggs and a quarter of a pound of cold water, and season to your liking with pepper and salt. Work it up as if you were kneading dough for bread; roll it out in the form of sausages, and let the pan you fry them in be hot, with a bit of butter in it.

Sausages for Scotch collops.

Take beef suet and some veal, with a little winter savory, sage, thyme, and some grated nutmeg, beaten cloves, mace, and a little salt and pepper. Let these be well beaten together; then add two eggs beat, and heat all together. Roll them up in grated bread, fry, and send them up.

Veal Sausages.

Take half a pound of the lean of a leg of veal; cut it in small pieces, and beat it very fine in a stone mortar, picking out all the little strings. Shred one pound and half of beef-suet very small; season it with pepper, salt, cloves, and mace, but twice as much mace as cloves, some sage, thyme, and sweet marjoram, according to your palate. Mix all these well with the yolks of twelve eggs; roll them to your fancy, and fry them in lard.

Sausages without skins.

Take a pound and quarter of the lean of a leg of veal and a pound and quarter of the lean of a hind loin of pork; pick the meat from the skins before you weigh it; then take two pounds and half of fresh beef-suet picked clean from the skins, and an ounce and half of red sage leaves, picked from the stalks; wash and mince them as fine as possible; put them to the meat and suet, and mince as fine as you can. Add to it two ounces of white salt and half an ounce of pepper. Pare all the crust from a stale penny French roll, and soak the crumb in water till it is wet through; put it into a clean napkin, and squeeze out all the water. Put the bread to the meat, with four new-laid eggs beaten; then with your hands work all these things to-gether, and put them into a clean earthen pan, pressed down close. They will keep good for a week. When you use this meat, divide a pound into eighteen parts; flour your hands a little, and roll it up into pretty thick sausages, and fry them in sweet butter; a little frying will do.

Spinach, the best mode of dressing.

Boil the spinach, squeeze the water from it completely, chop it a little; then put it and a piece of butter in a stewpan with salt and a very little nutmeg; turn it over a brisk fire to dry the remaining water. Then add a little flour; mix it well, wet it with a little good broth, and let it simmer for some time, turning it now and then to prevent burning.

To dress it *maigre*, put cream instead of broth, and an onion with a clove stuck in it, which you take out when you serve the spinach. Garnish with fried bread. Observe that if you leave water in it, the spinach cannot ever be good.

Another way.

Clean it well, and throw it into fresh water; then squeeze and drain it quite dry. Chop it extremely small, and put it into a pan with cream, fresh butter, salt, and a very small quantity of pepper and nutmeg: add an onion with two cloves stuck in it, and serve it up very hot, with fried bread sippets of triangular shape round the dish.

Spinach, to stew.

Pick the spinach very carefully; put it into a pan of water; boil it in a large vessel with a good deal of salt to preserve the green colour, and press it down frequently that it may be done equally. When boiled enough to squeeze easily, drain it from the water, and throw it into cold water. When quite cold, make it into balls, and squeeze it well. Then spread it on a table and chop it very fine; put a good piece of butter in a stewpan, and lay the spinach over the butter. Let it dry over a slow fire, and add a little flour; moisten with half a pint of beef jelly and a very little warm water: add a little cayenne pepper. This spinach should be very like thick melted butter, and as fine and smooth as possible.

Another way.

Take some fine spinach, pick and wash it extremely clean. When well boiled, put it into cold water, and squeeze it in a cloth very dry; chop it very small; put it in a stewpan with a piece of butter and half a pint of good cream; stir it well over the fire, that it may not oil; and put in a little more cream just as you are going to dish it.

Sweetbreads, ragout of.

Wash your sweetbreads; put them into boiling water, and, after blanching them, throw them into cold water; dry them with a linen cloth; and put them in a saucepan over the fire with salt, pepper, melted bacon, and a faggot of sweet-herbs. Shake them together, and put some good gravy to moisten them; simmer over the fire, and thicken to your liking.

Another.

Take sweetbreads and lamb's fry, and parboil them, cutting them into slices, and cocks'-combs sliced and blanched, and season them with pepper and salt, and other spices; fry them in a little lard; drain and toss them in good gravy, with two shalots, a bunch of sweet-herbs, mushrooms, and truffles. Thicken it with a glass of claret; garnish with red beet root.

Savoury Toasts, to relish Wine.

Cut six or seven pieces of bread about the size of two fingers, and fry them in butter till they are of a good colour; cut as many slices of ham of the same size, and put them into a stewpan over a slow fire, for an hour; when they are done take them out, and stir into the stewpan a little flour; when of a good colour moisten it with some broth, without salt; then skim off the fat, and strain the sauce through a sieve. Dish the ham upon the fried bread, and pour the sauce over.

Another Savoury Toasts to relish Wine.

Rasp some crumb of bread; put it over the fire in butter; put over it a minced veal kidney, with its fat, parsley, scallions, a shalot, cayenne pepper and salt, mixed with the whites and yolks of four eggs beat: put this forcemeat on fried toasts of bread, covering the whole with grated bread, and passing the salamander over it. Serve it with a clear beef gravy sauce under it.

Tomata to eat with roast meat.

Cover the bottom of a flat saucepan with the tomatas, that they may lie one upon another; add two or three spoonfuls of water, a little salt and pepper, to your taste; cover the pan, and stew them; in six or seven minutes turn them, and let them stew till they are soft. Send them up with their liquor.

Tongues, to cure. No. 1.

Take two fine bullocks' tongues; wash them well in spring water; dry them thoroughly with a cloth, and salt them with common salt, a quarter of a pound of saltpetre, a quarter of a pound of treacle, and a quarter of a pound of gunpowder. Let them lie in this pickle for a month; turn and rub them every day; then take them out and dry them with a cloth; rub a little gunpowder over them, and hang them up for a month, when they will be fit to eat, previously soaking a few hours as customary.

Tongues, to cure. No. 2.

One pound of bay salt, half a pound of saltpetre, two ounces of sal prunella, two pounds of coarse sugar; make your brine strong enough with common salt to float an egg. The quantity of water is seven quarts, boil all together, and scum it well for half an hour. When cold, put the tongues in, and wash them in warm water before dressing. For table be sure never to let them boil, but simmer slowly for four or five hours.

Tongues, to cure. No. 3.

Take two fine neats' tongues; cut off the roots, and cut a nick in the under side; wash them clean, and dry with a cloth. Rub them with common salt, and lay them on a board all night. Next day take two ounces of bay salt, one of sal prunella, and a handful of juniper-berries, all bruised fine; mix them with a quarter of a pound of coarse sugar and one pound of common salt. Rub the tongues well with this mixture; lay them in a long pan, and turn and rub them daily for a fortnight. Take them out of the pickle, and either dry or dress them.

Tongues, to cure. No. 4.

Mix some well bruised bay salt, and a little saltpetre, with common salt, and with a linen cloth rub the tongues and salt them, most particularly the roots; and as the brine consumes put some more, till the tongues are hard and stiff. When they are salted, roll them up, and dry them in bran.

Tongues, to cure. No. 5.

Have the roots well cleansed from the moisture, and with warm water wash and open the porous parts, that the salt may penetrate, and dry them well. Cover them for a week with a pickle made of common salt, and bay salt well boiled in it; then rub them with saltpetre, and to make them of a good red colour you must take them out, and rub and salt them well so that the salt penetrates, pressing them down hard with a board that, when they are put to dry, they may keep their due proportion. The usual way of drying them is with burnt sawdust, which, with the salt, gives the dusky colour that appears on the outside before they are boiled.

Tongues, to cure. No. 6.

Well rub into the tongue two ounces of saltpetre, a pound of common salt, and a quarter of a pound of treacle; and baste every day for three weeks.

Tongue, to smoke.

Wipe the tongue dry, when taken out of the pickle; glaze it over with a brush dipped in pyroligneous acid, and hang it up in the kitchen.

Tongue, to bake.

Season your tongues with pepper, salt, and nutmeg; lard them with large lardoons, and have them steeped all night in vinegar, claret, and ginger. Season again with whole pepper, sliced nutmeg, whole cloves, and salt. Bake them in an earthen pan; serve them up on sippets, and lay your spice over them, with slices of lemon and some sausages.

Tongue, to boil.

Put a good quantity of hay with your tongues, tying them up in a cloth, or else in hay. Boil them till they are tender and of a good colour, and they will eat short and mellow.

Tongue, to pot.

Prick the tongues with a skewer, and salt them with bay-salt and saltpetre, to make them red. Boil them till they will just peel; season with mace and a little pepper, to your liking; bake them in a pot well covered with butter, and they will keep as long as any potted meat.

Tongue and Udder, to roast.

Have the tongue and udder boiled and blanched, the tongue being salted with saltpetre; lard them with the whole length of large lardoons, and then roast them on a spit, basting them with butter: when roasted, dress them with grated bread and flour, and serve up with gravy, currant-jelly by itself, and slices of lemon.

Sheep's Tongue, or any other, with Oysters.

Boil six tongues in salt and water till they are sufficiently tender to peel. Slice them thin, and with a quart of large oysters put them in a dish, with some whole spice and a little claret, and let them stew together. Then put in some butter, and three yolks of eggs well beaten. Shake them all well together, and put some sippets and lay your tongues upon them.

Tripe, to dress.

Take of the finest tripe, and, when properly trimmed, cut it in pieces about four inches square; put it in a stewpan, with as much white wine as will almost cover it: slice in three or four race of ginger, quarter in a nutmeg, put in a good deal of salt, a bundle of herbs, rosemary, thyme, sweet marjoram, and onion. When this has stewed gently a good while, take out a pint of the clearest liquor, free from fat or dross, and dissolve in it some anchovies finely picked. Take up the tripe, a bit at a time, with a fork, and lay it in a warmed dish; pour on it the liquor in which the anchovies were dissolved. Sprinkle on it a little lemon juice. Those who are fond of onions or garlic may make either the prevailing ingredient.

Tripe, to fricassee.

Cut into slices the fat part of double tripe; dip them into eggs or batter, and fry them to lay round the dish. Cut the other part into long slips, and into dice, and toss them up with onion, chopped parsley, melted butter, yolks of eggs, and a little vinegar. Season with pepper and salt, and serve up.

Truffles and Morels, to stew.

Well wash the truffles, cut them into slices, of the size and about the thickness of half-a-crown; put them into a stewpan, with a pinch of salt and cayenne pepper, and a little butter, to prevent their being burnt. Let them stew ten minutes; have ready a good brown sauce of half a pint of beef and the same of veal jelly, thickened with a little butter and flour; add to it any trimmings of the truffles or morels, and boil them also in it; put in one pinch of cayenne pepper. Strain the truffles or morels from the butter they were first stewed in; throw them into the sauce; warm the whole again, and serve hot.

Veal, to boil.

Veal should be boiled well; a knuckle of six pounds will take very nearly two hours. The neck must be also well boiled in a good deal of water; if boiled in a cloth, it will be whiter. Serve it with tongue, bacon, or pickled pork, greens of any sort, brocoli, and carrots, or onion sauce, white sauce, oyster sauce, parsley and butter, or white celery sauce.

Veal, to collar.

Bone and wash a breast of veal; steep it in three waters, and dry it with a cloth; season it with savoury spice, some slices of bacon, and shred sweet-herbs; roll them in a collar of cloth, and boil it in salt and water, with whole spice; skim it clean and take it up, and when cold put it in the pickle.

Another way.

Take the meat of a breast of veal; make a stuffing of beef-suet, crumb of bread, lemon peel, parsley, pepper, and salt, mixed up with two eggs; lay it over the meat, and roll it up. Boil an hour and a half, and send it to table with oyster sauce.

Veal, to roast.

Veal will take a quarter of an hour to a pound: paper the fat of the loin and fillet; stuff the fillet and shoulder with the following ingredients: a quarter of a pound of suet, chopped fine, parsley, and sweet-herbs chopped, grated bread, lemon-peel, pepper, salt, nutmeg, and yolk of egg; butter may supply the want of suet. Roast the breast with the caul on it till almost done; take it off, flour and baste it. Veal requires to be more done than beef. For sauce use salad pickles, brocoli, cucumbers, raw or stewed, French beans, peas, cauliflower, celery, raw or stewed.

Veal, roasted, ragout of.

Cut slices of veal about the size of two fingers and at least as long as three; beat them with a cleaver till they are no thicker than a crown-piece; put upon every slice some stuffing made with beef-suet, ham, a little thyme, parsley, scallions, and a shalot. When the whole is minced, add the yolks of two eggs, half a table-spoonful of brandy, salt, and pepper; spread it on the veal and roll it. Cover each piece with a thin slice of bacon, and tie it carefully. Then put them on a small delicate spit covered with paper; and, when they are done, take off the paper carefully, grate bread over them, and brown them at a clear fire. Serve them with a gravy sauce.

Veal, to stew.

Cut the veal into small pieces; season with an onion, some salt and pepper, mace, lemon-peel, and two or three shalots; let them stew in water, with a little butter, or port wine, if you like. When enough done, put in some yolks of eggs beaten, and boil them quick. Dish and serve them up.

Veal, with Rice, to stew.

Boil half a pound of rice in three quarts of water in a small pan with some good broth, about a pint, and slices of ham at the bottom, and two good onions. When it is almost done, spread it, about twice the thickness of a crown-piece, over a silver or delft dish in which it is to be served [it must be a dish capable of bearing the fire]. Lay slices of veal and ham alternately—the veal having already been dressed brown. Cover the meat with rice in such a manner that it cannot be seen; put your dish upon a hot stove; brown the rice with a salamander; drain off the fat that may be in the dish, and serve it dry, or, if it is preferred, with any of the good sauces, for which there are directions, poured under it.

Veal served in paper.

Cut some slices of veal from the fillet, about an inch thick, in a small square, about the size of a small fricandeau; make a box of paper to fit neatly; rub the outside with butter, and put in your meat, with sweet oil or butter, parsley, scallions, shalots, and mushrooms, all stewed very fine, salt, and whole pepper. Set it upon the gridiron, with a sheet of oiled paper under it, and let it do by a very slow fire, lest the paper burn. When the meat is done on one side turn it on the other. Serve it in the box, having put over it very gently a dash of vinegar.

Bombarded Veal.

Take a piece of a long square of bacon; cut it in thin slices; do the same with veal, and lay the slices on your bacon. Having made a piece of good forcemeat, spread it thin on your veal, having previously seasoned the latter with pepper and salt. Roll these up one by one; spit them on a lark spit, quite even; wash them over with eggs and crumbs of bread; then roast them, and serve up with a good ragout.

Veal Balls.

Take two pounds of veal; pick out the skin and bones; mix it well with the crust of a French roll, soaked in hot milk, half a pound of veal suet, two yolks of eggs, onion, and chopped parsley; season with pepper and salt. Roll the balls in raspings; fry them of a gold colour: boil the bones and the bits of skin to make the gravy for them.

Breast of Veal.

To fricassee it like fowls, parboil it; turn it a few times over the fire with a bit of butter, a bunch of parsley, scallions, some mushrooms, truffles, and morels. Shake in a little flour; moisten with some good stock broth; and when the whole is done and skimmed, thicken it with the yolks of three eggs beat with some milk; and, before it is served, add a very little lemon juice.

Breast of Veal, with Cabbage and Bacon.

Cut the breast of veal in pieces, and parboil it; parboil also a cabbage and a bit of streaked bacon, cut in slices, leaving the rind to it. Tie each separately with packthread, and let them stew together with good broth; no salt or pepper, on account of the bacon. When the whole is done, take out the meat and cabbage, and put them into the terrine you serve to table. Take the fat off the broth, put in a little cullis, and reduce the sauce over the stove. When of a proper thickness pour it over the meat, and serve up.

Breast of Veal en fricandeau.

Lard your veal, and take a ragout of asparagus, (for which see Ragouts,) and lay your veal, larded or glazed, upon the ragout. The same may be done with a ragout of peas.

Breast of Veal, glazed brown.

Take a breast of veal, cut in pieces, or whole if you prefer it. Stir a bit of butter and a spoonful of flour over the fire, and, when it is of a good colour, put in a pint of broth, and afterwards the veal. Stew it over a slow fire, and season with pepper and salt, a bunch of parsley, scallions, cloves, thyme, laurel, basil, and half a spoonful of vinegar. When the meat is done and well glazed, skim the sauce well, and serve it round it.

Breast of Veal, to stew with Peas.

Cut the nicest part of the breast of veal, with the sweetbread; roast it a little brown; take a little bit of the meat that is cut off the ends, and fry it with butter, salt, pepper, and flour; take a little hot water just to rinse out the gravy that adheres to the frying-pan, and put it into a stewpan, with two quarts of hot water, a bundle of parsley, thyme, and marjoram, a bit of onion or shalot, plenty of lemon-peel, and a pint of old green peas, the more mealy the better. Let it stew two or three hours, then rub it through a sieve with a spoon; it should be all nice and thick; then put it again in the stewpan with the meat, having ready some hot water to add to the gravy in case it should be wanted. A thick breast will take two hours, and must be turned every now and then. Boil about as many nice young peas as would make a dish, the same as for eating; put them in about ten minutes before you take it up, skimming all the fat nicely off; and season it at the same time with salt and cayenne to your taste.

Another way.

Cut your veal into pieces, about three inches long; fry it delicately; mix a little flour with some beef broth, with an onion and two cloves; stew this some time, strain it, add three pints or two quarts of peas, or heads of asparagus, cut like peas. Put in the meat; let it stew gently; add pepper and salt.

Breast of Veal ragout.

Bone and cut out a large square piece of the breast of veal; cut the rest into small pieces, and brown it in butter, stewing it in your ragout for made dishes;

thicken it with brown butter, and put the ragout in the dish. Lay diced lemon, sweetbreads, sippets, and bacon, fried in batter of eggs; then lay on the square piece. Garnish with sliced oranges.

Veal Collops, with Oysters.

Cut thin slices out of a leg of veal, as many as will make a dish, according to the number of your company. Lard one quarter of them, and fry them in butter; take them out of the pan and keep them warm. Clean the pan, and put into it half a pint of oysters, with their liquor, and some strong broth, one or two shalots, a glass of white wine, two or three anchovies minced, and some grated nutmeg; let these have a boil up, and thicken with five eggs and a piece of butter. Put in your collops, and shake them together till the sauce is tolerably thick. Set them on the stove again to stew a little; then serve up.

Veal Collops, with white sauce.

Cut veal that has been already roasted into neat small pieces, round or square; season them with a little pepper and salt; pass them quick of a pale colour in a bit of butter of the size of a walnut; add the yolks of five eggs, and half a pint of cream, with a very small onion or two, previously boiled; toss them up quick, and serve hot.

Veal Cutlets, to dress.

Cut the veal steaks thin; hack and season them with pepper, salt, and sweet-herbs. Wash them over with melted butter, and wrap white paper buttered over them. Roast or bake them; and, when done, take off the paper, and serve them with good gravy and Seville orange-juice squeezed on.

Another way.

Take the best end of a neck of veal and cut your cutlets; four ribs will make eight cutlets. Beat them out very thin, and trim them round. Take chopped parsley, thyme, shalots, and mushrooms, pass them over the fire, add a little juice of lemon, lemon-peel, and grated nutmeg. Dip in the cutlets, crumb them, and boil them over a gentle fire. Save what you leave from dipping them in, put some brown sauce to it, and put it under them when going to table, first taking care to remove the grease from it. Lamb cutlets are done the same way.

Veal Cutlets, larded.

Cut a neck of veal into bones; lard one side, and fry them off quick. Thicken a piece of butter, of the size of a large nut, with a little flour, and whole onion. Put in as much good gravy as will just cover them, and a few mushrooms and forcemeat balls. Stove them tender; skim off all grease; squeeze in half a lemon, and serve them up.

Fillet of Veal, to farce or roast.

Mince some beef suet very small, with some sweet marjoram, winter savory, and thyme; season with salt, cloves, and mace, well beaten; put in grated bread; mix them all together with the yolk of an egg; make small holes in the veal, and stuff it very thick with these. Put it on the spit and roast it well. Let the sauce consist of butter, gravy, and juice of lemon, very thick. Dish the veal, and pour the sauce over it, with slices of lemon laid round the dish.

Fillet of Veal, to boil.

Cut out the bone of a fillet of veal; put it into good milk and water for a little while: make some forcemeat with boiled clary, raw carrots, beef suet, grated bread, sweet-herbs, and a good quantity of shrimps, nutmeg, and mace, the yolks of three eggs boiled hard, some pepper and salt, and two raw eggs; roll it up in butter, and stuff the veal with it. Boil the veal in a cloth for two hours, and scald four or five cucumbers, in order to take out the pulp the more easily. This done, fill them with forcemeat, and stew them in a little thin gravy. For sauce take strong white gravy, thickened with butter, a very little flour, nutmeg, mace, and lemon-peel, three anchovies dissolved in lemon-juice, some good cream, the yolk of an egg beaten, and a glass of white wine. Serve with the cucumbers.

Half a Fillet of Veal, to stew.

Take a stewpan large enough for the piece of veal, put in some butter, and fry it till it is firm, and of a fine brown colour all round; put in two carrots, two large onions, whole, half a pound of lean bacon, a bunch of thyme and of parsley, a pinch of cayenne pepper and of salt: add a cupful of broth, and let the whole stew over a very slow fire for one hour, or according to the size of your piece of veal, until thoroughly done. Have ready a pint of jelly soup, in which stew a table-spoonful of mustard and the same of truffles cut in small pieces; add one ounce of butter and a dessert spoonful of flour to thicken; unite it well together; put in a glass of white wine, and boil. When ready to serve, pour it over the veal; let there be sauce sufficient to fill the dish; the veal must be strained from the vegetables, and great care taken that the sauce is well passed through the sieve, to keep it clear from grease.

Knuckle of Veal, white.

Boil a knuckle of veal in a little water kept close from the air, with six onions and a little whole pepper, till tender. The sauce to be poured over it, when dished in a little of its own liquor—two or three anchovies, a little mace, half a pint of cream, and the yolk of an egg, thickened with a little flour.

Knuckle of Veal ragout.

Cut the veal into slices half an inch thick; pepper, salt, and flour them; fry them of a light brown; put the trimmings, with the bone broken, an onion sliced, celery, a bunch of sweet-herbs; pour warm water to cover them about an inch. Stew gently for two hours; strain it, and thicken with flour and butter, a spoonful of ketchup, a glass of wine, and the juice of half a lemon. Give it a boil, strain into a clean saucepan, put in the meat, and make it hot.

Leg of Veal and Bacon, to boil.

Lard the veal with bacon and lemon-peel; boil it with a piece of bacon, cut in slices; put the veal into a dish, and lay the bacon round it. Serve it up with green sauce made thus: beat two or more handfuls of sorrel in a mortar, with two pippins quartered, and put vinegar and sugar to it.

Loin of Veal, to roast.

Roast, and baste with butter; set a dish under your veal, with vinegar, a few sage leaves, and a little rosemary and thyme. Let the gravy drop on these, and, when the veal is roasted, let the herbs and gravy boil once or twice on the fire: serve it under the veal.

Loin of Veal, to roast with herbs.

Lard the fillet of a loin of veal; put it into an earthen pan; steep it three hours with parsley, scallions, a little fennel, mushrooms, a laurel-leaf, thyme, basil, and two shalots, the whole shred very fine, salt, whole pepper, a little grated nutmeg, and a little sweet oil. When it has taken the flavour of the herbs, put it upon the spit, with all its seasoning, wrapt in two sheets of white paper well buttered; tie it carefully so as to prevent the herbs falling out, and roast it at a very slow fire. When it is done take off the paper, and with a knife pick off all the bits of herbs that stick to the meat and paper, and put them into a stewpan, with a little gravy, two spoonfuls of verjuice, salt, whole pepper, and a bit of butter, about as big as a walnut, rolled in flour. Before you thicken the sauce, melt a little butter; mix it with the yolk of an egg, and rub the outside of the veal, which should then be covered with grated bread, and browned with a salamander. Serve it up with a good sauce under, but not poured over so as to disturb the meat.

Loin of Veal, fricassee of.

Well roast a loin of veal, and let it stand till cold. Cut it into slices; in a saucepan over the stove melt some butter, with a little flour, shred parsley, and chives. Turn the stewpan a little for a minute or so, and pepper and salt the veal. Put it again into the pan, and give it three or four turns over the stove with a little broth, and boil it a little: then put three or four yolks of eggs beaten up to a cream, and some parsley shred, to thicken it, always keeping it stirred over the fire till of sufficient thickness; then serve it up.

Loin of Veal Bechamel.

When the veal is nicely roasted, cut out part of the fillet down the back; cut it in thin slices, and put some white sauce to what you have cut out. Season it with the juice of lemon and a little pepper and salt; put it into the veal, and cover the top with crumbs of bread that has been browned, or salamander it over with crumbs, or leave the skin of the veal so that you can turn it over when the seasoning part is put in.

Neck of Veal, stewed with Celery.

Take the best end of a neck, put it into a stewpan with beef broth, salt, whole pepper, and two cloves, tied in a bit of muslin, an onion, and a piece of lemon-peel. Add a little cream and flour mixed, some celery ready boiled, and cut into lengths; and boil it up.

Veal Olives. No. 1.

are done the same way as the beef olives, only cut off a fillet of veal, fried of a fine brown. The same sauce is used as for beef, and, if you like, small bits of curled bacon may be laid in the dish. Garnish with lemon and parsley.

Veal Olives. No. 2.

Wash eight or ten Scots collops over with egg batter; season and lay over a little forcemeat; roll them up and roast them; make a good ragout for them; garnish with sliced orange.

Veal Olives. No. 3.

Take a good fillet of veal, and cut large collops, not too thin, and hack them well; wash them over with the yolk of an egg; then spread on a good layer of forcemeat, made of veal pretty well seasoned. Roll them up, and wash them with egg; lard them over with fat bacon, tie them round, if you roast them; but, if to be baked, you need only wash the bacon over with egg. Garnish with slices of lemon, and for sauce take thick butter and good gravy, with a piece of lemon.

Veal Olives. No. 4.

Lay over your forcemeat; first lard your collops, and lay a row of large oysters; and then roll them up, and roast or bake them. Make a ragout of oysters, sweetbreads fried, a few morels and mushrooms, and lay in the bottom of your dish, and garnish with fried oysters and grated bread.

Veal Rumps.

Take three veal rumps; parboil and put them into a little pot, with some broth, a bunch of parsley, scallions, a clove of garlic, two shalots, a laurel leaf, thyme, basil, two cloves, salt, pepper, an onion, a carrot, and a parsnip: let them boil till they are thoroughly done, and the sauce is very nearly consumed. Take them out, let them cool, and strain the sauce through a rather coarse sieve, that none of the fat may remain. Put it into a stewpan, with the yolks of three eggs beat up, and a little flour, and thicken it over the fire. Then dip your veal rumps into it, and cover them with grated bread; put them upon a dish, and brown them with a salamander. Serve them with sour sauce, for which see the part that treats of Sauces.

Shoulder of Veal, to stew.

Put it in an earthen pan, with a gill of water, two spoonfuls of vinegar, salt, whole pepper, parsley and scallions, two cloves of garlic, a bay leaf, two onions, two heads of celery, three cloves, and a bit of butter. Cover the pan close, and close the edges with flour and water. Stew it in an oven three hours; then skim and strain the sauce, and serve it over the veal.

Veal Steaks.

Cut a neck of veal into steaks, and beat them on both sides: beat up an egg, and with a feather wet your steaks on both sides. Add some parsley, thyme, and a little marjoram, cut small, and seasoned with pepper and salt. Sprinkle crumbs of bread on both sides of the steaks, and put them up quite tight and close into paper which has been rubbed with butter. They may be either broiled or baked in a pan.

Veal Sweetbreads, to fry.

Cut each of your sweetbreads in three or four pieces and blanch them: put them for two hours in a marinade made with lemon-juice, salt, pepper, cloves, a bay leaf, and an onion sliced. Take the sweetbreads out of the marinade, and dry them with a cloth; dip them in beaten yolk of eggs, with crumbs of bread; fry them in lard till they are brown; drain them; fry some parsley, and put it in the middle of the dish, and serve them.

Veal Sweetbreads, to roast.

Lard your sweetbreads with small lardoons of bacon, and put them on a skewer; fasten them to the spit and roast them brown. Put some good gravy into a dish; lay in the sweetbreads, and serve them very hot. You ought to set your sweetbreads and spit them; then egg and bread them, or they will not be brown.

Vegetables, to stew.

Cut some onions, celery, turnips, and carrots, into small squares, like dice, but not too small; stew them with a bunch of thyme in a little broth and butter; fry them till they are of a fine brown colour; turn them with a fork, till quite soft; if they are not done enough, put a little flour from the dredging-box to brown them; skim the sauce well, and pass it through a sieve; add a little cayenne pepper and salt; put the vegetables in, and serve them up.

Haunch of Venison, to roast. No. 1.

Butter and sprinkle your fat with salt; lay a sheet of paper over it; roll a thin sheet of paste and again another sheet of paper over the paste, and with a pack-thread tie and spit it. Baste the sheet of paper with butter, and let the venison roast till done enough. Be careful how you take off the papers and paste, basting it with some butter during that time, and dredge up: then let it turn round some time to give the fat a colour. The object of pasting is to save the fat. Have currant-jelly with it, and serve it up.

Haunch of Venison, to roast. No. 2.

Let your haunch be well larded with thick bacon; seasoning it with fine spices, parsley, sweet-herbs, cut small, pepper, and salt. Pickle it with vinegar, onions, salt, pepper, parsley, sweet basil, thyme, and bay-leaves: and, when pickled enough, spit it, and baste it with the pickle. When roasted, dish it up with vinegar, pepper, and thick sauce.

Haunch of Venison, to roast. No. 3.

Have the haunch well and finely larded with bacon, and put paper round it: roast and serve it up with sauce under it, made of good cullis or broth, gravy of ham, capers, anchovies, salt, pepper, and vinegar.

Venison, to boil.

Have your venison a little salted, and boil it in water. Meanwhile boil six cauliflowers in milk and water; and put them into a large pipkin with drawn butter; keep them warm, and put in six handfuls of washed spinach, boiled in strong broth; pour off the broth, and put some drawn butter to it; lay some sippets in the dish, and lay your spinach round the sides; have the venison laid in the middle, with the cauliflower over it; pour your butter also over, and garnish with barberries and minced parsley.

Haunch of Venison, to broil.

Take half a haunch, and cut it into slices of about half an inch thick; broil and salt them over a brisk fire, and, when pretty well soaked, bread and serve them up with gravy: do the same with the chine.

Venison, to recover when tainted.

Boil bay salt, ale, and vinegar together, and make a strong brine; skim it, and let it stand till cool, and steep the venison for a whole day. Drain and press it dry: parboil, and season it with pepper and salt.

Another way.

Tie your venison up in a clean cloth; put it in the earth for a whole day, and the scent will be gone.

Red Deer Venison, to pot.

Let the venison be well boned and cut into pieces about an inch thick, and round, of the diameter of your pot. Season with pepper and salt, something higher than you would pasty, and afterwards put it into your pots, adding half a quarter of butter, and two sliced nutmegs, cloves and mace about the same quantity of each, but rather less of the cloves. Then put into your pots lean and fat, so that there may be fat and lean mixed, until the pots are so nearly filled as to admit only a pint of butter more to be put into each. Make a paste of rye-flour, and stop your pots close on the top. Have your oven heated as you would for a pasty; put your pots in, and let them remain as long as for pasty; draw them out, and let them stand half an hour; afterwards unstop them, and turn the pots upside down; you may remove the contents, if you like, into smaller pots; in which case take off all the butter, letting the gravy remain, and using the butter for the fresh pots; let them remain all night; the next day fill them with fresh butter. To make a pie of the same, proceed in the same way with the venison, only do not season it so high; but put in a liberal allowance of butter.

Venison, excellent substitute for.

Skin a loin of mutton; put to it a quarter of a pint of port wine, half a pint of spring water, two spoonfuls of vinegar, an onion with three cloves, a small bunch of thyme and parsley, a little pepper and salt, to your taste. Stew them with the mutton very slowly for two hours and a half; baste it with the liquor very often; skim off the fat, and send the gravy in the dish with the mutton. Sauce—the same as for venison.

Water Cresses, to stew.

When the cresses are nicely picked and well washed, put them into a stewpan with a little butter under them. Let them stew on a clear fire until almost done; then rub them through a sieve; put them again into a pan, with a dust of flour, a little salt, and a spoonful of good cream: give it a boil, and dish it up with sippets. The cream may be omitted, and the cresses may be boiled in salt and water before they are rubbed through the sieve, and afterwards stewed, but it takes the strength out, therefore it is best not to boil them first.

POULTRY.

Chicken, to make white.

FEED them in the coop on boiled rice; give them no water at all to drink. Scalded oatmeal will do as well.

Chicken, to fricassee. No. 1.

Empty the chicken, and singe it till the flesh gets very firm. Carve it as neatly as possible; divide the legs at the joints into four separate pieces, the back into two, making in all ten pieces. Take out the lungs and all that remains within; wash all the parts of the chicken very thoroughly in lukewarm water, till all the blood is out. Put the pieces in boiling water, sufficient to cover them, about four tea-cupfuls, and let them remain there ten minutes; take them out, preserve the water, and put them into cold water. When quite cool, put two ounces of fresh butter into a stewpan with half a pint of mushrooms, fresh or pickled; if pickled, they must be put into fresh cold water two or three hours before; the water to be changed three times; put into the stewpan two bunches of parsley and two large onions; add the chicken, and set the stewpan over the fire. When the chickens have been fried lightly, taking care they are not in the least browned, dust a little salt and flour over them; then add some veal jelly to the water in which they were blanched; let them boil about three quarters of an hour in that liquor, skimming off all the butter, and scum very cleanly; then take out the chicken, leaving the sauce or liquor, and lay it in another stewpan, which place in a basin of hot water near the fire. Boil down the sauce or liquor, adding some more veal jelly, till it becomes strong, and there remains sufficient sauce for the dish; add to this the yolk of four eggs and three table-spoonfuls of cream: boil it, taking great care to keep it constantly stirring; and, when ready to serve, having placed the chicken in a very hot dish, with the breast in the middle, and the legs around, pour the sauce well over every part. The sauce should be thicker than melted butter, and of a yellow colour.

Chicken, to fricassee. No. 2.

Cut the chicken up in joints; put them into cold water, and set them on the fire till they boil; skim them well. Save the liquor. Skin, wash, and trim the joints; put them into a pan, with the liquor, a small bunch of parsley and thyme, a small onion, and as much flour and water as will give it a proper thickness, and let them boil till tender. When going to table, put in a yolk of egg mixed with a little good cream, a little parsley chopped very fine, juice of lemon, and pepper and salt to your taste.

Chicken, to fricassee. No. 3.

Take two chickens and more than half stew them; cut them into limbs; take the skin clean off, and all the inside that is bloody. Put them into a stewpan, with half a pint of cream, about two ounces of butter, into which shake a little flour, some mace, and whole pepper, and a little parsley boiled and chopped fine. Thicken it up with the yolks of two eggs; add the juice of a lemon, and three spoonfuls of good white gravy.

Chicken, to fricassee. No. 4.

Have a frying-pan, with sufficient liquor to cover your chicken cut into pieces; half of the liquor to be white wine and water. Take one nutmeg sliced, half a dozen cloves, three blades of mace, and some whole pepper; boil all these together in a frying-pan; put half a pound of fresh butter and skim it clean; then put in your chickens, and boil them till tender; add a small quantity of parsley. Take four yolks and two whites of eggs; beat them well with some thick butter, and put it to your chicken in the pan; toss it over a slow fire till thick, and serve it up with sippets.

Chicken, white fricassee of.

Cut in pieces chickens or rabbits; wash and dry them in a cloth; flour them well, and fry in clarified butter till they are a little brown, but, if not enough done, put them in a stewpan, and just cover them with strong veal or beef broth. Put in with them a bunch of thyme, an onion stuck with cloves, a little pepper and salt, and a blade of mace. Cover and stew till tender, and till the liquor is reduced about one half. Put in a quarter of a pound of butter, the yolk of two eggs beat, and a quarter of a pint of cream. Stir well; let it boil; if not thick enough, shake in some flour; and then put in juice of lemon.

Cream of Chicken, or Fowl.

For this purpose fowls are preferable, because the breasts are larger. Take two chickens, cut off the breast, and roast them; the remainder put in a stewpan with two pounds of the sinewy part of a knuckle of veal. Boil the whole together to make a little clear good broth: when the breasts are roasted, and your broth made, take all the white of the breast, put it in a small stewpan, and add to it the broth clean and clear. It will be better to cut the white of the chickens quite fine, and, when you find that it is boiled soft, proceed in the same manner as for cream of rice and pass it. Just in the same way, make it of the thickness you judge proper, and warm in the same manner as the cream of rice: put in a little salt if it is approved of.

Chickens, to fry.

Scald and split them; put them in vinegar and water, as much as will cover them, with a little pepper and salt, an onion, a slice or two of lemon, and a sprig or two of thyme, and let them lie two hours in the pickle. Dry them with a cloth; flour and fry them in clarified butter, with soft bread and a little of the pickle.

Chickens, to heat.

Take the legs, wings, brains, and rump, and put them into a little white wine vinegar and claret, with some fresh butter, the water of an onion, a little pepper and sliced nutmeg, and heat them between two dishes.

Chickens, dressed with Peas.

Singe and truss your chickens; boil one half and roast the other. Put them into a small saucepan, with a little water, a small piece of butter, a little salt, and a bundle of thyme and parsley. Set them on the fire, and put in a small lump of sugar. When they boil, set them over a slow fire to stew. Lay your boiled chickens in a dish; put your peas over them; then lay the roasted ones between, and send to table.

Chicken and Ham, ragout of.

Clear a chicken which has been dressed of all the sauce that may be about it. If it has been roasted, pare off the brown skin, take some soup, veal jelly, and cream, and a table-spoonful of mushrooms; if pickled, wash them in several waters to take out the vinegar: put them in the jelly, and keep this sauce to heat up. Cut up the chicken, the wings and breast in slices, the merrythought also, and divide the legs. Heat the fowl up separately from the sauce in a little thin broth: prepare six or eight slices of ham stewed apart in brown gravy; dip each piece of the fowl in the white sauce, and lay them in the middle of the dish with a piece of the ham alternately one beside another, taking care that as little of the white sauce as possible goes on the ham, to preserve its colour. Lay the legs one on each side of the meat in the middle; and pour the sauce in the middle, taking care not to pour it over the ham.

Chicken, or Ham and Veal patés.

Cut up into small dice some of the white of the chicken, or the most delicate part of veal already dressed; take sufficient white sauce, with truffles, morels, and mushrooms, and heat it up to put in the patés. When ready, pour it amply into them, and serve up hot.

Another.

Take the white of a chicken or veal, cut it up in small dice; do the same with some ham or tongue; warm it in a little broth, and take a good white sauce, such as is used for pheasants, and heat it up thoroughly.

Duck, to boil.

Pour over it boiling milk and water, and let it lie for an hour or two. Then boil it gently for a full half hour in plenty of water. Serve with onion sauce.

Duck, to boil, à la Française.

To a pint of rich beef gravy put two dozen of roasted peeled chesnuts, with a few leaves of thyme, two small onions if agreeable, a race of ginger, and a little whole pepper. Lard a fine tame duck, and half roast it; put it into the gravy; let it stew ten minutes, and add a pint of port wine. When the duck is done, take it out; boil up your gravy to a proper thickness, but skim it very clean from the fat; lay your duck in the dish, and pour the sauce over it.

Duck à la braise.

Lard the duck; lay a slice or two of beef at the bottom of the pan, and on these the duck, a piece of bacon, and some more beef sliced, an onion, a carrot, whole pepper, a slice of lemon, and a bunch of sweet-herbs. Cover this close, and set it over the fire for a few minutes, shaking in some flour: then pour in a quart of beef broth or boiling water, and a little heated red wine. Stew it for half an hour; strain the sauce, and skim it; put to it some more wine if necessary, with cayenne, shalot, a little mint, juice of a lemon, and chopped tarragon. If agreeable to your taste, add artichoke bottoms boiled and quartered.

Duck, to hash.

When cut in pieces, flour it; put it into a stewpan with some gravy, a little red wine, shalot chopped, salt and pepper; boil these; put in the duck; toss it up, take out the lemon, and serve with toasted sippets.

Duck, to stew with Cucumbers.

Half roast the duck, and stew it as before. Slice some cucumbers and onions; fry and drain them very dry; put them to the duck, and stew all together.

Duck, to stew with Peas.

Half roast the duck, put it into some good gravy with a little mint and three or four sage-leaves chopped. Stew this half an hour; thicken the gravy with a little flour; throw in half a pint of green peas boiled, or some celery, in which case omit the mint.

Fowls, to fatten in a fortnight.

Gather and dry, in proper season, nettle leaves and seed; beat them into powder, and make it into paste with flour, adding a little sweet olive-oil. Make this up into small crams: coop the birds up and feed them with it, giving them water in which barley has been boiled, and they will fatten in the above-mentioned time.

Fowl, to make tender.

Pour down the throat of the fowl, about an hour before you kill it, a spoonful of vinegar, and let it run about again. When killed, hang it up in the feathers by the legs in a smoky chimney; then pluck and dress it. This method makes fowls very tender.

Fowl, to roast with Anchovies.

Put a bit of butter in your stewpan with a little flour; keep stirring this over the fire, but not too hot, till it turns of a good gold colour, and put a little of it into your gravy to thicken it.

Fowl with Rice, called Pilaw.

Boil a pint of rice in as much water as will cover it. Put in with it some whole black pepper, a little salt, and half a dozen cloves, tied up in a bit of cloth. When the rice is tender take out the cloves and pepper, and stir in a piece of butter. Boil a fowl and a piece of bacon; lay them in a dish, and cover them with the rice. Lay round the dish and upon the rice hard eggs cut in halves and quarters, and onions, first boiled and then fried.

Fowl, to hash.

Cut the fowl in pieces; put it in some gravy, with a little cream, ketchup, or mushroom-powder, grated lemon-peel, a few oysters and their liquor, and a piece of butter mixed with flour. Keep stirring it till the butter is melted. Lay sippets in the dish.

Fowl, to stew.

Take a fowl, two onions, two carrots, and two turnips; put one onion into the fowl, and cut all the rest into four pieces each. Add two or three bits of bacon or ham, a bay-leaf, and as much water as will prevent their burning when put into an earthen vessel; cover them up close, and stew them for three hours and a half on a slow fire. Serve up hot or cold.

Goose, to stuff.

Having well washed your goose, dry it, and rub the inside with pepper and salt. Crumble some bread, but not too fine; take a piece of butter and make it hot; cut a middle-sized onion and stew in the butter. Cut the liver very small, and put that also in the butter for about a minute just to warm, and pour it over the head. It must then be mixed up with an egg and about two spoonfuls of cream, a little nutmeg, ginger, pepper and salt, and a small quantity of summer savory.

Another way.

Chop fine two ounces of onions, and an ounce of green sage leaves; add four ounces of bread crumbs, the yolk and white of an egg, a little salt and pepper, and sometimes minced apples.

Goose's liver, to dress.

When it is drawn, leave the gall sticking to it; lay it in fresh water for a day, and change the water several times. When you use it, wipe it dry, cut off the gall, and fry it in butter, which must be made very hot before the liver is put in: it must be whole and fried brown—no fork stuck in it. Serve with a little ketchup sauce.

Pigeons, to boil.

Chop sweet-herbs and bacon, with grated bread, butter, spice, and the yolk of an egg; tie both ends of the pullets, and boil them. Garnish with sliced lemon and barberries.

Pigeons, to broil.

Cut their necks and wings close, leaving the skin of the neck to enable you to tie close, and with some grated bread put an anchovy, the two livers of pigeons, half a grated nutmeg, a quarter of a pound of butter, a very little thyme, a little pepper and salt, and sweet marjoram shred. Mix all together, and into each bird put a piece of the size of a walnut, after sewing up the vents and necks, and, with a little nutmeg, pepper, and salt, strewed over them, broil them on a slow charcoal fire, basting and turning very often. Use rich gravy or melted butter for sauce, and season to your taste.

Pigeons, to jug.

Pick and draw the pigeons, and let a little water pass through them; parboil and bruise the liver with a spoon; mix pepper, salt, grated nutmeg, parsley shred fine, and lemon-peel, suet cut small, in quantity equal to the liver, the yolks of two eggs boiled hard and also cut fine; mix these with two raw eggs, and stuff the birds, tying up the necks and vents. After dipping the pigeons into water, season them with salt and pepper; then put them into a jug, with two or three pieces of celery, stopping it very close, to prevent the steam escaping. Set them in a kettle of cold water; lay a tile on the top, and boil three hours; take them out, and put in a piece of butter rolled in flour; shake it round till thick, and pour it over the pigeons.

Pigeons, to pot.

Truss and season them with savoury spice; put them into a a pot or pan, covering them with butter, and bake them. Take out, drain, and, when cold, cover them with clarified butter. Fish may be potted in the same way, but always bone them when baked.

Pigeons, to stew. No. 1.

Truss your pigeons as for boiling. Take pepper, salt, cloves, mace, some sweet-herbs, a little grated bread, and the liver of the birds chopped very fine; roll these up in a bit of butter, put it in the stomach of the pigeons, and tie up both ends. Make some butter hot in your stewpan, fry the pigeons in it till they are brown all over, putting to them two or three blades of mace, a few peppercorns, and one shalot. Take them out of the liquor, dust a little flour into the stewpan, shaking it about till it is brown. Have ready a quart of small gravy and a glass of white wine; let it just boil up: strain out all the spice, and put the gravy and pigeons into the stewpan. Let them simmer over the fire two hours; put in some pickled mushrooms, a little lemon juice, a spoonful of ketchup, a few truffles and morels. Dish and send to table with bits of bacon grilled. Some persons add forcemeat balls, but they are very rich without.

Pigeons, to stew. No. 2.

Shred the livers and gizzards, with as much suet as there is meat; season with pepper, salt, parsley, and thyme, shred small; fill the pigeons with this stuffing; lay them in the stewpan, breasts downward, with as much strong broth as will cover them. Add pepper, salt, and onion, and two thin rashers of bacon. Cover them close; let them stew two hours or more, till the liquor is reduced to one half, and looks like gravy, and the pigeons are tender; then put them in a dish with sippets. If you have no strong broth, you may stew in water; but you must not put so much water as broth, and they must stew more slowly.

Pigeons, to stew. No. 3.

Cut six pigeons with giblets into quarters, and put them into a stewpan, with two blades of mace, salt, pepper, and just water sufficient to stew them without burning. When tender, thicken the liquor with the yolk of an egg and three spoonfuls of fresh cream, a little shred thyme, parsley, and a bit of butter. Shake all together, and garnish with lemon.

Pigeons, biscuit of.

Wash, clean, and parboil, your pigeons, and stew them in strong broth. Have a ragout made for them of strong gravy, with artichoke bottoms and onions, seasoning them with the juice of lemons, and lemons diced, truffles, mushrooms, morels, and bacon cut as for lard. Pour the broth into a dish with dried sippets, and, after placing your pigeons, pour on the ragout. Garnish with scalded parsley, lemons, and beet-root.

Pigeons, en compote. No. 1.

The pigeons must be young and white, and the inside entirely taken out. Let none of the heart or liver remain, which is apt to render them bitter. Make some forcemeat of veal, and fill the pigeons with it; then put them in a braise, with some bacon, a slice of lemon, a little thyme, and bay-leaf, and let them stew gently for an hour. The sauce is made of cucumbers and mushrooms, and they must be sweated in a little butter till tender; then strain it off the butter, and put in some strong gravy and a little flour to thicken it. Lastly, add the yolks of two eggs and a little good cream, which, when put to it, must be well stirred, and not suffered to boil, as it would curdle and spoil the sauce.

Pigeons, en compote. No. 2.

Have the birds trussed with their legs in their bodies, but stuffed with forcemeat; parboil and lard them with fat bacon; season with pepper, spices, parsley, and minced chives; stew them very gently. While they are stewing, make a ragout of fowls' livers, cocks'-combs, truffles, morels, and mushrooms, and put a little bacon in the frying-pan to melt; put them in, and shake the pan three or four times round; then add some rich gravy, and let it simmer a little, and put in some veal cullis and ham to thicken it. Drain the pigeons, and put them into this ragout; let them just simmer; take them up, put them into your dish, and pour the ragout over.

Pigeons, en compote. No. 3.

Lard, truss, and force them; season and stew them in strong broth. Have a ragout garnished with sippets, sweetbreads, and sprigs of parsley; then fry the pigeons in a batter of eggs and sliced bacon. You may garnish most dishes in the same way.

Pigeons, à la Crapaudine.

Cut the birds open down the back, and draw the legs through the skin inside, as you would do a boiled fowl, then put into a roomy saucepan some butter, a little parsley, thyme, shalots, and, if you can have them, mushrooms, all chopped together very fine. Put the pigeons in this, and let them sweat in the butter and herbs for about five minutes. While they are warm and moist with the herbs and butter, cover them all over with fine bread crumbs; sprinkle a little salt upon them, and boil them on a slow fire. The sauce may be either of mushrooms or cucumbers, made by sweating whichever you choose in butter till quite tender, then adding a little gravy, cream, and flour.

Pigeons in disguise.

Draw, truss, and season the pigeons with salt and pepper, and make a nice puff; roll each pigeon in a piece of it; tie them in a cloth, but be careful not to let the paste break. Boil them in plenty of water for an hour and a half; and when you untie them take great care they do not break; put them into a dish, and pour a little good gravy to them.

Pigeons in fricandeau.

Draw and truss the pigeons with the legs in the bellies, larding them with bacon, and slit them. Fry them of a fine brown in butter: put into the stewpan a quart of good gravy, a little lemon-pickle, a tea-spoonful of walnut ketchup, cayenne, a little salt, a few truffles, morels, and some yolks of hard eggs. Pour your sauce with its ingredients over the pigeons, when laid in the dish.

Pigeons aux Poires.

Let the feet be cut off, and stuff them with forcemeat, in the shape of a pear, rolling them in the yolk of an egg and crumbs of bread, putting in at the lower end to make them look like pears. Rub your dish with a piece of butter, and then lay them over it, but not to touch each other, and bake them. When done, lay them in another dish, and pour some good gravy into it, thickening with the yolk of an egg; but take care not to pour it over the pigeons.

Another way.

Cut off one leg; truss the pigeons to boil, and let the leg come out of the vent; fill them with forcemeat: tie them with packthread, and stew them in good broth.

Roll the pigeons in yolks of eggs, well beaten with crumbs of bread. Lard your stewpan, but not too hot, and fry your birds to the colour of a popling pear; lay them in a dish, and send up gravy and orange in a terrine with them.

Pigeons, Pompeton of.

Butter your pan, lay in it some sliced bacon, and cover all the inside of it with forcemeat. Brown the pigeons off in a pan, and put them in a good ragout, stewing them up together, and put also a good ladleful of ragout to the forcemeat: then lay your pigeons breast downward, and pour over them the ragout that remains; cover them with forcemeat, and bake them. Turn them out, and serve up.

Pigeons au Soleil.

Make some forcemeat, with half a pound of veal, a quarter of a pound of mutton, and two ounces of beef, and beat them in a mortar with salt, pepper, and mace, till they become paste. Beat up the yolks of four eggs, put them into a plate, and mix two ounces of flour and a quarter of a pound of grated bread. Set on your stewpan with a little rich beef gravy; tie up three or four cloves in a piece of muslin, and put into it; then put your pigeons in, and stew them till nearly done; set them before the fire to keep warm, and with some good beef dripping in your pan, enough to cover the birds, set it on the fire; when boiling, take one at a time, and roll it in the meat that was beaten, then in the yolk of an egg, till they are quite wet; strew them with bread and flour in boiling dripping, and let them remain till brown.

Pigeons à la Tatare, with Cold Sauce.

Singe and truss the pigeons as for boiling, and beat them flat, but not so as to break the skin; season them with salt, pepper, cloves, and mace. Dip them in melted butter and grated bread; lay them on a gridiron, and turn them often. Should the fire not be clear, lay them upon a sheet of paper buttered, to keep them from being smoked. For sauce, take a piece of onion or shalot, an anchovy, and two spoonfuls of pickled cucumbers, capers, and mushrooms: mince these very small by themselves; add a little pepper and salt, five spoonfuls of oil, one of water, and the juice of a lemon, and mix them well together with mustard. Pour the sauce cold into the dish, and lay the birds, when broiled, upon it.

Pigeons, Surtout of.

Take some large tame pigeons; make forcemeat thus: parboil and bruise the livers fine; beat some boiled ham in a mortar; mix these with some mushrooms, a little chopped parsley, a clove of garlic shred fine, two or three young onions minced fine, a sweetbread of veal, parboiled and minced very fine, pepper, and salt. Fill the pigeons with this stuffing; tie them close, and cover each pigeon with the forcemeat: tie them up in paper to keep it on, and while roasting have some essence of ham heated; pour it into your dish, and lay your pigeons upon it.

To preserve tainted Poultry.

Have a large cask that has been just emptied, with part of a stave or two knocked out at the head, and into the others drive hooks to hang your fowls, but not so as to touch one another, covering the open places with the staves or boards already knocked out, but leaving the bung-hole open as an air vent. Let them dry in a cool place, and in this way you may keep fish or flesh.

Pullets with Oysters.

Boil your pullets. Put a quart of oysters over the fire till they are set; strain them through a sieve, saving the liquor, and put into it two or three blades of mace, with a little thyme, an onion, parsley, and two anchovies. Boil and strain all these off, together with half a pound of butter; draw it up, and squeeze into it half a lemon. Then let the oysters be washed, and set one by one in cold water; put them in the liquor, having made it very hot, and pour it over the pullets. Garnish, if you please, with bacon and sausages.

Pullets to bone and farce.

Bone the pullets as whole as you possibly can, and fill the belly with sweetbreads, mushrooms, chesnuts, and forcemeat balls; lard the breast with gross lard, pass them off in a pan, and either roast or stew them, making a sauce with mushrooms and oysters, and lay them under.

Rabbits, to boil.

Truss and lard them with bacon, boiling them white. Take the liver, shred with it fat bacon for sauce, and put to it very strong broth, vinegar, white wine, salt, nutmeg, mace, minced parsley, barberries, and drawn butter. Lay your rabbits in the dish, and let the sauce be poured over them. Garnish the dish with barberries and lemon.

Rabbits, to boil with Onions.

Truss the rabbits close; well wash; boil them white; boil the onions by themselves, changing the water three times. Strain them well, and chop and butter them, putting in a quarter of a pint of cream; then serve up the rabbits covered with onions.

Rabbits, brown fricassee of.

Fry your rabbits brown, and stew it in some gravy, with thyme, an onion, and parsley, tied together. Season, and thicken it with brown thickening, a few morels, mushrooms, lemon, and forcemeat balls.

Rabbits, white fricassee of. No. 1.

Cut the rabbits in slices; wash away the blood; fry them on a slow fire, and put them into your pan with a little strong broth; seasoning, and tossing them up with oysters and mushrooms. When almost done, put in a pint of cream, thickened with a piece of butter and flour.

Rabbits, white fricassee of. No. 2.

Take the yolks of five eggs and a pint of cream; beat them together, and put two ounces of butter into the cream, until the rabbits are tender. Put in this liquor to the rabbits, and keep tossing them over the fire till they become thickened, and then squeeze in a lemon; add truffles, mushrooms, morels, artichoke bottoms, pallets, cocks-combs, forcemeat balls, or any of these.

Rabbits, white fricassee of. No. 3.

Cut them in the same manner as for eating, and put them into a stewpan, with a pint of veal gravy, a little beaten mace, a slice of lemon-peel, and anchovy, and season with cayenne pepper and salt. Stew over a slow fire, and, when done enough, thicken the gravy with butter and flour; then strain and add to it two eggs, mixed with a glass of cream, and a little nutmeg. Take care not to let it boil.

Turkey, to boil.

Fill a large turkey with oysters; take a breast of veal, cut in olives; bone it, and season it with pepper, salt, nutmegs, cloves, mace, lemon-peel, and thyme, cut small; take some lean veal to make forcemeat, with the ingredients before mentioned, only adding shalot and anchovies; put some in the olives and some in the turkey, in a cloth; roast or bake the olives. Take three anchovies, a little pepper, a quarter of a pint of gravy, as much white wine; boil these with a little thyme till half is consumed; then put in some butter, meat, oysters, mushrooms, fried balls, and bacon; put all these in a pan, and pour on the turkey; lay the olives round, and garnish the dish with pickles and lemon. If you want sauce, add a little gravy, and serve it up.

Turkey, with Oysters.

Boil your turkey, and serve with the same sauce as for pullets, only adding a few mushrooms.

Turkey à la Daube.

Bone a turkey, and season it with pepper and salt; spread over it some slices of ham, over them some forcemeat, over that a fowl, boned, and seasoned as the turkey, then more ham and forcemeat, and sew it up. Cover the bottom of a stewpan with veal and ham cut in slices; lay in the turkey breast downward: chop all the bones to pieces, and lay them on the turkey; cover the pan close, and set it over the fire for five minutes. Put as much clear broth as will cover it, and let it do for two hours. When it is more than half done, put in one ounce of the best isinglass and a bundle of sweet-herbs; skim off all the fat, and, when it is cold, break it with whites of eggs as you do other jelly. Put part of it into a pan or mould that will hold the turkey, and, when it is cold, lay the turkey upon it with the breast downward; then cover it with the rest of the jelly. When you serve it, turn it out whole upon the dish.

Roasted Turkey, delicate Gravy for.

Prepare a very rich brown gravy with truffles cut in it; slit the skins off some chesnuts with a knife, and fry them in butter till thoroughly done, but not burned, and serve them whole in the sauce. There may be a few sausages about the turkey.

Turkey or Veal stuffing.

Mix a quarter of a pound of beef suet, the same quantity of bread crumbs, two drachms of parsley, a drachm and a half of sweet marjoram, or lemon-thyme, and the same of grated lemon-peel; an onion or shalot chopped fine, a little salt and pepper, and the yolks of two eggs, all pounded well together. For a boiled turkey, add the soft part of a dozen oysters, a little grated ham or tongue, and an anchovy, if you please.

GAME.

Hare, to dress.

Stuff and lard the hare, trussing it as for roasting: put it into a fish-kettle, with two quarts of strong beef gravy, one of red wine, a bunch of sweet-herbs, some slices of lemon, pepper, salt, a few cloves, and a nutmeg. Cover it up close, and let it simmer over a slow fire till three parts done. Take it up, put it into a dish, and strew over it crumbs of bread, a few sweet-herbs chopped fine, some grated lemon-peel, and half a nutmeg. Set it before the fire, and baste it till it is of a fine light brown; and, while it is doing, skim the gravy, thicken it with the yolk of an egg and a piece of butter rolled in flour, and, when done, put it in a dish, and the rest in a boat or terrine.

Hare, to roast.

Take half a pint of cream, grate bread into it; a little winter savory, thyme, and parsley; shred these very fine; half a nutmeg grated, and half of the hare's liver, shred; beat an egg, yolk and white together, and mix it in with it, and half a spoonful of flour if you think it too light. Put it into the hare and sew it up. Have a quart of cream to baste it with. When the hare is roasted, take some of the best of the cream out of the dripping-pan, and make it fine and smooth by beating it with a spoon. Have ready melted a little thick butter, and mix it with the cream, and a little of the pudding out of the hare's belly, as much as will make it thick.

Another way.

Lard the hare well with bacon; make a pudding of grated bread, and chop small the heart and liver, parboiled, with beef-suet and sweet-herbs. With the marrow mix some eggs, spice, and cream; then sew it in the belly of the hare; roast, and serve it up with butter, drawn with cream, gravy, or claret.

Hare, to hash.

Cut the hare into small pieces, and, if any stuffing is left, rub it small in gravy, and put to it a glass of red wine, a little pepper, salt, an onion, and a slice of lemon. Toss it up till hot through, and then take out the lemon and onion.

Hare, to jug. No. 1.

Cut and put it into a jug, with the same ingredients as for stewing, but no water or beer; cover it closely; set it in a kettle of boiling water, and keep it boiling three hours, or until the hare is tender; then pour your gravy into the stewpan, and put to it a glass of red wine and a little cayenne; but if necessary put a little more of the gravy, thicken it with flour; boil it up; pour it over the hare, and add a little lemon-juice.

Hare, to jug. No. 2.

Cut and joint the hare into pieces; scald the liver and bruise it with a spoon; mix it with a little beaten mace, grated lemon-peel, pepper, salt, thyme, and parsley shred fine, and a whole onion stuck with a clove or two; lay the head and neck at the bottom of the jar; lay on it some seasoning, a very thin slice of fat bacon, then some hare, and bacon, seasoned well in. Stop close the jug or jar with a cork, to prevent any water getting in or the steam evaporating; set it in a pot of hot water, and let it boil three hours; then have ready some strong beef gravy boiling, and pour it into the jug till the hare is just covered; shake it, pour it into your dish, and take out the onion.

Hare, to jug. No. 3.

Cut the hare in pieces, but do not wash it; season with an onion shred fine, a bunch of sweet-herbs, such as thyme, parsley, sweet marjoram, and the peel of one lemon. Cut half a pound of fat bacon into thin slices; then put it into a jug, first a layer of hare and then one of bacon; proceed thus till the jug is full: stop it close, that no steam may escape; then put it in a pot of boiling water, and let it boil three hours. Take up the jug; put in a quarter of a pound of butter mixed with flour; set it in your kettle again for a quarter of an hour, then put it in your dish. Garnish with lemon-peel.

Hare, to jug. No. 4.

Cut the hare in pieces, and half season and lard them. Put the hare into a large-mouthed jug, with two onions stuck with cloves, and a faggot of sweet-herbs; close down, and let it boil three hours. Take it out, and serve up hot.

Hare, to mince.

Boil the hare with onions, parsley, and apples, till tender; shred it small, and put in a pint of claret, a little pepper, salt, and nutmeg, with two or three anchovies, and the yolks of twelve eggs boiled hard and shred very small; stirring all well together. In serving up, put sufficient melted butter to make it moist. Garnish the dish with whites of eggs, cut in half, and some of the bones.

Hare, to stew.

Cut off the legs and shoulders, and cut out the back bone; cut into slices the meat that comes off the sides: put all these into a vessel with three quarters of a pint of small beer, the same of water, a large onion stuck with cloves, whole pepper, some salt, and a slice of lemon. Let this stew gently for an hour closely covered, and then put a quart of good gravy to it, stewing it gently two hours longer, till tender. Take out the hare, and rub half a spoonful of smooth flour in a little gravy; put it to the sauce and boil it up; add a little cayenne and salt if necessary;

put in the hare, and, when hot through, serve it up in a terrine stand.

Hare stuffing.

Two ounces of beef suet, three ounces of bread crumbs, a drachm of parsley, half a drachm of shalot, the same of marjoram, lemon-thyme, grated lemon-peel, and two yolks of egg.

Partridge, to boil.

Cover them with water, and fifteen minutes will boil them. Sauce—celery, liver, mushroom, or onion sauces.

Partridge, to roast.

Half an hour will be sufficient; and for sauce, gravy and bread sauce.

Partridge à la Paysanne.

When you have picked and drawn them, truss and put them on a skewer, tie them to a spit, and lay them to roast. Put a piece of fat bacon on a toasting fork, and hold it over the birds, that as it melts it may drop upon them while roasting. After basting them well in this manner, strew over a few crumbs of bread and a little salt, cut fine some shalots, with a little gravy, salt and pepper, and the juice of half a lemon. Mix all these over the fire; thicken them up; pour them into a dish, and lay your partridges upon them.

Partridge à la Polonaise.

Pick and draw a brace of partridges, and put a piece of butter in their bellies; nut them on the spit, and cover them with slices of bacon, and over that with paper, and lay them down to a moderate fire. While roasting, cut same shalots and parsley very small; mix these together, adding slices of ginger with pepper and salt; take a piece of butter, and work them up into a stiff paste. When the birds are nearly done, take them up; gently raise the wings and legs, and under each put a piece of paste; then hold them tight together, and squeeze over them a little orange juice and a good deal of zest from the peel. Serve them up hot with good gravy.

Partridge à la Russe.

Pick, draw, and cut into quarters some young partridges, and put them into white wine; set a stewpan with melted bacon over a brisk fire; then put your partridges in, turning them two or three times. Add a glass of brandy; set them over a slow fire, and, when they have stewed some time, put in a few mushrooms cut into slices, with good gravy. Simmer them briskly, and skim the fat off as it rises. When done, put in a piece of butter rolled in flour, and squeeze in the juice of lemon.

Partridge rolled.

Lard some young partridges with ham and bacon, and strew over some salt and pepper, with beaten mace, sweet-herbs cut small, and some shred lemon-peel.

Take some thin beef steaks, taking care that they have no holes in them, and strew over some seasoning, squeezing over some lemon-juice. Lay a partridge upon each steak, roll it up, and tie it round to keep it together, and pepper the outside. Set on a stewpan, with some slices of bacon and an onion cut in pieces; then carefully lay the partridges in, put some rich gravy to them, and stew gently till they are done. Take the partridges out of the beef; lay them in a dish, and pour over them some rich essence of ham.

Partridge stewed.

Stuff the craws with bread crumbs, grated lemon-peel, a bit of butter, shalot chopped, parsley, nutmeg, salt and pepper, and yolk of egg; rub the inside with pepper and salt. Half roast them; then stew them with rich gravy and a little Madeira, a piece of lemon-peel, an onion, savory, and spice, if necessary, for about half an hour. Take out the lemon-peel and onion, and thicken with a little flour; garnish with hard yolks of eggs; add artichoke bottoms boiled and quartered.

Salme of Partridges.

Cut up the partridges neatly into wings, legs, and breast; keep the backs and rumps apart to put into sauce; take off all the skin very clean, so that not a bit remains; then pare them all round, put them in a stewpan, with a little jelly gravy, just to cover them; heat them thoroughly, taking care they do not burn; strain off the gravy, and leave the partridge in the pan away from the fire, covering the pan. Take a large onion, three or four slices of ham, free from all fat, one carrot, cut in dice, a dessert-spoonful of mushrooms, clear washed from vinegar if they are pickled, two cloves, a little parsley and thyme, and a bit of butter, of the size of a walnut; fry these lightly; add a glass and a half of white wine, together with the jelly in which the partridges were heated, and as much more as will make up a pint of rich sauce, thickened with a little flour and butter; put in the parings of the birds except the claws; let them stew for an hour and a half on the corner of the stove; skim very clear; put in one lump of sugar, and strain the whole through a sieve; put the saucepan containing the partridges in boiling water, till thoroughly heated; lay the different parts of the birds neatly in a very hot dish; pour the sauce over them; have some slices of bread cut oval, rather broad at one end, neatly fried; lay them round the dish, and serve up.

Partridge, to pot.

For two brace of partridges take a small handful of salt, and of pepper, mace, and cloves, a quarter of an ounce each. With these, when well mixed, rub the birds thoroughly, inside and outside. Take a large piece of butter, season it well, put it into them, and lay them in pots, with the breasts downward. The pots must be large enough to admit the butter to cover them while they bake. Set them in a moderate oven; let them stand two hours; then take them out, and let them well drain from the gravy. Put them again into the pots; clear the butter in which they were baked through a sieve, and fill up the pots with it.

Partridge Pie.

Bone your partridges, and stuff them with forcemeat, made of breast of chicken and veal, ham and beef-suet, all chopped very fine, but not pounded in a mortar, which would spoil it. Season with mace, pepper, salt, a very little shalot, and lemon-peel. Put the whole into a stewpan; keep it stirred; add three eggs; have a raised crust, and lay thin slices of good fat bacon at the bottom and all round.

Pheasant, to boil.

Boil the birds in abundance of water; if they are large, they will require three quarters of an hour; if small, about half an hour. For sauce—stewed white celery, thickened with cream, and a bit of butter rolled in flour; pour this over them.

Pheasant, with white sauce.

Truss the bird with the legs inward, (like a fowl for boiling); singe it well; take a little butter and the fat of some bacon, and fry the pheasant white; when sufficiently firm, take it out of the pan; then put a spoonful of flour into the butter; fry this flour white; next add a pint of veal or game jelly; put in a few mushrooms, if pickled to be well washed; cut small a bunch of parsley, a large onion, a little thyme, one clove, a pinch of salt, cayenne pepper, and a small lump of sugar; stew the bird in this sauce till done; this may be known by putting a fork into the flesh, and seeing that no blood issues out; then skim off the fat and drain the pheasant; then strain and boil the gravy in which it has been stewed; have ready a few mushrooms fried white in butter; then thicken the gravy with the yolk of four eggs and two table-spoonfuls of cream, throw in the mushrooms, place the pheasant in a hot dish, pour the sauce over it, and serve it up.

Pheasant à la Braise.

Put a layer of beef, the same of veal, at the bottom of the stewpan, with a thin slice of bacon, a little bit of carrot, an onion stuck with cloves, a bunch of sweet-herbs, some black and white pepper, and a little beaten mace, and put in your pheasant; put over it a layer of veal and the same of beef; set it on the fire for five or six minutes; then pour two quarts of boiling water, cover it down close, and put a damp cloth round the outside of the cover to prevent the steam escaping: it must stew gently for an hour and a half; then take up the pheasant and keep it hot, and let the gravy stew till reduced to about a pint; strain it off, and put it into a saucepan, with a sweetbread, which must have been stewed with the bird, some liver of fowls, morels, truffles, artichoke bottoms, and the tops of asparagus, and let these simmer in the gravy; add two spoonfuls of red wine and of ketchup, and a piece of butter rolled in flour; let them stew for five or six minutes: lay the pheasant in the dish, pour the ragout over it, and lay forcemeat balls round it.

Pheasant à l'Italienne.

Cut the liver small: and to one bird take but six oysters; parboil them, and put them into a stewpan with the liver, a piece of butter, some parsley, green onions, pepper and salt, sweet-herbs, and a little allspice; let them stand a little over the fire, and stuff the pheasant with them; then put it into a stewpan, with some oil, green onions, sweet basil, parsley, and lemon juice, for a few minutes; take them off, cover your pheasant with slices of bacon, and put it upon a spit, tying some paper round it while roasting. Then take some oysters, and stew them in their own liquor a little, and put in your stewpan four yolks of eggs, half a lemon cut in dice, a little beaten pepper, scraped nutmeg, parsley cut small, an anchovy cut small, a rocambole, a little oil, a small glass of white wine, a little of ham cullis; put the sauce over the fire to thicken, then put in the oysters, and make the sauce relishing, and, when the pheasant is done, lay it in the dish, and pour the sauce over it.

Pheasant, Puré of.

Chop the fleshy parts of a pheasant, the wings, breast, and legs, very fine, and pound them well in a mortar. Warm a pint of veal jelly, and stew the bird in it. Strain the whole through a sieve. Mix it all to the consistency of mashed potatoes. Serve in a dish with fried bread round it.

Widgeon, to dress.

To eat widgeon in perfection, half roast the birds. When they come to table, slice the breast, strew on pepper and salt, pour on a little red wine, and squeeze the juice of an orange or lemon over; put some gravy to this; set the plate on a lamp; cut up the bird; let it remain over the lamp till enough done, turning it. A widgeon will take nearly twenty minutes to roast, to eat plain with good gravy only.

Wild Duck, to roast.

It will take full twenty minutes—gravy sauce to eat with it.

Woodcocks and Snipes, to roast.

Twenty minutes will roast the woodcocks, and fifteen the snipes. Put under either, while roasting, a toast to receive the trail, which lay under them in the dish. Melted butter and good gravy for sauce.

Woodcocks à la Française.

Pick them, then draw and truss them; let their breasts be larded with broad pieces of bacon; roast and serve them up on toasts dipped in verjuice.

Woodcocks, to pot.

The same as you pot pigeons.

SAUCES.

Essence of Anchovies.

TAKE two pounds of anchovies, one ounce of bay salt, three pints of spring water, half a gill of red port, half a gill mushroom ketchup; put them into a saucepan until the anchovies are all dissolved; let them boil; strain off the liquor with a one hair sieve, and be careful not to cork it until it is quite cold.

Anchovy Pickle.

Take two pounds of bay salt, three quarters of a pound of saltpetre, three pints of spring water, and a very little bole armeniac, to grate on the liquor to give it a colour; it must not be put to the anchovies until it is cold.

If anchovies are quite dry, put them into a jar, with a layer of bay salt at the bottom, and a little on the top.

Anchovy Sauce.

Take one or two anchovies; scale, split, and put them into a saucepan, with a little water, or good broth, a spoonful of vinegar, and a small round onion. When the anchovy is quite dissolved, strain off the liquor, and put into your melted butter to your taste.

To recover Anchovies.

When anchovies have, through the loss of the pickle, become rusty or decayed, put two pounds of saltpetre to a gallon of water, and boil it till reduced to a fourth part, continuing to skim it as it rises; then add a quarter of an ounce of crystal tartar; mix these, and stir them well. Take away the spoiled fish, put them together lightly, and pour in the new pickle, mixed with a pint of good old pickle, and stop them up close for twenty-four days. When you open them again, cover them with fine beaten bay salt; let them remain about four days; and, as you take them out for use, cover them carefully down.

Bacchanalian Sauce.

Take a spoonful of sweet oil, a gill of good broth, and a pint of white wine vinegar, adding two glasses of strong white wine: boil them together till half is consumed; then put in some shalot, garden cresses, tarragon, chervil, parsley, and scallions, all shred very fine, with some large pepper. Let the whole boil up, and serve it. A little cullis added will improve it.

Bechamel, or White Sauce. No. 1.

Take half a quarter of a pound of butter, three pounds of veal, cut into small slices, a quarter of a pound of ham, some trimmings of mushrooms, truffles, and morels, two white onions, a bunch of parsley, and thyme, put the whole into a stewpan, and set it on the fire till the meat is made firm; then put in three spoonfuls of flour, moistened with boiling hot thin cream. Keep this sauce rather thin, so that while you reduce it the ingredients may have time to be stewed thoroughly. Season with a little salt and cayenne pepper, and strain it through a sieve. This is excellent for pouring over roast veal instead of butter, and is a good sauce for hashed veal, for any white meat, and for all sorts of vegetables.

Bechamel. No. 2.

Two pounds of lean veal, cut in square pieces, half an inch thick; half a pound of lean ham. Melt in your stewpan two ounces of butter; simmer it until nearly ready to catch the stewpan, which must be avoided: add three table-spoonfuls of flour. When well mixed, add three pints of broth, or water, pouring in a little at a time that the thickening may be smooth. Stir till it boils; set it on the corner of the hob to boil gently for two hours. Season with an onion, twelve peppercorns, a few mushrooms, a faggot of parsley, a sprig of thyme, and a bay-leaf. Let the sauce be reduced to a quart; skim off the fat; and strain through a tamis.

Bechamel. No. 3.

Proceed much in the same way as for the brown sauce, (see Cullis) only it is not to be drawn down brown, but filled up and thickened with flour and water, some good cream added to it, and then strained.

Sauce for Beef Bouilli.

Four hard eggs well mixed up with half a table-spoonful of made mustard, eight capers, and one table spoonful of Reading sauce.

Sauce for boiled Beef à la Russe.

Scrape a large stick of horseradish, tie it up in a cloth, and boil it with the beef; when boiled a little, put it into some melted butter; boil it some time, and send it up in the butter. Some persons like to have it sent up in vinegar.

Bread Sauce. No. 1.

Put into half a pint of water a good sized piece of bread-crumb, not new, with an onion, a blade of mace, a few peppercorns, in a bit of cloth; boil them a few minutes; take out the onion and spice, mash the bread smooth, add a little salt and a piece of butter.

Bread Sauce. No. 2.

Take a French roll, or white bread crumb; set it on the fire, with some good broth or gravy, a small bag of peppercorns, and a small onion; add a little good cream, and a little pepper and salt; you may rub it through a sieve or not.

Bread Sauce. No. 3.

Take the crumb of a French roll; put it into a saucepan, with two large onions, some white peppercorns, and about a pint of water. Let it boil over a slow fire till the onions are very tender; then drain off the water; rub the bread and onions through a hair sieve; put the pulp into a stewpan, with a bit of butter, a little salt, and a gill of cream; and keep it stirring till it boils.

Bread Sauce. No. 4.

Put bread crumbs into a stewpan with as much milk as will soak them; moisten with broth; add an onion and a few peppercorns. Let it boil or simmer till it becomes stiff: then add two table-spoonfuls of cream, melted butter, or good broth. Take out the onion and peppercorns when ready to serve.

Bread Sauce for Pig.

To the sauce made as directed in No. 1 add a few currants picked and washed, and boil them in it.

Browning for made dishes.

Beat four ounces of loaf sugar very fine: put it into an iron frying-pan, with an ounce of butter; set it over a clear fire, mixing it well all the time: when it begins to be frothy, the sugar is dissolving; hold it high over the fire. When the butter and sugar is of a deep brown, pour in a little white wine; stir it well; add a little more wine, stirring it all the time. Put in the rind of a lemon, a little salt, three spoonfuls of mushroom ketchup, half an ounce of whole allspice, four shalots peeled; boil them slowly eight minutes, then pour into a basin, cover it close, and let it stand till next day. Skim and bottle it. A pint of white wine is the proper quantity for these ingredients.

Another.

Take some brown sugar, put a little water to it, set it on the fire, and let it boil till it nearly comes to burning, but it must not quite burn, as it would then be bitter: put some water to it, and when cold strain it off, and put it in a bottle. When you want to give a higher colour to gravy or sauce, you will find this very useful.

Butter, to burn.

Put your butter into a frying-pan over a slow fire; when it is melted, dust in some flour, and keep stirring it till it is thick and brown: then thicken some with it.

Butter, to clarify.

Let it slowly melt and then stand a little; and when it is poured into pots, leave the milk, which will settle at the bottom.

Another way.

Melt the butter, and skim it well before it is poured upon any thing.

Plain melted Butter—very simple, but rarely well done.

Keep either a plated or tin saucepan for the sole purpose of melting butter. Put into it a little water and a dust of flour, and shake them together. Cut the butter in slices; as it melts, shake it one way; let it boil up, and it will be smooth and thick.

Another.

Mix a little flour and water out of the dredger, that it may not be lumpy; then put in a piece of butter, set it over a quick fire; have it on and off every instant to shake it, and it will not oil, but will become thick and smooth.

To thicken Butter for Peas, &c.

Put two or three spoonfuls of water in a saucepan, sufficient to cover the bottom. When it boils, put half a pound of butter; when it is melted, take off the saucepan, and shake it round a good while, till very smooth.

Caper Sauce.

Chop half of the capers, and the rest put in whole; chop also a little parsley very fine, with a little bread grated very fine, and add salt: put these into smooth melted butter.

Carp Sauce.

One pint of Lisbon wine, with a small quantity of mace, cloves, and cinnamon, three anchovies, a bit of bay-leaf, a little horseradish not 'scraped, and a slice or two of onion; let the whole boil about a quarter of an hour, and, when cold, mix as much flour with the sauce as will make it of a proper thickness. Set it over the stove; keep it stirred till it boils. Just before you serve up, put in a quarter of a pint of cream, more or less according to the thickness of your sauce.

Boil the carp in as much water as will cover them, with some wine, a little vinegar, and slices of lemon and onion.

Another.

Four large anchovies, eight spoonfuls of white wine, four of vinegar, two onions, whole, a nutmeg quartered, some mace, whole pepper, two or three cloves; boil it nearly half away, then strain it off, thicken it with butter and flour, and three spoonfuls of thick cream; the sauce should not be too thick.

Light brown Sauce for Carp.

To the blood of the carp put thyme, parsley, onions, and anchovies; chop all these small, and put them together in a saucepan. Add half a pint of white wine, a quarter of a pint of elder vinegar, and a little tarragon vinegar: mix all these together, set the pan on the fire, and boil till it is almost dry. Mix some melted butter with the sauce, and pour it on the fish, being plain boiled.

Sauce for Carp and Tench.

Boil a pint of strong gravy drawn from beef, with three or four anchovies, a small bit of lemon-peel and horseradish, a little mushroom ketchup, and a great deal of black pepper. When boiled enough, strain it off, and when it is cold take off all the fat. Then add nearly half a pound of butter, well mixed with flour, to make it of a proper thickness. When it boils, add a cupful of red wine and a little lemon-juice.

White Sauce for Carp.

Boil half a pint of white wine, a quarter of a pint of elder vinegar, a little tarragon vinegar, half a pint of water, a bunch of sweet-herbs, an onion stuck with cloves, and some mace, till the goodness is out of the ingredients. Thicken with melted butter, the yolk of an egg beat, and a quarter of a pint of good cream.

Dutch Sauce for Carp or Tench.

Take six fine anchovies well washed and picked, put them in a stewpan, add to them four spoonfuls of vinegar, eight spoonfuls of water, one large onion sliced, two or three blades of mace, and four or five cloves. Let them stand one hour before the sauce is wanted; set them on the stove, and give them a boil up; strain the liquor into a clean stewpan; then add the yolks of four eggs well beaten; put to it some good thick melted butter; add half a pint of very nice thick cream. Mix all these well together; put it on a slow fire; stir it till it boils; season to your taste.

Carp Sauce, for Fish.

Put a little lean bacon and some slices of veal at the bottom of a stewpan, with three or four pieces of carp, four anchovies, an onion, two shalots, and tarragon, or any root to flavour to your taste. Let it remain over a very slow fire for half an hour, and, when it begins to thicken, or to stick to the pan, moisten it with a large glass of white wine, two spoonfuls of cullis, and the same quantity of broth. Skim and strain it through a sieve; it will want no salt.

Cavechi, an Indian Pickle. No. 1.

This is excellent for sauce. Into a pint of vinegar put two cloves of garlic, two spoonfuls of red pepper, two large spoonfuls of India soy, and four of walnut pickle, with as much cochineal as will colour it, two dozen large anchovies boned and dissolved in the juice of three lemons, and one spoonful of mustard. Use it as an addition to fish and other sauce, or in any other way, according to your palate.

Cavechi. No. 2.

Take three cloves, four scruples of coriander seed, bruised ginger, and saffron, of each ten grains, three cloves of garlic, and one pint of white wine vinegar. Infuse all together by the fireside for a fortnight. Shake it every day; strain off the liquor, and bottle it for use. You may add to it a pinch of cayenne.

Cavechi. No. 3.

One pint of vinegar, half an ounce of cayenne, two table-spoonfuls of soy, two of walnut pickle, two of ketchup, four cloves of garlic, and three shalots cut small; mix them well together.

Celery Sauce, white.

Make some strong boiled gravy, with veal, a good deal of spice, and sweet-herbs; put these into a stewpan with celery cut into pieces of about two or three inches in length, ready boiled, and thicken it with three quarters of a pound of butter rolled in flour, and half a pint of cream. Boil this up, and squeeze in some lemon-juice; pour some of it into the dish.

This is an excellent sauce for boiled turkey, fowl, or veal. When the stuffing is made for turkey, make some of it into balls, and boil them.

Celery Sauce, brown.

Put the celery, cut into pieces about an inch long, and the onions sliced, with a small lump of butter; stew them on a slow fire till quite tender; add two spoonfuls of flour, half a pint of veal or beef broth, salt, pepper, and a little milk or cream. Boil it a quarter of an hour.

Sauce for boiled Chickens.

Take the yolks of four eggs, three anchovies, a little of the middle of bacon, and the inside of half a lemon; chop them all very fine; add a little thyme and sweet marjoram; thicken them all well together with butter, and pour it over the chickens.

Another.

Shred some anchovies very fine, with the livers of the chickens and some hard eggs; take a little of the boiling water in which the chickens were boiled, to melt the butter. Add some lemon juice, with a little of the peel cut small.

Sauce for cold Chicken or Game.

Chop a boned anchovy or two, some parsley, and a small onion; add pepper, oil, vinegar, mustard, and ketchup, and mix them all together.

White Sauce for Chickens.

Half a pint of cream, with a little veal gravy, three tea-spoonfuls of the essence of anchovies, half a tea-spoonful of vinegar, one small onion, one dozen cloves: thicken it with flour and butter; rub it through a sieve, and add a table-spoonful of sherry.

Consommé.

To make this foundation of all sauces, take knuckle of veal and some new ham. One pound of ham will be sufficient for six pounds of veal, with onions and roots of different sorts, and draw it down to a light colour: fill up with beef broth, if there is not enough. When the scum rises, skim it well, and let it simmer gently for three or four hours, keeping it well skimmed. Strain it off for use.

Cream Sauce for White Dishes.

Put a bit of butter into a stewpan, with parsley, scallions, and shalots, the whole shred fine, and a clove of garlic entire; turn it a few times over the fire; shake in some flour, and moisten it with two or three spoonfuls of good cream. Boil it a quarter of an hour, strain off the sauce, and, when you are ready to use it, put in a little good butter, with some parsley parboiled and chopped very fine, salt, and whole pepper, thickening it over the fire.

Cullis, to thicken Sauces.

Take carrot, turnip, onion; put them in the bottom of a stewpan; slice some veal and ham, and lay over your carrot, with thyme, parsley, and seasoning; put this over a fire gently; when it sticks to the bottom, pour in some good stock, put in the crumb of some French rolls, boil them up together, strain it through a sieve, and rub the bread through; this will thicken any brown sauce.

Fish cullis must be as above, only with fish instead of meat.

Brown Cullis.

Take two pounds of veal and half a pound of ham, with two or three onions; put a little bit of butter in the bottom of your stewpan, and lay in it the veal and ham cut small, with the onions in slices, a little of the spices of different sorts, and a small piece of bay leaf. Let it stew gently over the stove until it comes to a fine colour; then fill it up with broth, but, if you have no broth, with water; then make some smooth flour and water, and put it to it, until you find it thick enough: let it boil gently half an hour; skim the grease from it, and strain it.

Another.

Put a piece of butter in a stewpan; set it over a fire with some flour to it; keep it stirring till it is of a good colour; then put some gravy to it; this cullis will thicken any sauce.

Cullis à la Reine, or Queen's Stock.

Cut some veal into thin slices; beat them, and lay them in a stewpan, with some slices of ham; cut a couple of onions small, and put them in; cut to pieces half a dozen mushrooms and add them to the rest, with a bunch of parsley; and set them on a very gentle stove fire to stew. When they are quite done, and the liquor is rich and high tasted, take out all the meat, and put in some grated bread; boil up once, stirring them thoroughly.

Turkey Cullis.

Roast a large turkey till it is brown; cut it in pieces; put it into a marble mortar, with some ham, parsley, chives, mushrooms, a handful of each, and a crust of bread; beat them up into a paste. Take it out, and put it into a deep stewpan, with a pint of veal broth; stir it all well together; cover it, and set it over the stove; turn it constantly, adding more veal broth. When thoroughly dissolved, pass it through a hair sieve, and keep it for use. It will give any sauce a fine flavour; but cullises are generally used for the sorts of meat of which they are made. Some of the above, for instance, would make an excellent sauce for a turkey, added to any other gravy; then put them over a slow fire to stew gently. Take the flesh of a fine fowl, already roasted, from the bones; beat it in a marble mortar; add this to the cullis in the stewpan. Stir it well together, but take great care that it does not boil; pound three dozen of sweet almonds blanched to a thin paste, in a marble mortar, with a little boiled milk; add it to the cullis, and, when the whole is dissolved, it is fit for use. This is good for all white sauces and white soups.

Cullis of Veal, or any other Meat.

Put some small pieces of veal into a stewpan, with the like quantity of ham, about a pound to a quarter of a pint of water. Stew gently with onions and different herbs, till all the juice of the meat is extracted; then boil it quicker, till it begins to stick to the dish. Take the meat and vegetables out of the pan; add a little butter and flour to the gravy; boil it till it becomes of a good colour; then add, if you like, some good broth; put the meat in again to simmer for two hours; skim it well; strain through a sieve, and keep it for use.

Dandy Sauce, for all sorts of Poultry and Game.

Put a glass of white wine into a stewpan, with half a lemon cut in slices, a little rasped bread, two spoonfuls of oil, a bunch of parsley and scallions, a handful of mushrooms, a clove of garlic, a little tarragon, one clove, three spoonfuls of rich cullis, and a thin slice of fine smoked ham. Let the whole boil together till it is of a fine rich consistency; pass it through the sieve; then give it another turn over the fire, and serve it up hot.

Devonshire Sauce.

Cut any quantity of young walnuts into small pieces; sprinkle a little salt on them; next day, pound them in a mortar and squeeze the juice through a coarse thin cloth, such as is used for cheese. To a pint of juice add a pound of anchovies, and boil them slowly till the anchovies are dissolved. Strain it; add half a pint of white wine vinegar, half an ounce of mace, half an ounce of cloves, and forty peppercorns; boil it a quarter of an hour, and, when cold, rack it off and bottle it. A quarter of a pint of vinegar put to the dregs that have been strained off, and well boiled up, makes an excellent seasoning for the cook's use in hashes, fish sauce, &c.

Sauce for Ducks.

Stew the giblets till the goodness is extracted, with a small piece of lean bacon, either dressed or not, a little sprig of lemon-thyme, some parsley, three or four sage leaves, a small onion quartered, a few peppercorns, and plenty of lemon-peel. Stew all these well together; strain and put in a large spoonful of port wine, a little cayenne pepper and butter, and flour it to thicken.

Dutch Sauce.

Put into a saucepan some vinegar and water with a piece of butter; thicken it with the yolks of two eggs; squeeze into it the juice of a lemon, and strain it through a sieve.

Dutch Sauce for Fish.

Slice a little horseradish, and put it into a quarter of a pint of water, with five or six anchovies, half a handful of white peppercorns, a small onion, half a bay-leaf, and a very little lemon peel, cut as thin as possible. Let it boil a quarter of an hour; then strain and thicken with flour and butter and the yolk of an egg. Add a little elder vinegar, and then squeeze it through a tamis. It must not boil after being strained, or it will curdle.

Dutch Sauce for Meat or Fish.

Put two or three table-spoonfuls of water, as many of vinegar, and as many of broth, into a saucepan, with a piece of butter; thicken it with the yolks of two eggs. If for fish, add four anchovies; if not, leave them out. Squeeze into it the juice of a lemon, and strain it through a sieve.

Dutch Sauce for Trout.

Put into a stewpan a tea-spoonful of floor, four of vinegar, a quarter of a pound of butter, the yolks of five eggs, and a little salt. Set it on the fire, and keep continually stirring. When thick enough, work it well that you may refine it; pass it through a sieve; season with a little cayenne pepper, and serve up.

Egg Sauce.

Take two or three eggs, or more if you like, and boil them hard; chop the whites first and then the yolks with them, and put them into melted butter.

The Exquisite.

Put a little cullis into a stewpan, with a piece of butter the size of a walnut rolled in twice as much flour, salt, and large pepper, the yolks of two eggs, three or four shalots cut small, and thicken it over the fire. This sauce, which should be very thick, is to be spread over meat or fish, which is afterwards covered with finely grated bread, and browned with a hot salamander.

Fish Sauce. No. 1.

One pound of anchovies, stripped from the salt, and rinsed in a little port wine, a quarter of an ounce of mace, twelve cloves, two races of ginger sliced, a small onion or shalot, a small sprig of thyme, and winter savory, put into a quart of port wine, and half a pint of vinegar. Stew them over a slow fire covered close; strain the liquor through a hair sieve, cover it till cold, and put it in dry bottles. By adding a pint of port wine and the wine strained that the anchovies were rinsed in you may make an inferior sort. When used, shake it up: take two spoonfuls to a quarter of pound of butter; if not thick enough add a little flour.

Fish Sauce. No. 2.

Take a pint of red wine, twelve anchovies, one onion, four cloves, a nutmeg sliced, as much beaten pepper as will lie upon a half-crown, a bit of horseradish sliced, a little thyme, and parsley, a blade of mace, a gill of vinegar, two bay-leaves. Simmer these all together until the anchovies are dissolved; then strain it off, and, when cold, bottle it up close. Shake the bottle up when you use it; take two table-spoonfuls to a quarter of a pound of butter, without flour and water, and let it boil.

Fish Sauce. No. 3.

Take chili pods, bruise them well in a marble mortar, strain off the juice. To a pint bottle of juice add a table-spoonful of brandy and a spoonful of salt. The refuse put into vinegar makes good chili vinegar. This is an excellent relishing sauce.

Fish Sauce. No. 4.

Take some gravy, an onion sliced, some anchovies washed, thyme, parsley, sliced horseradish, and seasoning; boil these together. Strain off the liquor; put into it a bit of thickening and some butter. Draw this up together, and squeeze in a lemon. You may add shrimps or oysters. If for lobster sauce, you must cut your lobster in slices, and beat the spawn in a mortar, with a bit of lobster, to colour your sauce.

Fish Sauce. No. 5.

A faggot of sweet-herbs, some onion, and anchovy, with a slice of lemon, boiled in small gravy or water; strain, and thicken it with butter and flour, adding a spoonful of soy, or more, if agreeable to your taste.

Fish Sauce. No. 6.

Take some of the liquor in which you boil the fish; add to it mace, anchovies, lemon-peel, horseradish, thyme, a little vinegar, and white wine; thicken it up with butter, as much as will serve for the fish. If it is for salmon, put in oysters, shrimps, and cockles; take away the liquor, and boil the whole in vinegar.

Fish Sauce. No. 7.

Take a quarter of a pint of vinegar, the same of white wine, a quarter of an ounce of mace, the same of cloves, pepper, and six large anchovies, a stick of horseradish, an onion, a sprig of thyme, and a bit of lemon-peel; boil all together over the fire; strain it off, and melt your butter for the sauce.

Fish Sauce. No. 8.

Take half a pint of cream and half a pint of strong broth; thicken them with flour and butter, and when it boils put in it a little anchovy and lemon-juice, and put it over your fish.

Fish Sauce. No. 9.

To every pint of walnut liquor put one pound of anchovies; boil them till quite dissolved, and strain off the liquor. To a quart of the liquor put one pint of vinegar, a quarter of an ounce of a mixture of cloves, mace, allspice, and long pepper, and a dozen shalots. Boil again till they are very tender; strain off the liquor, and bottle it for use. This is an excellent sauce.

Fish Sauce. No. 10.

Boil a bit of horseradish and anchovy in gravy with a little lemon-peel and mace; add some cream; thicken it with flour and butter. If you have no gravy, ketchup is a good substitute; but a little always put in is good.

Fish Sauce. No. 11.

Boil a piece or two of horseradish in gravy; put into it a bit of mace and lemon-peel; add a little anchovy, either before or after it has been boiled; thicken with cream, and add a spoonful of elderberry vinegar: let the acid be the last thing for fear of curdling it. If you have no gravy, ketchup and water is a good substitute.

Fish Sauce. No. 12.

Take a quarter of a pint of gravy, well boiled with a bit of onion, lemon-peel, and horseradish, four or five cloves, a blade of mace, and a spoonful of ketchup; boil it till it is reduced to four or five spoonfuls; then strain it off, and put to it four or five spoonfuls of cream; thicken it with butter, and put in a spoonful of elder vinegar or lemon-juice: anchovies are sometimes added.

Fish Sauce. No. 13.

Take two quarts of claret or port, a pint, or more, to your taste, of the best vinegar, which should be tart, one pound of anchovies unwashed, the pickle of them and all, half an ounce of mace, half a quarter of an ounce of cloves, six or eight races of ginger, a good piece of horseradish, a spoonful of cayenne pepper, half the peel of a lemon, a bunch of winter savory and thyme, and three or four onions, a piece of garlic, and one shalot. Stew all these over a slow fire for an hour; then strain the liquor through a coarse sieve, and bottle it. You may stew the ingredients over again with more wine and vinegar for present use. When you use it, it must be put into the saucepan with the butter, instead of water, and melt it together. If you keep it close stopped, it will be good many years.

Fish Sauce. No. 14.

Take twenty-four large anchovies, bones and all, ten or twelve shalots, a handful of horseradish, four blades of mace, one quart of Rhenish, or any white wine, one pint of water, one lemon cut in slices, half a pint of anchovy liquor, one pint of claret, twelve cloves, half a tea-spoonful of cayenne pepper: boil them till reduced to a quart; strain off and bottle the liquor. Two spoonfuls will be sufficient to one pound of butter.

Fish Sauce. No. 15.

A spoonful of red wine, and the same of anchovy liquor, put into melted butter.

An excellent white Fish Sauce.

An anchovy, a glass of white wine, a bit of horseradish, two or three blades of mace, an onion stuck with cloves, a piece of lemon-peel, two eggs, a quarter of a pint of good broth, two spoonfuls of cream, a large piece of butter, with some flour mixed well in it; keep stirring it till it boils; add a little ketchup, and a small dessert spoonful of the juice of a lemon, and stir it the whole time to prevent curdling. Serve up hot.

Another.

Take eight spoonfuls of white wine, three of vinegar, one of soy or ketchup, three anchovies, one onion, a few sweet-herbs, a little mace, cloves, and white pepper; let it stew gently till it is reduced to six spoonfuls; then strain it off, and add half a pound of fresh butter rolled in a little flour, and six spoonfuls of cream. Let it boil after the cream and butter are added.

White Sauce, with Capers and Anchovies, for any White Fish.

Put a bit of butter, about the size of an egg, rolled in flour, into a stewpan; dilute it with a large wine glass of veal broth, two anchovies, cut fine, minced parsley, and two spoonfuls of cream. Stew it slowly, till it is of the proper consistency.

Fish Stock.

Put into a pot a scate, cut in pieces, with turnips, carrots, thyme, parsley, and onion. Cut in pieces an eel or two, and some flounders; put them into a stewpan with a piece of butter; stew them down till they go to pieces; put them to your scate; boil the whole well, and strain it off.

Forcemeat Balls, for Sauces.

To make forcemeat balls for soups, without grease, commonly called *quenelles*, soak the crumb of two penny rolls in milk for about half an hour; take it out, and squeeze out the milk; put the bread into a stewpan, with a little white sauce, made of veal jelly, a little butter, flour, and cream, seasoned, a spoonful of beef or mutton jelly, some parsley, shalots, and thyme, minced very fine. Stew these herbs in a little butter, to take off their rawness. Set them to reduce the panada of bread and milk, which you must keep constantly stirring with a wooden spoon, when the panada begins to get dry in the pan, which prevents its sticking; when quite firm, take it from the fire, and mix with it the yolks of two eggs. Let it cool, and use when wanted.

This panada must always be prepared beforehand, in order to have it cold, for it cannot be used warm; when cold, roll it into balls, but let them be small; pound the whole as large as possible in a mortar, for the more they are pounded the more delicate they are. Then break two eggs, and pound them likewise; season with a pinch of cayenne pepper, salt, and spices, in powder. When the whole is well mixed together, try a small bit, rolling it with a little flour, then putting it into boiling water with a little salt; if it should not be firm enough, add another egg, without beating the white. When the whole is mixed once more, rub it through a sieve, roll it into balls, and serve up hot in sauces.

White Sauce, for Fowls.

Some good veal gravy, boiled with an anchovy or onion, some lemon-peel, and a very little ketchup. Put in it the yolk of hard egg to thicken it, and add what cream you think proper.

Another.

Take a pint of milk, the yolks of two eggs, well beaten, a spoonful of mushroom pickle, a little salt, nutmeg, a small piece of butter, rolled in flour; stir all together till thick. Pour it over the fowls, and garnish with lemon or parsley.

White Sauce, for boiled Fowls.

Have ready a sauce, made of one pint of veal jelly, half a quarter of a pound of butter, two small onions, and a bunch of parsley; then put three table-spoonfuls of flour, half a pint of boiling hot cream, the yolks of three eggs, a pinch of cayenne pepper, and the same of salt; boil all up together, till of a tolerable thickness; keep it hot, and take care that it does not curdle. Make ready some slices of truffles, about thirty-four, the size and thickness of a shilling, boil them in a little meat jelly; strain them, and add the truffles to the sauce previously made. When ready to serve, pour the sauce and truffles over whatever meat they are destined for.

Sauce, for roasted Fowls of all kinds, or roasted Mutton.

Cut some large onions into square pieces; cut some fat bacon in the same manner, and a slice of lean ham; put them in a stewpan; shake them round constantly, to prevent their burning. When they are of a fine brown colour, put in some good cullis, more or less, according to the quantity you want to make. Let them stew very gently, till the onions are tender; then put in two tea-spoonfuls of mustard, and one table-spoonful of vinegar. Serve it hot.

A very good general Sauce.

Take some mint, balm, basil, thyme, parsley, and sage; pick them from the stalks, cut them very fine, slice two large onions very thin; then put all the ingredients into a marble mortar, and beat them till they are quite mixed; add some cayenne pepper and salt; beat all these well together, and mix them by degrees in some good cullis, till it is of the thickness of cream. Put them in a stewpan, boil them up; strain the gravy from the herbs, pressing it from them very hard with the back of a spoon; add to the gravy half a glass of wine, half a spoonful of salad oil, the squeeze of a lemon, and a pinch of sugar. This sauce is excellent for most dishes.

Genoese Sauce for stewed Fish.

This sauce is made by stewing fish. Make marinade of carrots, parsley roots, onions, mushrooms, a bay-leaf, some thyme, a blade of mace, a few cloves, and some spices: fry the whole white in butter; pour in a pint of white wine, or less, according to the quantity of sauce required; put in the fish, and let it stew thoroughly to make the sauce. Then take a little browned flour and butter, and mix it with the reserved liquor; add three or four spoonfuls of gravy from veal jelly; let these stew very gently on the corner of the stove; skim off the grease; put in a little salt and cayenne pepper, and add two spoonfuls of the essence of anchovy and a quarter of a pound of butter kneaded with flour. Squeeze in the juice of a whole lemon, and cover the stewed fish with this sauce, which ought to be made thick and mellow.

German Sauce.

Put the same quantity of meat jelly and fresh made broth into a stewpan, with a little parsley parboiled and chopped, the livers of two roasted or boiled fowls, an anchovy, and some capers, the whole shred very fine, a bit of butter about the size of an egg, half a clove of garlic, salt, and a little cayenne pepper. Thicken it over the fire.

Exceedingly good with poultry, pigeons, &c.

Beef Gravy.

Cut in pieces some lean beef, according to the quantity of gravy you may want; put it into a stewpan, with an onion or two, sliced, and a little carrot; cover it close, set it over a gentle fire, and pour off the gravy as it draws from it. Then let the meat brown; keep turning it to prevent its burning, pour over some boiling water, and add a few cloves, peppercorns, a bit of lemon, and a bunch of sweet-herbs. Gently simmer it, and strain it with the gravy that was drawn from the meat, some salt, and a spoonful of ketchup.

Beef Gravy, to keep for use.

Cover a piece of six or eight pounds with water; boil it for twenty minutes or half an hour: then take out the meat, beat it thoroughly, and cut it in pieces, to let out the gravy. Put it again into the water, with a bunch of sweet-herbs, an onion stuck with cloves, a little salt, and some whole pepper. Let it stew, but not boil, till the meat is quite consumed; pass it through a sieve, and let it stand in a cool place.

It will keep for a week, if the weather is not very hot. If you want to use this for a hash of brown meat, put a little butter in your frying-pan, shake in a little flour as it boils, and add a glass of claret: if for a white sauce to fowls or veal, melt the butter in the gravy, with a glass of white wine, two spoonfuls of cream, and the yolks of four or six eggs, according to the quantity of sauce required.

Brown Gravy.

Put a piece of butter, about the size of a hen's egg, into a saucepan; when it is melted, shake in a little flour, and let it brown; then by degrees stir in the following ingredients: half a pint of small beer, the same quantity of water, an onion, a piece of lemon-peel cut small, three cloves, a blade of mace, some whole pepper, a spoonful of mushroom-pickle, the same quantity of ketchup, and an anchovy. Let the whole boil together a quarter of an hour; strain it off, and it will be a good sauce.

Another.

Take the glaze that remains at the bottom of the pot after you have stewed any thing à la braise, provided it be not tainted game; skim it, and strain it through a sieve; then put in a bit of butter about the size of a walnut, mixed with flour; thicken it over the fire, and add the juice of a lemon, and a little salt and cayenne pepper.

Green Sauce for Green Geese, or Ducklings.

Half a pint of the juice of sorrel, with a little grated nutmeg, some bread crumb, and a little white wine; boil it a quarter of an hour, and sweeten with sugar, adding scalded gooseberries and a piece of butter.

Another.

Pound a handful of spinach and another of sorrel together in a mortar; squeeze and put them into a saucepan; warm, but do not let it boil.

Ham Sauce.

When your ham is almost done, let the meat be picked clean from the bone, and mash it well; put it into a saucepan with three spoonfuls of gravy; set it over a slow fire, stirring it all the while, otherwise it will stick to the bottom. When it has been on for some time, add a small bundle of sweet-herbs, pepper, and half a pint of beef gravy; cover it up; stew it over a gentle fire, and when quite done strain off the gravy.

This is very good for veal.

Sauce for Hare or Venison.

In a little port wine and water melt some currant jelly, or send in the jelly only; or simmer port wine and sugar for twenty or thirty minutes.

Harvey's Sauce.

Three table-spoonfuls of walnut ketchup, two of essence of anchovies, one tea-spoonful of soy, and one of cayenne pepper. Mix these together; put them, with a clove of garlic, into a pint bottle, and fill it up with white wine vinegar.

Sauce for Hashes or Fish, and good with any thing and every thing.

Take two or more spoonfuls of good cullis, according to the quantity you intend to make, a glass of white wine, a shalot, a small onion, a few mushrooms, truffles, morels, and a bunch of sweet-herbs, with a little grated lemon-peel, a slice of ham, and the yolk of an egg. Thicken it with a bit of butter rolled in flour, and let it stew till the ingredients are quite soft.

Sauce for White Hashes or Chickens.

A pint of new milk, the yolk of two eggs, well beaten, two ounces of butter, well mixed with flour; mix it all together in a saucepan, and, when it boils, add two spoonfuls of mushroom ketchup; it must be stirred all the time, or it will not do. If used for cold veal or lamb, the meat must be cut as thin as possible, the sauce made first to boil, and then the meat put into it, till it is hot enough for table.

Horseradish Sauce.

A tea-spoonful of mustard, one table-spoonful of vinegar, three of thick cream, and a little salt; grate as much horseradish into it as will make it as thick as onion sauce. A little shalot may be added.

Italian Sauce.

Put into a stewpan two spoonfuls of sweet oil, a handful of mushrooms cut small, a bunch of parsley, scallions, and half a laurel-leaf, two cloves, and a clove of garlic; turn the whole a few times over the fire, and shake in a little flour. Moisten it with a glass of white wine and twice as much good cullis; let it boil half an hour; skim away the fat, allowing it to cool a little for that purpose; set it on again, and serve it; it will be found to eat well with any white meat.

Ketchup.

Put a pint of the best white wine vinegar into a wide-mouthed quart bottle; add twelve cloves of shalots, peeled and bruised; take a quarter of a pint of the strongest red wine and boil it a little; wash and bone about a dozen anchovies, let them dissolve in the wine, and, when cold, put them into the vinegar bottle, stopping it close with a cork, and shaking it well. Into the same quantity of wine put a spoonful of pepper bruised, a few races of split ginger, half a spoonful of cloves bruised, and a few blades of large mace, and boil them till the strength of the spice is extracted. When the liquor is almost cold, cut in slices two large nutmegs, and when quite cold put into it some lemon-peel. Put that into the bottle, and scrape thin a large, sound horseradish root, and put that also into the bottle; stop it down close; shake it well together every day for a fortnight, and you may then use it.

Lemon Sauce.

Pare a lemon, and cut it in slices; pick out the seeds and chop them small: then boil the lemon and bruise it. Mix these in a little gravy; and add it to some melted butter, with a little lemon-peel chopped fine.

Liver Sauce for boiled Fowls.

Boil the liver just enough to spread; add a little essence of anchovy and grated lemon-peel, the yolk of a hard egg, and the juice of a lemon: mix it well together, and stir it into some butter.

Lobster Sauce. No. 1.

Pull the lobster to pieces with a fork; do not chop it; bruise the body and the spawn with the back of a spoon; break the shell; boil it in a little water to give it a colour; strain it off. Melt some butter in it very smooth, with a little horseradish, and a little cayenne pepper; mix the body of the lobster well with the butter; then add the meat, and give it a boil, with a spoonful of ketchup and a spoonful of gravy.

Lobster Sauce. No. 2.

Put the red spawn of a hen lobster in a mortar; add half an ounce of butter; pound it smooth, and run it through a hair sieve with the back of a spoon. Cut the meat of the lobster into small pieces, and add as much melted butter to the spawn as will suffice; stir it till thoroughly mixed; then put to it the meat of the lobster, and warm it on the fire; but do not let it boil.

Lobster Sauce. No. 3.

Take the spawn of one large lobster, and bruise it well in a mortar: take a sufficient quantity of strong veal gravy, the yolk of an egg, and a little cream, and thicken with flour and butter.

The Marchioness's Sauce.

Put as much bread rasped very fine as you can take at two handfuls into a stewpan, with a bit of butter of the size of a walnut, a kitchen-spoonful of sweet oil, a shalot cut small, salt and large pepper, with a sufficient quantity of lemon-juice to lighten the whole. Stir it over the fire till it thickens. This sauce may be served with all sorts of meat that require a sharp relishing sauce.

Meat Jelly for Sauces.

Every sort of dish requires good sauce, and for every sauce it is absolutely necessary to have a good meat jelly. The following may be depended upon as being excellent: a shin of beef, about eight pounds, rather more than less; a knuckle of veal, about nine pounds; a neck of mutton, about nine pounds; two fowls; four calves' feet: carefully cut off all fat whatever, and stew over a stove as slowly as possible, till the juice is entirely extracted. This will produce about seven quarts of jelly. No pepper, salt, or herbs of any kind. These should be added in using the jelly, whether for soups, broths, or sauces; but the pure jelly is the thing to have as the foundation for every species of cookery.

Another.

Three shanks, or two pounds, of mutton in two quarts of water; stew down to a pint and a half, with a carrot, and an onion.

A Mixed Sauce.

Take parsley, scallions, mushrooms, and half a clove of garlic, the whole shred fine; turn it a few times over the fire with butter; shake in a little flour, and moisten it with good broth: when the sauce is consumed to half the original quantity, add two pickled gherkins cut small, and the yolks of three eggs beaten up with some more broth; a little salt and cayenne will complete the sauce.

Mushroom Ketchup. No. 1.

Take a bushel of the large flaps of mushrooms, gathered dry, and bruise them with your hands. Put some of them into an earthen pan; throw some salt over them; then put in more mushrooms, then more salt, till you have done. Add half an ounce of beaten mace and cloves, and the same quantity of allspice; and let them stand five or six days, stirring them every day. Tie a paper over and bake for four hours in a slow oven; strain out the liquor through a cloth, and let it stand to settle. Pour it off clear from the sediment: to every gallon of liquor put a quart of red wine; if not salt enough, add a little more salt, with a race of ginger cut small, and half an ounce of cloves and mace, and boil till reduced nearly one third. Strain it through a sieve into a pan; next day pour it from the settlings, and bottle it for use.

Mushroom Ketchup. No. 2.

Mash your mushrooms with a great deal of salt; let them stand two days; strain them, and boil the liquor once or twice, observing to scum it well. Then put in black pepper and allspice, a good deal of each, and boil them together. Bottle the liquor, and put five or six cloves into each bottle.

Mushroom Ketchup. No. 3.

Pick the mushrooms clean, but by no means wash them; put them into an earthen pipkin with salt, cover them close with a coarse paste, and put them in the oven for seven hours or thereabout. Squeeze them a little, and pour off the liquor, which must be put upon fresh mushrooms, and bake these as long as the first. Then pour off the liquor, after pressing, and boil it well with salt sufficient to keep. Boil it half away till it appears clammy. When cold, bottle it up.

Mushroom Ketchup. No. 4.

Into a quart of red wine put some flaps of mushrooms, half a pound of anchovies, some thyme, two onions sliced, parsley, cloves, and mace. Let them stew gently on the fire; then strain off the liquor, a spoonful of which, with a little gravy, butter, and lemon, will make excellent fish sauce, and be always ready.

Mushroom Sauce.

Mix a little flour with a good piece of butter; boil it up in some cream, shaking the saucepan; then throw in some mushrooms with a little salt and nutmeg: boil this up; or, if you like it better, put the mushrooms in butter melted with a little veal gravy, some salt, and grated nutmeg.

Sauce for roasted Mutton.

Wash an anchovy clean; put to it a glass of red wine, some gravy, a shalot cut small, and a little lemon-juice. Stew these together; strain them, and mix the liquor with the gravy that runs from the mutton.

Onion Sauce.

Let the onions be peeled; boil them in milk and water, and put a turnip into the pot; change the water twice: pulp them through a colander, or chop them as you please; then put them into a saucepan, with butter, cream, a little flour, and some pepper and salt.

Brown Onion Sauce.

Peel and slice the onions, to which put an equal quantity of cucumber or celery, with an ounce of butter, and set them on a slow fire; turn the onions till they are highly browned; stir in half an ounce of flour; add a little broth, pepper, and salt; boil it up for a few minutes; add a spoonful of claret or port, and some mushroom ketchup. You may sharpen it with a little lemon-juice. Rub through a tamis.

Oyster Sauce. No. 1.

Take two score of oysters, put them, with their own liquor, a few peppercorns, and a blade of mace, into a saucepan, and let them simmer a little over the fire, just to plump them; then with a fork shake each in the liquor so as to take off all the grit; strain the liquor, add to it a little good gravy and two anchovies, and thicken it with flour and butter, nearly as thick as custard.

Oyster Sauce. No. 2.

Wash the oysters from their liquor; strain it, and put that and the oysters into a little boiled gravy and just scald them: add a piece of butter mixed with flour, cream, and ketchup. Shake all up; let it boil, but not much, lest the oysters grow hard and shrink; but be very careful they are enough done, as nothing is more disagreeable than the oysters tasting raw.

Pepper-pot.

A good stock made with beef bones or mutton, one small carrot, one onion, three turnips, two heads of celery, a little thyme and sweet-herbs; season to your taste; boil these, and put them through a tamis; then add a little flour and butter; make up some flour and water in little balls, and boil them in the pepper-pot.

Sauce for Pike, or any other fresh-water Fish.

Take half a pint of good beef broth, three table-spoonfuls of cream, one onion sliced fine, a middling sized stick of horseradish scraped, seven or eight pepper-corns, three or four cloves, two anchovies; boil well in a piece of butter as big as a walnut well rolled in flour.

Pike should be boiled with the scales on.

Sauce Piquante.

Pound a table-spoonful of capers and one pound of minced parsley as fine as possible, add the yolks of three hard eggs; rub them together with a table-spoonful of mustard. Bone six anchovies, pound them, and rub them through a hair sieve; mix with these two spoonfuls of oil, one of vinegar, one of shalot, and a few grains of cayenne pepper. Rub all together in a mortar till thoroughly incorporated; then stir them into half a pound of good gravy, or melted butter, and pass the whole through a sieve.

Sauce Piquante, to serve hot.

Put into a stewpan a bit of butter, with two onions sliced, a carrot, a parsnip, a little thyme, laurel, basil, two cloves, two shalots, a clove of garlic, parsley, and scallions; turn the whole over the fire till it is well coloured; then shake in some flour, and moisten it with some broth, a spoonful of white wine vinegar, and a squeeze of a lemon, and strain it through a sieve, adding a little cayenne and salt. It is good with every thing.

Another.

Simmer a gill of white wine with as much broth, and, when it is consumed to half, put in a shalot, a little garlic, and some salad herbs shred very fine; let it boil, and then add a bit of butter of the size of a walnut, mixed with flour, salt, and whole pepper, thickening the whole over the fire.

Sauce Piquante, to serve cold.

Shred very fine all sorts of garden-herbs, thyme, sage, parsley, chervil, half a clove of garlic, and two shalots; dilute the whole with a small tea-spoonful of mus-tard, salad oil, a little vinegar, the squeeze of a lemon; add a little salt and cayenne. You may add an anchovy: this is excellent with cold partridge or game, or any hot or cold veal.

Poivrade Sauce.

Boil half a pint of the best vinegar, half a pint of water, two large onions, half a handful of horseradish, and a little pounded white pepper, some salt and shalot, all together a quarter of an hour. If you would have it clear, strain and bottle it: if you chuse, add a little gravy when you use it.

Poor Man's Sauce.

A handful of parsley leaves picked from the stalks, shred fine, and a little salt strewed over; shred six young green onions, put them to the parsley, with three table-spoonfuls of oil, and five of vinegar, some ground black pepper, and salt. Pickled French beans or gherkins, cut fine, may be added, or a little grated horseradish.

Quin's Fish Sauce.

A pint of old mushroom ketchup, a pint of old walnut pickle, six anchovies finely pounded, six cloves of garlic, three pounded, three not, and half a tea-spoonful of cayenne pepper.

Ragout Sauce.

One ounce of salt; half an ounce of mustard; a quarter of an ounce of allspice; black pepper ground, and lemon-peel grated, half an ounce each; of ginger and nutmeg grated, a quarter of an ounce each; cayenne pepper two drachms. Pound all these, and pass them through a sieve, infused in a quart of vinegar or wine, and bottle them for use.

Spice in ragout is indispensable to give it a flavour, but not a predominating one.

Sauce de Ravigotte.

Pick some parsley, sage, mint, thyme, basil, and balm, from the stalks, and cut them fine; slice two large onions very thin: put all these into a mortar, beat them thoroughly, and add pepper and salt, some rocambole, and two blades of mace cut fine. Beat these well, and mix them by degrees with gravy till of the thickness of butter; put them into a stewpan, and boil them up. Strain the gravy from the herbs; add to it a glass of wine and a spoonful of oil; beat these together, and pour it into a sauce-boat.

Sauce Ravigotte à la Bourgeoise.

Tie some parsley, sage, mint, thyme, and basil, in a bunch; put them into a saucepan of boiling water, and let them boil about a minute; take them out, squeeze the water from them, chop them very fine, and add a clove of garlic and two large onions minced very fine. Put the whole into a stewpan, with half a pint of broth, some pepper, and salt; boil it up, and add a spoonful of vinegar.

Relishing Sauce.

Put a wine glass of good stock jelly, made into broth, into a stewpan, half a spoonful of the best white wine vinegar, a little salt, a few whole peppercorns, and a bit of butter, the size of a walnut, mixed up with a little flour in balls, some tarragon, chervil, pimpernel, thyme, and shalot, with garden cresses; boil these herbs in water, having cut them very small; put them into the sauce, and thicken it to a thin creamy consistency over the fire. This sauce is good with any thing, fish, flesh, or fowl.

Sauce à-la-Remoulade. No. 1.

Take two large spoonfuls of capers cut fine, as much parsley, two anchovies, washed and boned, two cloves of garlic, and a little shalot; cut them separately, and then mix them together; put a little rich gravy into a stewpan, with two spoonfuls of oil, one of mustard, and the juice of a large lemon. Make it quite hot, and put in your other ingredients, with salt, pepper, and the leaves of a few sweet-herbs, picked from their stalks. Stir it well together, and let it be four minutes over a brisk fire.

Sauce à-la-Remoulade. No. 2.

Put into a stewpan a shalot, parsley, scallions, a little bit of garlic, two anchovies, some capers, the whole shred very fine. Dilute it with a little mustard, oil, and vinegar, and two table-spoonfuls of good cullis.

Sauce à-la-Remoulade. No. 3.—For cold Chicken, or Lobster Salad.

Two yolks of eggs boiled hard must be bruised very fine, with a tea-spoonful of cold water; add a tea-spoonful of mustard, and two table-spoonfuls of salad oil. When these are well mixed, add a tea-spoonful of chopped parsley, one clove of shalot, and a little tarragon; these must be chopped very fine, and well mixed; then add three table-spoonfuls of vinegar and one of cream. The chicken or lobster should be cut in small thick pieces (not sliced) and placed, with small quarters of lettuces and hard eggs quartered, alternately, so as to fill the dish in a varied form. The sauce is then poured over it.

Rice Sauce.

Steep a quarter of a pound of rice in a pint of milk, with onion, pepper, &c. When the rice is boiled quite tender, take out the spice, rub it through a sieve, and add to it a little milk or cream. This is a very delicate white sauce.

Richmond Sauce, for boiled Chicken.

Half a pint of cream, the liver of the chicken, a little parsley, an anchovy, some caper liquor, the yolks of two hard-boiled eggs, a little pepper, salt, nutmeg, and juice of lemon, with a piece of butter, about the size of a walnut, to thicken it. Send it up hot, with the chicken.

Sauce for any kind of roasted Meat.

While the mutton, beef, hare, or turkey, is roasting, put a plate under it, with a little good broth, three spoonfuls of red wine, a slice of onion, a little grated cheese, an anchovy, washed and minced, and a bit of butter; let the meat drop into it. When it is taken up, put the sauce into a pan that has been rubbed with onion; give it a boil up; strain it through a sieve, and serve it up under your roast, or in a boat.

Sauce Robert.

Melt an ounce of butter, and put to it half an ounce of onion, mixed fine; turn it with a wooden spoon till it takes a light brown colour; stir into it a table-spoonful of mushroom ketchup, and the same quantity of port wine. Add half a pint of broth, a quarter of a tea-spoonful of pepper, and the same of salt; give them a boil; add a tea-spoonful of mustard, the juice of half a lemon, and one or two tea-spoonfuls of vinegar or tarragon.

Another.

Cut a few large onions and some fat bacon into square pieces; put these together into a saucepan over a fire, and shake them well to prevent their burning. When brown, put in some good veal gravy, with a little pepper and salt; let them stew gently till the onions are tender; then add a little salt, vinegar, and mustard, and serve up.

Sauce for Salad.

The yolk of one egg, one tea-spoonful of mustard, one tea-spoonful of tarragon vinegar, three table-spoonfuls of oil, one table-spoonful of common vinegar, chives, according to taste.

Shalot Sauce, for boiled Mutton.

Mince four shalots fine, put them into a stewpan, with about half a pint of the liquor in which the mutton is boiled; put in a table-spoonful of vinegar, a quarter of a tea-spoonful of pepper, a little salt, a bit of butter, of the size of a walnut, rolled in flour; shake them together, and boil.

Spanish Sauce.

Put a cullis (that is always the stock or meat jelly,) in good quantity into a stewpan, with a glass of white wine, the same quantity of fresh made broth, a bunch of parsley, and shalots, one clove of garlic, half a laurel leaf, parsley, scallions, onions, any other root you please for the sake of flavour, such as celery or carrots. Boil it two hours over a slow fire, take the fat off, and strain it through a sieve; and then add salt, large pepper, and the least sprinkle of sugar.

This is very good with beef, mutton, and many sorts of game, venison and hare in particular; for which substitute a glass of red wine instead of white.

Sauce for Steaks.

A glass of small beer, two anchovies, a little thyme, parsley, an onion, some savory, nutmeg, and lemon-peel; cut all these together, and, when the steaks are ready, pour the fat out of the pan, and put in the small beer, with the other ingredients and a piece of butter rolled in flour: let it simmer, and strain it over the steaks.

Sultana Sauce.

Put a pint of cullis into a stewpan with a glass of white wine, two slices of peeled lemons, two cloves, a clove of garlic, half a laurel-leaf, parsley, scallions, onions, and turnip. Boil it an hour and a half over a slow fire, reducing it to a creamy consistency; strain it very carefully through a sieve, and then add a little salt, the yolk of an egg boiled hard and chopped, and a little boiled parsley shred fine.

This sauce is very good with poultry.

Tomata Ketchup.

Take a quart of tomata pulp and juice, three ounces of salt, one ounce of garlic pounded, half an ounce of powdered ginger, and a quarter of an ounce of cloves; add two ounces of anchovies or a wine-glassful of the essence, as sold in the shops. Boil all in a tin saucepan half an hour; strain it through a fine hair sieve. To the strained liquor add a quarter of a pint of vinegar, half a pint of white wine, half a quarter of an ounce of mace, which is to be pounded, and a tea-spoonful of cayenne pepper. Let the whole simmer together over a gentle fire twenty minutes; then strain it through fine lawn or muslin. When cold bottle it up, and be careful to keep it close corked. It is fit for use immediately.

The best way to obtain the pulp and juice free from the skin and seeds is to rub it through a hair sieve.

Tomata Sauce. No. 1.

Roast the tomatas before the fire till they are very tender; save all the liquor that runs from them while roasting; then with a spoon gently scoop out the pulp from the skins; avoid touching them with your fingers: add to the pulp a small quantity of shred ginger, and a few young onions cut very small. Salt it well, and mix the whole together with vinegar, or the best common wine. Put it into pint bottles, as it keeps best with only a bladder tied over.

This is to mix with all other sauces in the small cruet for fish.

Tomata Sauce. No. 2.

Take twelve or fifteen tomatas, ripe and red; cut them in half, and squeeze out all the water and seeds; add capsicums, and two or three table-spoonfuls of beef gravy; set them on a slow fire or stove, for an hour, till melted; rub them through a tamis into a clean stewpan, with a little white pepper and salt; then simmer for a few minutes. The French cooks add a little tarragon vinegar, or a shalot.

Tomata Sauce. No. 3.

When the fruit is ripe, bake it tender, skin, and rub the pulp through a sieve. To every pound of pulp add a quart of chili vinegar, one ounce of garlic, one of shalots, both sliced, half an ounce of salt, a little cayenne pepper, and the juice of three lemons. Boil all together for twenty minutes.

Savoury Jelly for a Turkey.

Spread some slices of veal and ham in the bottom of a stewpan, with a carrot and turnip, and two or three onions. Stew upon a slow fire till the liquor is of as deep a brown as you wish. Add pepper, mace, a very little isinglass, and salt to your taste. Boil ten minutes; strain through a French strainer; skim off all the fat; put in the whites of three eggs, and pass all through a strainer till it is quite clear.

Sauce for Turkey or Chicken.

Boil a spoonful of the best mace very tender, and also the liver of the turkey, but not too much, which would make it hard; pound the mace with a few drops of the liquor to a very fine pulp; then pound the liver, and put about half of it to the mace, with pepper, salt, and the yolk of an egg, boiled hard, and then dissolved; to this add by degrees the liquor that drains from the turkey, or some other good gravy. Put these liquors to the pulp, and boil them some time; then take half a pint of oysters and boil them but a little, and lastly, put in white wine, and butter wrapped in a little flour. Let it boil but a little, lest the wine make the oysters hard; and just at last scald four spoonfuls of good cream, and add, with a little lemon-juice, or pickled mushrooms will do better.

Sauce for boiled Turkey or Fowl.

Take an anchovy, boil it in a quarter of a pint of water; put to it a blade of mace and some peppercorns; strain it off; then put to it two spoonfuls of cream, with butter and flour.

Venison Sauce.

Take vinegar, water, and claret, of each a glassful, an onion stuck with cloves, salt, anchovies, pepper and cloves, of each a spoonful; boil all these together, and strain through a sieve.

Sweet Venison Sauce.

Take a small stick of cinnamon, and boil it in half a pint of claret; then add as much finely grated bread-crumbs as will make a thick pap; and, after it has boiled thoroughly, sweeten it with the powder of the best sugar.

Walnut Ketchup. No. 1.

Take walnuts when they are fit to pickle, beat them in a mortar, press out the juice through a piece of cloth, let it stand one night, then pour the liquor from the sediment, and to every pint put one pound of anchovies; let them boil together till the anchovies are dissolved; then skim, and to every pint of liquor add an eighth of an ounce of mace, the same of cloves and Jamaica pepper, half a pint of common vinegar, half a pound of shalots, with a few heads of garlic, and a little cayenne. Boil all together till the shalots are tender, and when cold bottle up for use.

A spoonful of this ketchup put into good melted butter makes an excellent fish-sauce; it is equally fine in gravy for ducks or beef-steaks.

Walnut Ketchup. No. 2.

Take half a bushel of green walnuts, before the shell is formed, and grind them in a crab-mill, or beat them in a marble mortar. Squeeze out the juice, through a coarse cloth, wringing the cloth well to get out all the juice, and to every gallon put a quart of wine, a quarter of a pound of anchovies, the same quantity of bay salt, one ounce of allspice, half an ounce of cloves, two ounces of long pepper, half an ounce of mace, a little ginger, and horseradish, cut in slices. Boil all together till reduced to half the quantity; pour it into a pan, when cold, and bottle it. Cork it tight, and it will be fit for use in three months.

If you have any pickle left in the jar after the walnuts are used, put to every gallon two heads of garlic, a quart of red wine, and of cloves, mace, long, black, and Jamaica pepper, one ounce each; boil them all together till reduced to half the quantity; pour the liquor into a pan; bottle it the next day for use, and cork it tight.

Walnut Ketchup. No. 3.

Pound one hundred walnuts very fine, put them in a glazed pan with a quart of vinegar; stir them daily for ten days; squeeze them very dry through a coarse cloth. Boil the liquor, and skim it as long as any thing will rise; then add spice, ginger, anchovies instead of salt, and boil it up for use.

Walnut Ketchup. No. 4.

Take one hundred walnuts, picked in dry weather, and bruise them well in a mortar. Squeeze out the juice; add a large handful of salt; boil and skim it well; then put into the juice an equal quantity of white wine vinegar, or the vinegar in which pickled walnuts have been steeped, a little red wine, anchovies unwashed, four or five cloves of garlic, as many blades of mace, two dozen cloves, and a little whole pepper. Boil it six or seven minutes, and when cold bottle it. If higher spiced the better.

Walnut Ketchup. No. 5.

Pound your walnuts; strew some salt upon them, and let them stand a day or two; strain them; to every pint of juice put half a pound of anchovies, and boil them in it till they are dissolved. Then strain the liquor, and to every pint add two drachms of mace, the same quantity of cloves, some black pepper, one ounce of dried shalots, and a little horseradish.

White Sauce.

Put some good veal or fowl cullis into a stewpan, with a piece of crumb of bread, about the size of a tea-cup, a bunch of parsley, thyme, scallions, a clove of garlic, a handful of butter, mushrooms, and a glass of white wine: let the whole boil till half the quantity is consumed. Strain it through a coarse sieve, keeping the vegetables apart; then add to it the yolks of three eggs beaten up in three table-spoonfuls of cream, and thicken it over the fire, taking care to keep it continually stirred lest the eggs should curdle. You may either add your vegetables or not.

This sauce may be used with all sorts of meat or fish that are done white.

Another.

Take some cream, a very little shalot, and a little salt; when warmed upon the fire add a piece of butter rolled in flour; stir it gently one way, and make it the consistency of cream. This sauce is excellent for celery, chickens, veal, &c.

White Wine sweet Sauce.

Break a stick of cinnamon, and set it over the fire in a saucepan, with enough water to cover it; boil it up two or three times; add a quarter of a pint of wine and about two spoonfuls of powdered sugar, and break in two bay-leaves; boil all these together; strain off the liquor through a sieve; put it in a sauceboat or terrine, and serve up.

CONFECTIONARY.

Almacks.

TAKE plums, or apricots, baking pears, and apples, of each a pound; slice the pears and apples, and open the plums; put them in layers in an earthen mug, and set it in a slow oven. When the fruit is soft, squeeze it through a colander; add a pound of sugar; place it on the fire, and let it simmer, till it will leave the pan clear. Then put it into an earthen mould to cut out for use, or drop it on a plate, and let it stand till it is so dry that paper will not stick to it, then put it by for use. You must stir it all the time it is on the fire, or it will burn.

Almond Butter.

Put half a pound of blanched almonds, finely beaten, into a quart of cream and a pint of milk mixed well together. Strain off the almonds, and set the cream over the fire to boil. Take the yolks of twelve eggs and three whites well beaten; let it remain over the fire; keep stirring till it begins to curdle. Put it into a cloth strainer and tie it up, letting it stand till the thin has drained off. When cold, break it with a spoon, and sweeten with sifted sugar.

Almond Cheesecakes.

Take a quarter of a pound of Jordan almonds and twelve or fourteen apricot or peach kernels; blanch them all in cold water, and beat them very fine with rose-water and a little sack. Add a quarter of a pound of fine powder sugar, by degrees, and beat them very light: then put a quarter of a pound of the best butter just melted, with two or three spoonfuls of sweet thick cream; beat them well again. Then, add four eggs, leaving out the whites, beaten as light as possible. When you have just done beating, put a little grated nutmeg. Bake them in a nice short crust; and, when they are just going into the oven, grate over them a little fine sugar.

Almond Cream.

Beat half a pound of fine almonds, blanched in cold water, very fine, with orange-flower water. Take a quart of cream boiled, cooled, and sweetened; put the almonds into it by degrees, and when they are well mixed strain it through canvass, squeezing it very well. Then stir it over the fire until it thickens; if you like it richly perfumed, add one grain of ambergris, and if you wish to give it the ratafia flavour, beat some apricot kernels with it.

Unboiled Almond Cream.

Take half a pound of almonds; blanch them, and cut out all their spots: then beat them very fine, in a clean stone or wooden mortar, with a little rose-water, and mix them with one quart of sweet cream. Strain them as long as you can get any out. Take as much fine sugar as will sweeten it, a nutmeg cut into quarters, some large mace, three spoonfuls of orange-flower water, as much rose-water, with musk or ambergris dissolved in it; put all these things into a glass churn; shake them continually up and down till the mass is as thick as butter; before it is broken, pour it all into a clean dish; take out the nutmeg and the mace; when it is settled smooth, scatter some comfits or scrape some hard sugar upon it.

Almond Paste, for Shapes, &c.

Blanch half a pound of almonds in cold water; let them lie twenty-four hours in cold water, then beat them in a mortar, till they are very fine, adding the whites of eggs as you beat them. Put them in a stewpan over a stove fire, with half a pound of double-refined sugar, pounded and sifted through a lawn sieve; stir it while over the fire, till it becomes a little stiff; then take it out, and put it between two plates, till it is cold. Put it in a pan, and keep it for use. It will keep a great while in a cool place. When you use it, pound it a little in a mortar, or mould it in your hands; then roll it out thin in whatever shape you choose, or make it up into walnuts or other moulds; press it down close that it may receive the impression of the nut, &c., and with a pin take it out of the mould and turn it out upon copper sheets, and so proceed till you have a sufficient quantity. The mould should be lightly touched with oil. Bake them of a light brown; fill them with sweetmeats, &c. and such as should be closed, as nuts, &c. cement together with isinglass boiled down to a proper consistence.

Almond Puffs.

Take one pound of fine sugar, and put water to it to make a wet candy: boil it till pretty thick; then put in a pound of beaten almonds, and mix them together, still keeping it stirred over a slow fire, but it must not boil, till it is as dry as paste. Then beat it a little in a mortar; put in the peel of a lemon grated, and a pound of sifted sugar; rub them well together, and wet this with the froth of whites of eggs.

Another way.

Blanch and beat fine two ounces of sweet almonds, with orange-flower water, or brandy; beat the whites of three eggs to a very high froth, and then strew in a little sifted sugar till it is as stiff as paste. Lay it in cakes, and bake it on paper in a cool oven.

Angelica, to candy.

Take the youngest shoots; scrape and boil them in water till tender, and put them on a cloth to drain. Make a very strong syrup of sugar; put in the angelica while the syrup is hot, but not boiling. Set it in a tin before the fire, or in the sun, for three or four days, to dry.

Apples, to do.

Scoop as many apples as you choose to do; dip them several times in syrup, and fill them with preserved raspberries or apricots; then roll them in paste, and when baked put on them either a white iceing, or with the white of an egg rub them over; sift on sugar, and glaze them with a hot salamander.

Pippins, to candy.

Take fine large pippins; pare and core them whole into an earthen platter: strew over them fine sugar; and sprinkle on the sugar a little rose-water. Bake them in an oven as hot as for manchet, and stop it up close. Let them remain there half an hour; then take them out of the dish, and lay them on the bottom of a sieve; leave them three or four days, till quite dry, when they will look clear as amber, and be finely candied.

Pippins, to dry.

Take two pounds of fine sugar and a pint of water; let it boil up and skim it; put in sixteen quarters of Kentish pippins pared and cored, and let them boil fast till they are very clear. Put in a pint of jelly of pippins, and boil it till it jellies; then put in the juice of a lemon; just let it boil up, and put them in bottles. You may put in the rind of an orange, first boiled in water, then cut in long thin pieces, and put it into the sugar at the same time with the pippins.

Apples, to preserve green.

Take green apples the size of a walnut, codlings are the best, with the stalks on; put them into spring water with vine leaves in a preserving pan, and cover them close; set them on a slow fire. When they are soft, take off the skins, and put them with vine leaves in the same water as before, and when quite cold put them over the fire till they are quite green. Then put them into a dish without liquor; sift loaf sugar over them while they are hot; when dry, they make a good syrup.

Golden Pippins, to preserve.

Into a pint of clear spring water put a pound of double-refined sugar, and set it on the fire. Neatly pare and take out the stalks and eyes of a pound of pippins; put them into the sugar and water; cover them close, and boil them as fast as you can for half a quarter of an hour. Take them off a little to cool; set them on again to boil as fast and as long as they did before. Do this three or four times till they are very clear; then cover them close.

Crabs, to preserve.

Gently scald them two or three times in a thin syrup; when they have lain a fortnight, the syrup must be made rich enough to keep, and the crabs scalded in it.

Siberian Crabs, to preserve (transparent.)

Take out the core and blossom with a bodkin; make a syrup with half their weight of sugar; put in the apples, and keep them under the syrup with a spoon, and they will be done in ten minutes over a slow fire. When cold, tie them down with brandy paper.

Another way.

To each pound of fruit add an equal quantity of sugar, which clarify with as little water as possible, and skim it thoroughly; then put in the fruit, and boil it gently till it begins to break. Take out the apples, boil the syrup again till it grows thick, and then pour it over them. They are not to be pared; and half the stalk left on.

Golden Pippins, to stew.

Cut the finest pippins, and pare them as thin as you can. As you do them, throw them into cold water to preserve their colour. Make a middling thick syrup, of about half a pound of sugar to a pint of water, and when it boils up skim it, and throw in the pippins with a bit of lemon-peel. Keep up a brisk fire; throw the syrup over the apples as they boil, to make them look clear. When they are done, add lemon-juice to your taste; and when you can run a straw through them they are done enough. Put them, without the syrup, into a bowl; cover them close, and boil the syrup till you think it sufficiently thick: then take it off, and throw it hot upon the pippins, keeping them always under it.

Apple Cheese.

Seven pounds of apples cored, one pound and three quarters of sugar, the juice and peel of two lemons; boil these in a stewpan till quite a thick jelly. Bake the apple till soft; break it as smooth as possible; put it into pots, and tie down close.

Conserve of Apples.

Take as many golden rennets as will fill the dish that is to go to table; pick them of a size; pare them, and take out the cores at the bottom, that they may appear whole at the top. With the cores and about half a glass of water make a syrup; when it is half done, put in your apples, and let them stew till they are done. Be careful not to break them; place them in your dish; that your syrup may be fine, add the white of an egg well beaten; skim it, and it will be clarified. Squeeze into it the juice of a lemon, with the peel cut in small shreds. This should boil a minute; then throw over the syrup, which should be quite a jelly.

Apple Demandon.

The whites of seven or eight very fresh eggs, put into a flat dish, with a very little finely sifted sugar, and beaten to a very thick froth. It will require to be beaten full half an hour before it becomes of a sufficient substance. It is then to be put over the apple and custard, and piled up to some height; after which place it in a very quick oven, and let it remain till it becomes partially of a light brown colour.

It should be done immediately before it is sent up to table.

Apple Fraise.

Pare six large apples, take out the cores, cut them in slices, and fry them on both sides with butter; put them on a sieve to drain; mix half a pint of milk and two eggs, with flour, to batter, not too stiff; put in a little lemon-peel, shred very fine, and a little beaten cinnamon. Put some butter into a frying-pan, and make it hot; put in half the batter, and lay the apples on it; let it fry a little to set it; then put the remaining batter over it; fry it on one side; then turn it, and fry the other brown: put it into a dish; strew powder-sugar over it, and squeeze on it the juice of a Seville orange.

Apple Fritters.

Pare six large apples and cut out the cores; cut them in slices as thick as a half-crown piece. Mix half a pint of cream and two eggs with flour into a stiff batter, put in a glass of wine or brandy, a little lemon-peel, shred very fine, two ounces of powder-sugar: mix it well up, and then put in the apples. Have a pan of hog's lard boiling hot; put in every slice singly as fast as you can, and fry them quick, of a fine gold colour on both sides; then take them out, and put them on a sieve to drain; lay them on a dish, and sprinkle them with sugar. For fritters be careful that the fat in which you fry them is quite sweet and clean.

Apple Jelly. No. 1.

Pare and slice pippins, or sharp apples, into a stewpan, with just as much water as will cover them; boil them as fast as possible till half the liquid is wasted; then strain them through a jelly-bag, and to every pint of juice put three quarters of a pound of sugar. Boil it again till it becomes jelly; put lemon-juice and lemon-peel to the palate. Some threads of lemon-peel should remain in the jelly.

Apple Jelly. No. 2.

Take about a half sieve of john apples, or golden pippins; pare them, and put them in a clean bright copper pan; add as much river water as will cover them; set them over a charcoal fire, turning them now and then, till they are boiled tender. Put a hair-sieve over a pan, and throw them on to drain; then put the apples in a large pan or mortar, and beat them into pulp. Put them back into the copper pan, adding about half the water that came from them; then set them on the fire, and stir them till they boil two or three minutes. Strain them into a flannel jelly-bag; it should run out quite slowly, and be thick like syrup; you should allow it six or eight hours to run or drop. Then measure the jelly into a bright copper pan, and to each pint add one pound of treble-refined sugar; put it on a slow fire till the sugar is melted; then let the fire be made up, that it may boil; keep skimming it constantly. When you hold up the skimmer near the window, or in the cool, and you perceive it hangs about half an inch, with a drop at the end, then add the juice of half a lemon, if a small quantity. Take it off the fire, and pour it into gallipots.

The apples that are supposed to have the most jelly in them in this country are the john apple. The best time to make the jelly is the autumn; the riper they get, the less jelly. If the flannel bag is quite new, it should be washed in several clean warm waters, without soap. The jelly, if well made, should appear like clear water, about the substance of currant-jelly.

Apple Jelly. No. 3.

Take apples, of a light green, without any spot or redness, and rather sour; cut them in quarters, taking out the cores, and put them into a quart of water; let them boil to a pulp, and strain it through a hair-sieve, or jelly-bag. To a pint of liquor take a pound of double-refined sugar; wet your sugar, and boil it to a thick syrup, with the white and shell of an egg: then strain your syrup, and put your liquor to it. Let it boil again, and, as it boils, put in the juice of a lemon and the peel, pared extremely thin, and cut as fine as threads; when it jellies, which you may know by taking up some in your spoon, put it in moulds; when cold, turn it out into your dish; it should be so transparent as to let you see all the flowers of your china dish through it, and quite white.

Crab Jam or Jelly.

Pare and core the crabs; to fifteen pounds of crabs take ten pounds of sugar, moistened with a little water; boil them well, skimming the top. When boiled tender, and broke to the consistency of jam, pour it into your pans, and let it stand twenty-four hours. It is better the second year than the first. The crabs should be ripe.

Pippin or Codling-Jelly.

Slice a pound of pippins or codlings into a pint of clear spring water; let them boil till the water has extracted all the flavour of the fruit; strain it out, and to a pint of this liquor take a pound of double-refined sugar, boiled to sugar again; then put in your codling liquor; boil it a little together as fast as you can. Put in your golden pippins; boil them up fast for a little while; just before the last boiling, squeeze in the juice of a lemon; boil it up quick once more, taking care the apples do not lose their colour; cut them, and put them in glasses with the jelly. It makes a very pretty middle or corner dish.

Apples and Pears, to dry.

Take Kirton pippins or royal russets, golden pippins or nonpareils; finely pare and quarter the russets, and pare and take out the core also of the smaller apples. Take the clean tops of wicker baskets or hampers, and put the apples on the wickers in a cool oven. Let them remain in till the oven is quite cold: then they must be turned as you find necessary, and the cool oven repeated till they are properly dry. They must stand some time before they are baked, and kept carefully from the damp air. The richer the pears the better; but they must not be over-ripe.

Apricots in Brandy.

The apricots must be gathered before they are quite ripe, and, as the fruit is usually riper on one side than the other, you must prick the unripe side with the point of a penknife, or a very large needle. Put them into cold water, and give them a great deal of room in the preserving-pan; and proceed in the same manner as directed for peaches. If they are not well coloured, it is owing to an improper choice of the fruit, being too ripe or too high coloured, provided the brandy be of the right sort.

Apricot Chips.

Cut apricots when ripe in small thin pieces; take double-refined sugar, pounded very small and sifted through a fine sieve, and strew a little at the bottom of a silver basin; then put in your chips, and more of your sugar. Set them over a chaffing-dish of coals, shaking your basin, lest the chips should stick to the bottom, till you put in your sugar. When your sugar is all candied, lay them on glass plates; put them in a stove, and turn them out.

Apricot Burnt Cream.

Boil a pint of cream with some bitter almonds pounded, and strain it off. When the cream is cold, add to it the yolks of four eggs, with half a spoonful of flour, well mixed together; set it over the fire; keep stirring it till it is thick. Add to it a little apricot jam; put it in your dish; sift powdered sugar over it, and brown it with your salamander.

Apricots, to dry.

Pare and stone a pound of apricots, and put to them three quarters of a pound of double-refined sugar, strewing some of the sugar over the apricots as you pare them, that they may not lose colour. When they are all pared put the remainder of the sugar on them; let them stand all night, and in the morning boil them on a quick fire till they are clear. Then let them stand till next day covered with a sheet of white paper. Set them on a gentle fire till scalding hot; let them stand three days in the syrup; lay them out on stone plates; put them into a stove, and turn them every day till they are dry.

Apricot Jam.

Take two pounds of apricot paste in pulp and a pint of strong codling liquor; boil them very fast together till the liquor is almost wasted; then put to it one pound and a half of fine sugar pounded; boil it very fast till it jellies; put it into pots, and it will make clear cakes in the winter.

Apricot and Plum Jam.

Stone the fruit; set them over the fire with half a pint of water; when scalded, rub them through a sieve, and to every pound of pulp put a pound of sifted loaf-sugar. Set it over a brisk fire in a preserving-pan; when it boils, skim it well, and throw in the kernels of the apricots and half an ounce of bitter almonds blanched; boil it together fast for a quarter of an hour, stirring it all the time.

Apricot Paste.

Take ripe apricots, pare, stone, and quarter them, and put them into a skillet, setting them on embers, and stirring them till all the pieces are dissolved. Then take three quarters of their weight in fine sugar, and boil it to a candy; put in the apricots, and stir it a little on the fire; then turn it out into glasses. Set it in a warm stove; when it is dry on one side, turn the other. You may take apricots not fully ripe, and coddle them, and that will do also.

Another.

Pare and stone your apricots; to one pound of fruit put one pound of fine sugar, and boil all together till they break. Then to five pounds of paste put three pounds of codling jelly, and make a candy of three pounds of fine sugar. Put it in all together; just scald it, and put it in little pots to dry quickly. Turn it out to dry on plates or glasses.

Apricots, to preserve.

Stone and pare four dozen of large apricots, and cover them with three pounds of fine sugar finely beaten; put in some of the sugar as you pare them. Let them stand at least six or seven hours; then boil them on a slow fire till they are clear and tender. If any of them are clear before the rest, take them out and put them in again. When the rest are ready, let them stand closely covered with paper till next day. Then make very strong codling jelly: to two pounds of jelly add two pounds of sugar, which boil till they jelly; and while boiling make your apricots scalding hot; put the jelly to the apricots, and boil them, but not too fast. When the apricots rise in the jelly and jelly well, put them in pots or glasses, and cover closely with brandy paper.

Another way.

Cut in half, and break in pieces, ripe apricots; put them in a preserving pan, simmer for a few minutes, and pass through a fine hair sieve: no water to be used. Add three quarters of a pound of white powdered sugar to a pound of fruit; put in the kernels; mix all together, and boil for twenty minutes: well skim when it begins to boil. Put it into pots; when cold, cover close with paper dipped in brandy, and tie down with an outer cover of paper.

Apricots, to preserve whole.

Gather the fruit before it is too ripe, and to one pound put three quarters of a pound of fine sugar. Stone and pare the apricots as you put them into the pan; lay sugar under and over them, and let them stand till next day. Set them on a quick fire, and let them just boil; skim well; cover them till cold, or till the following day; give them another boil; put them in pots, and strew a little sugar over them while coddling, to make them keep their colour.

Apricots, to preserve in Jelly.

To a pound of apricots, before they are stoned and pared, weigh a pound and a quarter of the best pounded sugar. Stone and pare the fruit, and, as you pare, sprinkle some sugar under and over them. When the sugar is pretty well melted, set them on the fire and boil them. Keep out some sugar to strew on them in the boiling, which assists to clear them. Skim very clear, and turn the fruit with a ladle or a feather. When clear and tender, put them in glasses; add to the syrup a quarter of a pint of strong pippin liquor, and nearly the weight of it in sugar; let it boil awhile, and put it to the apricots. The fire should be brisk, as the sooner any sweetmeat is done the clearer and better it will be. Let the liquor run through a jelly-bag, that it may clear before you put the syrup to it, or the syrup of the apricots to boil.

French Bances.

Take half a pint of water, a bit of lemon-peel, a piece of butter the size of a walnut, and a little orange-flower water; boil them gently three or four minutes; take out the lemon-peel, and add to it by degrees half a pint of flour: keep it boiling and stirring until it is a stiff paste; then take it off the fire, and put in six eggs, well beaten, leaving out three whites. Beat all very well for at least half an hour, till it is a stiff light paste; then take two pounds of hog's-lard; put it in a stewpan; give it a boil up, and, if the bances are of a right lightness, fry them; keep stirring them all the time till they are of a proper brown. A large dish will take six or seven minutes boiling. When done, put them in a dish to drain; keep them by the fire; strew sugar over them; and, when you are going to fry them, drop them through the handle of a key.

Barberries, to preserve.

Tie up the finest maiden barberries in bunches; to one pound of them put two pounds and a quarter of sugar; boil the sugar to a thick syrup, and when thick enough stir it till it is almost cold. Put in the barberries; set them on the fire, and keep them as much under the syrup as you can, shaking the pan frequently. Let them just simmer till the syrup is hot through, but not boiling, which would wrinkle them. Take them out of the syrup, and let them drain on a lawn sieve; put the syrup again into the pot, and boil it till it is thick. When half cold put in the barberries, and let them stand all night in the preserving-pan. If the syrup has become too thin, take out the fruit and boil it again, letting it stand all night: then put it into pots, and cover it with brandy paper.

Biscuits.

Take one pound of loaf sugar, finely beaten and sifted; then take eight eggs, whites and all; beat them in a wooden bowl for an hour; then take a quarter of a pound of blanched almonds, beat them very small with some rose-water; put them into the bowl, and beat them for an hour longer; then shake in five ounces of fine flour and a spoonful of coriander seed, and one of caraways. Beat them half an hour; butter your plates, and bake them.

Another way.

Take one pound of flour; mix it stiff with water; then roll it very thin; cut out the biscuits with cutters, and bake them.

Dutch Biscuits.

Take the whites of six eggs in fine sugar, and the whites of four in flour; then beat your eggs with the sugar and flour well with a whisk: butter your pans, and only half fill them; strew them over with sugar before you put them in the oven; grate lemon-peel over them.

Ginger Biscuits.

One pound of flour, half a pound of butter, half a pound of loaf sugar, rather more than one ounce of ginger powdered, all well mixed together. Let it stand before the fire for half an hour; roll it into thin paste, and cut out with a coffee-cup or wine-glass: bake it for a few minutes.

Lemon Biscuits.

Blanch half a pound of sweet almonds in cold water; beat them with the whites of six eggs, first whipped up to a froth; put in a little at a time as they rise; the almonds must be very fine. Then add one pound of double-refined sugar, beaten and sifted; put in, by degrees, four ounces of fine flour, dried well and cold again; the yolks of six eggs well beaten; the peels of two large lemons finely grated: beat these all together about half an hour; put them in tin pans; sift on a little sugar. The oven must be pretty quick, though you keep the door open while you bake them.

Another way.

Take three pounds of fine sugar, and wet it with a spoonful and a half of gum-dragon, and put in the juice of lemons, but make the mass as stiff as you can: mix it well, and beat it up with white of eggs. When beaten very light, put in two grains of musk and a great deal of grated lemon; drop the paste into round papers, and bake it.

Ratafia Biscuits.

Blanch two ounces of bitter almonds in cold water, and beat them extremely fine with orange-flower water and rose-water. Put in by degrees the whites of five eggs, first beaten to a light froth. Beat it extremely well; then mix it up with fine sifted sugar to a light paste, and lay the biscuits on tin plates with wafer paper. Make the paste so light that you may take it up with a spoon. Lay it in cakes, and bake them in a rather brisk oven. If you make them with sweet almonds only, they are almond puffs or cakes.

Table Biscuits.

Flour, milk, and sugar, well mixed together. Shape the biscuits with the top of a glass, and bake them on a tin.

Blancmange. No. 1.

To one pint of calves' foot or hartshorn jelly add four ounces of almonds blanched and beaten very fine with rose and orange-flower water; let half an ounce of the almonds be bitter, but apricot kernels are better. Put the almonds and jelly, mixed by degrees, into a skillet, with as much sugar as will sweeten it to your taste. Give it two or three boils; then take it up and strain it into a bowl; add to it some thick cream: give it a boil after the cream is in, and keep it stirred while on the fire. When strained, put it into moulds.

Blancmange. No. 2.

Boil three ounces of isinglass in a quart of water till it is reduced to a pint; strain it through a sieve, and let it stand till cold. Take off what has settled at the bottom: then take a pint of cream, two ounces of almonds, and a few bitter ones; sweeten to your taste. Boil all together over the fire, and pour it into your moulds. A laurel leaf improves it greatly.

Blancmange. No. 3.

Take an ounce of isinglass dissolved over the fire in a quarter of a pint of water, strain it into a pint of new milk; boil it, and strain again; sweeten to your taste. Add a spoonful of orange-flower water and one of mountain. Stir it till it is nearly cold, and put it into moulds. Beat a few bitter almonds in it.

Blancmange. No. 4.

Into two quarts of milk put an ounce of isinglass, an ounce of sugar, half the peel of a lemon, and a bit of cinnamon. Keep stirring till it boils.

Dutch Blancmange.

Steep an ounce of the best isinglass two hours in a pint of boiling water. Take a pint of white wine, the yolks of eight eggs well beaten, the juice of four lemons and one Seville orange, and the peel of one lemon; mix them together, and sweeten to your taste. Set it on a clear fire; keep it stirred till it boils, and then strain it off into moulds.

Bread.

Forty pounds of flour, a handful of salt, one quart of yest, three quarts of water; stir the whole together in the kneading trough. Strew over it a little flour, and let it stand covered for one hour. Knead it and make it into loaves, and let them stand a quarter of an hour to rise, before you put them in the oven.

Diet Bread, which keeps moist.

Three quarters of a pound of lump sugar, dissolved in a quarter of a pint of water, half a pound of the best flour, seven eggs, taking away the whites of two; mix the liquid sugar, when it has boiled, with the eggs: beat them up together in a basin with a whisk; then add by degrees the flour, beating all together for about ten minutes; put it into a quick oven. An hour bakes it.

Tin moulds are the best: the dimensions for this quantity are six inches in length and four in depth.

Potato Bread.

Boil a quantity of potatoes; drain them well, strew over them a small quantity of salt, and let them remain in the vessel in which they were boiled, closely covered, for an hour, which makes them mealy: then peel and pound them as smooth as flour. Add eight pounds of potatoes to twelve of wheaten flour; and make it into dough with yest, in the way that bread is generally made. Let it stand three hours to rise.

Rice Bread.

Boil a quarter of a pound of rice till it is quite soft; then put it on the back of a sieve to drain. When cold, mix it with three quarters of a pound of flour, a tea-cupful of milk, a proper quantity of yest, and salt. Let it stand for three hours; then knead it very well, and roll it up in about a handful of flour, so as to make the outside dry enough to put into the oven. About an hour and a quarter will bake a loaf of this size. When baked, it will produce one pound fourteen ounces of very good bread; it is better when the loaves are not made larger than the above-mentioned quantity will produce, but you may make any quantity by allowing the same proportion for each loaf. This bread should not be cut till it is two days old.

Rye Bread.

Take one peck of wheaten flour, six pounds of rye flour, a little salt, half a pint of good yest, and as much warm water as will make it into a stiff dough. Let it stand three hours to rise before you put it into the oven. A large loaf will take three hours to bake.

Scotch short Bread.

Melt a pound of butter, pour it on two pounds of flour, half a tea-cupful of yest, two ounces of caraway seeds, one ounce of Scotch caraways; sweeten to your taste with lump sugar, then knead it well together and roll it out, not too thin; cut in quarters and pinch it round: prick it well with a fork.

Buttered Loaves.

Take three quarts of new milk; put in as much runnet as will turn it; whey the curds very clean; break them small with your hands; put in nine yolks of eggs and one white, a handful of grated bread, half a handful of flour, and a little salt. Mix these well together, working it well with your hands; roll it into small loaves, and bake them in a quick oven three quarters of an hour. Then take half a pound of butter, four spoonfuls of clear water, half a nutmeg sliced very thin, and a little sugar. Set it on a quick fire, stirring it quickly, and let it boil till thick. When the loaves are baked, cut out the top and stir up the crumb with a knife; then pour some of the butter into each of them, and cover them up again. Strew a little sugar on them: before you set them in the oven, beat the yolk of an egg and a little beer together, and with a feather smear them over with it.

Egg Loaf.

Soak crumb of bread in milk for three hours; strain it through a sieve; then put in a little salt, some candied citron and lemon-peel cut small, and sugar to your taste. Put to your paste the yolks only of six or eight new-laid eggs, and beat it till the eggs are mixed. Whip the whites of the eggs till they are frothed; add to the other ingredients, and mix them well. Butter the pan or dish in which you bake your loaf. When baked, turn it out into your dish, scrape some fine sugar upon it, and glaze with a hot shovel.

Buns. No. 1.

Two pounds of flour, a quarter of a pound of butter; rub the butter in the flour like grated bread; set it to the fire to dry: put in one pound of currants and a quarter of a pound of moist sugar, with a few caraway seeds, and two spoonfuls of good yest; make the dough into small buns; set them to rise half an hour: you may put two or three eggs in if you like.

Buns. No. 2.

One pound of fine flour, two pounds of currants, a few caraway seeds, a quarter of a pound of moist sugar, a pint of new milk, and two table-spoonfuls of yest; mix all well together in a stiff paste, and let it stand half an hour to rise; then roll them out, and put them in your tins; let them stand another half hour to rise before you bake them. The above receipt answers equally well for a cake baked in a tin.

Buns. No. 3.

Take flour, butter, and sugar, of each a quarter of a pound, four eggs, and a few caraway seeds. This quantity will make two dozen. Bake them on tins.

Bath Buns.

Take a quarter of a pound of loaf sugar finely powdered, the same quantity of butter, and nearly double of flour dried before the fire, a walnut-shell full of caraway-seeds just bruised, and one egg. Work all these up together into a paste, the thickness of half-a-crown, and cut it with a tea-cup, flour a tin; lay the cakes upon it; take the white of an egg well beat and frothed; lay it on them with a feather, and then grate upon them a little fine sugar.

Another way.

Take one pound of fine flour, dry it well by the fire, sift it, and rub into it a pound of butter, the yolks of four eggs, the whites of two, both beaten light, three spoonfuls of cream, and the like quantity of white wine and ale yest. Let this sponge stand by the fire to rise; then beat it up extremely well and light with your hand; grate in a nutmeg; continue beating till it is ready for the oven; then add a pound of rough caraway seeds, keeping a few out to strew on the top of the cakes before they are put into the oven.

Plain Buns.

Take three pounds of flour, six ounces of butter, six ounces of sugar sifted fine, six eggs, both yolks and whites. Beat your eggs till they will not slip off the spoon; melt the butter in a pint of new milk, with which mix half a pint of good yest; strain it into the flour, and throw in half an ounce of caraway seeds. Work the whole up very light; set it before the fire to rise; then make it up into buns of the size of a penny roll, handling them as little as possible. Twenty minutes will bake them sufficiently.

Butter, to make without churning.

Tie up cream in a fine napkin, and then in a coarse cloth, as you would a pudding: bury it two feet under ground; leave it there for twelve hours, and when you take it up it will be converted into butter.

Black Butter.

To one quart of black gooseberries put one pint of red currants, picked into an earthen jar. Stop it very close, and set it in a pot of cold water over the fire to boil till the juice comes out. Then strain it, and to every pint of liquor put a pound of sugar; boil and skim it till you think it done enough: put it in flat pots, and keep it in a dry place. It will either turn out or cut in slices.

Spanish Butter.

Take two gallons of new milk, boil it, and, when you take it off the fire, put in a quart of cream, giving it a stir; then pour it through a sieve into an earthen pan: lay some sticks over your pan, and cover it with a cloth; if you let it stand thus two days, it will be the better. Skim off the cream thick, and sweeten it to your taste; you may put in a little orange-flower water, and whip it well up.

Cake.

Five pounds of flour dried, six pounds of currants, a quart of boiled cream, a pound and a half of butter, twenty eggs, the whites of six only, a pint of ale yest, one ounce of cinnamon finely beaten, one ounce of cloves and mace also well beaten, a quarter of a pound of sugar, a little salt, half a pound of orange and citron. Put in the cream and butter when it is just warm; mix all well together, and let it stand before the fire to rise. Put it into your hoop, and leave it in the oven an hour and a quarter. The oven should be as hot as for a manchet.

An excellent Cake.

Beat half a pound of sifted sugar and the same quantity of fresh butter to a cream, in a basin made warm; mixing half a pound of flour well dried, six eggs, leaving out four whites, and one table-spoonful of brandy. The butter is to be beaten in first, then the flour, next the sugar, the eggs, and lastly, the brandy. Currants or caraways may be added at pleasure. It must be beaten an hour, and put in the oven immediately.

A great Cake.

Take six quarts of fine flour dried in an oven, six pounds of currants, five pounds of butter, two pounds and a half of sugar, one pound of citron, three quarters of a pound of orange-peel, and any other sweetmeat you think proper; a pound of almonds ground very small, a few coriander seeds beat and sifted, half an ounce of mace, four nutmegs, sixteen eggs, six of the whites, half a pint of sack, and half a pint of ale yest.

Light Cake.

One pound of the finest flour, one ounce of powdered sugar, five ounces of butter, three table-spoonfuls of fresh yest.

A nice Cake.

Take nine eggs; beat the yolks and whites separately; the weight of eight eggs in sugar, and five in flour: whisk the eggs and the sugar together for half an hour; then put in the flour, just before the oven is ready to bake it. Both the sugar and the flour must be sifted and dried.

A Plain Cake.

Take a pound of flour, well dried and sifted; add to it one pound of sugar also dried and sifted; take one pound of butter, and work it in your hands till it is like cream; beat very light the yolks of ten eggs and six whites. Mix all these by degrees, beating it very light, and a little sack and brandy. It must not stand to rise. If you choose fruit, add one pound of currants, washed, picked, and dried.

A very rich Cake.

Two pounds and a half of fresh butter, twenty-four eggs, three-pounds of flour, one pound and a half of sugar, one ounce of mixed spice, four pounds of currants, half a jar of raisins, half of sweet almonds, a quarter of a pound of citron, three quarters of orange and lemon, one gill of brandy, and one nutmeg. First work the butter to a cream; then beat the sugar well in; whisk the eggs half an hour; mix them with the butter and sugar; put in the spice and flour; and, when the oven is ready, mix in the brandy, fruit, and sweetmeats. It will take one hour and a half beating. Let it bake three hours.

Cake without butter.

Beat up eight eggs for half an hour. Have ready powdered and sifted one pound of loaf sugar; shake it in, and beat it half an hour longer. Put to it a quarter of a pound of sweet almonds beat fine with orange-flower water; grate the rind of a lemon into the almonds, and squeeze in the juice. Mix all together. Just before you put it in the oven, add a quarter of a pound of dry flour; rub the hoop or tin with butter. An hour and a half will bake it.

Another.

Take ten eggs and the whites of five; whisk them well, and beat in one pound of finely sifted sugar, and three quarters of a pound of flour: the flour to be put in just before the cake is going to the oven.

Almond Cake.

Take a pound of almonds; blanch them in cold water, and beat them as small as possible in a stone mortar with a wooden pestle, putting in, as you beat them, some orange-flower water. Then take twelve eggs, leaving out half of the whites; beat them well; put them to your almonds, and beat them together, above an hour, till it becomes of a good thickness. As you beat it, sweeten it to your taste with double-refined sugar powdered, and when the eggs are put in add the peel of two large lemons finely rasped. When you beat the almonds in the mortar with orange-water, put in by degrees about four spoonfuls of citron water or ratafia of apricots, or, for want of these, brandy and sack mixed together, two spoonfuls of each. The cake must be baked in a tin pan; flour the pan before you put the cake into it. To try if it is done enough, thrust a straw through it, and if the cake sticks to the straw it is not baked enough; let it remain till the straw comes out clean.

Another.

Take twelve eggs, leaving out half the whites; beat the yolks by themselves till they look white; put to them by degrees one pound of fine sifted sugar; put in, by a spoonful at a time, three quarters of a pound of fine flour, well dried and sifted, with the whites of the eggs well beaten, and continue this till all the flour and the whites are in. Then beat very fine half a pound of fine almonds, with sack and brandy, to prevent their oiling; stir them into the cake. Bake it three quarters of an hour. Ratafia cake is made in the same manner, only keep out two ounces of the almonds, and put in their stead two of apricot kernels; if you have none, use bitter almonds.

Almond Cakes.

Take one pound of almonds, blanch them; then take one pound of double-refined sugar, beaten very small; crack the almonds, one by one, upon the tops; put them into the sugar; mix them, and then beat them well together till they will work like paste. Make them into round cakes; take double-refined sugar, pounded and sifted, beat together with the white of an egg, and, when the cakes are hardened in the oven, take them out, and cover one side with sugar with a feather; then put them into the oven again, and, when one side is hardened, take them out and do the same on the other side. Set them in again to harden, and afterwards lay them up for use.

Clear Almond Cakes.

Take the small sort of almonds; steep them in cold water till they will blanch, and as you blanch them throw them into water. Wipe them dry, and beat them in a stone mortar, with a little rose-water, and as much double-refined sugar, sifted, as will make them into clear paste. Roll them into any size you please; then dry them in an oven after bread has been drawn, so that they may be dry on both sides;

when they are cold, make a candy of sugar; wet it a little with rose-water; set it on the fire; stir it till it boils, then take it off, and let it cool a little. With a feather spread it over the cakes on one side; lay them upon papers on a table; take the lid of a baking-pan, put some coals on it, and set it over the cakes to raise the candy quickly. When they are cold, turn the other side, and serve it in the same manner.

Apple Cake.

Take one pound and a half of white sugar, two pounds of apples, pared and cut thin, and the rind of a large lemon; put a pint of water to the sugar, and boil it to a syrup; put the apples to it, and boil it quite thick. Put it into a mould to cool, and send it cold to table, with a custard, or cream poured round it.

Another.

One pound of apples cut and cored, one pound of sugar put to a quarter of a pint of water, so as to clarify the sugar, with the juice and peel of a lemon, and a little Seville orange. Boil it till it is quite stiff; put it in a mould; when cold it will turn out. You may put it into a little warm water to keep it from breaking when taken out.

Apricot Clear Cakes.

Make a strong apple jelly, strain it, and put apricots into it to boil. Slit the apricots well, cover them with sugar, and boil them clear. Strain them, and put them in the candy when it is almost boiled up; and then put in your jelly, and scald it.

Biscuit Cake.

Take eggs according to the size of the cake, weigh them, shells and all; then take an equal weight of sugar, sifted very fine, and half the weight of fine flour, well dried and sifted. Beat the whites of the eggs to snow; then put the yolks in another pan; beat them light, and add the sugar to them by degrees. Beat them until very light; then put the snow, continuing to beat; and at last add by degrees the flour. Season with lemon-peel grated, or any peel you like; bake it in a slow oven, but hot enough to make it rise.

Bread Cake.

Take two pounds of flour, a quarter of a pound of butter, four eggs, one spoonful of good yest, half a pound of currants, half a pound of Lisbon sugar, some grated lemon-peel, and nutmeg. Melt the butter and sugar in a sufficient quantity of new milk to make it of a proper stiffness. Set it to rise for two hours and a half before the fire, and bake it in an earthen pan or tin in a quick oven, of a light brown.

Caraway seeds may be added—two ounces to the above quantity.

Breakfast Cakes.

To a pound of fine flour take two ounces of fresh butter, which rub very well in with a little salt. Beat an egg smooth, and mix a spoonful of light yest with a little warm milk. Mix as much in the flour as will make a batter proper for fritters; then beat it with your hand till it leaves the bottom of the bowl in which it is made. Cover it up for three or four hours; then add as much flour as will form a paste proper for rolling up; make your cakes half an hour before you put them into the oven; prick them in the middle with a skewer, and bake them in a quick oven a quarter of an hour.

Excellent Breakfast Cakes.

Water the yest well that it may not be bitter; change the water very often; put a very little sugar and water to it just as you are going to use it; this is done to lighten and set it fermenting. As soon as you perceive it to be light, mix up with it new milk warmed, as if for other bread; put no water to it; about one pound or more of butter to about sixteen or eighteen cakes, and a white of two of egg, beat very light; mix all these together as light as you can; then add flour to it, and beat it at least a quarter of an hour, until it is a tough light dough. Put it to the fire and keep it warm, and warm the tins on which the cakes are to be baked. When the dough has risen, and is light, beat it down, and put it to the fire again to rise, and repeat this a second time; it will add much to the lightness of the cakes. Make them of the size of a saucer, or thereabouts, and not too thick, and bake them in a slow oven. The dough, if made a little stiffer, will be very good for rolls; but they must be baked in a quicker oven.

Bath Breakfast Cakes.

A pint of thin cream, two eggs, three spoonfuls of yest, and a little salt. Mix all well together with half a pound of flour. Let it stand to rise before you put it in the oven. The cakes must be baked on tins.

Butter Cake.

Take four pounds of flour, one pound of currants, three pounds of butter, fourteen eggs, leaving out the whites, half an ounce of mace, one pound of sugar, half a pint of sack, a pint of ale yest, a quart of milk boiled. Take it off, and let it cool. Rub the butter well in the floor; put in the sugar and spice, with the rest of the ingredients; wet it with a ladle, and beat it well together. Do not put the currants till the cake is ready to go into the oven. Butter the dish, and heat the oven as hot as for wheaten bread. You must not wet it till the oven is ready.

Caraway Cake. No. 1.

Melt two pounds of fresh butter in tin or silver; let it stand twenty-four hours; then rub into it four pounds of fine flour, dried. Mix in eight eggs, and whip the whites to a froth, a pint of the best yest, and a pint of sack, or any fine strong sweet wine. Put in two pounds of caraway seeds. Mix all these ingredients thoroughly; put the paste into a buttered pan, and bake for two hours and a half. You may mix with it half an ounce of cloves and cinnamon.

Caraway Cake. No. 2.

Take a quart of flour, a quarter of a pint of good ale yest, three quarters of a pound of fresh butter, one quarter of a pound of almonds, three quarters of a pound of caraway comfits, a handful of sugar, four eggs, leaving out two of the whites, new milk, boiled and set to cool, citron, orange, and lemon-peel, at your discretion, and two spoonfuls of sack. First rub your flour and yest together, then rub in the butter, and make it into a stiff batter with the milk, eggs, and sack; and, when you are ready to put it into the oven, add the other ingredients. Butter your hoop and the paper that lies under. This cake will require about three quarters of an hour baking; if you make it larger, you must allow more time.

Caraway Cake. No. 3.

Take four quarts of flour, well dried, and rub into it a pound and a quarter of butter. Take a pound of almonds, ground with rose-water, sugar, and cream, half an ounce of mace, and a little cinnamon, beaten fine, half a pound of citron, six ounces of orange-peel, some dried apricots, twelve eggs, four of the whites only, half a pound of sugar, a pint of ale yest, a little sack, and a quart of thick cream, well boiled. When your cream is nearly cold, mix all these ingredients well together with the flour; set the paste before the fire to rise; put in three pounds of double-sugared caraways, and let it stand in the hoop an hour and a quarter before it is put into the oven.

Small Caraway Cakes.

Take one quart of fine flour, fourteen ounces of butter, five or six spoonfuls of ale yest, three yolks of eggs, and one white; mix all these together, with so much cream as will make it into a paste; lay it before the fire for half an hour; add to it a handful of sugar, and half a pound of caraway comfits; and when you have worked them into long cakes, wash them over with rose-water and sugar, and pick up the top pretty thick with the point of a knife. Your oven must not be hotter than for manchet.

Cocoa-nut Cakes.

Grate the cocoa-nut on a fine bread grater; boil an equal quantity of loaf-sugar, melted with six table-spoonfuls of rose-water; take off all the scum; throw in the grated cocoa-nut, and let it heat thoroughly in the syrup, and keep constantly stirring, to prevent its burning to the bottom of the pan. Have ready beaten the yolks of eight eggs, with two table-spoonfuls of rose-water; throw in the cocoa-nut by degrees, and keep beating it with a wooden slice one hour; then fill your pans, and send them to the oven immediately, or they will be heavy.

Currant clear Cakes.

Take the currants before they are very ripe, and put them into water, scarcely enough to cover them; when they have boiled a little while, strain them through a woollen bag; put a pound and a quarter of fine sugar, boiled to a candy; then put a pint of the jelly, and make it scalding hot: put the whole into pots to dry, and, when jellied, turn them on glasses.

Egg Cake.

Beat eight eggs, leaving out half the whites, for half an hour; half a pound of lump-sugar, pounded and sifted, to be put in during that time; then, by degrees, mix in half a pound of flour. Bake as soon after as possible. Butter the tin.

Enamelled Cake.

Beat one pound of almonds, with three quarters of a pound of fine sugar, to a paste; then put a little musk, and roll it out thin. Cut it in what shape you please, and let it dry. Then beat up isinglass with white of eggs, and cover it on both sides.

Epsom Cake.

Half a pound of butter beat to a cream, half a pound of sugar, four eggs, whites and yolks beat separately, half a quartern of French roll dough, two ounces of caraway seeds, and one tea-spoonful of grated ginger: if for a plum-cake, a quarter of a pound of currants.

Ginger Cakes.

To a pound of sugar put half an ounce of ginger, the rind of a lemon, and four large spoonfuls of water. Stir it well together, and boil it till it is a stiff candy; then drop it in small cakes on a wet table.

Ginger or Hunting Cakes. No. 1.

Take three pounds of flour, two pounds of sugar, one pound of butter, two ounces of ginger, pounded and sifted fine, and a nutmeg grated. Rub these ingredients very fine in the flour, and wet it with a pint of cream, just warm, sufficiently to roll out into thin cakes. Bake them in a slack oven.

Ginger or Hunting Cakes. No. 2.

Rub half a pound of butter into a pound of flour; add a quarter of a pound of powder-sugar, one ounce of ginger, beat and sifted, the yolks of three eggs, and one gill of cream. A slow fire does them best.

Ginger or Hunting Cakes. No. 3.

One ounce of butter, one ounce of sugar, twelve grains of ginger, a quarter of a pound of flour, and treacle sufficient to make it into a paste; roll it out thin, and bake it.

Gooseberry clear Cakes.

Take the gooseberries very green; just cover them with water, and, when they are boiled and mashed, strain them through a sieve or woollen bag, and squeeze it well. Then boil up a candy of a pound and a quarter of fine sugar to a pint of the jelly; put it into pots to dry in a stove, and, when they jelly, turn them out on glasses.

Jersey Cake.

To a pound of flour take three quarters of a pound of fresh butter beaten to a cream, three quarters of a pound of lump sugar finely pounded, nine eggs, whites and yolks beaten separately, nutmeg to your taste. Add a glass of brandy.

Jersey Merveilles.

One pound of flour, two ounces of butter, the same of sugar, a spoonful of brandy, and five eggs. When well mixed, roll out and make into fancy shapes, and boil in hot lard. The Jersey shape is a true-lover's knot.

London Wigs.

Take a quarter of a peck of flour; put to it half a pound of sugar, and as much caraways, smooth or rough, as you like; mix these, and set them to the fire to dry. Then make a pound and half of butter hot over a gentle fire; stir it often, and add to it nearly a quart of milk or cream; when the butter is melted in the cream, pour it into the middle of the flour, and to it add a couple of wine-glasses of good white wine, and a full pint and half of very good ale yest; let it stand before the fire to rise, before you lay your cakes on the tin plates to bake.

Onion Cake.

Slice onions thin; set them in butter till they are soft, and, when they are cold, put into a pan to a quart basin of these stewed onions three eggs, three spoonfuls of fine dried bread crumbs, salt, and three spoonfuls of cream. Put common pie-crust in a tin; turn it up all round, like a cheesecake, and spread the onions over the cake; beat up an egg, and with a brush spread it in, and bake it of a fine yellow.

Orange Cakes.

Put the Seville oranges you intend to use into water for two days. Pare them very thick, and boil the rind tender. Mince it fine; squeeze in the juice; take out all the meat from the strings and put into it. Then take one-fourth more than its weight in double-refined sugar; wet it with water, and boil it almost to sugar again. Cool it a little; put in the orange, and let it scald till it looks clear and sinks in the syrup, but do not let it boil. Put it into deep glass plates, and stove them till they are candied on the tops. Turn them out, and shape them as you please with a knife. Continue to turn them till they are dry; keep them so, and between papers.

Lemon cakes are made in the same way, only with half the juice.

Another way.

Take three large oranges; pare and rub them with salt; boil them tender and cut them in halves; take out the seeds; then beat your oranges, and rub them through a hair sieve till you have a pound; add one pound and a quarter of double-refined sugar, boiled till it comes to the consistency of sugar, and put in a pint of strong juice of pippins and juice of lemon; keep stirring it on the fire till the sugar is completely melted.

Orange Clove Cake.

Make a very strong jelly of apples, and to every pint of jelly put in the peel of an orange. Set it on a quick fire, and boil it well; then run it through a jelly-bag and measure it. To every pint take a pound of fine sugar; set it on the fire, make it scalding hot, and strain it from the scum. Take the orange-peel, boiled very tender, shred it very small, and put it into it; give it another scald, and serve it out.

Lemon clove cake may be done the same way, but you must scald the peel before the sugar is put in.

Orange-flower Cakes.

Dip sugar in water, and let it boil over a quick fire till it is almost dry sugar again. To half a pound of sugar, when it is perfectly clear, add seven spoonfuls of water; then put in the orange-flowers: just give the mixture a boil up; drop it on china or silver plates, and set them in the sun till the cakes are dry enough to be taken off.

Plum Cake. No. 1.

Take eight pounds and three quarters of fine flour well dried and sifted, one ounce of beaten mace, one pound and a half of sugar. Mix them together, and take one quart of cream and six pounds of butter, put together, and set them over the fire till the butter is melted. Then take thirty-three eggs, one quart of yest, and twelve spoonfuls of sack; put it into the flour, stir it well together, and, when well mixed, set it before the fire to rise for an hour. Then take ten pounds of currants washed and dried, and set them to dry before the fire, one pound of citron minced, one pound of orange and lemon-peel together, sliced. When your oven is ready, stir your cake thoroughly; put in your sweetmeats and currants; mix them well in, and put into tin hoops. The quantity here given will make two large cakes, which will take two hours' baking.

Plum Cake. No. 2.

One pound of fine flour well dried and sifted, three quarters of a pound of fine sugar, also well dried and sifted. Work one pound to a cream with a noggin of brandy; then add to it by degrees your sugar, continuing to beat it very light. Beat the yolks of ten eggs extremely light; then put them into the butter and sugar, a spoonful at a time; beat the whites very light, and when you add the flour, which should be by degrees, put in the whites a spoonful at a time; add a grated nutmeg and a little beaten mace, and a good pound of currants, washed, dried, and picked, with a little of the flour rubbed about them. Work them into the cake. Cut in thin slices a quarter of a pound of blanched almonds, and two ounces of citron and candied orange-peel. Between every layer of cake, as you put it into the hoop, put in the sweetmeats, and bake it two hours.

Plum Cake. No. 3.

Rub one pound of butter into two pounds of flour; take one pound of sugar, one pound of currants, and mix them with four eggs; make them into little round cakes, and bake them on tins. Half this quantity is sufficient to make at a time.

Clear Plum Cake.

Make apple jelly rather strong, and strain it through a woollen bag. Put as many white pear plums as will give a flavour to the jelly; let it boil; strain it again through the bag, and boil up as many pounds of fine sugar for a candy as you had pints of jelly; and when your sugar is boiled very high, add your jelly; just scald it over the fire; put it in little pots, and let it stand with a constant fire.

Portugal Cakes.

Put one pound of fine sugar, well beaten and sifted, one pound of fresh butter, five eggs, and a little beaten mace, into a flat pan: beat it up with your hand until it is very light; then put in by degrees one pound of fine flour well dried and sifted, half a pound of currants picked, washed, and well dried; beat them together till very light; bake them in heart pans in a slack oven.

Potato Cakes.

Roast or bake mealy potatoes, as they are drier and lighter when done that way than boiled; peel them, and beat them in a mortar with a little cream or melted butter; add some yolks of eggs, a little sack, sugar, a little beaten mace, and nutmeg: work it into a light paste, then make it into cakes of what shape you please with moulds. Fry them brown in the best fresh butter; serve them with sack and sugar.

Pound Cake.

Take a pound of flour and a pound of butter; beat to a cream eight eggs, leaving out the whites of four, and beat them up with the butter. Put the flour in by degrees, one pound of sugar, a few caraway seeds, and currants, if you like; half a pound will do.

Another.

Take half a pound of butter, and half a pound of powdered lump-sugar; beat them till they are like a cream. Then take three eggs, leaving out the whites of two; beat them very well with a little brandy; then put the eggs to the butter and sugar; beat it again till it is come to a cream. Shake over it half a pound of dried flour; beat it well with your hand; add half a nutmeg, half an ounce of caraway seeds, and what sweetmeat you please. Butter the mould well.

Pound Davy.

Beat up well ten eggs and half a pound of sugar with a little rose-water; mix in half a pound of flour, and bake it in a pan.

Clear Quince Cakes.

Take the apple quince, pare and core it; take as many apples as quinces; just cover them with water, and boil till they are broken. Strain them through a sieve or woollen bag, and boil up to a candy as many pounds of sugar as you have of jelly, which put in your jelly; just let it scald over the fire, and put it into paste in a stove. The paste is made thus: Scald quinces in water till they are tender; then pare and scrape them fine with a knife and put them into apple jelly; let it stand till you think the paste sufficiently thickened, then boil up to a candy as many pounds of sugar as you have of paste.

Ratafia Cakes.

Bitter and sweet almonds, of each a quarter of a pound, blanched and well dried with a napkin, finely pounded with the white of an egg; three quarters of a pound of finely pounded sugar mixed with the almonds. Have the whites of three eggs beat well, and mix up with the sugar and almonds; put the mixture with a tea-spoon on white paper, and bake it in a slow heat; when the cakes are cold, they come off easily from the paper. When almonds are pounded, they are generally sprinkled with a little water, otherwise they become oily. Instead of water take to the above the white of an egg or a little more; to the whole of the above quantity the whites of four eggs are used.

Rice Cake.

Ground rice, flour and loaf-sugar, of each six ounces, eight eggs, leaving out five of the whites, the peel of a lemon grated: beat all together half an hour, and bake it three quarters of an hour in a quick oven.

Another.

Take one pound of sifted rice flour, one pound of fine sugar finely beaten and sifted, and sixteen eggs, leaving out half the whites; beat them a quarter of an hour at least, separately; then add the sugar, and beat it with the eggs extremely well and light. When they are as light as possible, add by degrees the rice-flour; beat them all together for an hour as light as you can. Put in a little orange-flower water, or brandy, and candied peel, if you like; the oven must not be too hot.

Rock Cakes.

One pound of flour, half a pound of clarified butter, half a pound of currants, half a pound of sugar; mix and pinch into small cakes.

Royal Cakes.

Take three pounds of very fine flour, one pound and a half of butter, and as much currants, seven yolks and three whites of eggs, a nutmeg grated, a little rose-water, one pound and a half of sugar finely beaten; knead it well and light, and bake on tins.

Savoy or Sponge Cake.

Take twelve new-laid eggs, and their weight in double refined sugar; pound it fine, and sift it through a lawn sieve; beat the yolks very light, and add the sugar to them by degrees; beat the whole well together till it is extremely light. Whisk the whites of the eggs to a strong froth; then mix all together by adding the yolks and the sugar to the whites. Have ready the weight of seven eggs in fine flour very well dried and sifted; stir it in by degrees, and grate in the rind of a lemon. Butter a mould well, and bake in a quick oven. About half an hour or forty minutes will do it.

Another.

Take one pound of Jordan and two ounces of bitter almonds; blanch them in cold water, and beat them very fine in a mortar, adding orange-flower and rose-water as you beat them to prevent their oiling. Then beat eighteen eggs, the whites separately to a froth, and the yolks extremely well, with a little brandy and sack. Put the almonds when pounded into a dry, clean, wooden bowl, and beat them with your hand extremely light, with one pound of fine dried and sifted sugar; put the sugar in by degrees, and beat it very light, also the peels of two large lemons finely grated. Put in by degrees the whites of the eggs as they rise to a froth, and in the same manner the yolks, continuing to beat it for an hour, or until it is as light as possible. An hour will bake it; it must be a quick oven; you must continue to beat the cake until the oven is ready for it.

Seed Cake. No. 1.

Heat a wooden bowl, and work in three pounds of butter with your hands, till it is as thin as cream; then work in by degrees two pounds of fine sugar sifted, and eighteen eggs well beaten, leaving out four of the whites; put the eggs in by degrees. Take three pounds of the finest flour, well dried and sifted, mixed with one ounce and a half of caraway seeds, one nutmeg, and a little mace; put them in the flour as you did the sugar, and beat it well up with your hands; put it in your hoop; and it will take two hours' baking. You may add sweetmeats if you like. The dough must be made by the fire, and kept constantly worked with the hands to mix it well together. If you have sweetmeats, put half a pound of citron, a quarter of a pound of lemon-peel, and put the dough lightly into the hoop, just before you send it to the oven, without smoothing it at top, for that makes it heavy.

Seed Cake. No. 2.

Take a pound and a half of butter; beat it to a cream with your hand or a flat stick; beat twelve eggs, the yolks in one pan and the whites in another, as light as possible, and then beat them together, adding by degrees one pound and a half of well dried and sifted loaf-sugar, and a little sack and brandy. When the oven is nearly ready, mix all together, with one pound and a half of well dried and sifted flour, half a pound of sliced almonds, and some caraway seeds: beat it well with your hand before you put it into the hoop.

Seed Cake. No. 3, called Borrow Brack.

Melt one pound and a half of butter in a quart of milk made warm. Mix fourteen eggs in half a pint of yest. Take half a peck of flour, and one pound of sugar, both dried and sifted, four ounces of caraway seeds, and two ounces of beaten ginger. Mix all well together. First put the eggs and the yest to the flour, then add the butter and the milk. Make it into a paste of the substance of that for French bread; if not flour enough add what is sufficient; and if too much, put some warm new milk. Let it stand for above half an hour at the fire, before you make it up into what form you please.

Shrewsbury Cakes.

Take three pounds and a half of fresh butter, work the whey and any salt that it may contain well out of it. Take four pounds of fine flour well dried and sifted, one ounce of powdered cinnamon, five eggs well beaten, and two pounds of loaf-sugar well dried and sifted. Put them all into the flour, and work them well together into a paste. Make it into a roll; cut off pieces for cakes and work them well with your hands. This quantity will make above six dozen of the size of those sold at Shrewsbury. They require great care in baking; a short time is sufficient, and the oven must not be very hot.

Sponge Cake.

Take seven eggs, leaving out three whites; beat them well with a whisk; then take three quarters of a pound of lump-sugar beat fine: put to it a quarter of a pint of boiling water, and pour it to the eggs; then beat it half an hour or more; when you are just going to put it in the oven, add half a pint of flour well dried. You must not beat it after the flour is in. Put a paper in the tin. A quick oven will bake this quantity in an hour. It must not be beaten with a spoon, as it will make it heavy.

Another.

Take twelve eggs, leaving out half the whites; beat them to froth; shake in one pound of lump-sugar, sifted through a fine sieve, and three quarters of a pound of flour well dried; put in the peel of two lemons grated and the juice of one; beat all well in with a fork.

Sugar Cakes.

Take half a pound of sugar, half a pound of butter, two ounces of flour, two eggs, but the white of one only, a little beaten mace, and a little brandy. Mix all together into a paste with your hands; make it into little cakes, and bake them on tins. You may put in six ounces of currants, if you like.

Little Sugar Cakes.

Take double-refined sugar and sift it very fine; beat the white of an egg to a froth; take gum-dragon that has been steeped in juice of lemon or orange-flower water, and some ambergris finely beaten with the sugar. Mix all these together in a mortar, and beat it till it is very white; then roll it into small knobs, or make it into small loaves. Lay them on paper well sugared, and set them into a very gentle oven.

Sweet Cakes.

Take half a pound of butter, and beat it with a spoon till it is quite soft; add two eggs, well beaten, half a pound of currants, half a pound of powdered sugar, and a pound of flour, mixed by degrees with the butter. Drop it on, and bake them. Blanched almonds, powdered to paste, instead of currants, are excellent.

Tea Cakes.

Take loaf sugar, finely powdered, and butter, of each a quarter of a pound, about half a pound of flour, dried before the fire, a walnut-shellful of caraway seeds, just bruised, and one egg. Work all together into a paste, adding a spoonful of brandy. Roll the paste out to the thickness of a half-crown, and cut it with a tea-cup. Flour a tin, and lay the cakes upon it. Take the white of an egg, well beaten and frothed, dip a feather in this, and wash them over, and then grate upon them a little fine sugar. Put them into a slackish oven, till they are of a very pale brown.

Dry Tea Cakes.

Boil two ounces of butter in a pint of skimmed milk; let it stand till it is as cold as new milk; then put to it a spoonful of light yest, a little salt, and as much flour as will make it a stiff paste. Work it as much, or more, than you would do brown bread; let it lie half an hour to rise; then roll it into thin cakes; prick them very well quite through, to prevent their blistering, and bake them on tin plates in a quick oven. To keep crisp, they must be hung up in the kitchen, or where there is a constant fire.

Thousand Cake.

One pound of flour, half a pound of butter, six ounces of sugar, five eggs, leaving out three whites; rub the flour, butter, and sugar, well together; pour the eggs into it; work it up well; roll it out thin, and cut them with a glass of what size you please.

Tunbridge Cakes.

One pound and a half of flour, one pound of butter; rub the butter into the flour; strew in a few caraways, and add the yolks of two eggs, first beaten, and as much water as will make it into a paste: roll it out thin, and prick it with a jagging iron; run the cakes into what shape you please, or cut them with a glass. Just as you put them into the oven, sift sugar on them, and a very little when they come out. The oven must be as hot as for manchets. Bake them on paper.

Veal Cake.

Take thin slices of veal, and fat and lean slices of ham, and lay the bottom of a basin or mould with one slice of each in rows. Chop some sweet-herbs very small, and fill the basin with alternate layers of veal and ham, sprinkling every layer with the herbs. Season to your taste; and add some hard yolks of eggs. When the basin is full, pour in some gravy. Put a plate on the top, and a weight on it to keep the meat close. Bake it about an hour and a half, and do not turn it out till next day.

Yorkshire Cakes.

Take two pounds of flour, three ounces of butter, the yolks of two eggs, three spoonfuls of yest that is not bitter; melt the butter in half a pint of milk; then mix them all well together; let it stand one hour by the fire to rise; then roll the dough into cakes pretty thin. Set them a quarter of an hour longer to the fire to rise; bake them on tins in a moderate oven; toast and butter them as you do muffins.

Calves' Foot Jelly. No. 1.

To two calves' feet put a gallon of water, and boil it to two quarts; run it through a sieve, and let it stand till it is cold; then take off all the fat, and put the jelly in a pan, with a pint of white wine, the juice of two lemons, sugar to your taste, and the whites of six eggs. Stir these together near half an hour, then strain it through a jelly-bag; put a piece of lemon-peel in the bag; let it pass through the bag till it is clear. If you wish this jelly to be very clear and strong, add an ounce of isinglass.

Calves' Foot Jelly. No. 2.

Boil four calves' feet in three quarts of water for three or four hours, or till they will not hold together, now and then skimming off the fat. The liquor must be reduced to a quart. When you have quite cleared it from the fat, which must be done by papering it over, add to it nearly a bottle of white wine, sherry is the best, the juice of four or five lemons, the peel also pared very thin, so that no white is left on it, and sugar to your taste. Then beat up six whites of eggs to a stiff froth, and with a whisk keep stirring it over the fire till it boils. Then pour it into the jelly-bag, and keep changing it till it comes clear. This quantity will produce about a quart of jelly strong enough to turn out of moulds.

Calves' Foot Jelly. No. 3.

Take two feet to two quarts of water; reduce it to three pints of jelly. Then add the juice and peel of four lemons, one ounce of isinglass, the shells and whites of four eggs, a little cinnamon, mace, and allspice, and a good half pint of Madeira.

Calves' Foot Jelly. No. 4.

Stew a calf's foot slowly to a jelly. Melt it with a little wine, sugar, and lemon-peel.

Cheese, to make.

Strain some milk into a cheese tub, as warm as you can from the cow; put into it a large quantity of strong runnet, about a spoonful to sixty quarts; stir it well with a fleeting dish; and cover it close with a wooden cover, made to fit your tub. About the middle of June, let it stand thus three quarters of an hour, in hotter weather less, in cold weather somewhat longer. When it is come, break it pretty small with a dish, and stir it gently till it is all come to a curd; then press it down gently with your dish and hand, so that the whey do not rise over it white; after the whey is pretty well drained and the curd become tolerably hard, break it into a vat very small, heaped up as high as possible, and press it down, at first gently and then harder, with your hands, till as much whey as possible can be got out that way, and yet the curd continues at least two inches above the vat; otherwise the cheese will not take press, that is, will be sour, and full of eyes and holes.

Then put the curd into one end of a good flaxen cloth, and cover it with the other end, tucking it in with a wooden cheese knife, so as to make it lie smooth and keep the curd quite in; then press it with a heavy weight or in a press, for five or six hours, when it will be fit to turn into a dry cloth, in which press it again for four hours. Then take it out, salt it well over, or it will become maggoty, and put it into the vat again for twelve hours. Take it out; salt it a second time; and leave it in a tub or on a dresser four days, turning it every day. This done, wash it with cold water, wipe it with a dry cloth, and store it up in your cheese-loft, turning and wiping it every day till it is quite dry. The reason of mouldiness, cracks, and rottenness within, is the not well pressing, turning, or curing, the curd and cheese.

The best Cheese in the world.

To make a cheese in the style of Stilton cheese, only much better, take the new milk of seven cows, with the cream from the milk of seven cows. Heat a gallon of water scalding hot, and put into it three or four handfuls of marigolds bruised a little; strain it into the tub containing the milk and cream, and put to it some runnet, but not so much as to make it come very hard. Put the curd into a sieve to drain; do not break it all, but, as the whey runs out, tie up the cloth, and let it stand half an hour or more. Then cut the curd in pieces; pour upon it as much cold water as will cover it, and let it stand half an hour. Put part of it into a vat or a hoop nearly six inches deep; break the top of it a little, just to make it join with the other, and strew on it a very little salt; then put in the other part, lay a fifty-pound weight upon it, and let it stand half an hour. Turn it, and put it into the press. Turn it into wet clean cloths every hour of the day. Next morning salt it; and let it lie in the salt a night and a day. Keep it swathed tight, till it begins to dry and coat, and keep it covered with a clean cloth for a long time.

The month of August is the best time for making this cheese, which should be kept a year before it is cut.

Cheese, to stew.

Scrape some rich old cheese into a saucepan, with a small piece of butter and a spoonful of cream. Let it stew till it is smooth; add the yolk of one egg; give it a boil all together. Serve it up on a buttered toast, and brown it with a salamander.

Cream Cheese.

Take a basin of thick cream, let it stand some time; then salt it, put a thin cloth over a hair-sieve, and pour the cream on it. Shift the cloth every day, till it is proper; then wrap the cheese up to ripen in nettle or vine leaves.

Another.

Take a quart of new milk and a quart of cream; warm them together, and put to it a spoonful of runnet; let it stand three hours; then take it out with a skimming-dish; break the curd as little as possible; put it into a straw vat, which is just big enough to hold this quantity; let it stand in the vat two days; take it out, and sprinkle a little salt over it; turn it every day, and it will be ready in ten days.

Princess Amelia's Cream Cheese.

Wash the soap out of a napkin; double it to the required size, and put it wet into a pewter soup-plate. Put into it a pint of cream; cover it, and let it stand twenty-four hours unless the weather is very hot, in which case not so long. Turn the cheese in the napkin: sprinkle a little salt over it, and let it stand twelve hours. Then turn it into a very dry napkin out of which all soap has been washed, and salt the other side. It will be fit to eat in a day or two according to the weather. Some keep it in nut leaves to ripen it.

Irish Cream Cheese.

Take a quart of very thick cream, and stir well into it two spoonfuls of salt. Double a napkin in two, and lay it in a punch-bowl. Pour the cream into it; turn the four corners over the cream, and let it stand for two days. Put it into a dry cloth within a little wooden cheese-vat; turn it into dry cloths twice a day till it is quite dry, and it will be fit to eat in a few days. Keep it in clean cloths in a cool place.

Rush Cheese.

Take a quart of cream, put to it a gill of new milk; boil one half of it and put it to the other; then let it stand till it is of the warmth of new milk, after which put in a little earning, and, when sufficiently come, break it as little as you can; put it into a vat that has a rush bottom, lay it on a smooth board, and turn it every day till ripe.

Winter Cream Cheese.

Take twenty quarts of new milk warm from the cow; strain it into a tub; have ready four quarts of good cream boiled to put to it, and about a quart of spring water, boiling hot, and stir all well together; put in your earning, and stir it well in; keep it by the fire till it is well come. Then take it gently into a sieve to whey it, and after that put it into a vat, either square or round, with a cheese-board upon it, of two pounds weight at first, which is to be increased by degrees to six pounds; turn it into dry cloths two or three times a day for a week or ten days, and salt it with dry salt, the third day. When you take it out of the vat, lay it upon a board, and turn and wipe it every other day till it is dry. It is best to be made as soon as the cows go into fog.

The cheeses are fit to eat in Lent, sometimes at Christmas, according to the state of the ground.

To make Cream Cheese without Cream.

Take a quart of milk warm from the cow and two quarts of boiling water. When the curd is ready for the cheese-vat, put it in, without breaking it, by a dishful at a time, and fill it up as it drains off. It must not be pressed. The cheese-vat should have holes in it all over like a colander. Take out the cheese when it will bear it, and ripen it upon rushes: it must be more than nine inches deep.

Damson Cheese.

Take the damsons full ripe, and squeeze out the stones, which put into the preserving-pan, with as much water as will cover them: let them simmer till the stones are quite clear, and put your fruit into the liquor. Take three pounds of good powder sugar to six pounds of fruit; boil it very fast till quite thick; then break the stones, and put the whole kernels into it, before you put it into moulds for use.

Another.

Boil up one pound of damsons with three quarters of a pound of sugar; when the fruit begins to break, take out the stones and the skins; or, what is a better way, pulp them through a colander. Then peel and put in some of the kernels; boil it very high; it will turn out to the shape of any pots or moulds, and is very good.

French Cheese.

Boil two pints of milk and one of cream, with a blade of mace and a little cinnamon: put the yolks of three eggs and the whites of two, well beaten, into your milk, and set on the fire again, stirring it all the while till it boils. Take it off, and stir it till it is a little cooled; then put in the juice of two lemons, and let it stand awhile with the lemons in it. Put it in a linen strainer, and hang it up to drain out the whey. When it is drained dry, take it down, and put to it a spoonful or two of rose-water, and sweeten it to your taste: put it into your pan, which must be full of holes; let it stand a little; put it into your dish with cream, and stick some blanched almonds about it.

Italian Cheese.

One quart of cream, a pint of white wine, the juice of three lemons, a little lemon-peel, and sugar to your taste; beat it with a whisk a quarter of an hour; then pour it on a buttered cloth, over a sieve, to drain all night, and turn it out just before it is sent to table. Strew comfits on the top, and garnish as you like.

Lemon Cheese—very good.

Into a quart of thick sweet cream put the juice of three lemons, with the rind finely grated; sweeten it to your taste; beat it very well; then put it into a sieve, with some fine muslin underneath it, and let it stand all night. Next day turn it out, and garnish with preserved orange or marmalade.

Half the above quantity makes a large cheese. Do not beat it till it comes to butter, but only till it is near coming. It is a very pretty dish.

Cheesecake. No. 1.

Take four quarts of new milk and a pint of cream; put in a blade or two of mace, with a bag of ambergris; set it with as much runnet as will bring it to a tender curd. When it has come, break it as you would a cheese, and, when you have got what whey you can from it, put it in a cloth and lay it in a pan or cheese-hoop, placing on it a weight of five or six pounds, and, when you find it well pressed out, put it into an earthen dish, bruising it very small with a spoon. Then take two ounces of almonds, blanch and beat them with rose-water and cream; mix these well together among your curd; sweeten them with loaf-sugar; put in something more than a quarter of a pound of fresh butter, with the yolks of six eggs mixed together. When you are ready to put it into crust, strew in half a pound of currants; let the butter boil that you make your crust with; roll out the cakes very thin. The oven must not be too hot, and great care must be taken in the baking. When they rise up to the top they are sufficiently done.

Cheesecake. No. 2.

Blanch half a pound of the best sweet almonds, and beat them very fine. Add two spoonfuls of orange-flower or rose-water, half a pound of currants, half a pound of the finest sugar, beaten and sifted, and two quarts of thick cream, which must be kept stirred over a gentle fire. When almost cold, add eight eggs, leaving out half the whites, well beaten and strained, a little beaten mace and finely powdered cinnamon, with four well pounded cloves. Mix them well into the rest of the ingredients, keeping it still over the fire as before. Pour it well beaten into puff-paste for the oven, and if it be well heated they will be baked in a quarter of an hour.

Cheesecake. No. 3.

Take two quarts of milk, make it into curd with a little runnet; when it is drained as dry as possible, put to it a quarter of a pound of butter; rub both together in a marble mortar till smooth; then add one ounce of almonds blanched; beat two Naples biscuits, and about as much crumb of roll; put seven yolks of eggs, but only one white; season it with mace and a little rose-water, and sweeten to your taste.

Cheesecake. No. 4.

Break one gallon of milk with runnet, and press it dry; then beat it in a mortar very small; put in half a pound of butter, and beat the whole over again until it is as smooth as butter. Put to it six eggs, leaving out half the whites; beat them very light with sack and rose-water, half a nutmeg grated, half a quarter of a pound of almonds beaten fine with rose-water and a little brandy. Sweeten to your taste; put in what currants you like, make a rich crust, and bake in a quick oven.

Cheesecake. No. 5.

A quart of milk with eight eggs beat together; when it is come to a curd, put it into a sieve, and strain the whey out. Beat a quarter of a pound of butter with the curd in a mortar, with three eggs and three spoonfuls of sugar; pound it together very light; add half a nutmeg and a very little salt.

Cheesecake. No. 6.

Take a pint of milk, four eggs well beaten, three ounces of butter, half a pound of sugar, the peel of a lemon grated; put all together into a kettle, and set it over a clear fire; keep stirring it till it begins to boil; then mix one spoonful of flour with as much milk as will just mix it, and put it into the kettle with the rest. When it begins to boil, take it off the fire, and put it into an earthen pan; let it stand till the next morning; then add a quarter of a pound of currants, a little nutmeg, and half a glass of brandy.

Almond Cheesecake.

Blanch six ounces of sweet and half an ounce of bitter almonds; let them lie half an hour on a stove or before the fire; pound them very fine with two table-spoonfuls of rose or orange-flower water; put in the stewpan half a pound of fresh butter, add to this the almonds, six ounces of sifted loaf-sugar, a little grated lemon-peel, some good cream, and the yolks of four eggs; rub all well together with the pestle; cover the pattypans with puff paste, fill them with the mixture, and bake it half an hour in a brisk oven.

Cocoa-nut Cheesecakes.

Take a cocoa-nut, which by many is thought far superior to almonds; grate it the long way; put to it some thick syrup, mixing it by degrees. Boil it till it comes to the consistence of cheese; when half cold add to it two eggs; beat it up with rose-water till it is light: if too thick, add a little more rose-water. When beaten up as light as possible, pour it upon a fine crust in cheesecake pans, and, just before they are going into the oven, sift over some fine sugar, which will raise a nice crust and much improve their appearance. The addition of half a pound of butter just melted, and eight more eggs, leaving out half of the whites, makes an excellent pudding.

Cream Cheesecake.

Two quarts of cream set on a slow fire, put into it twelve eggs very well beat and strained, stir it softly till it boils gently and breaks into whey and a fine soft curd; then take the curd as it rises off the whey, and put it into an earthen pan; then break four eggs more, and put to the whey; set it on the fire, and take off the curd as before, and put it to the rest: then add fourteen ounces of butter, half a pound of light Naples biscuit grated fine, a quarter of a pound of almonds beat fine with rose-water, one pound of currants, well washed and picked, some nutmeg grated, and sugar to your taste: a short crust.

Curd Cheesecake.

Just warm a quart of new milk; put into it a spoonful of runnet, and set it near the fire till it breaks. Strain it through a sieve; put the curd into a pan, and beat it well with a spoon. Melt a quarter of a pound of butter, put in the same quantity of moist sugar, a little grated nutmeg, two Naples biscuits, grated fine, the yolks of four eggs beat well, and the whites of two, a glass of raisin wine, a few bitter almonds, with lemon or Seville orange-peel cut fine, a quarter of a pound of currants plumped; mix all well together, and put it into the paste and pans for baking.

Lemon Cheesecake.

Grate the rind of three to the juice of two lemons; mix them with three sponge biscuits, six ounces of fresh butter, four ounces of sifted sugar, half a gill of cream, and three eggs well beaten. Work them well, and fill the pan, which must be lined with puff-paste; lay on the top some candied lemon-peel cut thin.

Another.

Boil the peel of two lemons till tender; pound it in a mortar very fine; blanch and pound a few almond kernels with the peel. Mix a quarter of a pound of loaf sugar, a quarter of a pound of butter, the yolks of six eggs, all together in the mortar, and put it in the puff-paste for baking. This quantity will make twelve or fourteen cakes.

Orange Cheesecake.

Take the peel of one orange and a half and one lemon grated; squeeze out the juice; add a quarter of a pound of sugar, and a quarter of a pound of melted butter, four eggs, leaving out the whites, a little Naples biscuit grated, to thicken it, and a little white wine. Put almonds in it if you like.

Scotch Cheesecake.

Put one ounce of butter into a saucepan to clarify; add one ounce of powder sugar and two eggs; stir it over a slow fire until it almost boils, but not quite. Line your pattypans with paste; bake the cakes of a nice brown, and serve them up between hot and cold.

Cherries, to preserve. No. 1.

Take either morella or carnation; stone the fruit; to morella cherries take the jelly of white currants, drawn with a little water, and run through a jelly-bag; to a pint and a half of jelly, add three pounds of fine sugar. Set it on a quick fire; when it boils, skim it, and put in a pound of stoned cherries. Let them not boil too fast at first; take them off at times; but when they are tender boil them very fast till they are very clear and jelly; then put them into pots or glasses. The carnation cherries must have red currant jelly; if you have not white currant jelly for the morella, codling jelly will do.

Cherries, to preserve. No. 2.

To three quarters of a pound of cherries stoned take one pound and a quarter of sugar; leave out a quarter of a pound to strew on them as they boil. Put in the preserving-pan a layer of cherries and a layer of sugar, till they are all in; boil them quick, keeping them closely covered with white paper, which take off frequently, and skim them; strew the sugar kept out over them; it will clear them very much. When they look clear they are done enough. Take them out of the syrup quite clear from the skim; strain the syrup through a fine sieve; then put to it a quarter of a pint of the juice of white currants, put them into the pan again, and boil it till it is a hanging jelly. Just before it is quite done put in the cherries; give them a boil, and put them into pots. There must be fourteen spoonfuls of water put in at first with the cherries.

Cherries, to preserve. No. 3.

Stone the cherries, and to twelve pounds of fruit put nine pounds of sugar; boil the sugar-candy high; stir it well; throw in the cherries; let them not boil too fast at first, stirring them often in the pan; afterwards boil them fast till they become tender.

Morella Cherries, to preserve.

When you have stalked and stoned your cherries, put to them an equal weight of sugar: make your syrup, skim it, and take it off the fire. Skim it again well, and put in your cherries, shaking them with care in the pan. Boil them, not on a quick fire, lest the fruit should crack; and take them off the fire several times. Let them boil till done; put your cherries into pots; strain the syrup through muslin, and boil it again till thoroughly done.

Morella Cherries, to preserve in Brandy.

Take two pounds of morella cherries, when not too ripe, but finely coloured, weighed with their stalks and stones. Put a quart of water and twelve ounces of double-refined sugar into a preserving-pan, and set it over a clear charcoal fire. Let it boil a quarter of an hour; skim it clean, and set it by till cold. Then take away the stalks and stones, and, when the syrup is quite cold, put the stoned cherries into the syrup, set them over a gentle fire, and let them barely simmer till their skins begin to rise. Take them from the fire; pour them into a basin; cut a piece of paper round of the size of the basin; lay it close upon the cherries while hot, and let them stand so till next day. Set a hair sieve in a pan, and pour the cherries into it; let them drain till the syrup is all drained out: boil the syrup till reduced to two-thirds, and set it aside till cold. Put your cherries into a glass jar; put to them a spoonful of their own syrup and one of brandy, and continue to do so till the jar is filled within two inches of the top: then put over it a wet bladder, and a piece of leather over that; tie it down close, and keep it in a warm place.

If you do not mind the stones, merely cut off the stalks of the cherries.

Brandy Cherries.

To each bottle of brandy add half a pound of white sugar-candy: let this dissolve; cut the large ripe morella cherries from the tree into a glass or earthen jar, leaving the stalks about half the original length. When the jar is full, pour upon the cherries the brandy as above. Let the fruit be completely covered, and fill it up as the liquor settles. Cork the jar, and tie a leather over the top. Apricot kernels blanched and put in are an agreeable addition.

Cherries, to dry.

Stone the cherries, and to ten pounds when stoned put three pounds of sugar finely beaten. Shake the cherries and sugar well together; when the sugar is quite dissolved, give them a boil or two over a slow fire, and put them in an earthen pot. Next day scald them, lay them on a sieve, and dry them in the sun, or in a oven, not too hot. Turn them till they are dry enough, then put them up; but put no paper.

Liquor for dried Cherries.

Take some red currants, and boil them in water till it is very red; then put it to your cherries and sugar it; this makes them of a good colour.

Cherry Jam.

Take twelve pounds of stoned cherries; boil and break them as they boil, and, when you have boiled all the juice away, and can see the bottom of the pan, put in three pounds of sugar finely beaten: stir it well in; give the fruit two or three boils, and put it in pots or glasses, and cover with brandy paper.

Cocoa.

Take three table-spoonfuls of cocoa and one dessert spoonful of flour; beat them well together, and boil in a pint and a half of spring water, upon a slow fire, for two or three hours, and then strain it for use.

Cocoa-Nut Candy.

Grate a cocoa-nut on a fine bread grater; weigh it, and add the same quantity of loaf-sugar: melt the sugar with rose-water, of which, for a small cocoa-nut, put six table-spoonfuls. When the syrup is clarified and boiling, throw in the cocoa-nut by degrees; keep stirring it all the time, whilst boiling, with a wooden slice, to prevent it burning to the bottom of the pan, which it is very apt to do, unless great care is taken. When the candy is sufficiently boiled, spread it on a pasteboard previously rubbed with a wet cloth, and cut it in whatever shape you please.

To know when the candy is sufficiently boiled, drop a small quantity on the pasteboard, and if the syrup does not run from the cocoa-nut, it is done enough; when the candy is cold, put it on a dish, and keep it in a dry place.

Coffee, to roast.

For this purpose you must have a roaster with a spit. Put in no more coffee than will have room enough to work about well. Set it down to a good fire; put in every now and then a little fresh butter, and mix it well with a spoon. It will take five or six hours to roast. When done, turn it out into a large dish or a dripping-pan, till it is quite dry.

Another way.

Take two pounds of coffee, and put it into a roaster. Roast it one hour before a brisk fire; add two ounces of butter, and let it roast till it becomes of a fine brown. Watch, that it does not burn. Two hours and a half will do it. Take half a pound for eight cups.

Coffee to make the foreign way.

Take Demarara—Bean Dutch coffee—in preference to Mocha coffee; wash it well. When it is very clean, put it in an earthen vessel, and cover it close, taking great care that no air gets to it; then grind it very thoroughly. Put a good half pint of coffee into a large coffee-pot, that holds three quarts, with a large table-spoonful of mustard; then pour upon it boiling water. It is of great consequence that the water should boil; but do not fill the coffee-pot too full, for fear of its boiling over, and losing the aromatic oil. Then pour the whole contents backwards and forwards several times into a clean cup or basin, wiping the basin or cup each time—this will clear it sufficiently. Let it then stand ten minutes, after which, when cool, pour it clear off the grounds steadily, into clean bottles, and lay them down on their sides, well corked. Do not throw away your coffee grounds, but add another table-spoonful of mustard to them, and fill up the vessel with boiling water, doing as before directed. Be sure to cork the bottles well; lay them down on one side, and before you want to use them set them up for a couple of hours, in case any sediment should remain. Let it come to the boil, always taking care that it is neither smoked nor boils over. All coffee should be kept on a lamp while you are using it.

By following this receipt as much coffee will be obtained for threepence as you would otherwise get for a shilling; and it is the best possible coffee.

To make Cream rise in cold weather.

Dip each pan or bowl into a pail of boiling water before you strain the milk into it. Put a close cover over each for about ten minutes: the hot steam causes the cream to rise thick and rich.

Cream, to fry.

Take two spoonfuls of fine flour and the yolks of four eggs; grate in the rind of one lemon; beat them well with the flour, and add a pint of cream. Mix these very well together; sweeten to your taste, and add a bit of cinnamon. Put the whole in a stewpan over a slow fire; continue to stir it until it is quite hot; but it must not boil. Take out the cinnamon; beat two eggs very well, and put them into the cream; butter a pewter dish; pour the cream in it; put it into a warm oven to set, but not to colour it. When cold, cut it into pieces, and have ready a stewpan or frying-pan, with a good deal of lard; dredge the cream with flour; fry the pieces of a light brown, grate sugar over them, glaze with a salamander, and serve them very hot.

Artificial Cream and Curd.

A pint of good new milk, nine whites of eggs beat up, and well stirred and mixed with the milk; put it on a slow fire to turn; then take it off, and drain it through a fine sieve, and set it into a basin or mould. To make the cream for it, take a pint of milk and the yolks of four eggs well beat, boil it with a bit of cinnamon over a slow fire; keep it constantly stirring; when it is as thick as rich cream, take it off, and stir it a little while afterwards.

Cream of Rice.

Wash and well clean some very good rice; put it into a stewpan, with water, and boil it gently till quite soft, with a little cinnamon, if agreeable to the taste. When the rice is boiled quite soft, take out the cinnamon. Then take a large dish, and set it on a table: have a clean tamis—a new one would be better—a tamis is only the piece of flannel commonly used in kitchens for passing sauces through— and give one end of the tamis to a person on the opposite side of the table to hold, while you hold the other end with your left hand. Having a large wooden spoon in your right, you put two or three spoonfuls of boiled rice into this tamis, which is held over the large dish, and rub the rice upon it with the spoon till it passes through into the dish. Whatever sticks to the tamis take off with a silver spoon and put into the dish. When you have passed the quantity you want, put it in a basin. It should be made fresh every day. Warm it for use in a small silver or tin saucepan, adding a little sugar and Madeira, according to your taste.

Almond Cream.

Make this in the manner directed for pistachio cream, adding half a dozen bitter almonds to the sweet.

Barley Cream.

Take half a pint of pearl barley, and two quarts of water. Boil it half away, and then strain it out. Put in some juice of lemons; sweeten it to your taste. Steep two ounces of sweet almonds in rose-water; and blanch, stamp, and strain them through into the barley, till it is as white as milk.

French Barley Cream.

Boil your barley in two or three waters, till it looks white and tender; pour the water clean from the barley, and put as much cream as will make it tolerably thick, and a blade or two of mace, and let it boil. To a pint and a half of cream put two ounces of almonds, blanched and ground with rose-water. Strain them with cold cream; put the cream through the almonds two or three times, wringing it hard. Sweeten to your taste; let it boil; and put it in a broad dish.

Chocolate Cream.

Boil a quart of thick cream, scraping into it one ounce of chocolate. Add about a quarter of a pound of sugar; when it is cold put nine whites of eggs; whisk it, and, as the froth rises, put it into glasses.

Citron Cream.

To a quarter of a pound of citron pounded put three gills of cream: mill it up with a chocolate-stick till the citron is mixed; put it in sugar if needful.

Clotted Cream.

Set the milk in the usual way; when it has stood twelve hours, it is, without being skimmed, to be placed in a stove and scalded, of course not suffered to boil, and then left to stand again for twelve hours; then take off the cream which floats at the top in lumps, for which reason it is called clotted cream; it may be churned into butter; the skim milk makes cheese.

Coffee Cream.

Take two ounces of whole coffee, one quart of cream, about four ounces of fine sugar, a small piece of the yellow rind of a lemon, with rather less than half an ounce of the best picked isinglass. Boil these ingredients, stirring them now and then, till the cream is highly flavoured with the coffee. It might, perhaps, be better to flavour the cream first, and then dissolve the isinglass and put it to it. Take it off the fire; have ready the yolks of six eggs beaten, which add to the cream, and continue to beat it till it is about lukewarm, lest the eggs should turn the cream. Strain the whole through a fine sieve into the dish in which you mean to serve it, which must be first fixed into a stewpan of boiling water, that will hold it so commodiously, that the bottom only will touch the water, and not a drop of the water come to the cream. Cover the cream with the lid of a stewpan, and in that lid put two or three bits of lighted charcoal, moving them from one part to another, that it may all set alike; it should only simmer. When it has done in this manner for a short time, take off the cover of the stewpan; if not done enough, cover it again, and put fresh charcoal; it should be done so as to form a weak jelly. Take it off, and keep it in a cool place till you serve it. If you wish to turn it out in a mould, boil more isinglass in it. Tea cream is made in the same manner.

Eringo Cream.

Take a quarter of a pound of eringoes, and break them into short pieces; put to them a pint of milk; let it boil till the eringoes are very tender; then pour the milk from them; put in a pint of cream to the eringoes; let them boil; put in an egg, beaten well, to thicken, and dish it up.

Fruit Cream.

Scald your fruit; when done, pulp it through a sieve; let it stand till almost cold; then sweeten it to your taste; put it into your cream, and make it of whatever thickness you please.

Preserved Fruit Creams.

Put half a pound of the pulp of any preserved fruit in a large pan: add to it the whites of three eggs, well beaten; beat these well together for an hour. Take it off with a spoon, and lay it up high on the dish or glasses. Raspberries will not do this way.

Italian Cream.

Boil a pint of cream with half a pint of new milk; when it boils throw in the peel of an orange and a lemon, with a quarter of a pound of sugar, and a small pinch of salt. When the cream is impregnated with the flavour of the fruit, mix and beat it with the yolks of eight eggs; set it on the fire to be made equally thick; as soon as it is thick enough for the eggs to be done, put into it an ounce of dissolved isinglass; drain it well through a sieve: put some of the cream into a small mould, to see if it is thick enough: if not, add more isinglass. Lay this preparation in a mould in some salt or ice; when it is quite stiff, and you wish to send it up, dip a napkin in hot water, and put it round the mould, which turn upside down in the dish.

Another.

Put two table-spoonfuls of sifted sugar, half of a gill of white wine, with a little brandy, a table-spoonful of lemon-juice, and the rind of a lemon, in a basin, with a pint of cream well whipped together; put thin muslin in the shape or mould, and set it in a cold place, or on ice, till wanted.

Lemon Cream. No. 1.

Take five large lemons and rasp off all the outside; then squeeze the lemons, and put what you have rasped off into the juice; let it stand two or three hours, if all night the better. Take eight whites of eggs and one yolk, and beat them well together; put to it a pint of spring water: then mix them all, and sweeten it with double-refined sugar according to your taste. Set it over a chaffing-dish of coals, stirring it till it is of a proper thickness; then dish it out. Be sure not to let it boil.

Lemon Cream. No. 2.

Pare three smooth-skinned lemons; squeeze out the juice; cut the peel in small pieces, and put it to the juice. Let it stand two or three hours closely covered, and, when it has acquired the flavour of the peel, add to it the whites of five eggs and the yolks of three. Beat them well with two spoonfuls of orange-flower water; sweeten with double-refined sugar; strain it; set it over a slow fire, and stir it carefully till it is as thick as cream; then pour it into glasses.

Lemon Cream. No. 3.

Set on the fire three pints of cream; when it is ready to boil, take it off, and squeeze a lemon into it. Stir it up; hang it up in a cloth, till the whey has run out; sweeten it to your taste, and serve it up.

Lemon Cream. No. 4.

Take the sweetest cream, and squeeze in juice of lemon to your taste: put it into a churn, and shake it till it rises or ferments. Sweeten it to your taste, but be sure not to put any sugar before you churn it, for that will hinder the fermentation.

Lemon Cream. No. 5.

Pare two lemons, and squeeze to them the juice of one larger or two smaller; let it remain some time, and then strain the juice to a pint of cream, and add the yolks of four eggs beaten and strained; sweeten it, and stir it over the fire till thick. You may add a little brandy, if agreeable.

Lemon Cream without Cream.

Squeeze three lemons, and put the parings into the juice; cover and let it remain three hours; beat the yolks of two eggs and the whites of four; sweeten this; add a little orange-flower water, and put it to the lemon-juice. Set the whole over a slow fire till it becomes as thick as cream, and take particular care not to let it boil.

Lemon Cream frothed.

Make a pint of cream very sweet, and add the paring of one lemon; let it just boil; put the juice of one large lemon into a glass or china dish, and, when the cream is nearly cold, pour it out of a tea-pot upon the juice, holding it as high as possible. Serve it up.

Orange Cream.

Squeeze the juice of four oranges to the rind of one; pat it over the fire with about a pint of cream, and take out the peel before the cream becomes bitter. Boil the cream, and, when cold, put to it the yolks of four eggs and the whites of three, beaten and strained, and sugar to your taste. Scald this, but keep stirring all the time, until of a proper thickness.

Orange Cream frothed.

Proceed in the same way as with the lemon, but put no peel in the cream; merely steep a bit a short time in the juice.

Imperial Orange Cream.

Take a pint of thick sweet cream, and boil it with a little orange-peel. When it just boils, take it off the fire, and stir it till it is no hotter than milk from the cow. Have ready the juice of four Seville oranges and four lemons; strain the juice through a jelly-bag, and sweeten it well with fine sugar, and a small spoonful of orange-flower water. Set your dish on the ground, and, your juice being in it, pour the cream from as great a height as you can, that it may bubble up on the top of the cream; then set it by for five or six hours before you use it, if the weather is hot, but in winter it may stand a whole night.

Pistachio Cream.

Take a quarter of a pound of pistachio-nuts and blanch them; then beat them fine with rose-water; put them into a pint of cream; sweeten it, let it just boil, and put it into glasses.

Raspberry Cream.

To one pint of cream put six ounces of jam, and pulp it through a sieve, adding the juice of a lemon; whisk it fast at the edge of your dish; lay the froth on the sieve, and add a little more of the juice. When no more froth will rise, put your cream into a dish or cups; heap the froth well on.

Ratafia Cream.

Boil three or four laurel-leaves in one pint of cream, and strain it; when cold, add the yolks of three eggs beaten and strained; then sweeten it; put in it a very little brandy; scald it till thick, and keep stirring it all the time.

Rice Cream.

Boil a quart of milk with a laurel-leaf; pour it on five dessert spoonfuls of ground rice; let it stand two hours; then put it into a saucepan, and boil it till it is tender, with rather less than a quarter of a pound of sugar. Beat the yolks of two eggs, and put them into it when it is almost cold; and then boil till it is as thick as a cream. When it is sent to table, put in a few ratafia biscuits.

Runnet Whey Cream.

Turn new milk from the cow with runnet; press the whey from it; beat the curd in a mortar till it is quite smooth; then mix it with thick cream, and froth it with a froth-stick; add a little powdered sugar.

Snow Cream.

Sweeten the whites of four eggs, add a pint of thick sweet cream and a good spoonful of brandy. Whisk this well together; take off the froth, and lay it upon a sieve; when all the froth that will rise is taken off, pour what has run through to the rest. Stir it over a slow fire, and let it just boil; fill your glasses about three parts full, and lay on the froth.

Strawberry Cream.

Exactly the same as raspberry.

Sweetmeat Cream.

Slice preserved peaches, apricots, or plums, into good cream, sweetening it with fine sugar, or the syrup in which they were preserved. Mix these well together, and put it into glasses.

Whipt Cream, to put upon Cake.

Sweeten a pint of cream to your taste; grate in the peel of a lemon, and steep it some hours before you make use of your cream. Add the juice of two lemons; whip it together; and take off the top into a large piece of fine muslin, or gauze, laid within a sieve. Let this be done the night before it is to be used. In summer it may be done in the morning of the same day; but the whipt cream must be drained from the curd before it is put upon the cake.

Cucumbers, to preserve green.

Take fine large green cucumbers; put them in salt and water till they are yellow; then green them over fresh salt and water in a little roch alum. Cover them close with abundance of vine leaves, changing the leaves as they become yellow. Put in some lemon-juice; and, when the cucumbers are of a fine green, take them off and scald them several times with hot water, or make a very thin syrup, changing it till the raw taste of the cucumbers is taken away. Then make a syrup thus: to a pound of cucumbers take one pound and a half of double-refined sugar; leave out the half pound to add to them when boiled up again; put lemon-peel, ginger cut in slices, white orris root, and any thing else you like to flavour with; boil it well; when cool, put it to the cucumbers, and let them remain a few days. Boil up the syrup with the remainder of the sugar; continue to heat the syrup till they look clear. Just before you take the syrup off, add lemon-juice to your taste.

Cream Curd.

Boil a pint of cream, with a little mace, cinnamon, and rose-water, and, when as cool as new milk, put in half a spoonful of good runnet. When it turns, serve it up in the cream dish.

Lemon Curd.

To a pint of cream, when it boils, put in the whites of six eggs, and one lemon and a half; stir it until it comes to a tender curd. Then put it into a holland bag, and let it drain till all the whey is out of it; beat the curd in a mortar with a little sugar; put it in a basin to form; about two or three hours before you use it, turn it out, and pour thick cream and sugar over it.

Paris Curd.

Put a pint of cream on the fire, with the juice of one lemon, and the whites of six eggs; stir it till it becomes a curd. Hang it all night in a cloth to drain; then add to it two ounces of sweet almonds, with brandy and sugar to your taste. Mix it well in a mortar, and put it into shapes.

Currants, to bottle.

Gather your fruit perfectly dry, and not too ripe; cut each currant from the stalk separately, taking care not to bruise them; fill your bottles quite full, cork them lightly, set them in a boiler with cold water, and let them simmer a quarter of an hour, or according to the nature and ripeness of the fruit. By this process the fruit will sink; pour on as much boiling water as will cover the surface and exclude air. Should they mould, move it off when you use the fruit, and you will not find the fruit injured by it. Cork your bottles quickly, after you take them out of the water; tie a bladder over, and put them in a dry place. This method answers equally well for gooseberries, cherries, greengages, and damsons.

Another way.

Gather the currants quite dry; clip them off the stalks; if they burst in pulling off they will not do. Fill some dry common quart bottles with them, rosin the corks well over, and then tie a bladder well soaked over the cork, and upon the leather; all this is absolutely necessary to keep the air out, and corks in; place the bottles, with the corks downwards, in a boiler of cold water, and stuff hay between them to keep them steady. Make a fire under them, and keep it up till the water boils; then rake it out immediately, and leave the bottles in the boiler till the water is quite cold. Put them into the cellar in any vessel that will keep them steadily packed, the necks always downward. When a bottle is opened, the currants must be used at once. The bottles will not be above half full when taken out of the boiler, and they must not be shaken more than can be avoided.

This process answers equally well for apricots, plums, and cherries.

Currants or Barberries, to dry in bunches.

When the currants, or barberries, (which should be maiden barberries) are stoned and tied up in bunches, take to one pound of them a pound and a half of sugar. To each pound of sugar put half a pint of water; boil the syrup well, and put the fruit into it. Set it on the fire; let it just boil, and then take it off. Cover it close with white paper; let it stand till next day; then make it scalding hot, and let it stand two or three days, covered close with paper. Lay it in earthen plates; sprinkle over it fine sugar, put it on a stove to dry; lay it on sieves till one side is dry; then turn and sift sugar on it. When dry enough lay it between papers.

Currants, to ice.

Take the largest and finest bunches of currants you can get; beat the white of an egg to a froth; dip them into it; lay them, so as not to touch, upon a sieve: sift double-refined sugar over them very thick, and let them dry in a stove or oven.

White Currants, to preserve.

Take the largest white currants, but not the amber colour; strip them, and to two quarts of currants put a pint of water; boil them very fast, and run them through a jelly-bag to a pint of juice. Put a pound and half of sugar, and half a pound of stoned currants; set them on a brisk fire, and let them boil very fast till the currants are clear and jelly very well; then put them into glasses or pots, stirring them as they cool, to make them mix well. Paper them down when just cold.

Red Currants, to preserve.

Mash the currants and strain them through a thin strainer; to a pint of juice take a pound and a half of sugar and six spoonfuls of water. Boil it up and skim it well. Put in half a pound of stoned currants; boil them as fast as you can, till the currants are clear and jelly well; then put them into pots or glasses, and, when cold, paper them as other sweetmeats. Stir all small fruits as they cool, to mix them with the jelly.

Another way.

Take red and white currants; squeeze and drain them. Boil two pints of juice with three pounds of fine sugar: skim it; then put in a pound of stoned currants; let them boil fast till they jelly, and put them into bottles.

Currant Jam.

To a pound of currants put three quarters of a pound of lump sugar. Put the fruit first into the preserving-pan, and place the sugar carefully in the middle, so as not to touch the pan. Let it boil gently on a clear fire for about half an hour. It must not be stirred. Skim the jelly carefully from the top, and add a quarter of a pound of fruit to what remains from the jelly; stir it well, and boil it thoroughly. The proportion of fruit added for the jam must always be one quarter. In making jelly or jam, it is an improvement to add to every five pounds of currants one pound of raisins.

Currant Jam or Jelly.

Take two pounds of currants and half a pound of raspberries: to every pound of fruit add three quarters of a pound of good moist sugar. Simmer them slowly; skim the jam very nicely; when boiled to a sufficient consistency, put it into jars, and, when cold, cover with brandy paper.

Black or red Currant Jelly.

Strip the fruit when full ripe; put it into a stone jar; put the jar, tied over with white paper, into a saucepan of cold water, and stew it to boiling on the stove. Strain off the liquor, and to every pint of red currants weigh out a pound of loaf-sugar, if black, three quarters of a pound; mix the fruit and the sugar in lumps, and let it rest till the sugar is nearly dissolved. Then put it in a preserving-pan, and simmer and skim it till it is quite clear. When it will jelly on a plate, it is done, and may be put in pots.

Currant Juice.

Take currants, and squeeze the juice out of them; have some very dry quart bottles, and hold in each a couple of burning matches. Cork them up, to keep the smoke confined in them for a few hours, till the juice is put in them. Fill them to the neck with the currant juice; then scald them in a copper or pot with hay between. The water must be cold when the bottles are put in: let them have one boil.

Another way.

Boil a pint of currant juice with half a pint of clarified sugar; skim it; add a little lemon to taste, and mix with a quart of seed.

Currant Paste.

Mash red and white currants; strain them through a linen bag; break in as much of the strained currants as will make the juice thick enough of seeds; add some gooseberries boiled in water. Boil the whole till it jellies; let it stand to cool; then put a pound of sugar to every pint, and scald it.

Custard. No. 1.

One quart of cream, twelve eggs, the whites of four, the rind of one lemon, boiled in the cream, with a small quantity of nutmeg, and a bay-leaf, bitter and sweet almonds one ounce each, a little ratafia and orange-flower water; sweeten to your taste. The cream must be quite cold before the eggs are added. When mixed, it must just be made to boil, and then fill your cups.

Custard. No. 2.

Take one pint of cream, boil in it a few laurel-leaves, a stick of cinnamon, and the rind of a lemon; when nearly cold, add the yolks of seven eggs, well beaten, and six ounces of lump sugar; let it nearly boil; keep stirring it all the while, and till nearly cold, and add a little brandy.

Custard. No. 3.

A quart of cream, and the yolks of nine eggs, sugared to your taste; if eggs are scarce, take seven and three whites; it must not quite boil, or it will curdle; keep it stirred all the time over a slow fire. When it is nearly cold, add three table-spoon-fuls of ratafia; stir till cold, otherwise it will turn. It is best without any white of eggs.

Custard. No. 4.

Take a pint of cream; blanch a few sweet almonds, and beat them fine; sweeten to your palate. Beat up the yolks of five eggs, stir all together, one way, over the fire, till it is thick. Add laurel-leaves, bitter almonds, or ratafia, to give it a flavour; then put it into cups.

Custard. No. 5.

Make some rice, nicely boiled, into a good wall round your trifle dish; strew the rice over with pink comfits; then pour good custard into the rice frame, and stripe it across with pink and blue comfits alternately.

Almond Custard.

Blanch and pound fine, with half a gill of rose-water, six ounces of sweet and half an ounce of bitter almonds; boil a pint of milk; sweeten it with two ounces and a half of sugar; rub the almonds through a sieve, with a pint of cream; strain the milk to the yolks of eight eggs, well beaten—three whites if thought necessary—

stir it over a fire till of a good thickness; when off the fire, stir it till nearly cold to prevent its curdling.

To bottle Damsons.

Take ripe fruit; wipe them dry, and pick off the stalks; fill your bottles with them. The bottles must be very clean and dry. Put the corks lightly into them, to keep out the steam when simmering: then set them up to the necks in cold water, and let them simmer a quarter of an hour, but not boil, or the fruit will crack. Take them out, and let them stand all night. Next day, cork them tight, rosin the corks, and keep them in a dry place.

Damsons, to dry.

Pick out the finest damsons, and wipe them clean. To every pound of fruit take half a pound of sugar; wet the damsons with water; and put them into the sugar with the insides downward. Set them on the fire till the sugar is melted; let them lie in the sugar till it has thoroughly penetrated them, heating them once a day. When you take them out, dip them in hot water, and lay them to dry.

Damsons, to preserve without Sugar.

When the damsons are quite ripe, wipe them separately, and put them into stone jars. Set them in an oven four or five times after the bread is drawn. When the skins shrivel they are done enough; if they shrink much, you must fill up the jar with more fruit, and cover them at last with melted suet.

Dripping, to clarify for Crust.

Boil beef dripping in water for a few minutes; let it stand till cold, when it will come off in a cake. It makes good crust for the kitchen.

Dumplings.

Take of stale bread, suet, and loaf-sugar, half a pound each; make the whole so fine as to go through a sieve. Mix it with lemon-juice, and add the rind of a lemon finely grated. Make it up into dumplings, and pour over them sweet sauce without wine.

Currant Dumplings.

A quarter of a pound of apple, a quarter of a pound of currants, three eggs, some sugar, bitter almonds, lemon or orange peel, and a little nutmeg. Boil an hour and a half.

Drop Dumplings.

To a piece of fresh butter, of the size of an egg, take three spoonfuls of flour, and three yolks of eggs; stir the butter and eggs well together; add a little salt and nutmeg, and then put the flour to it. Drop the batter with a small spoon into boiling water, and let it boil four or five minutes; pour the water from the dumplings, and eat them with a ragout, or as a dish by itself.

Another way.

Break two eggs into half a pint of milk, and beat them up; mix with flour, and put a little salt. Set on the fire a saucepan with water, and, when it boils, drop the batter in with a large spoon, and boil them quick for five minutes. Take them out carefully with a slice, lay them on a sieve for a minute to dry, put them into a dish, cut a piece of butter in thin slices, and stir among them. Send them up as hot as you can.

Kitchen hard Dumplings.

Mix flour and water with a little salt into a stiff paste. Put in a few currants for change, and boil them for half an hour. It improves them much to boil them with beef or pork.

Yest Dumplings.

A table-spoonful of yest, three handfuls of flour, mix with water and a little salt. Boil ten minutes in a deep pot, and cover with water when they rise. The dough to be made about the size of an apple. The quantity mentioned above will make a dozen of the proper size.

Another way.

Make nice light dough, by putting your flour into a platter; make a hollow in the middle of it, and pour in a little good small beer warmed, an egg well beaten, and some warm milk and water. Strew salt upon the flour, but not upon the mix-ture in the middle, or it will not do well. Then make it into as light a dough as you can, and set it before the fire, covered with a cloth, a couple of hours, to rise. Make it into large dumplings, and set them before the fire six or seven minutes; then put them into boiling water with a little milk in it. A quarter of an hour will do them.

Eggs.

Eggs left till cold will reheat to the same degree as at first. For instance, an egg boiled three minutes and left till cold will reheat in the same time and not be harder. It may be useful to know this when fresh eggs are scarce.

Whites of Eggs.

Beat up the whites of twelve eggs with rose-water, some fine grated lem-on-peel, and nutmeg; sweeten to your taste, and well mix the whole. Boil it in four bladders, tied up in the shape of an egg, till hard; they will take half an hour. When cold, lay them in a dish; mix half a pint of good cream, a gill of sack, and half the juice of a Seville orange; sweeten and mix it well, and pour it over the eggs.

Another way.

Beat two whites in a plate in a cool place till quite stiff and they look like snow.

Lay it on the lid of a stewpan; put it in a cool oven, and bake it of a light brown for about ten minutes.

Figs, to dry.

Take figs when thoroughly ripe, pare them very thin, and slit them at the top. To one pound of fruit put three quarters of a pound of sugar, and to the sugar a pint of water; boil the syrup at first a little, skim it very clean, and set it over coals to keep it warm. Have ready some warm water, and when it boils put in your figs; let them boil till tender; then take them up by the stalk, and drain them clean from water. Put them into the syrup over the fire for two or three hours, turning them frequently; do the same morning and evening, keeping them warm, for nine days, till you find them begin to candy. Then lay them out upon glasses. Turn them often the first day, on the next twice only; they will quickly dry if they are well attended to. A little ambergris or musk gives the fruit a fine flavour. Peaches and plums may be done the same way.

Small Flowers, to candy.

Take as much fine sugar as you think likely to cover the flowers, and wet it for a candy. When boiled pretty thick, put in your flowers, and stir, but be careful not to bruise them. Keep them over the fire, but do not let them boil till they are pretty dry; then rub the sugar off with your hands as soon as you can, and take them out.

Flowers in sprigs, to candy.

Dissolve gum arabic in water, and let it be pretty thin; wet the flowers in it, and put them in a cloth to dry. When nearly dry, dip them all over in finely sifted sugar, and hang them up before the fire, or, if it should be a fine sunshiny day, hang them in the sun till they are thoroughly dry, and then take them down. The same may be done to marjoram and mint.

Dutch Flummery.

Steep two ounces of isinglass two hours in a pint of boiling water; take a pint of white wine, the yolks of eight eggs, well beaten, the juice of four lemons, with the rind of one. Sweeten it to your taste; set it over the fire, and keep it stirring till it boils.

Hartshorn Flummery. No. 1.

Take half a pound of hartshorn; boil it in four quarts of water, till reduced to one quarter or less; let it stand all night. Blanch a quarter of a pound of almonds, and beat them small; melt the jelly, mix with it the almonds, strained through a thin strainer or hair sieve; then put a quarter of a pint of cream, a little cinnamon, and a blade of mace; boil these together, and sweeten it. Put it into china cups, and, when you use it, turn it out of the cups, and eat it with cream.

Hartshorn Flummery. No. 2.

Put one pound of hartshorn shavings to three quarts of spring water; boil it very gently over a slow fire till it is reduced to one quart, then strain it through a fine sieve into a basin; let it stand till cold; then just melt it, and put to it half a pint of white wine, a pint of good thick cream, and four spoonfuls of orange-flower water. Scald the cream, and let it be cold before you mix it with the wine and jelly; sweeten it with double-refined sugar to your taste, and then beat it all one way for an hour and a half at least, for, if you are not careful in thus beating, it will neither mix nor even look to please you. Dip the moulds first in water, that they may turn out well. Keep the flummery in cups a day before you use it; when you serve it, stick it with blanched almonds, cut in thin slices. Calves' feet may serve instead of hartshorn shavings.

Hartshorn Flummery. No. 3.

Take one pound of hartshorn shavings, and put to it three quarts of water; boil it till it is half consumed; then strain and press out the hartshorn, and set it by to cool. Blanch four ounces of almonds in cold water, and beat them very fine with a little rose and orange-flower water. Make the jelly as warm as new milk, and sweeten it to your taste with the best sugar; put it by degrees to the almonds, and stir it very well until they are thoroughly mixed. Then wring it through a cloth, put it into cups, and set it by to jelly. Before you turn them out, dip the outside in a little warm water to loosen them; stick them with blanched almonds, cut in thin long pieces. Three ounces of sweet almonds, and one of apricot or peach kernels, make ratafia flummery. If you have none of the latter, use bitter almonds.

Fondues.

Boil a quarter of a pound of crumb of bread in milk; beat it with a wooden spoon; grate half a pound of Cheshire cheese, add the yolks of three eggs, and a quarter of a pound of butter; beat all well together. Beat up three whites of eggs to a thick froth; put this in last, and beat the whole well together. Bake in two paper cases or a dish, in a quick oven, for twenty minutes.

Yorkshire Fritters.

To two quarts of flour take two spoonfuls of yest, mixed with a little warm milk. Let it rise. Take nine eggs, leaving out four whites, and temper your dough to the consistence of paste. Add currants or apples, and a little brandy or rose-water. Roll the fritters thin, and fry them in lard.

Fruit, to preserve.

Strip the fruit, put it into a stone jar, set the jar in a saucepan of water, and stew it to boiling on the stove. Strain off the liquor, and to every pint allow a pound of loaf sugar. Mix the fruit and the sugar in lumps in a stone vessel, but not till the sugar is nearly dissolved: then put it in a preserving-pan, and simmer and strain it till it is quite clear. When it will jelly on a plate, it is done, and may be put into pots.

Fruit, to preserve green.

Take green pippins, pears, plums, apricots, or peaches; put them into a preserving-pan; cover them with vine-leaves, and then with clear spring water. Put on the cover of the pan, and set them over a very clear fire; take them off as soon as they begin to simmer, and take them carefully out with a slice. Then peel and preserve them as other fruit.

Fruit of all sorts, to scald.

Put your fruit into scalding water, sufficient nearly to cover it; set it over a slow fire, and keep it in a scald till tender, turning the fruit where the water does not cover. When it is very tender, lay paper close to it, and let it stand till it is cold. Then, to a pound of fruit put half a pound of sugar, and let it boil, but not too fast, till it looks clear. All fruit must be done whole, excepting pippins, and they are best in halves or quarters, with a little orange-peel and the juice of lemon.

Gingerbread. No. 1.

To a pound and a half of flour add one pound of treacle, almost as much sugar, an ounce of beaten ginger, two ounces of caraway seeds, four ounces of citron and lemon-peel candied, and the yolks of four eggs. Cut your sweetmeats, mix all, and bake it in large cakes, or tin plates.

Gingerbread. No. 2.

Into one pound and a half of flour work three quarters of a pound of butter; add three quarters of a pound of treacle, two ounces of sugar, half an ounce of ginger, a little orange-peel beaten and sifted. Some take a pound and a quarter of treacle and two ounces of ginger.

Gingerbread. No. 3.

Two pounds of flour, two ounces of caraway seeds, one tea-spoonful of powdered ginger, half a spoonful of allspice, and the same of pearl-ash, two ounces of preserved orange, the same of lemon-peel, and half a pound of butter; mix these ingredients well together, and make it into a stiff paste with treacle, as stiff as you would make paste for a tart; then put it before the fire to rise for one hour, after which you may roll it out, and cut it into cakes, or mould it, as you like.

Gingerbread. No. 4.

Take a pound of treacle and half a pound of butter; melt them together over a fire; have ready a pound and a half of flour well dried, into which put at least half an ounce of ginger well beaten and sifted, as many coriander seeds, half a pound of sugar, a little brandy, and some candied orange-peel; then mix the warm treacle and butter with the flour; make it into flat cakes, and bake it upon tins.

Gingerbread. No. 5.

Two pounds of flour well dried, one pound of treacle, one pound of sugar, one nutmeg, four ounces of sweetmeats, one ounce of beaten ginger, one pound of fresh butter, melted with the treacle, and poured hot upon the other ingredients; make it into a paste, and let it lie till quite cold; then roll it out, and bake it in a slow oven.

Gingerbread. No. 6.

One pound of treacle, the same weight of flour, butter and sugar of each a quarter of a pound, ginger and candied lemon-peel of each half an ounce. Rub the butter, ginger, and sugar, well together, before you put in the treacle.

Thick Gingerbread.

To a pound and a half of flour take one pound of treacle, almost as much sugar, an ounce of beaten ginger, two ounces of caraway seed, four ounces of citron and lemon-peel candied, and the yolks of four eggs. Cut the sweetmeats; well mix the whole; and bake in large cakes on tin plates.

Gingerbread Cakes or Nuts.

Melt half a pound of butter, and put to it half a pound of treacle, two spoonfuls of brandy, and six ounces of coarse brown sugar. Mix all these together in a saucepan, and let the whole be milk warm; then put it to a pound and a quarter of flour, half an ounce of ginger, some orange-peel finely grated, and as much candied orange as you like.

Gingerbread Nuts.

A quarter of a pound of treacle, the same of flour, one ounce of butter, a little brown sugar, and some ginger. Mix all together, and bake the nuts on tins. Sweetmeat is a great addition.

Gooseberries, to bottle.

Pick them in dry weather before they are too large; cut them at both ends with scissars, that they may not be broken; put them into very dry bottles, and fill them up to the neck with cold spring water. Put the bottles up to their necks in water, in a large fish-kettle, set it on the fire, and scald them. Take it off immediately when you perceive the gooseberries change colour. Next day, if the bottles require filling, have ready some cold spring water which has been boiled, and fill half way up the neck of the bottles; then pour in a little sweet oil, just sufficient to cover the water at the top of the bottle, and tie them over with a bladder.

Gooseberries in Jelly.

Make as much thick syrup as will cover the quantity of gooseberries you intend to do; boil and skim it clear: set it by till almost cold. Have ready some green hairy gooseberries, not quite ripe, and the skins of which are still rather hard; cut off the remains of the flower at one end, leaving the little stalk on at the other; with a small penknife slit down the side, and with the point of the knife carefully remove the seeds, leaving the pulp. Put the gooseberries into the syrup when lukewarm; set it on the fire, shake it frequently, but do not let it boil. Take it off, and let the gooseberries stand all night: with a spoon push them under the syrup, or cover them with white paper. Next day set them on the fire, scald them again, but they must not boil, and shake them as before. Proceed in the same manner a third time. The jelly to put them in must be made thus: Take three pints of the sharpest gooseberries you can get—they must be of the white sort—to one pint of water; and the quantity you make of this jelly must of course be proportioned to that of the fruit. Boil them half an hour, till all the flavour of the fruit is extracted; strain off the liquor; let it settle, pour off the clear, and to each pint add one pound of double-refined sugar. Boil it till it jellies, which you may see by putting a little into a spoon or cup. Put a little of the jelly at the bottom of the pot to prevent the gooseberries from sinking to the bottom; when it is set, put in the rest of the gooseberries and jelly. When cold, cover with brandy paper.

Gooseberries, to preserve.

Pick the white gooseberries, stamp and strain them; then take the largest of them when they just begin to turn; stone them, and to half a pound of gooseberries put a pound of the finest sugar, and beat it very fine. Take half a pound of the juice which you have strained; let it stand to settle clear; and set it, with six spoonfuls of water, on a quick fire; boil it as fast as you can; when you see the sugar, as it boils, look clear, they are enough; which will be in less than a quarter of an hour. Put them in glasses or pots, and paper them close. Next day, if they are not jellied hard enough, set them for a day or two in a hot stove, or in some warm place, but not in the sun; and, when jellied, put the papers close to them after being wetted and dried with a cloth.

Another way.

Stone your gooseberries, and as you stone them put them into water: then weigh them, and to eight ounces of gooseberries take twelve ounces of double-refined sugar. Put as much water as will make it a pretty thick syrup, and when boiled and skimmed let it cool a little; then put the gooseberries into the syrup, and boil them quick, till they look clear. Take them out one by one, and put them into glass bottles; then heat the syrup a little, strain it through muslin, pour it on the fruit, and it will jelly when cold.

Gooseberry Paste.

Pick off the eyes of the gooseberries, and put them in water scarcely sufficient to cover them; let them boil, and rub them through a sieve. Boil up a candy of sugar; put in your paste, and just scald it a little. Add one pound of sugar to a pint of the paste, and put into pots to dry in the stove: when candied over, turn them out on glasses.

Grapes, to dry.

Scald bunches of grapes in water till they will peel; when they are peeled and stoned, put them into fresh cold water, cover them up close, and set them over the fire till they begin to green. Then take them out of the water and put them to the syrup; after it has been well skimmed. Cut a paper that will exactly fit the skillet, and let it rest upon the syrup. Cover the skillet, and set it over a slow fire, till the grapes look green; put them into a thicker syrup, and, when they are as green as you wish them to be, take them out of the syrup, and let them dry in the stove in bunches.

Grapes, to preserve.

Stone your grapes, and peel off the skin; cover them and no more with codling jelly, and let them boil fast up: then take them off the fire, let them stand until they are cold, and boil them again till they become green. Put a pound of sugar to a pint of the grapes, and let them boil fast till they jelly.

Greengages, to preserve.

Gather the plums before they are too ripe, and take as much pump water as will cover them. Put to the water a quarter of a pound of double-refined sugar, boil it, and let it stand to be cold. Prick the greengages with a large needle in four places to the stone; wrap each of them lightly in a vine-leaf, and set them over a slow fire to green. Do so for three days running; on the last day, put in a spoonful of old verjuice or lemon-juice, and a small lump of alum. Next day draw them, and, after taking off the vine-leaves, put them in a thick syrup, first boiled and cleared. Finish them by degrees, by heating them a little every day till they look clear.

Another way.

Stone and split the fruit without taking off the skin. Weigh an equal quantity of sugar and fruit, and strew part of the sugar over the greengages, having first laid them on dishes, with the hollow part uppermost. Take the kernels from the stones, peel and blanch them. The next day, pour off the syrup from the fruit, and boil it very gently with the other sugar eight minutes. Skim it, and add the fruit and kernels. Simmer the whole till quite clear, taking off any scum that rises. Put the fruit, one by one, into small pots, and pour the syrup and kernels to it.

Hartshorn Jelly.

Boil one pound of hartshorn shavings over a very gentle fire, in two quarts of water, till it is reduced to one quart; let it settle, and strain it off. Put to this liquor the whites of eight or nine eggs, and four or five of their shells, broken very fine, the whites well beaten, the juice of seven or eight lemons, or part oranges; sweeten with the best sugar, and add above a pint of Rhenish or Lisbon wine. Mix all these well together, and boil over a quick fire, stirring all the time with a whisk. As soon as it boils up, strain it through a flannel bag, throwing it backward and forward till it is perfectly clear. Boil lemon-peel in it to flavour it. The last time of passing it through the bag, let it drip into the moulds or glasses.

Hedgehog.

Blanch two quarts of the best almonds in cold water; beat them very fine in a mortar, with a little canary wine and orange-flower water; make them into a stiff paste; then beat in the yolks of twelve eggs, leaving out five whites; add a pint of good cream; sweeten to your taste, and put in half a pound of good butter melted. Set it on a slow fire, and keep it constantly stirring till it is stiff enough. Make it up into the form of a hedgehog; stick it full of blanched almonds, slit and stuck up like the bristles; put it in a dish, and make hartshorn jelly, and put to it, or cold cream, sweetened with a glass of white wine, and the juice of a Seville orange; plump two currants for the eyes.

Ice and Cream.

Mix a little cream and new milk together in a dish; put in runnet, as for cheese-cakes; stir it together. Pour in some canary wine and sugar. Then put the whites of three eggs and a little rose-water to a pint of cream; whip it up to a froth with a whisk, and, as it rises, put it upon the runnet and milk. Lay in here and there bunches of preserved barberries, raspberry jam, or any thing of that sort you please. Whip up more froth, and put over the whole.

Lemon Ice.

Grate the peel of two lemons on sugar, and put it into a bowl, with the juice of four lemons squeezed, and well stir it about; then sweeten it with clarified sugar to your taste, and add to it three spoonfuls of water. Throw over a little salt on the ice; put the ice in the bottom of the pail; put the ice-pot on it, and cover it also with ice. Turn the pot continually, and in about a minute or two open it, and continue to stir it till it is frozen enough; after this stir every now and then.

Iceing for Cakes.

Beat the white of an egg to a strong froth; put in by degrees four ounces of fine sugar, beaten and sifted very fine, with as much gum as will lie on a sixpence. Beat it up for half an hour, and lay it over your cakes the thickness of a straw.

Another.

Take the whites of four eggs and a pound of double-refined sugar, pounded and sifted; beat the eggs a little; put the sugar in, and whip it as fast as possible; then wash your cake with rose-water, and lay the iceing on; set it in the oven with the lid down till it is hard.

Jaunemange.

Steep two ounces of isinglass for an hour in a pint of boiling water; put to it three quarters of a pint of white wine, the juice of two oranges and one lemon, the peel of a lemon cut very fine, and the yolks of eight eggs. Sweeten and boil it all together; strain it in a mould, and, when cold, turn it out. Make it the day before you use it.

Another way.

One ounce of isinglass, dissolved in a good half pint of water, the juice of two small lemons, the peel of half a lemon, the yolks of four eggs, well beaten, half a pound of sugar, half a pint of white wine: mix these carefully together, and stir them into the isinglass jelly over the fire. Let it simmer a few minutes; when a little cool, pour it into your moulds, taking care to wet them first; turn it out the next day.

Coloured Jelly, to mix with or garnish other Jelly.

Pare four lemons as thin as possible; put the rinds into a pint and a half of water; let them lie twelve hours: then squeeze the lemons; put the water and juice together; add three quarters of a pound of the best sugar, but if the lemons are large, it will require more sugar. When the sugar is quite melted, beat up the whites of six new-laid eggs to a froth; mix all together, and strain it through a hair sieve into a saucepan; set it on a slow fire, and keep it stirred till it is near boiling and grows thick. Then take it off, and keep stirring it the same way till it cools. The colouring is to be steeped in a cup of water, and then strained into the other ingredients. Care must be taken to stir it always one way. The eggs are the last thing put in; the whole must be well mixed with a whisk till thoroughly incorporated.

Gloucester Jelly.

Of rice, sago, pearl barley, candied eringo root, of each one ounce; add two quarts of water; simmer it over the fire till it is reduced to one quart; strain it. This will produce a strong jelly; a little to be dissolved in white wine or warm milk, and to be taken three or four times a day.

Another way.

Pearl barley, whole rice, sago, and candied eringo root, of each one ounce, and half an ounce of hartshorn shavings, put into two quarts of spring water; simmer very gently till reduced to one quart, and then rub it through a fine sieve. Half a coffee-cup to be taken with an equal quantity of milk in a morning fasting, and lie an hour after it, and to be taken twice more in the day. You may then put a small quantity of wine or brandy instead of milk.

Lemon Jelly.

Put the juice of four lemons, and the rind pared as thin as possible, into a pint of spring water, and let it stand for half an hour. Take the whites of five eggs; sweeten, and strain through a flannel bag. Set it over a slow fire, and stir it one way till it begins to thicken. You may then put it in glasses or dishes, and colour with turmeric.

Nourishing Jelly.

Dissolve two ounces of isinglass in a quart of port wine, with some cinnamon and sugar: sweeten to your taste with the best white sugar. It must not be suffered to boil, and will take two or three hours to dissolve, as the fire must be very slow: stir it often to prevent its boiling. It must be taken cold.

Orange Jelly. No. 1.

Squeeze the juice of nine or ten China oranges and one Seville orange through a sieve into an earthen pan, adding a quarter of a pound of double-refined sugar. Take an ounce and a half, good weight, of the best isinglass, the peel of seven of the oranges grated, and the bitter squeezed out through a towel; boil this peel in the isinglass, which must be put over the fire in about a pint of water just to melt it. Stir it all the time it is on the fire; strain and pour it to the juice of the oranges, which boil together for about ten minutes. When you take it off, strain it again, and put it into moulds.

Orange Jelly. No. 2.

Set on the fire one ounce of isinglass in a quarter of a pint of warm water till it is entirely dissolved. Take the juice of nine oranges; strain off clear half a pint of mountain wine, sweetened with lump sugar to your taste, and colour it with a very little cochineal. Boil all together for a few minutes, and strain it through a flannel bag, till it is quite clear: pour it to the peels, and let it stand till it is a stiff jelly.

Orange Jelly. No. 3.

One ounce of isinglass, dissolved in a pint of water, the juice of six China oranges, a bit of the rind, pared thin, sweetened to the taste, scalded, and strained. You may scoop the rind and fill the oranges, and, when cold, halve or quarter them.

Restorative Jelly.

Take two pounds of knuckle of veal and a pound and a half of lean beef; set it over the fire with four pints of water; cover it close, and stew it till reduced to half. While stewing, put in half an ounce of fine isinglass, picked small, a little salt, and mace. Strain it off clear, and when cold take off every particle of fat. Warm it in hot water, and not in a pan. Take a tea-cupful twice a day.

Strawberry Jelly.

Boil two ounces of isinglass in a quarter of a pint of water over a gentle fire, and skim it well. Mash a quart of scarlet strawberries in an earthen pan with a wooden spoon; then put in the isinglass, some powdered sugar, and the juice of a good lemon—this quantity is for six small moulds; if you do not find it enough, add a little more water; then run it through a tamis, changing it two or three times.

Wine Jelly.

On two ounces of isinglass and one ounce of hartshorn shavings pour one pint of boiling water; let it stand a quarter of an hour covered close; then add two quarts of water, and boil it well till the isinglass is dissolved; add a pint of dry wine, sugar to your taste, four lemons, and the whites of seven eggs well beaten. Boil it quick, and keep it stirring all the time; then pour it through a jelly-bag, and strain it two or three times till quite clear.

Lemons or Seville Oranges, to preserve.

Take fine large lemons or Seville oranges; rasp the outside skin very fine and thin; put them in cold water, and let them lie all night. Put them in fresh water, and set them on the fire in plenty of water, and, when they have had two or three boils, take them off, and let them lie all night in cold water. Then put them into fresh water, and let them boil till they are so tender that you can run a straw through them. If you think the bitterness not sufficiently out, put them again into cold water, and let them lie all night. Lemons need not soak so long as oranges. To four oranges or lemons put two pounds of the best sugar and a pint of water; boil and skim it clear, and when it is cold put in the oranges, and let them lie four or five days in cold syrup; then give them a boil every day till they look clear. Make some pippin or codlin jelly thus: to a pint of either put one pound of sugar, and let it boil till it jellies; then heat the oranges, and put them to the jelly and half their syrup; boil them very fast a quarter of an hour, and, just before you take them off the fire, put in the juice of two or three lemons; put them in pots or porringers, that will hold them single, and that will admit jelly enough. To four oranges or lemons, put a pound and a half of jelly and the same quantity of syrup, but boiled together, as directed for the oranges. Malaga lemons are the best; they are done in the same manner as the oranges, only that they do not require so much soaking.

Lemon Caudle.

Take a pint of water, the juice of two lemons, the rind of half a lemon pared as thin as possible from the white, a blade of mace, and some bread shred very small; sweeten to your taste. Set the whole on the fire to boil; when boiled enough, which you will perceive by the bread being soft, beat three or four eggs well together till they are as thin as water; then take a little out of the skillet and put to the eggs, and so proceed till the eggs are hot; then put them to the rest, stirring well to prevent curdling.

Lemon or Chocolate Drops.

Take half a pound of fine-sifted double-refined sugar; grate into it the yellow rind of a fair large lemon; whip the white of an egg to a froth, with which wet the sugar till it is as stiff as good working paste. Drop it as you like on paper, with a little sugar first sifted on it; bake in a very slow oven.

For chocolate drops, grate about an ounce of chocolate as you did of lemon-peel, which must then be left out.

Lemon Puffs.

Into half a pound of double-refined sugar, beat fine and sifted, grate the yellow rind of a large lemon. Whip up the white of an egg to a froth, and wet it with the froth, till it is as stiff as a good working paste. Lay the puffs on papers, and bake them in a very slow oven.

Lemon Tart.

A quarter of a pound of almonds blanched and beaten with a little sweet cream; put in half a pound of sugar, the yolks only of eight eggs, half a pound of butter, the peel of two lemons grated. Beat all together fine in a mortar; lay puff paste about the dish; bake it half an hour.

Lemon Solid.

Put the juice of a lemon, with the rind grated, into a dish: sweeten it to your taste; boil a quart of cream till it is reduced to three half pints; pour it upon the lemon, and let it stand to cool. It should be made the day before it is used.

Syrup of Lemons.

To three pounds of the best sugar finely beaten put one pint of lemon juice, set by to settle, and then poured off clear: put it in a silver tankard, and set that in a pot of boiling water. Let this boil till the sugar is quite dissolved, and when cold bottle it; take care that in the boiling not the least water gets in. Skim off any little scum that rises.

Macaroons.

Take half a pound of almonds, blanched and pounded, and half a pound of finely pounded lump sugar. Beat up the whites of two eggs to a froth; mix the sugar and almonds together; add the eggs by degrees; and, when they are well mixed, drop a spoonful on wafer-paper. They must be baked as soon as made in a slow oven.

Citron Marmalade.

Boil the citron very tender, cutting off all the yellow rind; beat the white very well in a wooden bowl; shred the rind, and to a pound of pulp and rind take a pound and a half of sugar, and half a pint of water. When it boils, put in the citron, and boil it very fast till it is clear; put in half a pint of pippin jelly, and boil it till it jellies very well; then add the lemon-juice, and put it into your pots or glasses.

Cherry Marmalade.

Take eight pounds of cherries, not too ripe; stone them; take two pounds of sugar beaten, and the juice of four quarts of currants, red and white. Put the cherries into a pan, with half a pound of the sugar, over a very hot fire; shake them frequently; when there is a good deal of liquor, put in the rest of the sugar, skimming it well and boiling it as fast as possible, till your syrup is almost wasted; then put in your currant juice, and let it boil quick till it jellies; keep stirring it with care; then put it in pots.

Another way.

Take five pounds of cherries stoned and two pounds of loaf sugar; shred your cherries, wet your sugar with the juice that runs from them, then put the cherries into the sugar, and boil them pretty fast, till they become a marmalade. When cold, put it into glasses for use.

Orange Marmalade. No. 1.

Pare your oranges very thin, and lay them in water two or three days, changing the water twice a day; then take them out, and dry them with a linen cloth. Take their weight in sugar beat fine; cut the oranges in halves, take out the pulp, pick out the seeds, and take off the skins carefully. Boil the rinds very tender in a linen cloth; cut them in strips whilst hot, and lay them in the pan in which you design to boil the marmalade. Put a layer of sugar, and a layer of orange rinds, alternately, till all are in; let them stand till the sugar is quite dissolved; add the juice of a lemon; set them on a stove, and let them boil fast till nearly done; then put in the pulp, and boil them again till quite done. Take them off, and add the juice of a lemon; let them stand in pots for a few days, and they will be fit for eating.

Lemon marmalade may be done in the same way, only with a much greater quantity of sugar, or sugar mixed with sugar-candy.

Orange Marmalade. No. 2.

Take six dozen Seville oranges; pare thin three dozen, the other three rasp thin, and keep the parings and raspings separate. Cut all the six dozen in halves; squeeze out the juice, but not too hard; scoop out the pulp with a tea-spoon; pick out the seeds, and keep the pulp. Boil the skins, changing the water two or three times, to take off the bitterness, till they are tender enough for a straw to pierce them. When they are boiled, scoop out and throw away the stringy part; boil the parings three times in different waters; beat the boiled skins very fine in a marble mortar; beat the boiled rinds in the same manner. The pulp, skin, rinds, and juice, must be all weighed, but not yet mixed; for each pound in the whole take one pound of loaf sugar, which must first be mixed with a little water, boiled alone, well skimmed, and thoroughly cleared. The pulp, skins, and juice, must then be put into this syrup, well mixed, and boiled together for about half an hour; after which put in the rasped rinds, beaten as above directed, and boil all together for a short time. Put the marmalade into small pots, and cover with brandy paper.

Orange Marmalade. No. 3.

Take a dozen of Seville oranges and their weight in sugar finely powdered. Pare the oranges as thin as possible; the first peel is not used in marmalade; it is better to grate off the outer peel and put them in water. Let them lie two or three days, changing the water every day; then cut the oranges in quarters, and take out all the pulp; boil the peels in several waters, till they are quite tender and not bitter. Then put to the sugar half a pint of water, and boil it to a syrup, till it draws as fine as a hair; put in the peels sliced very thin, and boil them gently about a quarter of an hour. While the peels are boiling, pick out all the seeds and skins from the pulp; then put the pulp to the orange-peel; let it boil till it is clear; put a little in a saucer, and when it jellies it is done enough.

Scotch Orange Marmalade.

Weigh the oranges, and take an equal weight of sugar; wipe the fruit with a wet cloth; grate them, cut them across, and squeeze them through a hair sieve. Boil the skins tender, so that the head of a pin will easily pierce them; take them off the fire, squeeze out the water, scrape the pulp from them, cut the skins into very thin chips, and let them boil until they are very transparent. Then put in the juice and so much of the gratings as you choose; let it all boil together till it will jelly, which you will know by letting a little of it cool in a saucer.

Red Quince Marmalade. No. 1.

Take one pound and a half of quinces, two pounds of sugar, a pint of water, and a quarter of a pint of the juice of quinces; boil it tender, and skim it well. When done enough, put into it a quarter of a pint of the juice of barberries. Skim it clear as long as any thing rises.

Red Quince Marmalade. No. 2.

Scald as many fine large quinces as you would use, and grate as many small ones as will make a quart of juice, or according to the quantity you want. Let this settle; after you have pressed it through a coarse cloth, strain it through a jelly-bag, that what you use may be perfectly clear. To every pint of this liquor put a pound and a half of sugar, and a pound and a half of the scalded quinces, which must be pared and cored before they are weighed. Set it at first on a pretty brisk fire; when it begins to boil, slacken the fire; and when it begins to turn red cover it close. As soon as it is of a fine bright red, take it off, as it turns of a blackish muddy colour in a moment if not carefully watched. A small bit of cochineal, tied up in a bit of rag and boiled with it, gives it a beautiful colour. Before you have finished boiling, add barberry juice, to your judgment, which improves the flavour.

Red Quince Marmalade. No. 3.

Pare the quinces, quarter them, and cut out all the hard part; to a pound of quinces put a pound and a half of sugar and half a pound of the juice of barberries, boiled with water, as you do jelly or other fruit, boiling it very fast, and break it very small; when it is all to pieces and jellied, it is enough. If you wish the marmalade to be of a green colour, put a few black bullaces to the barberries when you make the jelly.

White Quince Marmalade.

Pare and quarter the quinces, and put as much water as will cover them; boil them all to pieces to make jelly, and run it through a jelly-bag. Take a pound of quinces, quarter them, and cut out all the hard parts; pare them, and to a pound of fruit put a pound and a half of finely beaten sugar and half a pint of water. Let it boil till very clear; keep stirring it, and it will break as you wish it. When the sugar is boiled very thick, almost to a candy, put in half a pint of jelly, and let it boil very fast till it becomes a jelly. Take it off the fire, and put in juice of lemon; skim it well, and put it into pots or glasses.

Marchpane.

Blanch one pound of almonds as white as you can; take three quarters of a pound of fine white sugar well pounded; beat them up together with a little rose-water, to prevent the almonds from oiling. Take out the mixture, work it like paste, make it into cakes, lay them on wafers, and bake them. Boil rose-water and sugar till it becomes a syrup; when the cakes are almost done, spread this syrup all over them, and strew them with comfits.

Another way.

Take a pound of almonds finely beaten, and a pound of fine sugar, sifted through a hair sieve; mix these together; then add the whites of four eggs, beaten up to a froth; mix the whole well together, and scald it over your fire, still keeping it well-stirred, to prevent burning. Let it stand till cold; afterwards roll it on papers, and bake it.

Marrow Pasties.

Make the pasties small, the length of a finger; put in large pieces of marrow, first dipped in egg, and seasoned with sugar, beaten cloves, mace, and nutmeg. Strew a few currants on the marrow, and either bake or fry them.

Melons or Cucumbers, to preserve.

Cut and pare a thoroughly ripe melon into thick slices; put them into water till they become mouldy; then put them into fresh water over the fire to coddle, not to boil. Make a good syrup; when properly skimmed, and while boiling, put your melon in to boil for a short time. The syrup should be boiled every day for a fortnight; do not put it to the melon till a little cold: the last time you boil the syrup, put it into a muslin bag; add one ounce of ginger pounded and the juice and rind of two lemons; but, if a large melon, allow an additional ounce of ginger.

Melon Compote.

Cut a good melon as for eating; peel it, carefully taking off the green part entirely, but not more. Take out all the inside, and steep the slices for ten days in the best vinegar, keeping it well covered. Take out the slices, and put them over the fire in fresh vinegar; let them stew till quite tender. Then drain and dry them in a cloth; stick bits of cloves and cinnamon in them; lay them in a jar, and make a syrup, and pour over them. Tie the jar close down. This kind of sweetmeat is eaten in Geneva with roast meat, and is much better than currant jelly or apple sauce. The melon must be in good order, and within three or four days of being ripe enough to eat.

Mince Meat. No. 1.

One pound of beef, one pound and a half of suet, one pound of currants, half a pound of chopped raisins, one pound of sugar, if moist, half a pint of brandy, a pint of raisin wine, mace, cinnamon, allspice, and nutmeg, pounded together.

Sweetmeats, candied lemon, and fresh peel, may be added, when used for baking.

Mince Meat. No. 2.

One pound of beef suet, one pound of apples peeled and cored, one pound of raisins stoned and chopped very fine, the same of currants well picked, half a pound of sugar made very fine, a glass of brandy, a glass of wine, half an ounce of allspice, the juice of two large lemons, the rind chopped as fine as possible: add sweetmeats to your taste.

Mince Meat. No. 3.

Take one pound of beef and two pounds of suet shred fine, two pounds of currants, one pound of the best raisins stoned, but not chopped, three quarters of a pound of sugar, four fine pippins or russetings chopped fine, some grated lemon-peel, half an ounce of cinnamon, the same of nutmeg, a quarter of an ounce of mace, wine and brandy to your taste, and whatever sweetmeats you please.

Mince Meat without Meat. No. 1.

Twelve pounds of currants, very well washed, dried, and picked, six pounds of raisins stoned and chopped very small, a quarter of a pound of cloves, three ounces of mace, and two of nutmegs, pounded very fine, the rind of three large fresh lemons pared very thin and chopped fine, six pounds of powder sugar, a quart of sack, a quart of brandy, one hundred golden rennets, pared, cored, and chopped small: mix all well together, and let it stand two days, stirring it from the bottom twice or thrice a day. Add three whole dried preserved oranges and an equal weight of dried citron. Mix in the suet a day or two before you use it. Add lemon-juice to your taste, and that only to the quantity you mean to bake at once. Without suet these ingredients will keep for six months.

Mince Meat without Meat. No. 2.

To make a mince meat that will keep for five or six years, take four pounds of raisins of the sun, stoned and chopped very fine, five pounds of currants, three pounds of beef suet shred very fine, the crumb of a half-quartern loaf, three pounds of loaf-sugar, the peel of four lemons grated, half an ounce of nutmeg, a quarter of an ounce of mace, the same of cloves, and one pint of good brandy. When you make your pies, add about one third of apple chopped fine; and to each pie put six or eight small slices of citron and preserved orange-peel, with a table-spoonful of sweet wine, ratafia, and a piece of a large lemon mixed together.

Mince Meat without Meat. No. 3.

Three pounds of suet, three pounds of apples, pared and cored, three pounds of currants washed, picked, and dried, one pound and a half of sugar powdered, three quarters of a pound of preserved orange-peel, six ounces of citron, the juice of six lemons, one pint of sack and one of brandy, a quarter of an ounce of mace, the same of nutmeg, and of cloves and cinnamon half a quarter of an ounce each.

Lemon Mince Meat.

Cut three large lemons, and squeeze out the juice; boil the peels together with the pulp till it will pound in a mortar; put to it one pound of beef suet, finely chopped, currants and lump sugar, one pound of each; mix it all well together; then add the juice with a glass of brandy. Put sweetmeats to your taste.

Mirangles.

Put half a pint of syrup into a stewpan, and boil it to what is called blow; then take the whites of three eggs, put them in another copper pan, and whisk them very strong. When your sugar is boiled, rub it against the sides of the stewpan with a table-spoon; when you see the sugar change, quickly mix the whites of eggs with it, for if you are not quick your sugar will turn to powder. When you have mixed it as light as possible, put in the rind of one lemon; stir it as little as possible: take a board, about one foot wide and eighteen inches long, and put a sheet of paper on it. With your table-spoon drop your batter in the shape of half an egg: sift a little powdered sugar over them before you put them in the oven. Let your oven be of a moderate heat; watch them attentively, and let them rise, and just let the outside be a little hard, but not the least brown; the inside must be moist. Take them off with a knife, and just put about a tea-spoonful of jam in the middle of them; then put two of them together, and they will be in the shape of an egg; you must handle them very gently.

Moss.

Take as much white starch as sugar, and sift it; colour some of the sugar with turmeric, some with blue powder, some with chocolate, and some with the juice of spinach; and wet each by itself with a solution of gum-dragon. Strain and rub it through a hair sieve, and let them dry before you touch them.

Muffins.

Mix flour in a pan, with warm new milk and water, yest and salt, according to your judgment. Beat it up well with a wooden spoon till it is a stiff batter; then set it near the fire to rise, which will be in about an hour. It must then be well beaten down, and put to rise again, and, when very light, made into muffins, and baked in flat round irons made for the purpose. The iron must be made hot, and kept so with coals under it. Take out the batter with a spoon, and drop it on a little flour sprinkled lightly on a table. Then lay them on a trencher with a little flour; turn the trencher round to shape them, assisting with your hand if they need it. Then bake them; when one side is done, turn them with a muffin knife, and bake the other.

Oranges, to preserve.

Make a hole at the stalk end; take out all the seeds, but no pulp; squeeze out the juice, which must be saved to put to them, taking great care you do not loosen the pulp. Put them into an earthen pan, with water; boil them till the water is bitter, changing it three times, and, in the last water put a little salt, and boil them till they are very tender, but not to break. Take them out and drain them; take two pounds of sugar and a quart of pippin jelly; boil it to a syrup, skim it very clear, and then put in your oranges. Set them over a gentle fire till they boil very tender and clear; then put to them the juice that you took from them; prick them with a knife that the syrup may penetrate. If you cut them in halves, lay the skin side upwards, and put them up and cover them with the syrup.

Lemons and citrons may be done in the same way.

Whole Oranges, to preserve.

Take six oranges, rasp them very thin, put them in water as you do them, and let them lie all night. In the morning boil them till they are tender, and then put them into clear water, and let them remain so two or three days. Take the oranges, and cut a hole in the top, and pick out the seeds, but not the meat; then take three pounds of fine sugar, and make a thin syrup, and, when boiled and skimmed, put in your oranges, and let them boil till they are clear. Take them out, and let them stand three or four days; then boil them again till the syrup is rather thick. Put half a pound of sugar and half a pint of apple jelly to every orange, and let it boil until it jellies; put them into pots, and place any substance to keep down the orange in the pot till it cools.

Seville Oranges, to preserve.

Put Seville oranges in spring water, where let them remain three or four days, shifting the water every day. Take them out, and grate off a little of the outside rind very carefully without touching the white, only to take away a little of the bitter; make a thin syrup, and, when it is sufficiently cleared and boiled, take it off, and, when it is only warm, put the oranges in and just simmer them over the fire. Put them and the syrup into a pan, and in a day or two set them again on the fire, and just scald them. Repeat this a day afterwards; then boil a thick syrup; take the oranges out of the thin one, and lay them on a cloth to drain, covered over with another; then put them to the thick syrup, as you before did to the thin one, putting them into it just hot, and giving them a simmer. Repeat this in a few days if you think they are not sufficiently done. The insides must be left in.

Butter Orange.

Take a pint of the juice of oranges and eight new-laid eggs beaten well together; mix and season them to your taste with loaf-sugar; then set it on the fire; keep stirring till it becomes thick; put in a bit of butter of the size of a walnut, stirring it while on the fire; then dish it up.

Candied Orange.

Take twelve oranges, the palest you can get; take out the pulp, pick out the seeds and skins; let the outsides soak in water with a little salt all night: then boil them in a good quantity of spring water, till tender, which will be about nine or ten hours. Drain and cut them in very thin slices; add them to the pulp, and to every pound take one pound and a half of sugar beaten fine. Boil them together till clear, which will be in about three quarters of an hour.

Orange Cream.

Grate the peels of four Seville oranges into a pint of water, then squeeze the juice into the water. Well beat the yolks of four eggs; put all together; and sweeten with double-refined sugar. Press the whole hard through a strong strainer; set it on the fire, and stir it carefully one way, till it is as thick as cream.

Orange Jelly.

Dissolve two ounces of isinglass in a pint of water; add a pint of the juice of four China oranges, two Seville oranges, and two lemons. Grate the peel of them all, and sweeten to your palate.

Orange Paste.

Pick all the meat out of the oranges, and boil the rinds in water till they are very tender. Cut off all the outside, and beat the pulp in a mortar till it is very fine. Shred the outside in long thin bits, and mix it with the meat, when you have taken out all the seeds. To every pint of juice put half a pint of the pulp, and mix all together. Then boil up a candy of sugar; put in your paste, and just scald it; add a good pound of sugar to a pint of the paste; put it into a broad earthen pan, set it on a stove, let it remain till it candies; skim it off with a spoon, drop it on glasses to dry, and as, often as it candies keep skimming it.

Another way.

To six ounces of sugar put six ounces at least of fine flour, mixed with a little orange-flower water, but no eggs, as they would make it too dry. Moisten with water, taking care that it is neither too hard nor too soft. Rub the pan with a little fine oil.

Orange Puffs.

Pare off the yellow peel of a large Seville orange, but be careful not to touch the white; boil it in three several waters to take out the bitterness; it will require about three hours' boiling. Beat it very fine in a marble mortar, with four ounces of fine lump sugar, four ounces of fresh butter, the yolks of six eggs, four good spoonfuls of sweet thick cream, and one spoonful of orange-flower water. Beat all these ingredients so well together that you cannot discern a particle of the orange-peel. Roll out your puff paste as thin as possible, lay it in pattypans, fill them with the ingredients, but do not cover them. Bake them in an oven no hotter than for cheesecakes; but for frying you must make them with crust without butter, and fry them in lard.

Another way.

Take one pound of single-refined sugar sifted and the rind of an orange grated, a little gum-dragon, and beaten almonds rubbed through a sieve. Mix all these well together; wet it into paste, and beat it in a mortar; add whites of eggs whipped to a frost.

Orange Sponge.

Dissolve two ounces of isinglass in one pint of water; strain it through a sieve; add the juice of two China oranges and some lemon; sugar it to your taste. Whisk it till it looks like a sponge; put it into a mould, and turn it out.

Orange and Lemon Syrup.

To each pint of juice, which must be put into a large pan, throw a pound and a half of sugar, broken into small lumps, which must be stirred every day till dissolved, first carefully taking off the scum. Let the peel of about six oranges be put into twelve quarts, but it must be taken out when the sugar is melted, and you are ready to bottle it. Proceed in the same way with lemon, only taking two pounds of sugar to a pint of juice.

Oranges for a Tart.

Pare some oranges as thin as possible; boil them till they are soft. Cut and core double the number of good pippins, and boil them to pap, but so as that they do not lose their colour; strain the pulp, and add one pound of sugar to every pint. Take out the orange-pulp, cut the peel, make it very soft by boiling, and bruise it in a mortar in the juice of lemons and oranges; then boil it to a proper consistence with the apple and orange-pulp and half a pint of rose-water.

Orange Tart.

Take eight Seville oranges; cut them in halves, pick out all the seeds; then pick out all the orange as free from the white skins as possible. Take the seeds out of the cores, and boil them till tender and free from bitter. When done enough, dry them very well from the water, and beat five of the orange-peels in a marble mortar till quite smooth. Then take the weight of the oranges in double-refined sugar, beaten fine, and sifted; mix it with the juice, and pound all well in the mortar; the peel that was left unbeaten you slice into your tart. You may keep out as much sugar as will ice the tart. Make the crust for it with twelve ounces of flour, six ounces of butter, melted in water, and the yolks of two eggs, well beaten and mixed into your flour. Be sure to prick the crust well before it goes into the oven.

Half this quantity makes a pretty-sized tart.

Another way.

Take as many oranges as you require. Cut the peel extremely thin from the white, and shred it small. Clear the oranges entirely from the white, and cut them in small pieces like an apple, taking out the seeds. Sweeten as required, and bake in a nice paste. In winter, apples may be mixed.

Panada.

Take oatmeal, clean picked and well beaten; steep it in water all night; strain and boil it in a pipkin, with some currants, a blade or two of mace, and a little salt. When it is well boiled, take it off; and put in the yolks of two or three new-laid eggs, beaten with rose-water. Set it on a gentle fire, and stir it that it may not curdle. Sweeten with sugar, and put in a little nutmeg.

Pancakes. No. 1.

Mix a quart of milk with as much flour as will make it into a thin batter; break in six eggs; put in a little salt, a glass of raisin wine, a spoonful of beaten ginger; mix all well together; fry and sprinkle them with sugar.

In making pancakes or fritters, always make your batter an hour before you begin frying, that the flour may have time to mix thoroughly. Never fry them till they are wanted, or they will eat flat and insipid. Add a little lemon-juice or peel.

Pancakes. No. 2.

To a pint of cream put three spoonfuls of sack, half a pint of flour, six eggs, but only three whites; grate in some nutmeg, very little salt, a quarter of a pound of butter melted, and some sugar. After the first pancake, lay them on a dry pan, very thin, one upon another, till they are finished, before the fire; then lay a dish on the top, and turn them over, so that the brown side is uppermost. You may add or diminish the quantity in proportion. This is a pretty supper dish.

Pancakes. No. 3.

Break three eggs, put four ounces and a half of flour, and a little milk, beat it into a smooth batter; then add by degrees as much milk as will make it the thickness of good cream. Make the frying-pan hot, and to each pancake put a bit of butter nearly the size of a walnut; when melted, pour in the batter to cover the bottom of the pan; make them of the thickness of half a crown. The above will do for apple fritters, by adding one spoonful more flour; peel and cut your apples in thick slices, take out the core, dip them in the batter, and fry them in hot lard; put them in a sieve to drain; grate some loaf sugar over them.

French Pancakes.

Beat the yolks of eight eggs, which sweeten to your taste, nearly a table-spoonful of flour, a little brandy, and half a pint of cream. They are not to be turned in the frying-pan. When half done, take the whites beaten to a strong froth, and put them over the pancakes. When these are done enough, roll them over, sugar them, and brown them with a salamander.

Grillon's Pancakes.

Two soup-ladles of flour, three yolks of eggs, and four whole ones, two tea-spoonfuls of orange-flower water, six ratafia cakes, a pint of double cream; to be stirred together, and sugar to be shaken over every pancake, which is not to be turned—about thirty in number.

Quire of Paper Pancakes.

Take to a pint of cream eight eggs, leaving out two whites, three spoonfuls of fine flour, three of sack, one of orange-flower water, a little sugar, a grated nutmeg, a quarter of a pound of butter melted in the cream. Mix a little of the cream with flour, and so proceed by degrees that it may be smooth: then beat all well together. Butter the pan for the first pancake, and let them run as thin as possible to be whole. When one side is coloured, it is enough; take them carefully out of the pan, lay them as even on each other as possible; and keep them near the fire till they are all fried. The quantity here given makes twenty.

Rice Pancakes.

In a quart of milk mix by degrees three spoonfuls of flour of rice, and boil it till it is as thick as pap. As it boils, stir in half a pound of good butter and a nutmeg grated. Pour it into a pan, and, when cold, put in by degrees three or four spoonfuls of flour, a little salt, some sugar, and nine eggs, well beaten up. Mix them all together, and fry them in a small pan, with a little piece of butter.

Paste.

Take half a pound of good fresh butter, and work it to a cream in a basin. Stir into it a quarter of a pound of fine sifted sugar, and beat it together: then work with it as much fine flour as will make a paste fit to roll out for tarts, cheesecakes, &c.

Paste for baking or frying.

Take a proper quantity of flour for the paste you wish to make, and mix it with equal quantities of powdered sugar and flour; melt some butter very smooth, with some grated lemon-peel and an egg, well beat; mix into a firm paste; bake or fry it.

Paste for Pies.

French roll dough, rolled out with less than half the quantity of butter generally used, makes a wholesome and excellent paste for pies.

Paste for raised Pies.

Put four pounds of butter into a kettle of water; add three quarters of a pound of rendered beef suet; boil it two or three minutes; pour it on twelve pounds of flour, and work it into a good stiff paste. Pull it into lumps to cool. Raise the pie, using the same proportions for all raised pies according to the size required: bake in a hot oven.

Another way.

Take one pound of flour, and seven ounces of butter, put into boiling water till it dissolves: wet the flour lightly with it. Roll your paste out thick and not too stiff; line your tins with it; put in the meat, and cover over the top of the tin with the same paste.

This paste is best made over-night.

Paste for Tarts.

To half a pound of the best flour add the same quantity of butter, two spoonfuls of white sugar, the yolks of two eggs and one white; make it into a paste with cold water.

Paste for Tarts in pans.

Take a pound of flour, the same of butter, with five yolks of eggs, the white of one, and as much water as will wet it into a pretty soft paste. Roll it up, and put it into your pan.

Paste for very small Tartlets.

Take an egg or more, and mix it with some flour; make a little ball as big as a tea-cup; work it with your hands till it is quite hard and stiff; then break off a little at a time as you want it, keeping the rest of the ball under cover of a basin, for fear of its hardening or drying too much. Roll it out extremely thin; cut it out, and make it up in what shape you please, and harden them by the fire, or in an oven in a manner cold. It does for almonds or cocoa-nut boiled up in syrup rich, or any thing that is a dry mixture, or does not want baking.

Potato Paste.

Take two thirds of potato and one of ground rice, as much butter rubbed in as will moisten it sufficiently to roll, which must be done with a little flour. The crust is best made thin and in small tarts. The potatoes should be well boiled and quite cold.

Rice Paste.

Whole rice, boiled in new milk, with a reasonable quantity of butter, to such a consistency as to roll out when cold. The board must be floured while rolling.

Another way.

Beat up a quarter of a pound of rice-flour with two eggs; boil it till soft; then make it into a paste with very little butter, and bake it.

Paste Royal.

Mix together one pound of flour, and two ounces of sifted sugar; rub into it half a pound of good butter, and make it into a paste not over stiff. Roll it out for your pans. This paste is proper for any sweet tart or cheesecake.

Short or Puff Paste. No. 1.

Rub together six ounces of butter and eight of flour; mix it up with as little water as possible, so as to make a stiff paste. Beat it well, and roll it thin. This is the best crust of all for tarts that are to be eaten cold and for preserved fruit. Have a moderate oven.

Short Paste. No. 2.

Half a pound of loaf-sugar, and the same quantity of butter, to be rubbed into a pound of flour; then make it into paste with two eggs.

Short Paste. No. 3.

To a pound and a quarter of sifted flour rub gently in half a pound of fresh butter, mixed up with half a pint of spring water, and set it by for a quarter of an hour; then roll it out thin; lay on it in small pieces three quarters of a pound more of butter; throw on it a little more flour, roll it out thin three times, and set it by for an hour in a cold place.

Short Paste. No. 4.

Take one pound of flour, half a pound of fresh butter, and about four table-spoonfuls of pounded white sugar. Knead the paste with the yolks of two eggs well beaten up instead of water. Roll it very thin for biscuits or tarts.

Short Paste. No. 5.

Three ounces of butter to something less than a pound of flour and the yolk of one egg; the butter to be thoroughly worked into the flour; if you use sugar, there is no occasion for an egg.

Short Paste. No. 6.

Three quarters of a pound of butter, and the same of flour; mix the flour very stiff with a little water; put the butter in a clean cloth, and press it thoroughly to get from it all the water. Then roll out all the flour and water paste, and lay the butter upon it, double over the paste, and beat it with a rolling-pin. Double it up quite thick, lay it in a clean plate, and put it in a cool place for an hour. If it is not light when tried in the oven, it must be beaten again.

Short Paste. No. 7.

Rub into your flour as much butter as possible, without its being greasy; rub it in very fine; put water to make it into a nice light paste; roll it out; stick bits of butter all over it; then flour and roll it up again. Do this three times; it is excellent for meat-pies.

Short Paste, made with Suet.

To one pound of flour take about half a pound of beef suet chopped very small; pour boiling water upon it; let it stand a little time; then mix the suet with the flour, taking as little of the water as possible, and roll it very thin; put a little sugar and white of egg over the crust before it is baked.

Sugar Paste.

Take half a pound of flour, and the same quantity of sugar well pounded; work it together, with a little cream and about two ounces of butter, into a stiff paste; roll it very thin. When the tarts are made, rub the white of an egg, well beaten, over them with a feather; put them in a moderate oven, and sift sugar over them.

Peaches, to preserve in Brandy. No. 1.

The peaches should be gathered before they are too ripe; they should be of the hard kind—old Newington or the Magdalen peaches are the best. Rub off the down with a flannel, and loosen the stone, which is done by cutting a quill and passing it carefully round the stone. Prick them with a large needle in several places; put them into cold water; give them a great deal of room in the preserving-pan; scald them extremely gently: the longer you are scalding them the better, for if you do them hastily, or with too quick a fire, they may crack or break. Turn them now and then with a feather: when they are tender to the feel, like a hard-boiled egg that has the shell taken off, remove them from the fire, carefully take them out, and cover them up close with a flannel. You must in all their progress observe to keep the fruit covered, and, whenever you take it from the scalding syrup, cover it up with a cloth or flannel, or the air will change the colour. Then put to them a thin syrup cool. The next day, if you think the syrup too thin, drain it well from the peaches, and add a little more sugar; boil it up, and put it to them almost cold. To a pint of syrup put half a pint of the best pale brandy you can get, which sweeten with fine sugar. If the brandy is dark-coloured, it will spoil the look of the fruit. The peaches should be well chosen, and they should have sufficient room in the glass jars. When the liquor wastes, supply the deficiency by adding more syrup and brandy. Cover them with a bladder, and every now and then turn them upside down, till the fruit is settled.

Peaches, to preserve in Brandy. No. 2.

Scald some of the finest peaches of the white heart kind, free from spots, in a stewpan of water; take them out when soft, and put them into a large table-cloth, four or five times doubled. Into a quart of white French brandy put ten ounces of powdered sugar; let it dissolve, and stir it well. Put your peaches into a glass jar; pour the brandy on them; cover them very close with leather and bladder, and take care to keep your jar filled with brandy.

You should mix your brandy and sugar before you scald the peaches.

Peaches, to preserve in Brandy. No. 3.

Put Newington peaches in boiling water: just give them a scald, but do not let them boil; then take them out, and throw them into cold water. Dry them on a sieve, and put them in long wide-mouthed bottles. To half a dozen peaches take half a pound of sugar; just wet it, and make it a thick syrup. Pour it over the peaches hot; when cold, fill the bottles with the finest pale brandy, and stop them very close.

Pears, to pot.

Put in your fruit scored; cover them with apple jelly, and let them boil till they break; then put them in a hair sieve, and rub them through with a spoon till you think it thick enough. Boil up as many pounds of sugar to a candy as you have pints of paste, and when the sugar is put in the paste, just scald it, and put it into pots.

Pears, to stew.

Pare some Barland pears; take out the core, and lay them close in a tin saucepan, with a cover fitting quite exact; add the rind of a lemon cut thin and half its juice, a small stick of cinnamon, twenty grains of allspice, and one pound of loaf-sugar, to a pint and a half of water. Bake them six hours in a very slow oven. Prepared cochineal is often used for colouring.

Chicken Pie.

Parboil and neatly cut up your chickens; dry them, and set them over a slow fire for a few minutes; have ready some forcemeat, and with it some pieces of ham; lay these at the bottom of the dish, and place the chickens upon it; add some gravy well seasoned. It takes from an hour and a half to two hours.

Giblet Pie.

Let the giblets be well cleaned, and put all into a saucepan excepting the liver, with a little water and an onion, some whole pepper, a bunch of sweet-herbs, and a little salt. Cover them close, and let them stew till tender; then lay in your dish a puff paste, and upon that a rump-steak peppered and salted; put the seasoned giblets in with the liver, and add the liquor they were stewed in. Close the pie; bake it two hours; and when done pour in the gravy.

A Dutch pie is made in the same way.

Common Goose Pie.

Quarter a goose and season it well. Make a raised crust, and lay it in, with half a pound of butter at the top, cut into three pieces. Put the lid on, and bake it gently.

Rich Goose Pie.

After having boned your goose and fowl, season them well, and put your fowl into the goose, and into the fowl some forcemeat. Then put both into a raised crust, filling the corners with the forcemeat. Cut about half a pound of butter into three or four pieces, and lay on the top, and bake it well.

Ham and Chicken Pie.

Cut some thin slices from a boiled ham, lay them on a good puff paste at the bottom of your dish, and pepper them. Cut a fowl into four quarters, and season it with a great deal of pepper, and but a little salt; and lay on the top some hard yolks of eggs, a few truffles and morels, and then cover the whole with slices of ham peppered: fill the dish with gravy, and cover it with a good thick paste. Bake it well, and, when done, pour into it some rich gravy. If to be eaten cold, put no gravy.

Hare Pie.

Cut the hare into pieces; season it with salt, pepper, and nutmeg, and jug it with half a pound of butter. It must do above an hour, covered close in a pot of boiling water. Make some forcemeat, and add bruised liver and a glass of red wine. Let it be highly seasoned, and lay it round the inside of a raised crust; put the hare in when cool, and add the gravy that came from it, with some more rich gravy. Put the lid on, and bake it two hours.

Lumber Pie.

Take the best neat's tongue well boiled, three quarters of a pound of beef suet, the like quantity of currants, two good handfuls of spinach, thyme, and parsley, a little nutmeg, and mace; sweeten to your taste. Add a French roll grated and six eggs. Mix these all together, put them into your pie, then lay up the top. Cut into long slices one candied orange, two pieces of citron, some sliced lemon, add a good deal of marrow, preserved cherries and barberries, an apple or two cut into eight pieces, and some butter. Put in white wine, lemon, and sugar, and serve up.

Olive Pie.

Two pounds of leg of veal, the lean, with the skin taken out, one pound of beef suet, both shred very small and beaten; then put them together; add half a pound of currants and half a pound of raisins stoned, half a pound of sugar, eight eggs and the whites of four, thyme, sweet marjoram, winter savory, and parsley, a handful of each. Mix all these together, and make it up in balls. When you put them in the pie, put butter between the top and bottom. Take as much suet as meat; when it is baked, put in a little white wine.

Partridge Pie.

Truss the partridges the same way as you do a fowl for boiling; then beat in a mortar some shalots, parsley cut small, the livers of the birds, and double the quantity of bacon, seasoning them with pepper, salt, and two blades of mace. When well pounded, put in some fresh mushrooms. Raise a crust for the pie; cover the bottom with the seasoning; put in the partridges, but no stuffing, and put in the remainder of the seasoning between the birds and on the sides; strew over a little mace, pepper and salt, shalots, fresh mushrooms, a little bacon beaten very fine; lay a layer of it over them, and put the lid on. Two hours and a half will bake it, and, when done, take the lid off, skim off the fat, put a pint of veal gravy, and squeeze in the juice of an orange.

Rich Pigeon Pie.

Season the pigeons high; lay a puff paste at the bottom of the dish, stuffing the craws of the birds with forcemeat, and lay them in the dish with the breasts downward; fill all the spaces with forcemeat, hard-boiled yolks of eggs, artichoke bottoms cut in pieces, and asparagus tops. Cover, and bake it; when drawn, pour in rich gravy.

High Veal Pie.

Veal, forcemeat balls, yolks of eggs, oysters, a little nutmeg, cayenne pepper, and salt, with a little water put into the dish.

Vegetable Pie.

Stew three pounds of gravy beef, with some white pepper, salt, and mace, a bundle of sweet-herbs, a few sweet almonds, onions, and carrots, till the gravy is of a good brown colour. Strain it off; let it stand till cold; and take off all the fat. Have some carrots, turnips, onions, potatoes, and celery, ready cut; boil all these together. Boil some greens by themselves, and add them to the pie when served up.

A Yorkshire Christmas Pie.

Let the crust be made a good standing one; the wall and bottom must be very thick. Take a turkey and bone it, a goose, a fowl, a partridge, and a pigeon, and season all well. Take half an ounce of cloves, the same of black pepper, and two table-spoonfuls of salt, and beat them well together; let the fowls be slit down the back, and bone them; put the pigeon into the partridge, the partridge into the fowl, the fowl into the goose, and the goose into the turkey. Season all well first, and lay them in the crust; joint a hare, and cut it into pieces; season it, and lay it close on one side; on the other side woodcocks, or any other sort of game; let them also be well seasoned and laid close. Put four or five pounds of butter into the pie; cover it with a very rich paste, put it in a very hot oven, and four hours will bake it.

A bushel of flour is about the quantity required for the paste.

Pineapple, to preserve in slices.

Pare the pines, and cut them in slices of about the same thickness as you would apples for fritters. Take the weight of the fruit in the best sugar; sift it very fine, and put a layer of sugar, then a layer of pineapple; let it stand till the sugar is entirely dissolved. Then drain off the syrup, and lay the pine in the pot in which you intend to keep it; boil the syrup, adding a little more sugar and water to make it rich; pour it, but not too hot, upon the fruit. Repeat this in about ten days; look at it now and then, and, if the syrup ferments, boil it up again, skim it, and pour it warm upon the pine. The parings of the pineapple boil in the water you use for the syrup, and extract all the flavour from them.

Pineapple Chips.

Pare the pineapples; pick out the thistle part: take half its weight of treble-refined sugar; part the apple in halves; slice it thin; put it in a basin, with sifted sugar between; in twelve hours the sugar will be melted. Set it over a fire, and simmer the chips till clear. The less they boil the better. Next day, heat them; scrape off the syrup; lay them in glasses, and dry them on a moderate stove or oven.

Plums, to dry green.

Take green amber plums; prick them with a pin all over; make some water boiling hot, and put in the plums; be sure to have so much water as not to be made cold when the plums are put in. Cover them very close, and, when they are almost cold, set them on the fire again, but do not let them boil. Do so three or four times. When you see the thin skin cracked, put in some alum finely beaten, and keep them in a scald till they begin to green; then give them a boil closely covered. When they are green, let them stand in fresh hot water all night; next day, have ready as much clarified sugar, made into syrup, as will cover them; drain the plums, put them into the syrup, and give them two or three boils. Repeat this twice or three times, till they are very green. Let them stand in the syrup a week; then lay them out to dry in a hot stove. You may put some of them in codling jelly, and use them as a wet sweetmeat.

Green Plum Jam.

Take the great white plums before they begin to turn, when they are at their full growth, and to every pound of plums allow three quarters of a pound of fine sugar. Pare and throw the plums into water, to keep their colour; let your sugar be very finely pounded; cut your plums into slices, and strew the sugar over them. You must first take them out of the water, and put them over a moderate fire, and boil them till they are clear and will jelly. You may put in a few of the stones, if you like them.

Great White Plum, to preserve.

To one pound of plums put three quarters of a pound of fine sugar; dip the lumps of sugar in water just sufficient to wet it through; boil and skim it, till you think it enough. Slit the plums down the seam; put them in the syrup with the slit downward, and let them stew over the fire for a quarter of an hour. Skim them; take them off; when cold, turn them; cover them up for four or five days, turning them two or three times a day in the syrup; then put them in pots, not too many together.

Posset.

Take a quart of white wine and a quart of water; boil whole spice in them; then take twelve eggs, and put away half the whites; beat them very well, and take the wine from the fire; then put your eggs, being thoroughly beaten, to the wine. Stir the whole together; then set it on a very slow fire, stirring it the whole time, till it is thick. Sweeten it with sugar, and sprinkle on it beaten spice, cinnamon, and nutmeg.

Another way, richer.

Take two quarts of cream, and boil it with whole spice; then take twelve eggs, well beaten and strained; take the cream from the fire, and stir in the eggs, and as much sugar as will sweeten it according to the taste of those who are to drink it; then a pint of wine, or more—sack, sherry, or Lisbon. Set it on the fire again, and let it stand awhile; then take a ladle, and raise it up gently from the bottom of the skillet you make it in, and break it as little as you can, and do so till you see that it is thick enough. Then put it into a basin with a ladle gently. If you do it too much or too quickly it will whey, and that is not good.

Sack Posset.

To twelve eggs, beaten very much, put a pint of sack, or any other strong rich white wine. Stir them well, that they may not curd; put to them three pints of cream and half a pound of fine sugar, stirring them well together. When hot over the fire, put the posset into a basin, and set it over a boiling pot of water until it is like a custard; then take it off, and, when it is cool enough to eat, serve it with beaten spice, cloves, cinnamon, and nutmeg, strewed over it very thick.

Sack Posset, without milk.

Take thirteen eggs; beat them very well, and, while they are beating, take a quart of sack, half a pound of fine sugar, and a pint of ale, and let them boil a very little while; then put the eggs to them, and stir them till they are hot. Take it from the fire, and keep it stirring awhile; then put it into a fit basin, and cover it close with a dish. Set it over the fire again till it rises to a curd; serve it with beaten spice.

Sack Posset, or Jelly.

Take three pints of good cream and three quarters of a pound of fine sugar pounded, twenty eggs, leaving out eight of the whites; beat them very well and light. Add to them rather more than a pint of sack; beat them again well; then set it on a stove; make it so hot that you can just endure your finger at the bottom of the pan, and not hotter; stir it all one way; put the cream on the fire just to boil up, and be ready at the time the sack is so. Boil in it a blade of mace, and put it boiling hot to the eggs and sack, which is to be only scalding hot. When the cream is put in, just stir it round twice; take it off the fire; cover it up close when it is put into the mould or dish you intend it for, and it will jelly. Pour the cream to the eggs, holding it as high from them as possible.

Puffs.

Blanch a pound of almonds, and beat them with orange-flower water, or rose-water; boil a pound of sugar to a candy; put in the almonds, and stir them over the fire till they are stiff. Keep them stirred till cold; then beat them in a mortar for a quarter of an hour. Add a pound of sugar, and make it into a paste, with the whites of three eggs beaten to a froth, more or less, as you may judge necessary. Bake the puffs in a cool oven.

Cheese Puffs.

Scald green gooseberries, and pulp them through a colander. To six spoonfuls of this pulp add half a pound of butter beaten to a cream, half a pound of finely pounded and sifted sugar, put to the butter by degrees, ten eggs, half the whites, a little grated lemon-peel, and a little brandy or sack. Beat all these ingredients as light as possible, and bake in a thin crust.

Chocolate Puffs.

Take a pound of single-refined sugar, finely sifted, and grate as much chocolate as will colour it; add an ounce of beaten almonds; mix them well together; wet it with the froth of whites of eggs, and bake it.

German Puffs.

Take four spoonfuls of fine flour, four eggs, a pint of cream, four ounces of melted butter, and a very little salt; stir and beat them well together, and add some grated nutmeg. Bake them in small cups: a quarter of an hour will be quite sufficient: and the oven should be so quick as to brown both top and bottom. If well baked, they will be more than as large again. For sauce—melted butter, sack, and sugar. The above quantity will make fourteen puffs.

Spanish Puffs.

Take one pint of skim milk, and thicken it with flour; boil it very well till it is tough as paste, then let it cool, put it into a mortar, and beat it very well. Put in three eggs, and beat it again, then three eggs more, keeping out one white. Put in some grated nutmeg and a little salt. Have your pan over the fire, with some good lard; drop the paste in; fry the puffs a light brown, and strew sugar over them when you send them up.

Pudding.

Boil one pint of milk; beat up the yolks of five eggs in a basin with a little sugar, and pour the milk upon them, stirring it all the time. Prepare your mould by putting into it sifted sugar sufficient to cover it; melt it on the stove, and, when dissolved, take care that the syrup covers the whole mould. The flavour is improved by grating into the sugar a little lemon-peel. Pour the pudding into your mould, and place it in a vessel of boiling water; it must boil two hours; it may then be turned out, and eaten hot or cold.

Another way.

Grate a penny loaf, and put to it a handful of currants, a little clarified butter, the yolk of an egg, a little nutmeg and salt; mix all together, and make it into little balls. Boil them half an hour. Serve with wine sauce.

A good Pudding.

Take a pint of cream, and six eggs, leaving out two of the whites. Beat up the eggs well, and put them to the cream or milk, with two or three spoonfuls of flour, and a little nutmeg and sugar, if you please.

A very good Pudding.

Scald some green gooseberries, and pulp them through a colander; to six spoonfuls of this pulp add half a pound of butter beaten to a cream, half a pound of finely beaten and sifted sugar, put to the butter by degrees, ten eggs, half the whites, a little grated lemon-peel, a little brandy or sack: beat all these ingredients as light as possible; bake in a thin crust.

An excellent Pudding.

Cut French rolls in thin slices; boil a pint of milk, and poor over them. Cover it with a plate and let it cool; then beat it quite fine. Add six ounces of suet chopped fine, a quarter of a pound of currants, three eggs beat up, half a glass of brandy, and some moist sugar. Bake it full two hours.

A plain Pudding.

Three spoonfuls of flour, a pint of new milk, three eggs, a very little salt. Boil it for half an hour, in a small basin.

A scalded Pudding.

Take four spoonfuls of flour, and pour on it one pint of boiling milk. When cold, add four eggs, and boil it one hour.

A sweet Pudding.

Half a pound of ratafia, half a pint of boiling milk, more if required, stir it with a fork; three eggs, leaving out one white. Butter the basin, or dish, and stick jar-raisins about the butter as close as you please; then pour in the pudding and bake it.

All Three Pudding.

Chopped apples, currants, suet finely chopped, sugar and bread crumb, three ounces of each, three eggs, but only two of the whites; put all into a well floured bag, and boil it well two hours. Serve it with wine sauce.

Almond Pudding. No. 1.

Blanch half a pound of sweet almonds, with four bitter ones; pound them in a marble mortar, with two spoonfuls of orange-flower water, and two spoonfuls of rose-water; mix in four grated Naples biscuits, and half a pound of melted butter. Beat eight eggs, and mix them with a pint of cream boiled; grate in half a nutmeg, and a quarter of a pound of sugar. Mix all well together, and bake it with a paste at the bottom of the dish.

Almond Pudding. No. 2.

Take a pound of almonds, ground very small with a little rose-water and sugar, a pound of Naples biscuits finely grated, the marrow of six bones broken into small pieces—if you have not marrow enough, put in beef suet finely shred—a quarter of a pound of orange-peel, a quarter of citron-peel, cut in thin slices, and some mace. Take twenty eggs, only half as many whites; mix all these well together. Boil some cream, let it stand till it is almost cold; then put in as much as will make your pudding tolerably thick. You may put in a very few caraway seeds and a little ambergris, if you like.

Almond Pudding. No. 3.

Two small wine glasses of rose-water, one ounce of isinglass, twelve bitter almonds, blanched and shred; let it stand by the fire till the isinglass is dissolved; then put a pint of cream, and the yolks of six eggs, and sweeten to the taste. Set it on the fire till it boils; strain it through a sieve; stir it till nearly cold; then pour it into a mould wetted with rose-water.

Amber Pudding.

Half a pound of brown sugar, the same of butter, beat up as a cake, till it becomes a fine cream, six eggs very well beaten, and sweetmeats, if agreeable; mix all together. Three quarters of an hour will bake it; add a little brandy, and lay puff paste round the dish.

Princess Amelia's Pudding.

Pare eight or ten fair large apples, cut them into thin slices, and stew them gently in a very little water till tender; then take of white bread grated the quantity of half a threepenny loaf, six yolks and four whites of eggs beat very light, half a pint of cream, one large spoonful of sack or brandy, four spoonfuls of clarified butter; mix these all well together, and beat them very light. Sweeten to your taste, and bake in tea-cups: a little baking is sufficient. When baked, take them out of the cups, and serve them with sack, sugar, and melted butter, for sauce.

Apple Mignon.

Pare and core golden pippins without breaking the apple; lay them in the dish in which they are to be baked. Take of rice boiled tender in milk the quantity you judge sufficient; add to it half a pint of thick cream, with the yolks of five eggs; sweeten it to your taste, and grate in a little nutmeg; pour it over the apples in the dish; set it in a gentle oven. Three quarters of an hour will bake it. Glaze it over with sugar.

Apple Pudding. No. 1.

Coddle six large codlings till they are very soft over a slow fire to prevent their bursting. Rub the pulp through a sieve. Put six eggs, leaving out two whites, six ounces of butter beaten well, three quarters of a pound of loaf sugar pounded fine, the juice of two lemons, two ounces of candied orange and lemon-peel, and the peel of one lemon shred very fine. You must not put in the peel till it is going to the oven. Put puff paste round the dish; sift over a little sugar; an hour will bake it.

Apple Pudding. No. 2.

Prepare apples as for sauce; when cold, beat in two whole eggs, a little nutmeg, bitter almonds pounded fine, and sugar, with orange or lemon peel, and a little juice of either. Bake in a paste.

Apple Pudding. No. 3.

Take six apples; stew them in as little water as you can; take out the pulped part; add to it four eggs, and not quite half a pound of butter; sweeten it to your taste. Let your paste be good, and put it in a gentle oven.

Arrow-root Pudding.

Boil a pint of milk with eight bitter almonds pounded, a piece of cinnamon, and lemon-peel, for some time; then take a large table-spoonful of arrow-root, and mix it with cold milk. Mix this afterwards with the boiling milk. All these must become cold before you put in the eggs; then beat together three eggs, a little nutmeg and sugar, and the arrow-root, and strain through a sieve. Butter your mould, and boil the pudding half an hour. The mould must be quite full; serve with wine sauce, butter a paper to put over it, and then tie over a cloth.

Pearl Barley Pudding.

Boil three table-spoonfuls of pearl barley in a pint and a half of new milk, with a few bitter almonds, and a little sugar, for three hours. Strain it; when cold add two eggs; put some paste round the dish, and bake it.

Batter Pudding.

Make a batter, rather stiffer than pancake batter; beat up six eggs, leaving out three of the whites, and put them to the batter, with a little salt and nutmeg. This quantity is for a pint basin, and will take one hour to boil.

Another.

Three table-spoonfuls of flour, two eggs, and about a tea-cupful of currants; beat up well with a pint of milk, and bake in a slow oven.

Plain Batter Pudding, or with Fruit.

Put six large spoonfuls of flour into a pan, and mix it with a quart of milk, till it is smooth. Beat up the yolks of six and the whites of three eggs, and put in; strain it through a sieve; then put in a tea-spoonful of salt, one of beaten ginger, and stir them well together. Dip your cloth in boiling water; flour it, and pour in your pudding; tie it rather close, and boil it an hour. When sent to table, pour melted butter over it. You may put in ripe currants, apricots, small plums, damsons, or white bullace, when in season; but with fruit it will require boiling half an hour longer.

Norfolk Batter Pudding.

Yolks and whites of three eggs well beaten, three table-spoonfuls of flour, half a pint of milk, and a small quantity of salt; boil it half an hour.

Green Bean Pudding.

Boil and blanch old beans; beat them in a mortar, with very little pepper and salt, some cream, and the yolk of an egg. A little spinach-juice will give a fine colour; but it is good without. Boil it for an hour in a basin that will just hold it, and pour over it parsley and butter. Serve bacon to eat with it.

Beef Steak Pudding.

Cut rump-steaks, not too thick, into pieces about half the size of your hand, taking out all the skin and sinews. Add an onion cut fine, also potatoes (if liked,) peeled and cut in slices a quarter of an inch thick; season with pepper and salt. Lay a layer of steaks, and then one of potatoes, proceeding thus till full, occasionally throwing in part of the onion. Add half a gill of water or veal broth. Boil it two hours. You may put in, if you please, half a gill of mushroom ketchup, and a ta-ble-spoonful of lemon-pickle.

Bread Pudding.

Cut off all the crust from a twopenny loaf; slice it thin in a quart of milk; set it over a chaffing-dish of charcoal, till the bread has completely soaked up the milk; then put in a piece of butter; stir it well round, and let it stand till cold. Take the yolks of seven eggs and the whites of five, and beat them up with a quarter of a pound of sugar, with some nutmeg, cinnamon, mace, cloves, and lemon-peel, fine-ly pounded. Mix these well together, and boil it one hour. Prepare a sauce of white wine, butter, and sugar; pour it over, and serve up hot.

Another way.

Boil together half a pint of milk, a quarter of a pound of butter, and the same of sugar, and pour it over a quarter of a pound of crumb of bread. Beat up the yolks of four eggs and two whites; mix all well together; put the pudding in tea-cups, and bake in a moderate oven about an hour. Serve in wine sauce.

The above quantity makes five puddings.

Rich Bread Pudding.

Cut the inside of a rather stale twopenny loaf as fine as possible; pour over it boiled milk sufficient to allow of its being beaten, while warm, to the thickness of cream; put in a small piece of butter while hot; beat into it four almond macaroons; sweeten it to your taste. Beat four eggs, leaving out two whites; and boil it three quarters of an hour.

Bread and Butter Pudding.

Cut a penny loaf or French roll into thin slices of bread and butter, as for tea; butter the bottom of the dish, and cover it with slices of bread and butter; sprinkle on them a few currants, well washed and picked; then lay another layer of bread and butter; then again sprinkle a few currants, and so on till you have put in all the bread and butter. Beat up three eggs with a pint of milk, a little salt, grated nutmeg, or ginger, and a few bitter almonds, and pour it on the bread and butter. Put a puff paste round the dish, and bake it half an hour.

Raisin Bread Pudding.

Boil your bread pudding in a basin; put the stoned raisins in a circle at the top, and from it stripes down, when ready to serve up.

Buttermilk Pudding.

Take three quarts of new milk; boil and turn it with a quart of buttermilk: drain the whey from the curd through a hair sieve. When it is well drained, pound it in a marble mortar very fine; then put to it half a pound of fine beaten and sifted sugar. Boil the rind of two lemons very tender; mince it fine; add the inside of a roll grated, a large tea-cupful of cream, a few almonds, pounded fine, with a noggin of white wine, a little brandy, and a quarter of a pound of melted butter. The boats or cups you bake in must be all buttered. Turn the puddings out when they are baked, and serve them with a sauce of sack, butter, and sugar.

Carrot Pudding.

Take two or three large carrots, and half boil them; grate the crumb of a penny loaf and the red part of the carrots; boil as much cream as will make the bread of a proper thickness; when cold, add the carrots, the yolks of four eggs, beat well, a little nutmeg, a glass of white wine, and sugar to your taste. Butter the dish well, and lay a little paste round the edge. Half an hour will bake it.

Another way.

Take raw carrots, scraped very clean, and grate them. To half a pound of grated carrot put a pound of grated bread. Beat up eight eggs, leaving out the whites; mix the eggs with half a pint of cream, and then stir in the bread and carrots, with half a pound of fresh butter melted.

Charlotte Pudding.

Cut as many thin slices of white bread as will cover the bottom and line the sides of a baking-dish, having first rubbed it thick with butter; put apples in thin slices into the dish in layers till full, strewing sugar and bits of butter between. In the mean time, soak as many thin slices of bread as will cover the whole in warm milk, over which lay a plate and a weight to keep the bread close on the apples. Bake slowly three hours. To a middling-sized dish put half a pound of butter in the whole.

Cheese Pudding.

Boil a thick piece of stale loaf in a pint of milk; grate half a pound of cheese; stir it into the bread and milk; beat up separately four yolks and four whites of eggs, and a little pepper and salt, and beat the whole together till very fine. Butter the pan, and put into the oven about the time the first course is sent up.

Another way.

Half a pound of cheese—strong and mild mixed—four eggs and a little cream, well mixed. Butter the pan, and bake it twenty minutes. To be sent up with the cheese, or, if you like, with the tart.

Citron Pudding.

One spoonful of fine flour, two ounces of sugar, a little nutmeg, and half a pint of cream; mix them well together with the yolks of three eggs. Put it into tea-cups, and divide among them two ounces of citron, cut very thin. Bake them in a pretty quick oven, and turn them out on a china dish.

Cocoa-nut Pudding.

Take three quarters of a pound of sugar, one pound of cocoa-nut, a quarter of a pound of butter, eight yolks of eggs, four spoonfuls of rose-water, six Naples biscuits soaked in the rose-water; beat half the sugar with the butter and half with the eggs, and, when beat enough, mix the cocoa-nut with the butter; then throw in the eggs, and beat all together. For the crust, the yolks of four eggs, two spoonfuls of rose-water, and two of water, mixed with flour till it comes to a paste.

College Pudding. No. 1.

Beat up four eggs, with two ounces of flour, half a nutmeg, a little ginger, and three ounces of sugar pounded, beaten to a smooth batter; then add six ounces of suet chopped fine, six of currants well washed and picked, and a glass of brandy, or white wine. These puddings are generally fried in butter or lard, but they are better baked in an oven in pattypans; twenty minutes will bake them; if fried, fry them till of a nice light brown, or roll them in a little flour. You may add an ounce of orange or citron minced very fine. When you bake them, add one more egg, or two spoonfuls of milk.

College Pudding. No. 2.

Take of bread crumb, suet, very finely chopped, currants, and moist sugar, half a pound of each, and four eggs, leaving out one white, well beaten. Mix all well together, and add a quarter of a pint of white wine, leaving part of it for the sauce. Add a little nutmeg and salt. Boil it a full half hour in tea-cups; or you may fry it. This quantity will make six. Pour over them melted butter, sugar, and wine.

College Pudding. No. 3.

A quarter of a pound of biscuit powder, a quarter of a pound of beef suet, a quarter of a pound of currants, nicely picked and washed, nutmeg, a glass of raisin wine, a few bitter almonds pounded, lemon-peel, and a little juice. Fry ten minutes in beef dripping, and send to table in wine sauce. Half these ingredients will make eight puddings.

College Pudding. No. 4.

A quarter of a pound of grated bread, the same quantity of currants, the same of suet shred fine, a small quantity of sugar, and some nutmeg: mix all well together. Take two eggs, and make it with them into cakes; fry them of a light brown in butter. Serve them with butter, sugar, and wine.

New College Pudding.

Grate a penny white loaf, and put to it a quarter of a pound of currants, nicely picked and washed, a quarter of a pound of beef suet, minced small, some nutmeg, salt, and as much cream and eggs as will make it almost as stiff as paste. Then make it up in the form of eggs: put them into a stewpan, with a quarter of a pound of butter melted in the bottom; lay them in one by one; set them over a clear charcoal fire; and, when they are brown, turn them till they are brown all over. Send them to table with wine sauce.

Lemon-peel and a little juice may be added to the pudding.

Another way.

Take one pound of suet, half a pound of the best raisins, one pound of currants, half a pound of sugar, half a pound of flour, one nutmeg, a tea-spoonful of salt, two table-spoonfuls of brandy, and six eggs. Make them up the size of a turkey's egg; bake or fry them in butter.

Cottage Pudding.

Two pounds of potatoes, boiled, peeled, and mashed, one pint of milk, three eggs, and two ounces of sugar. Bake it three quarters of an hour.

Currant Pudding.

Take one pound of flour, ten ounces of currants, five of moist sugar, a little grated ginger, nutmeg, and sliced lemon-peel. Put the flour with the sugar on one side of the basin, and the currants on the other. Melt a quarter of a pound of butter in half a pint of milk; let it stand till lukewarm; then add two yolks of eggs and one white only, well beaten, and three tea-spoonfuls of yest. To prevent bitterness, put a piece of red-hot charcoal, of the size of a walnut, into the milk; strain it through a sieve, and pour it over the currants, leaving the flour and the sugar on the other side of the basin. Throw a little flour from the dredger over the milk; then cover it up, and leave it at the fire-side for half an hour to rise. Then mix the whole together with a spoon; put it into the mould, and leave it again by the fire to rise for another half hour.

Custard Pudding. No. 1.

Take three quarters of a pint of milk, three tea-spoonfuls of flour, and three eggs: mix the flour quite smooth with a little of the milk cold; boil the rest, and pour it to the mixed flour, stirring it well together. Then well beat the eggs, and pour the milk and flour hot to them. Butter a basin, pour in the pudding. Tie it close in a cloth, and boil it half an hour. It may be made smaller or larger, by allowing one egg to one tea-spoonful of flour and a quarter of a pint of milk, and proportionately shortening the time of boiling. It may be prepared for boiling any time, or immediately before it is put into the saucepan, as maybe most convenient.

The basin must be quite filled, or the water will get in.

Custard Pudding. No. 2.

Set on the fire a pint of milk, sweetened to your taste, with a little cinnamon, a few cloves, and grated lemon-peel. Boil it up, and pour it the moment it is taken off the fire upon the yolks of seven eggs and the whites of four, stirring it well, and pouring it in by degrees. Boil it in a well buttered basin, which will hold a pint and a half. Pour wine sauce over it.

Custard Pudding. No. 3.

Boil a pint of milk and a quarter of a pint of good cream; thicken with flour and water perfectly smooth; break in the yolks of five eggs, sweetened with powdered loaf sugar, the peel of a lemon grated, and half a glass of brandy. Line the dish with good puff paste, and bake for half an hour.

Custard Pudding. No. 4.

Take six eggs, one table-spoonful of flour, and a sufficient quantity of milk to fill the pan. Boil it three quarters of an hour.

Fish Pudding.

Pound fillets of whiting with a quarter of a pound of butter; add the crumb of two penny rolls, soaked in cold milk, pepper and salt, with seasoning according to the taste. Boil in a mould one hour and a quarter, and then turn it out, and serve up with sauce.

French Pudding.

Beat twelve eggs, leaving out half the whites, extremely well; take one pound of melted butter, and one pound of sifted sugar, one nutmeg grated, the peel of a small orange, the juice of two; the butter and sugar to be well beaten together; then add to them the eggs and other ingredients. Beat all very light, and bake in a thin crust.

Gooseberry Pudding.

Scald a quart of gooseberries, and pass them through a sieve, as you would for gooseberry fool; add three eggs, three table-spoonfuls of crumb of bread, three table-spoonfuls of flour, an ounce of butter, and sugar to your taste. Bake it in a moderate oven.

Another.

Scald the gooseberries, and prepare them according to the preceding receipt; mix them with rice, prepared as for a rice pudding, and bake it.

Hunter's Pudding.

One pound of raisins, one pound of suet, chopped fine, four spoonfuls of flour, four of sugar, four of good milk, and four eggs, whites and all, two spoonfuls of brandy or sack, and some grated nutmeg. It must boil four hours complete, and should have good room in the bag, as it swells much in the boiling.

Jug Pudding.

Beat the whites and yolks of three eggs; strain through a sieve; add gradually a quarter of a pint of milk; rub in a mortar two ounces of moist sugar and as much grated nutmeg as would cover a sixpence; then put in four ounces of flour, and beat it into a smooth batter by degrees; stir in seven ounces of suet and three ounces of bread crumb; mix all together half an hour before you put it into the pot. Boil it three hours.

Lemon Pudding.

Take two large lemons; peel them thin, and boil them in three waters till tender; then beat them in a mortar to a paste. Grate a penny roll into the yolks and whites of four eggs well beaten, half a pint of milk, and a quarter of a pound of sugar; mix them all well together; put it into a basin well buttered, and boil it half an hour.

Another way.

Three lemons, six eggs, a quarter of a pound of butter, some crumb of bread grated, with some lemon-peel and grated sugar.

Small Lemon Puddings.

One pint of cream, one spoonful of fine flour, two ounces of sugar, some nutmeg, and the yolks of three eggs; mix all well together; and stick in two ounces of citron. Bake in tea-cups in a quick oven.

Maccaroni Pudding.

Take three ounces of maccaroni, two ounces of butter, a pint and a half of milk boiled, four eggs, half a pound of currants. Put paste round the dish, and bake it.

Marrow Pudding.

Boil two quarts of cream with a little mace and nutmeg; beat very light ten eggs, leaving out half the whites; put the cream scalding to the eggs, and beat it well. Butter lightly the dish you bake it in; then slice some French roll, and lay a layer at the bottom; put on it lumps of marrow; then sprinkle on some currants and fine chopped raisins, then another layer of thin sliced bread, then marrow again, with the currants and raisins as before. When the dish is thus filled, pour over the whole the cream and eggs, which must be sweetened a little. An oven that will bake a custard will be hot enough for this pudding. Strew on the marrow a little powdered cinnamon.

Another way.

Boil up a pint of cream, then take it off; slice two penny loaves thin, and put them into the cream, with a quarter of a pound of fresh butter, stirring it till melted. Then put into it a quarter of a pound of almonds beaten well and small, with rose-water, the marrow of three marrow-bones, and the whites of five eggs, and two yolks. Season it with mace shred small, and sweeten with a quarter of a pound of sugar. Make up your pudding. The marrow should first be laid in water to take out the blood.

Nottingham Pudding.

Peel six apples; take out the core, but be sure to leave the apples whole, and fill up the place of the core with sugar. Put them in a dish, and pour over them a nice light batter. Bake it an hour in a moderate oven.

Oatmeal Pudding.

Steep oatmeal all night in milk; in the morning pour away the milk, and put some cream, beaten spice, currants, a little sugar if you like it; if not, salt, and as many eggs as you think proper. Stir it well together; boil it thoroughly, and serve with butter and sugar.

Orange Pudding. No. 1.

Take the yolks of twelve eggs and the whites of two, six ounces of the best sugar, beat fine and sifted, and a quarter of a pound of orange marmalade: beat all well together; set it over a gentle fire to thicken; put to it half a pound of melted butter, and the juice of a Seville orange. Bake it in a thin light paste, and take great care not to scorch it in the oven.

Orange Pudding. No. 2.

Grate off the rind of two large Seville oranges as far as they are yellow; put them in fair water, and let them boil till they are tender, changing the water two or three times. When they are tender, cut them open, take away the seeds and strings, and beat them in a mortar, with half a pound of sugar finely sifted, until it is a fine light paste; then put in the yolks of ten eggs well beaten, five or six spoonfuls of thick cream, half a Naples biscuit, and the juice of two more Seville oranges. Mix these well together, and melt a pound of the best butter, or beat it to a cream without melting: beat all light and well together, and bake it in a puff paste three quarters of an hour.

Orange Pudding. No. 3.

Grate the peel of four china oranges and of one lemon; boil it in a pint of cream, with a little cinnamon and some sugar. Scald crumb of white bread in a little milk; strain the boiled cream to the bread, and mix it together; add the yolks of six and the whites of three eggs; mix all well together. Put it into a dish rubbed with a little butter, and bake it of a nice brown colour. Serve with wine sauce.

Orange Pudding. No. 4.

Melt half a pound of fresh butter, and when cold take away the top and bottom; then mix the yolks of nine eggs well beaten, and half a pound of double-refined sugar, beaten and seared; beat all well together; grate in the rind of a good Seville orange, and stir well up. Put it into a dish, and bake it.

Orange Pudding. No. 5.

Simmer two ounces of isinglass in water; steep orange-peel in water all night; then add one pint of orange-juice, with the yolks of four eggs, and some white sugar. Bake a quarter of an hour or twenty minutes.

Orange Pudding. No. 6.

Cut two large china oranges in quarters, and take out the seeds; beat them in a mortar, with two ounces of sugar, and the same quantity of butter; then add four eggs, well beat, and a little Seville orange-juice. Line the dish with puff paste, and bake it.

Plain Orange Pudding.

Make a bread pudding, and add a table-spoonful of ratafia, the juice of a Seville orange and the rind, or that of a lemon cut small. Bake with puff paste round it; turn it out of the tin when sent to table.

Paradise Pudding.

Six apples pared and chopped very fine, six eggs, six ounces of bread grated very fine, six ounces of sugar, six ounces of currants, a little salt and nutmeg, some lemon-peel, and one glass of brandy. The whole to boil three hours.

Pith Pudding.

Take the pith of an ox; wipe the blood clean from it; let it lie in water two days, changing the water very often. Dry it in a cloth, and scrape it with a knife to separate the strings from it. Then put it into a basin; beat it with two or three spoonfuls of rose-water till it is very fine, and strain it through a fine strainer. Boil a quart of thick cream with a nutmeg, a blade of mace, and a little cinnamon. Beat half a pound of almonds very fine with rose-water; put them in the cream and strain it: beat them again, and again strain till you have extracted all their goodness; then put to them twelve eggs, with four whites. Mix all these together with the pith; add five or six spoonfuls of sack, half a pound of sugar, citron cut small, and the marrow of six bones; and then fill them. Half an hour will boil them.

Plum Pudding. No. 1.

Half a pound of raisins stoned, half a pound of suet, good weight, shred very fine, half a pint of milk, four eggs, two of the whites only. Beat the eggs first, mix half the milk with them, stir in the flour and the rest of the milk by degrees, then the suet and raisins, and a small tea-cupful of moist sugar. Mix the eggs, sugar, and milk, well together in the beginning, and stir all the ingredients well together.

A plum pudding should never boil less than five hours; longer will not hurt it. This quantity makes a large plain pudding: half might do.

Plum Pudding. No. 2.

One pound of jar raisins stoned and cut in pieces, one pound of suet shred small, with a very little salt to it; six eggs, beat with a little brandy and sack, nearly a pint of milk, a nutmeg grated, a very little flour, not more than a spoonful, among the raisins, to separate them from each other, and as much grated bread as will make these ingredients of the proper consistence when they are all mixed together.

Plum Pudding. No. 3.

Take half a pound of crumb of stale bread; cut it in pieces; boil half a pint of milk and pour over it; let it stand half an hour to soak. Take half a pound of beef suet shred fine, half a pound of raisins, half a pound of currants beat up with a little salt; mix them well together with a handful of flour. Butter the dish, and put the pudding in it to bake; but if boiled, flour the bag, or butter the mould, if you boil it in one. To this quantity put three eggs.

Plum Pudding. No. 4.

One pound of beef suet, one pound of raisins stoned, four table-spoonfuls of flour, six ounces of loaf-sugar, one tea-spoonful of salt, five eggs, and half a grated nutmeg. Flour the cloth well, and boil it six hours.

Plum Pudding. No. 5.

Take currants, raisins, suet, bread crumb, and sugar, half a pound of each, five eggs, two ounces of almonds blanched and shred very fine, citron and brandy to taste, and a spoonful of flour.

A rich Plum Pudding.

A pound and a quarter of sun raisins, stoned, six eggs, two spoonfuls of flour, a pound of suet, a little nutmeg, a glass of brandy: boil it five or six hours.

Potato Pudding. No. 1.

Boil two pounds of white potatoes; peel them, and bruise them fine in a mortar, with half a pound of melted butter, and the yolks of four eggs. Put it into a cloth, and boil it half an hour; then turn it into a dish; pour melted butter, with a glass of raisin wine, and the juice of a Seville orange, mixed together as sauce, over it, and strew powdered sugar all over.

Potato Pudding. No. 2.

Take four steamed potatoes; dry and rub them through a sieve; boil a quarter of a pint of milk, with spice, sugar, and butter; stir the potatoes in the milk, with the yolks of three eggs; beat the whites to a strong froth, and add them to the pudding. Bake it in a quick oven.

Potato Pudding. No. 3.

Boil three or four potatoes; mash and pass them through a sieve; beat them up with milk, and let it stand till cold. Then add the yolks of four eggs and sugar; beat up the four whites to a strong froth, and stir it in very gently before you put the pudding into the mould.

Potato Pudding. No. 4.

One pound of potatoes, three quarters of a pound of butter, one pound of sugar, eight eggs, a little mace, and nutmeg. Rub the potatoes through a sieve, to make them quite free from lumps. Bake it.

Potato Pudding. No. 5.

Mix twelve ounces of potatoes, boiled, skinned, and mashed, one ounce of suet, one ounce, or one-sixteenth of a pint, of milk, and one ounce of Gloucester cheese—total, fifteen ounces—with as much boiling water as is necessary to bring them to a due consistence. Bake in an earthen pan.

Potato Pudding. No. 6.

Potatoes and suet as before, and one ounce of red herrings, pounded fine in a mortar, mixed, baked, &c. as before.

Potato Pudding. No. 7.

The same quantity of potatoes and suet, and one ounce of hung beef, grated fine with a grater, and mixed and baked as before.

Pottinger's Pudding.

Three ounces of ground rice, and two ounces of sweet almonds, blanched and beaten fine; the rice must be boiled and beaten likewise. Mix them well together, with two eggs, sugar and butter, to your taste. Make as thin a puff paste as possible, and put it round some cups; when baked, turn them out, and pour wine sauce over them. This quantity will make four puddings.

Prune Pudding.

Mix a pound of flour with a quart of milk; beat up six eggs, and mix with it a little salt, and a spoonful of beaten ginger. Beat the whole well together till it is a fine stiff batter; put in a pound of prunes; tie the pudding in a cloth, and boil it an hour and a half. When sent to table, pour melted butter over it.

Quaking Pudding.

Boil a quart of milk with a bit of cinnamon and mace; mix about a spoonful of butter with a large spoonful of flour, to which put the milk by degrees. Add ten eggs, but only half the whites, and a nutmeg grated. Butter your basin and the cloth you tie over it, which must be tied so tight and close as not to admit a drop of water. Boil it an hour. Sack and butter for sauce.

Another way.

To three quarts of cream put the yolks of twelve eggs and three whites, and two spoonfuls of flour, half a nutmeg grated, and a quarter of a pound of sugar. Mix them well together. Put it into a bag, and boil it with a quick fire; but let the water boil before you put it in. Half an hour will do it.

Ratafia Pudding.

A quarter of a pound of sweet and a quarter of an ounce of bitter almonds, butter and loaf sugar of each a quarter of a pound; beat them together in a marble mortar. Add a pint of cream, four eggs, leaving out two whites, and a wine glassful of sherry. Garnish the dish with puff paste, and bake half an hour.

Rice Pudding.

Take a quarter of a pound of rice, a pint and a half of new milk, five eggs, with the whites of two. Set the rice and the milk over the fire till it is just ready to boil; then pour it into a basin, and stir into it an ounce of butter till it is quite melted. When cold, the eggs to be well beaten and stirred in, and the whole sweetened to the taste: in general, a quarter of a pound of sugar is allowed to the above proportions. Add about a table-spoonful of ratafia, and a little salt: a little cream improves it much. Put it into a nice paste, and an hour is sufficient to bake it.

The rice and milk, while over the fire, must be kept stirred all the time.

Another.

Boil five ounces of rice in a pint and a half of milk; when nearly cold, stir in two ounces of butter, two eggs, three ounces of sugar, spice or lemon, as you like. Bake it an hour.

Plain Rice Pudding.

Take a quarter of a pound of whole rice, wash and pick it clean; put it into a saucepan, with a quart of new milk, a stick of cinnamon, and lemon-peel shred fine. Boil it gently till the rice is tender and thick, and stir it often to keep it from burning. Take out the cinnamon and lemon-peel; put the rice into an earthen pan to cool; beat up the yolks of four eggs and the whites of two. Stir them into the rice; sweeten it to the palate with moist sugar; put in some lemon or Seville orange-peel shred very fine, a few bitter almonds, and a little grated nutmeg and ginger. Mix all well together; lay a puff paste round the dish, pour in the pudding, and bake it.

Another way.

Pour a quart of new milk, scalding hot, upon three ounces of whole rice. Let it stand covered for an hour or two. Scald the milk again, and pour it on as before, letting it stand all night. Next day, when you are ready to make the pudding, set the rice and milk over the fire, give it a boil up, sweeten it with a little sugar, put into it a very little pounded cinnamon, stir it well together; butter the dish in which it is to be baked, pour it in, and put it into the oven. This pudding is not long in baking.

Ground Rice Pudding.

Boil three ounces of rice in a pint of milk, stirring it all well together the whole time of boiling. Pour it into a pan, and stir in six ounces of butter, six ounces of sugar, eight eggs, but half of the whites only, and twenty almonds pounded, half of them bitter. Put paste at the bottom of the dish.

Rice Hunting Pudding.

To a pound of suet, half a pound of currants, a pound of jar raisins stoned, five eggs, leaving out two whites, half a pound of ground rice, a little spice, and as much milk as will make it a thick batter. Boil it two hours and a half.

Kitchen Rice Pudding.

Half a pound of rice in two quarts of boiling water, a pint and a half of milk, and a quarter of a pound of beef or mutton suet, shred fine into it. Bake an hour and a half.

Rice Plum Pudding.

Half a pound of rice boiled in milk till tender, but the milk must not run thin about it; then take half a pound of raisins, and the like quantity of currants, and suet, chopped fine, four eggs, leaving out half the whites, one table-spoonful of sugar, two of brandy, some lemon-peel, and spice. Mix these well together, and take two table-spoonfuls of flour to make it up. It must boil five or six hours in a tin or basin.

Small Rice Puddings.

Set three ounces of flour of rice over the fire in three quarters of a pint of milk; stir it constantly; when stiff, take it off, pour it into an earthen pan, and stir in three ounces of butter, and a large tea-cupful of cream; sweeten it to your taste with lump sugar. When cold, beat five eggs and two whites; grate the peel of half a lemon; cut three ounces of blanched almonds small, and a few bitter ones with them. Beat all well together; boil it half an hour in small basins, and serve with wine sauce.

Swedish Rice Pudding.

Wash one pound of rice six or eight times in warm water; put it into a stewpan upon a slow fire till it bursts; strain it through a sieve; add to the rice one pound of sugar, previously well clarified, and the juice of six or eight oranges, and of six lemons, and simmer it on the fire for half an hour. Cover the bottom and the edges of a dish with paste, taking care that the flour of which the paste is made be first thoroughly dried. Put in your rice, and decorate with candied orange-peel.

Rice White Pot.

Boil one pound of rice, previously well washed in two quarts of new milk, till it is much reduced, quite tender, and thick; beat it in a mortar, with a quarter of a pound of almonds blanched, putting it to them by degrees as you beat them. Boil two quarts of cream with two or three blades of mace; mix it light with nine eggs—only five whites—well beat, and a little rose-water; sweeten it to your taste. Cut some candied orange and citron very thin, and lay it in. Bake it in a slow oven.

Sago Pudding.

Boil a quarter of a pound of sago in a pint of new milk, till it is very thick; stir in a large piece of butter; add sugar and nutmeg to your palate, and four eggs. Boil it an hour. Wine sauce.

Spoonful Pudding.

A table-spoonful of flour, a spoonful of cream or milk, some currants, an egg, a little sugar and brandy, or raisin wine. Make them round and about the size of an egg, and tie them up in separate pudding-cloths.

Plain Suet Pudding, baked.

Four spoonfuls of flour, four spoonfuls of suet shred very fine, three eggs, mixed with a little salt, and a tea-cupful of milk. Bake in a small pie-dish, and turn it out for table.

Suet Pudding, boiled.

Shred a pound of beef suet very fine; mix it with a pound of flour, a little salt and ginger, six eggs, and as much milk as will make it into a stiff batter. Put it in a cloth, and boil it two hours. When done, turn it into a dish, with plain melted butter.

Tansy Pudding.

Beat sixteen eggs very well in a wooden bowl, leaving out six whites, with a little orange-flower water and brandy; then add to them by degrees half a pound of fine sifted sugar; grate in a nutmeg, and a quarter of a pound of Naples biscuit; add a pint of the juice of spinach, and four spoonfuls of the juice of tansy; then put to it a pint of cream. Stir it all well together, and put it in a skillet, with a piece of butter melted; keep it stirring till it becomes pretty thick; then put it in a dish, and bake it half an hour. When it comes out of the oven, stick it with blanched almonds cut very thin, and mix in some citron cut in the same manner. Serve it with sack and sugar, and squeeze a Seville orange over it. Turn it out in the dish in which you serve it bottom upwards.

Another way.

Take five ounces of grated bread, a pint of milk, five eggs, a little nutmeg, the juice of tansy and spinach, to your taste, a quarter of a pound of butter, some sugar, and a little brandy; put it in a saucepan, and keep it stirring on a gentle fire till thick. Then put it in a dish and bake it; when baked, turn it out, and dust sugar on it.

Tapioca Pudding.

Take a small tea-cupful of tapioca, and rather more than half that quantity of whole rice; let it soak all night in water, just enough to cover it; then add a quart of milk: let it simmer over a slow fire, stirring it every five minutes till it looks clear. Let it stand till quite cold; then add three eggs, well beaten with sugar, and grated lemon-peel, and bake it. It is equally good cold or hot.

Neat's Tongue Pudding.

Boil a neat's tongue very tender; when cold, peel and shred it very fine, after grating as much as will cover your hand. Add to it some beef suet and marrow. Take some oranges and citron, finely cut, some cloves, nutmeg, and mace, not forgetting salt to your taste, twenty-four eggs, half the whites only, some sack, a little rose-water, and as much boiled cream as will make the whole of proper thickness. Then put in two pounds of currants, if your tongue be large.

Quatre Fruits.

Take picked strawberries, black currants, raspberries, and the little black cherries, one pound of each, and two quarts of brandy. Infuse the whole together, and sweeten to taste. When it has stood a sufficient time, filter through a jelly-bag till the liquor is quite clear.

Quinces, to preserve.

Put a third part of the clearest and largest quinces into cold water over the fire, and coddle till tender, but not so as to be broken. Pare and cut them into quarters, taking out the core and the hard part, and then weigh them. The kernels must be taken out of the core, and tied up in a piece of muslin or gauze. The remaining two-thirds of the quinces must be grated, and the juice well squeezed out; and to a pound of the coddled quinces put a pint of juice; pound some cochineal, tie it up in muslin, and put it to the quinces and juice. They must be together all night; next day, put a pound of lump sugar to every pound of coddled quinces; let the sugar be broken into small lumps, and, with the quince juice, cochineal, and kernels, be boiled together until the quinces are clear and red, quite to the middle of each quarter. Take out the quarters, and boil the syrup for half an hour: put the quarters in, and let them boil gently for near an hour: then put them in a jar, boil the syrup till it is a thick jelly, and put it boiling hot over them.

Quinces, to preserve whole.

Pare the quinces very thin, put them into a well-tinned saucepan; fill it with hard water, lay the parings over the fruit, and keep them down; cover close that the steam may not escape, and set them over a slow fire to stew till tender and of a fine red colour. Take them carefully out, and weigh them to two pounds of quinces. Take two pounds and a half of double-refined sugar; put it into a preserving-pan, with one quart of water. Set it over a clear charcoal fire to boil; skim it clean, and, when it looks clear, put in the quinces. Boil them twelve minutes; take them off, and set them by for four hours to cool. Set them on the fire again, and let them boil three minutes; take them off, and let them stand two days; then boil them again ten minutes with the juice of two lemons, and set them by till cold. Put them into jars; pour on the syrup, cover them with brandy paper, tie them close with leather or bladder, and set them in a dry cool place.

Ramaquins. No. 1.

Take two ounces of Cheshire cheese grated, two ounces of white bread grated, two ounces of butter, half a pint of cream, and a little white pepper; boil all together; let it stand till cold; then take two yolks of eggs, beat the whole together, and put it into paper coffins. Twenty minutes will bake them.

Ramaquins. No. 2.

Take very nearly half a pound of Parmesan cheese, two ounces of mild Gloucester, four yolks of eggs, about six ounces of the best butter, and a good tea-cupful of cream. Beat the cheese first in a mortar; add by degrees the other ingredients, and in some measure be regulated by your taste, whether the proportion of any of them should be increased or diminished. A little while bakes them; the oven must not be too hot. They are baked in little paper cases, and served as hot as possible.

Ramaquins. No. 3.

Put to a little water just warm a little salt; stir in a quarter of a pound of butter; it must not boil. When well mixed, let it stand till cold: then stir in three eggs, one at a time, beating it well till it is quite smooth; then add three more eggs, beating it well, and half a pound of Parmesan cheese. Beat it well again, adding two yolks of eggs and a quarter of a pound of cold butter, and again beat it. Just before it is going into the oven, beat six eggs to a froth, and beat the whole together. Bake in paper moulds and in a quick oven. Serve as hot as possible.

Ramaquins. No. 4.

Take a quarter of a pound of Cheshire cheese, two eggs, and two ounces of butter; beat them fine in a mortar, and make them up in cakes that will cover a piece of bread of the size of a crown-piece. Lay them on a dish, not touching one another; set them on a chaffing-dish of coals, and hold a salamander over them till they are quite brown. Serve up hot.

Raspberries, to preserve.

Take the juice of red and white raspberries; if you have no white raspberries, put half codling jelly; put a pint and a half of juice to two pounds of sugar; let it boil, and skim it. Then put in three quarters of a pound of large red raspberries;

boil them very fast till they jelly and are very clear; do not take them off the fire, that would make them hard, and a quarter of an hour will do them. After they begin to boil fast, put the raspberries in pots or glasses; then strain the jelly from the seeds, and put it to them. When they begin to cool, stir them, that they may not lie at the top of the glasses; and, when cold, lay upon them papers wetted with brandy and dried with a cloth.

Another way.

Put three quarters of a pound of moist sugar to every quart of fruit, and let them boil gently till they jelly.

Raspberries, to preserve in Currant Jelly.

Strip the currants from the stalks; weigh one pound of sugar to one pound of fruit, and to every eight pounds of currants put one pound of raspberries, for which you are not to allow any sugar. Wet the sugar, and let it boil till it is almost sugar again; then throw in the fruit, and, with a very smart fire, let it boil up all over. Take it off, and strain it through a lawn sieve. You must not let it boil too much, for fear of the currants breaking, and the seeds coming through into the jelly. When it boils up in the middle, and the syrup diffuses itself generally, it is sufficiently done; then take it off instantly. This makes a very elegant, clear currant jelly, and may be kept and used as such. Take some whole fine large raspberries; stalk them; put some of the jelly, made as above directed, in your preserving-pan; sprinkle in the raspberries, not too many at a time, for fear of bruising them. About ten minutes will do them. Take them off, and put them in pots or glasses. If you choose to do more, you must put in the pan a fresh supply of jelly. Let the jelly nearly boil up before you put in the raspberries.

Raspberry Jam. No. 1.—Very good.

Take to each pound of raspberries half a pint of juice of red and white currants, an equal quantity of each, in the whole half a pint, and a pound of double-refined sugar. Stew or bake the currants in a pot, to get out the juice. Let the sugar be finely beaten; then take half the raspberries and squeeze through a coarse cloth, to keep back the seeds; bruise the rest with the back of a wooden spoon; the half that is bruised must be of the best raspberries. Mix the raspberries, juice, and sugar, together: set it over a good fire, and let it boil as fast as possible, till you see it will jelly, which you may try in a spoon.

Raspberry Jam. No. 2.

Weigh equal quantities of sugar and of fruit; put the fruit into a preserving-pan: boil it very quickly; break it; and stir it constantly. When the juice is almost wasted, add the sugar, and simmer it half an hour. Use a silver spoon.

Raspberry Jam. No. 3.

To six quarts of raspberries put three pounds of refined sugar finely pounded; strain half the raspberries from the seed; then boil the juice and the other half

together. As it jellies, put it into pots. The sugar should first be boiled separately, before the raspberries are added.

Raspberry Paste.

Break three parts of your raspberries red and white; strain them through linen; break the other part, and put into the juice; boil it till it jellies, and then let it stand till cold. To every pint put a pound of sugar, and make it scalding hot: add some codling jelly before you put in the seeds.

Apple Tart with Rice Crust.

Pare and quarter six russet apples; stew them till soft; sweeten with lump-sugar; grate some lemon-peel; boil a tea-cupful of rice in milk till it becomes thick: sweeten it well with loaf-sugar. Add a little cream, cinnamon, and nutmeg; lay the apple in the dish; cover it with rice; beat the whites of two eggs to a strong froth; lay it on the top; dust a little sugar over it, and brown it in the oven.

Another way.

Pare and core as many apples as your dish will conveniently bake; stew them with sugar, a bit of lemon-peel, and a little cinnamon. Prepare your rice as for a rice pudding. Fill your dish three parts full of apples, and cover it with the rice.

Rolls.

Take two pounds of flour; divide it; put one half into a deep pan; rub two ounces of butter into the flour; the whites of two eggs whisked to a high froth; add one table-spoonful of yest, four table-spoonfuls of cream, the yolk of one egg, a pint of milk, rather more than new milk warm. Mix the above together into a lather; beat it for ten minutes; then cover it, and set it before the fire for two hours to rise. Mix in the other half of the flour, and set it before the fire for a quarter of an hour. These rolls must be baked in earthenware cups, rubbed with a little butter, and not more than half filled with dough; they must be baked a quarter of an hour in a very hot oven.

Another way.

Take one quart of fine flour; wet it with warm milk, and six table-spoonfuls of small beer yest, a quarter of a pound of butter, and a little salt. Do not make the dough too stiff at first, but let it rise awhile; then work in the flour to the proper consistency. Set it to rise some time longer, then form your rolls of any size you please; bake them in a warmish oven; twenty minutes will bake the small and half an hour the large ones.

Excellent Rolls.

Take three pounds of the finest flour, and mix up the yolks of three eggs with the yest. Wet the flour with milk, first melting in the milk one ounce of butter, and add a little salt to the flour.

Little Rolls.

One pound of flour, two or three spoonfuls of yest, the yolks of two eggs, the white of one, a little salt, moistened with milk. This dough must be made softer than for bread, and beaten well with a spoon till it is quite light; let it stand some hours before it is baked; some persons make it over-night. The Dutch oven, which must first be made warm, will bake the rolls, which must be turned to prevent their catching.

Breakfast Rolls.

Rub exceedingly fine two ounces of good butter in a pound and three quarters of fine flour. Mix a table-spoonful of yest in half a pint of warm milk; set a light sponge in the flour till it rises for an hour; beat up one or two eggs in half a spoonful of fine sugar, and intermix it with the sponge, adding to it a little less than half a pint of warm milk with a tea-spoonful of salt. Mix all up to a light dough, and keep it warm, to rise again for another hour. Then break it in pieces, and roll them to the thickness of your finger of the proper length; lay them on tin plates, and set them in a warm stove for an hour more. Then touch them over with a little milk, and bake them in a slow oven with care. To take off the bitterness from the yest, mix one pint of it in two gallons of water, and let it stand for twenty-four hours; then throw off the water, and the yest is fit for use; if not, repeat it.

Another way.

With two pounds of flour mix about half a pound of butter, till it is like crumbled bread; add two whole eggs, three spoonfuls of good yest, and a little salt. Make it up into little rolls; set them before the fire for a short time to rise, but, if the yest is very good, this will not be necessary.

Brentford Rolls.

Take two pounds of fine flour; put to it a little salt, and two spoonfuls of fine sugar sifted; rub in a quarter of a pound of fresh butter, the yolks of two eggs, two spoonfuls of yest, and about a pint of milk. Work the whole into a dough, and set it to the fire to rise. Make twelve rolls of it; lay them on buttered tins, let them stand to the fire to rise till they are very light, then bake them about half an hour.

Dutch Rolls.

Into one pound of flour rub three ounces of butter; with a spoonful of yest, mixed up with warm milk, make it into light paste; set it before the fire to rise. When risen nearly half as big again, make it into rolls about the length of four inches, and the breadth of two fingers; set them again to rise before the fire, till risen very well; put them into the oven for a quarter of an hour.

French Rolls. No. 1.

Seven pounds of flour, four eggs leaving out two yolks—the whites of the eggs should be beaten to a snow—three quarters of a pint of ale yest. Beat the eggs and yest together, adding warm milk; put it so beat into the flour, in which must be well rubbed four ounces of butter; wet the whole into a soft paste. Keep beating it in the bowl with your hand for a quarter of an hour at least; let it stand by the fire half an hour, then make it into rolls, and put them into pans or dishes, first well floured, or, what is still better, iron moulds, which are made on purpose to bake rolls in. Let them stand by the fire another half hour, and put them, bottom upwards, on tin plates, in the middle of a hot oven for three quarters of an hour or more: take them out, and rasp them.

French Rolls. No. 2.

Take two or three spoonfuls of good yest, as much warm water, two or three lumps of loaf-sugar, and the yolk of an egg. Mix all together; let it stand to rise. Meanwhile take a quartern of the finest flour, and rub in about an ounce of butter. Then take a quart of new milk, and put into it a pint of boiling water, so as to make it rather warmer than new milk from the cow. Mix together the milk and yest, and strain through a sieve into the flour, and, when you have made it into a light paste, flour a piece of clean linen cloth well, lay it upon a thick double flannel, put your paste into the cloth, wrap it up close, and put it in an earthen pan before the fire till it rises. Make it up into ten rolls, and put them into a quick oven for a quarter of an hour.

French Rolls. No. 3.

To half a peck of the best flour put six eggs, leaving out two whites, a little salt, a pint of good ale yest, and as much new milk, a little warmed, as will make it a thin light paste. Stir it about with your hand, or with a large wooden spoon, but by no means knead it. Set it in a pan before the fire for about an hour, or till it rises; then make it up into little rolls, and bake it in a quick oven.

Milton Rolls.

Take one pound of fine rye flour, a little salt, the yolk of one egg, a small cupful of yest, and some warm new milk, with a bit of butter in it. Mix all together; let it stand one hour to rise; and bake your rolls half an hour in a quick oven.

Runnet.

Take out the stomachs of fowls before you dress them; wash and cleanse them thoroughly; then string them, and hang them up to dry. When wanted for use, soak them in water, and boil them in milk; this makes the best and sweetest whey.

Another way.

Take the curd out of a calf's maw; wash and pick it clean from the hair and stones that are sometimes in it, and season it well with salt. Wipe the maw, and salt it well, within and without, and put in the curd. Let it lie in salt for three or four days, and then hang it up.

Rusks.

Take flour, water, or milk, yest, and brown sugar; work it just the same as for bread. Make it up into a long loaf, and bake it. Then let it be one day old before you cut it in slices: make your oven extremely hot, and dry them in it for about two minutes, watching them all the time.

Another way.

Put five pounds of fine flour in a large basin; add to it eight eggs unbeat, yolks and whites; dissolve half a pound of sugar over the fire, in a choppin (or a Scotch quart) of new milk; add all this to the flour with half a mutchkin, (one English pint) of new yest; mix it well, and set it before a good fire covered with a cloth. Let it stand half an hour, then work it up with a little more flour, and let it stand half an hour longer. Then take it out of the basin, and make it up on a board into small round or square biscuits, place them upon sheets of white iron, and set them before the fire, covered with a cloth, till they rise, which will be in half an hour. Put them into the oven, just when the bread is taken out; shut the oven till the biscuits turn brown on the top; then take them out, and cut them through.

Rusks, and Tops and Bottoms.

Well mix two pounds of sugar, dried and sifted, with twelve pounds of flour, also well dried and sifted. Beat up eighteen eggs, leaving out eight whites, very light, with half a pint of new yest, and put it into the flour. Melt two pounds of butter in three pints of new milk, and wet the paste with it to your liking. Make it up in little cakes; lay them one on another; when baked, separate them, and return them to the oven to harden.

Sally Lunn.

To two pounds of fine flour put about two table-spoonfuls of fresh yest, mixed with a pint of new milk made warm. Add the yolks of three eggs, well beat up. Rub into the flour about a quarter of a pound of butter, with salt to your taste; put it to the fire to rise, as you do bread. Make it into a cake, and put it on a tin over a chaffing-dish of slow coals, or on a hot hearth, till you see it rise; then put it into a quick oven, and, when the upper side is well baked, turn it. When done, rasp it all over and butter it; the top will take a pound of butter.

Slip-Cote.

A piece of runnet, the size of half-a-crown, put into a table-spoonful of boiling water over-night, and strained into a quart of new milk, lukewarm, an hour before it is eaten.

Soufflé.

Two table-spoonfuls of ground rice, half a pint of milk or cream, and the rind of a lemon, pared very thin, sugar, and a bay-leaf, to be stewed together for ten minutes; take out the peel, and let it stand till cold; then add the yolks of four eggs, which have been well beaten, with sifted sugar; the four whites to be beaten separately to a fine froth, and added to the above, which must be gently stirred all together, put into a tin mould, and baked in a quick oven for twenty minutes.

Another way.

Make a raised pie of any size you think proper. Take some milk, a bay-leaf, a little cinnamon, sugar, and coriander seeds; boil it till it is quite thick. Melt a piece of butter in another stewpan, with a handful of flour well stirred in; let it boil some time; strain the milk through, and put all together, adding four or five eggs, beaten up for a long time; these are to be added at the last, and then baked.

Soufflé of Apples and Rice.

Prepare some rice of a strong solid substance; dress it up all round a dish, the same height as a raised crust, that is, about three inches high. Have some marmalade of apple ready made; mix with it six yolks of eggs, and a small piece of butter; warm it on the stove in order to do the eggs; then have eight whites of eggs well whipped, as for biscuits; mix them lightly with the apples, and put the whole into the middle of the rice. Set it in a moderately hot oven, and, when the soufflé is raised sufficiently, send it up quickly to table, as it would soon fall and spoil.

Strawberries, to preserve for eating with Cream.

Take the largest scarlet strawberries you can get, full red, but not too ripe, and their weight in double-refined sugar. Take more strawberries of the same sort; put them in a pot, and set them in water over the fire to draw out the juice. To every pound of strawberries allow full half a pint of this juice, adding to it nearly a quarter of a pound more sugar. Dip all the sugar in water; set it on the fire; and, when it is thoroughly melted, take it off, and stir it till it is almost cold. Then put in the strawberries, and boil them over a quick fire; skim them; and, when they look clear, they are done enough. If you think the syrup too thin, take out the fruit, and boil it more; but you must stir it till it is cold before you put the strawberries in again.

Strawberries, to preserve in Currant Jelly.

Boil all the ordinary strawberries you can spare in the water in which you mean to put the sugar to make the syrup for the strawberries. Take three quarters of a pound of the finest scarlet or pine strawberries; add to them one pound and a quarter of sugar, which dip in the above-mentioned strawberry liquor; then boil the strawberries quick, and skim them clear once. When cold, remove them out of the pan into a China bowl. If you touch them while hot, you break or bruise them. Keep them closely covered with white paper till the currants are ripe, every now and then looking at them to see if they ferment or want heating up again. Do it if required, and put on fresh papers. When the currants are ripe, boil up the strawberries; skim them well; let them stand till almost cold, and then take them out of the syrup very carefully. Lay them on a lawn sieve, with a dish under them to catch the syrup; then strain the syrup through another lawn sieve, to clear it of all the bits and seeds; add to this syrup full half a pint of red and white currant juice, in equal quantities of each; then boil it quick about ten minutes, skimming it well.

When it jellies, which you may know by trying it in a spoon, add the strawberries to it, and let them just simmer without boiling. Put them carefully into the pots, but, for fear of the strawberries settling at the bottom, put in a little of the jelly first and let it set; then put in the strawberries and jelly; watch them a little till they are cold, and, as the strawberries rise above the syrup, with a tea-spoon gently force them down again under it. In a few days put on brandy papers—they will turn out in a firm jelly.

Strawberries, to preserve in Gooseberry Jelly.

Take a quart of the sharpest white gooseberries and a quart of water; let them come up to a boil, and then strain them through a lawn sieve. To a pint of the liquor put one pound of double-refined sugar; let it boil till it jellies; skim it very well, and take it off; when cool, put in the strawberries whole and picked. Set them on the fire; let them come to a boil; take them off till cold; repeat this three or four times till they are clear; then take the strawberries out carefully, that they may not bruise or break, and boil the jelly till it is stiff. Put a little first in the bottom of your pots or glasses; when set, put in the rest, first mixed with the strawberries, but not till nearly cold.

Strawberry Jam—very good.

To one pound of scarlet strawberries, which are by far the best for the purpose, put a pound of powdered sugar. Take another half pound of strawberries, and squeeze all their juice through a cloth, taking care that none of the seeds come through to the jam. Then boil the strawberries, juice, and sugar, over a quick fire; skim it very clean; set it by in a clean China bowl, covering it close with writing paper; when the currants are ripe, add to the strawberries full half a pint of red currant juice, and half a pound more of pounded sugar: boil it all together for about ten or twelve minutes over a quick fire, and skim it very well.

Another way.

Gather the strawberries very ripe; bruise them fine; put to them a little juice of strawberries; beat and sift their weight in sugar, and strew it over them. Put the pulp into a preserving-pan; set it on a clear fire, and boil it three quarters of an hour, stirring it all the time. Put it into pots, and keep it in a dry place, with brandy paper over it.

Sugar, to clarify.

Break into pieces two pounds of double-refined sugar; put it into a stewpan, with a pint of cold spring water; when dissolved, set it over a moderate fire; beat about half the white of an egg; put it to the sugar, before it gets warm, and stir it well together. When it boils, take off the scum; keep it boiling till no scum rises and it is perfectly clear. Run it through a clean napkin; put it in a bottle well corked, and it will keep for months.

Syllabub.

Take a quart of cream with a slice or two of lemon-peel, to be laid to soak in the cream. Take half a pint of sack and six spoonfuls of white wine, dividing it equally into your syllabub. Set your cream over the fire, and make it something more than lukewarm; sweeten both sack and cream, and put the cream into a spouted pot, pouring it rather high from the pot into the vessel in which you intend to put it. Let it be made about eight or nine hours before you want it for use.

Another way.

Mix a quart of cream, not too thick, with a pint of white wine, and the juice of two lemons; sweeten it to your taste; put it in a broad earthen pan; then whisk it up. As the froth rises, take it off with a spoon, and put it in your glasses, but do not make it long before you want them.

Everlasting Syllabub—very excellent.

Take a quart and half a pint of cream, one pint of Rhenish wine, half a pint of sack, the juice of three lemons, about a pound of double-refined sugar, beaten fine and sifted before you put it into the cream. Grate off the rinds of the three lemons used, put it with the juice into the wine, and that to the cream. Then beat all together with a whisk just half an hour; take it up with a spoon, and fill your glasses. It will keep good nine or ten days, and is best three or four days old.

Solid Syllabub.

Half a pint of white wine, a wine-glass of brandy, the peel of a lemon grated and the juice, half a pound of powdered loaf-sugar, and a pint of cream. Stir these ingredients well together; then dissolve one ounce of isinglass in half a pint of water; strain it; and when cool add it to the syllabub, stirring it well all the time; then put it in a mould. It is better made the day before you want it.

Whipt Syllabub.

Boil a quart of cream with a bit of cinnamon; let it cool; take out the cinnamon, and sweeten to your taste. Put in half a pint of white wine, or sack, and a piece of lemon-peel. Whip it with a whisk to a froth; take it off with a spoon as it rises; lay it on the bottom of a sieve; put wine sweetened in the bottom of your glasses, and lay on the syllabub as high as you can.

Taffy.

Two pounds of moist sugar, an ounce of candied orange-peel, the same of citron, the juice of three lemons, the rind of two grated, and two ounces and a half of butter. Keep stirring these on the fire until they attain the desired consistency. Pour it on paper oiled to prevent its sticking.

Trifle. No. 1.

Take as many macaroons as the bottom of your dish will hold; peel off the wafers, and dip the cakes in Madeira or mountain wine. Make a very thick custard, with pounded apricot or peach kernels boiled in it; but if you have none, you may put some bitter almonds; pour the custard hot upon the maccaroons. When the custard is cold, or just before the trifle is sent to table, lay on it as much whipped syllabub as the dish can hold. The syllabub must be done with very good cream and wine, and put on a sieve to drain before you lay it on the custard. If you like it, put here and there on the whipped cream bunches of preserved barberries, or pieces of raspberry jam.

Trifle. No. 2.

Take a quart of sweet cream; boil it with a blade of mace and a little lemon-peel; sweeten it with sugar; keep stirring it till it is almost cold to prevent it from creaming at top; then put it into the dish you intend to serve it in, with a spoonful or less of runnet. Let it stand till it becomes like cheese. You may perfume it, or add orange-flower water.

Trifle. No. 3.

Cover the bottom of your dish with maccaroons and ratafia cakes; just wet them all through with mountain wine or raisin wine; then make a boiled custard, not too thick, and when cold pour it over them. Lay a whipped syllabub over that. You may garnish with currant jelly.

Trotter Jelly.

Boil four sheep's trotters in a quart of water till reduced to a pint, and strain it through a fine sieve.

Veal and Ham Patés.

Chop six ounces of ready dressed lean veal and three ounces of ham very small; put it into a stewpan, with an ounce of butter rolled in flour, half a gill of cream, the same quantity of veal stock, a little lemon-peel, cayenne pepper and salt, to which add, if you like, a spoonful of essence of ham and some lemon-juice.

Venison Pasty.

Bone a neck and breast of venison, and season them well with salt and pepper; put them into a pan, with part of a neck of mutton sliced and laid over them, and a glass of red wine. Cover the whole with a coarse paste, and bake it an hour or two; but finish baking in a puff paste, adding a little more seasoning and the gravy from the meat. Let the crust be half an inch thick at the bottom, and the top crust thicker. If the pasty is to be eaten hot, pour a rich gravy into it when it comes from the oven; but, if cold, there is no occasion for that. The breast and shoulder make a very good pasty. It may be done in raised crust. A middle-sized pasty will take three hours' baking.

Vol-au-Vent.

Take a sufficient quantity of puff-paste, cut it to the shape of the dish, and make it as for an apple pie, only without a top. When baked, put it on a sheet of writing paper, near the fire, to drain the butter, till dinner time. Then take two fowls, which have been previously boiled; cut them up as for a fricassee, but leave out the back. Prepare a sauce, the white sauce as directed for boiled fowls. Wash a table-spoonful of mushrooms in three or four cold waters; cut them in half, and add them also; then thoroughly heat up the sauce, and have the chicken also ready heated in a little boiling water, in which put a little soup jelly. Strain the liquor from the chicken; pour a little of the sauce in the bottom of the paste, then lay the wings, &c. in the paste; pour the rest of the sauce over them, and serve it up hot. The paste should be well filled to the top, and if there is not sauce enough more must be added.

Wafers.

Take a pint of cream, melt in it half a pound of butter, and set it to cool. When cold, stir into it one pound of well dried and sifted flour by degrees, that it may be quite smooth and not lumpy, also six eggs well beaten, and one spoonful of ale yest. Beat all these well together; set it before the fire, cover it, and let it stand to rise one hour, before you bake. Some order it to be stirred a little while to keep it from being hard at top. Sprinkle over a little powdered cinnamon and sugar, when done.

Sugar Wafers.

Take some double-refined sugar, sifted; wet it with the juice of lemon pretty thin, and then scald it over the fire till it candies on the top. Then put it on paper, and rub it about thin; when almost cold, pin up the paper across, and put the wafers in a stove to dry. Wet the outside of the paper to take them off. You may make them red with clear gilliflowers boiled in water, yellow with saffron in water, and green with the juice of spinach. Put sugar in, and scald it as though white, and, with a pin, mark your white ones before you pin them up.

Walnuts, to preserve.

Take fine large walnuts at the time proper for pickling; prick, with a large bodkin, seven or eight holes in each to let out the water; keep them in water till they change colour or no longer look green; then put them over a fire in cold water to boil, till they feel just soft, but not too soft. Spread them on a coarse cloth to cool, and take away the water; stick in each walnut three or four cloves, three or four splinters of cinnamon, and the same of candied orange; then put them in pots or glasses. Boil a syrup, but not thick, which, when cold, pour over the walnuts, and let it stand a day or two; then pour the syrup off; add some more sugar; boil it up once more, and pour it again over the walnuts. When cold, tie them up.

White Walnuts.

Take nuts that are neither too large nor too small; peel them to the white, taking off all the green with care, and throw them into pump water as you peel them; let them soak one night. Boil them quick in fair water, throwing in a handful or two of alum in powder, according to the quantity, that they may be very white. When boiled, put them in fresh water, and take them out again in a minute; lay them on a dry cloth to dry, and lard them with preserved citron; then put them in the syrup you have made for the purpose, while they were larding, and let them soak two or three days before you boil them quite; the syrup must be very clear. One hundred walnuts make about three pounds of sweetmeats.

Mustard Whey.

Take milk and water of each a pint, bruised mustard seed an ounce and a half; boil these together till the curd is perfectly separated: then strain the whey through a cloth, and add a little sugar, which makes it more palatable.

Yest.

Boil one ounce of hops in three quarts of water until reduced to about three pints. Pour it upon one pound of flour; make it into a batter; strain it through a colander, and, when nearly cold, put to it one pint of home-brewed yest. Put it into a bottle, and keep it for use. It should stand twenty-four or thirty hours before it is used.

Excellent Yest.

Put a pint of well boiled milk into a hasty-pudding, and beat it till cold and there are few lumps remaining; then put to it two spoonfuls of yest and two of white powdered sugar, and stir it well. Put it in a large bowl not far from the fire, and next morning you will find it risen and light. Put it all to your flour, which must be mixed with as much warm milk and water as is necessary to make it into dough, and put it to rise in the common way.

Potato Yest.

Boil rather more than a quarter of a peck of potatoes; bruise them through a colander; add half a pound of fine flour, and thin it with cold water till it is like a thick batter. Add three table-spoonfuls of good yest; let it stand for an hour, and make your bread.

This yest will always serve to make fresh from.

Another way.

Weigh four pounds of raw potatoes pared; boil them in five pints of water. Wash and rub them through a sieve with the water in which they were boiled. Add four table-spoonfuls of good brown sugar; when milk-warm, put to the mixture three pennyworth of fresh yest; stir it well, and let it work in an open vessel. It will be fit for use in about twelve or fourteen hours.

About a pint and a half of this mixture will raise eighteen pounds of coarse flour; it may be put to rise over-night and will be ready to knead the first thing in the morning. It should be left to rise in the loaf four or five hours, before it is put in the oven.

PICKLES.

General Directions.

STONE jars, well glazed, are best for all sorts of pickles, as earthen vessels will not resist the vinegar, which penetrates through them.

Never touch pickles with the hand, or any thing greasy; but always make use of a wooden spoon, and keep them closely tied down, in a cool, dry place.

When you add vinegar to old pickles, let it boil, and stand till cold before you use it: on the contrary, when you make pickles, put it on the ingredients boiling and done with the usual spices.

Green Almonds.

Boil a quantity of vinegar proportionate to that of the almonds to be pickled, skim it, and put into it salt, mace, ginger, Jamaica and white pepper. Put it into a jar, and let it stand till cold. Throw your almonds into the liquor, which must cover them.

Artichokes.

Artichokes should be laid about six hours in a very strong brine of salt and water. Then put them into a pot of boiling water, and boil them till you can draw the leaves from the bottom, which must be cut smooth and clean, and put into a pot, with whole black pepper, salt, cloves, mace, bay-leaves, and as much white wine vinegar as will cover them. Lastly, pour upon them melted butter an inch thick, and cover them down close. When you take out any for use, put them into boiling water, with a piece of butter to plump them, and you may use them for whatever you please.

Artichokes to boil in Winter.

Boil your artichokes for half a day in salt and water; put them into a pot of boiling water, allowing them to continue boiling until you can just draw off the leaves from the bottom; cut them very clean and smooth, and put them into the pot with cloves, mace, salt, pepper, two bay-leaves, and as much vinegar as will cover them. Pour melted butter over to cover them about an inch thick; tie and keep them close down for use, with a piece of butter to plump them. You may use these for what you like.

Asparagus.

Scrape the asparagus, and cut off the prime part at the ends; wipe them, and lay them carefully in a jar or jelly-pot, pour vinegar over them, and let them lie in this about fourteen days. Then boil fresh vinegar, and pour it on them hot; repeat this until they are of a good colour; add a little mace and nutmeg, and tie them down close. This does very well for a made dish when asparagus is not to be had.

Barberries. No. 1.

Gather the barberries when full ripe, picking out those that look bad. Lay them in a deep pot. Make two quarts of strong brine of salt and water; boil it with a pint of vinegar, a pound of white sugar, a few cloves, whole white pepper, and mace, tied in a bag; skim it, and when cold pour it on your barberries. Barberries with stones will pickle; they must be without stones for preserving.

Barberries. No. 2.

Colour the water of the worst barberries, and add salt till the brine is strong enough to bear an egg. Boil it for half an hour, skimming it, and when cold strain it over the barberries. Lay something on them to keep them in the liquor: put them into a glass, and cover with leather.

Barberries. No. 3.

Boil a strong brine of salt and water, let it stand till quite cold, and pour it upon the barberries.

Barberries. No. 4.

Put into a jar some maiden barberries, with a good quantity of salt; tie on a bladder, and when the liquor scums change it.

Beet-root.

Beet-root must be boiled in strong salt and water, to which add a pint of vinegar and a little cochineal. When boiled enough, take it off the fire, and keep it in the liquor in which it has been boiled. It makes a pretty garnish for a dish of fish, and is not unpleasant to eat.

Another.

Boil the root till tender, peel it, and, if you think proper, cut it into shapes. Pour over it a hot pickle of white wine vinegar, horseradish, a little ginger, and pepper.

Beet-root and Turnips.

Boil your beet-root in salt and water, with a little cochineal and vinegar; when half boiled, put in your turnips pared; when they are done enough, take them off, and keep them in the same liquor in which they were boiled.

Cabbage.

Shave the cabbage into long slips, or, if you like, cut it in quarters. Scald it in salt and water for about four minutes; then take it out, and let it cool. Boil some vinegar, salt, ginger, whole pepper, and mace; after boiling and skimming it, let it get cold, and then put in your cabbage, which, if covered down presently, will keep white.

Red Cabbage. No. 1.

Slice the cabbage very fine crosswise, put it on an earthen dish, sprinkle a handful of salt over it, cover it with another dish, and let it stand twenty-four hours. Then put it in a colander to drain, and lay it in your jar; take white wine vinegar enough to cover it, a little cloves, mace, and allspice. Put them in whole with one pennyworth of cochineal, bruised fine; boil it up, and put it over the cabbage, hot, or cold, which you like best. Cover it close with a cloth till it is cold, and then tie it over with leather.

Red Cabbage. No. 2.

Slice the cabbage into a colander, sprinkle each layer with salt, let it drain two days; then put it into wide-mouthed bottles, pour on it boiling vinegar, sufficient to cover it, and add a few slices of beet-root. Cover the bottle with bladder.

Red Cabbage. No. 3.

Take a firm cabbage cut in quarters; slice it; boil your vinegar with ginger and pepper; let it stand till cold; then pour it over your cabbage, and tie it down. It will be fit for use in three weeks.

Capers.

Capers are the produce of, a small shrub, but preserved in pickle, and are grown in some parts of England, but they come chiefly from the neighbourhood of Toulon, the produce of which is considered the finest of any in Europe. The buds are gathered from the blossom before they open, and then spread on the floor, where the sun cannot reach them, and there they are left till they begin to wither; they are then thrown into sharp vinegar, and in about three days bay salt is added in proper quantity, and when this is dissolved they are fit for packing for sale, and sent all over the world.

Capsicum.

Let the pods be gathered with the stalks on before they turn red, and with a penknife cut a slit down the side, and take out all the seed, but as little of the meat as possible. Lay them in strong brine for three days, changing the brine every day. Take them out, lay them on a cloth, and another over them. Boil the liquor, put into it some mace and nutmeg beaten small; put the pods into a jar; when the liquor is cold, pour it over them, and tie down with a bladder and leather.

Cauliflower.

Cut from the closest and whitest heads pieces about the length of your finger, and boil them in a cloth with milk and water, but not till tender. Take them out very carefully, and let them stand till cold. With the best white wine vinegar boil nutmeg, cut into quarters, mace, cloves, a little whole pepper, and a bay-leaf, and let it remain till cold. Pour this into the jar to your cauliflower, and in three or four days it will be ready for use.

Another way.

Having cut the flower in bunches, throw them for a minute into boiling salt and water, and then into cold spring water. Drain and dry them; cover with double-distilled vinegar; in a week put fresh vinegar, with a little mace and nutmeg, covering down close.

Clove Gilliflower, or any other Flower, for Salads.

Put an equal weight of the flowers and of sugar, fill up with white wine vinegar, and to every pint of vinegar put a pound of sugar.

Codlings.

The codlings should be the size of large walnuts; put vine leaves in the bottom of your pan, and lay in the codlings, covering with leaves and then with water; set them over a gentle fire till they may be peeled; then peel and put them into the water, with vine leaves at top and bottom, covering them close; set them over a slow fire till they become green, and, when they are cold, take off the end whole, cutting it round with a small knife; scoop out the core, fill the apple with garlic and mustard seed, put on the bit, and set that end uppermost in the pickle, which must be double-distilled vinegar cold, with mace and cloves.

Cucumbers. No. 1.

Gather young cucumbers, commonly called gherkins—the small long sort are considered the best—wipe them very clean with a cloth; boil some salt and water, and pour over them; keep them close covered. Repeat this every day till they are green, putting fresh water every other day: let them stand near the fire, just to keep warm; the brine must be strong enough to bear an egg. When they are green, boil some white wine vinegar, pour it over them, put some mace in with them, and cover them with leather. It is better to put the salt and water to them once only, and they should be boiled up over the fire, in the vinegar, in a bell-metal kettle, with some vine leaves over, to green them. A brass kettle will not hurt, if very clean, and the cucumbers are turned out of it as soon as off the fire.

Cucumbers. No. 2.

In a large earthen pan mix spring water and salt well together, taking two pounds of salt to every gallon of water. Throw in your cucumbers, wash them well, and let them remain for twelve hours; then drain and wipe them very dry, and put them into a jar. Put into a bell-metal pot a gallon of the best white wine vinegar, half an ounce of cloves and of mace, one ounce of allspice, one ounce of mustard-seed, a stick of horseradish sliced, six bay-leaves, a little dill, two or

three races of ginger, a nutmeg cut in pieces, and a handful of salt. Boil all together, and pour it over the cucumbers. Cover them close down, and let them stand
twenty-four hours, then pour off the vinegar from them, boil it, pour it over them
again, and cover them close: repeat this process every day till they are green. Then
tie them down with bladder and leather; set them in a cool dry place, and they will
keep for three or four years. Beans may be pickled in the same manner.

Cucumbers. No. 3.

Wipe the cucumbers clean with a coarse cloth, and put them into a jar. Take
some vinegar, into which put pepper, ginger, cloves, and a handful of salt. Pour it
boiling hot over the cucumbers, and smother them with a flannel: let them stand
a fortnight; then take off the pickle, and boil it again. Pour it boiling on the cucumbers, and smother them as before. The pickle should be boiled in a bell-metal
skillet. With two thousand cucumbers put into the pot about a pennyworth of
Roman vitriol.

Large Cucumbers, Mango of.

Take a cucumber, cut out a slip from the side, taking out the seeds, but be careful to let as much of the meat remain as you can. Bruise mustard seed, a clove of
garlic, some bits of horseradish, slices of ginger, and put in all these. Tie the piece
on again, and make a pickle of vinegar, whole pepper, salt, mace, and cloves: boil
it, and pour it on the mangoes, and continue this for nine days together. When
cold, cover them down with leather.

Another.

Scrape out the core and seed, filling them with whole pepper, a clove of garlic,
and other spice. Put them into salt and water, covered close up, for twenty-four
hours; then drain and wipe them dry. Boil as much vinegar with spice as will cover
them, and pour it on them scalding hot.

Cucumbers sliced.

Take cucumbers not full grown, slice them into a pewter dish; to twelve cucumbers put three or four onions sliced, and as you do them strew salt on them;
cover them with a pewter dish, and let them stand twenty-four hours. Then take
out the onions, strain the liquor from the cucumbers through a colander, and put
them in a well glazed jar, with a pickle made of white wine vinegar, distilled in a
cold still, with seasoning of mace, cloves, and pepper. The pickle must be poured
boiling hot upon them, and then cover them down as close as possible. In four or
five days take them out of the pickle, boil it, and pour it on as before, keeping the
jar very close. Repeat this three times; cover the jar with a bladder, and leather over
it; the cucumbers will keep the whole year, and be of a fine sea-green, but perhaps
not of so fine colour when first you open them; they will become so, however, if
the vinegar is really fine.

Cucumbers stuffed.

Take six or eight middling-sized cucumbers, the smoothest you can procure; pare them, cut a small piece off the end, and scoop out all the seeds; blanch them for three or four minutes in boiling water on the fire; then put them into cold water to make the forcemeat. Then take some veal off the leg, calf's udder, fat bacon, and a piece of suet, and put it in boiling water about four minutes; take it out, and chop all together; put some parsley, small green onions, and shalots, all finely chopped, some salt, pepper, and nutmeg, sufficient for seasoning it, some crumbs of bread that have been steeped in cream, the whites of two eggs, and four yolks beaten well in a mortar. Stuff your cucumbers with this, and put the piece you cut off each upon it again. Lay at the bottom of your stewpan some thin slices of bacon, with the skin of the veal, onions in slices, parsley, thyme, some cloves; put your cucumbers in your stewpan, and cover them with bacon, &c., as at the bottom, and then add some strong broth, just sufficient to cover them. Set them over a slow fire covered, and let them stew slowly for an hour. Make some brown gravy of a good colour, and well tasted; and, when your cucumbers are stewed, take them out, drain them well from all grease, and put them in your brown gravy; it must not be thick. Set it over the stove for two minutes, and squeeze in the juice of a lemon.

To make brown gravy, put into your stewpan a quarter of a pound of butter; set it over the fire, and, when melted, put in a spoonful of flour, and keep stirring it till it is as brown as you wish, but be careful not to let it burn; put some good gravy to it, and let it boil some time, with parsley, onions, thyme, and spices, and then strain it to your cucumbers.

Should any of the cucumbers be left at dinner, you may serve them up another way for supper; cut the cucumbers in two, lengthwise, or, if you like, in round slices; add yolks of eggs beaten, and dust them all well over with crumb of bread rubbed very fine; fry them very hot; make them of a good colour, and serve them in a dish, with fried parsley.

Cucumbers, to preserve.

Take some small cucumbers, and large ones that will cut in quarters, but let them be as green and as free from seeds as you can get them. Put them into a narrow-mouthed jar, in strong salt and water, with a cabbage-leaf to keep them from rising; tie a paper over them, and set them in a warm place till they are yellow. Then wash them out, and set them over the fire in fresh water, with a little salt and a fresh cabbage-leaf over them. Cover the pan very close, but be sure you do not let them boil. If they are not of a fine green, change the water, which will help them; then make them hot, and cover them as before. When you find them of a good green, take them off the fire, and let them stand till they are cold: then cut the large ones into quarters; take out the seeds and soft parts, put them into cold water, and let them stand two days; but change the water twice each day, to take out the salt; put a pound of refined sugar to a pint of water, and set it over the fire; when you have skimmed it clear, put in the rind of a lemon and an ounce of ginger, scraping off the outside. Take your syrup off as soon as it is pretty thick, and, when it is cold, wipe the cucumbers dry and put them into it. Boil the syrup once in two or three days for three weeks, and strengthen the syrup if required, for the greatest danger of spoiling them is at first. When you put the syrup to the cucumbers, wait till it is quite cold.

French Beans. No. 1.

Gather them when very slender; string and parboil them in very strong salt and water; then take them out, and dry them between two linen cloths. When they are well drained, put them into a large earthen vessel, and, having boiled up the same kind of pickle as for cucumbers, pour as much upon your beans as will cover them well. Strain the liquor from them three days successively; boil it up, and put your beans into the vinegar on the fire till they are warm through. After the third boiling, put them into jars for use, and tie them down.

French Beans. No. 2.

Take from the small slender beans their stalks, and let them remain fourteen days in salt and water; then wash and well cleanse them from the brine, and put them in a saucepan of water over a slow fire, covering them with vine-leaves. Do not let them boil, but only stew, until they are tender, as for eating; strain them off, lay them on a coarse cloth to dry, and put them into pots; boil and skim alegar, and pour it over, covering them close; keep boiling in this manner for three or four days, or until they become green; add spice, as you would to other pickles, and, when cold, cover with leather.

French Beans. No. 3.

Put in a large jar a layer of beans, the younger the better, and a layer of salt, alternately, and tie it down close. When wanted for use, boil them in a quantity of boiling water: change the water two or three times, always adding the fresh water boiling; then put them into cold water to soak out the salt, and cut them when you want them for dressing for table. They must not be soaked before they are boiled.

Herrings, to marinate.

Take a quarter of a hundred of herrings; cut off their heads and tails; take out the roes, and clean them; then take half an ounce of Jamaica and half an ounce of common pepper, an ounce of bay salt, and an ounce and a half of common salt; beat the pepper fine, mix it with the salt, and put some of this seasoning into the belly of each herring. Lay them in rows, and between every row strew some of the seasoning, and lay a bunch or two of thyme, parsley, and sage, and three or four bay-leaves. Cover your fish with good vinegar, and your pot with paste; put the pot into the oven after the household bread is drawn; let it remain all night; and, when it comes out of the oven, pour out all the liquor, take out the herbs; again boil up the liquor; add as much more vinegar as will cover the herrings, skim it clean, and strain it. When cold, pour it over your herrings.

Herrings, red, Trout fashion.

Cut off their heads, cleanse them well, and lay a row at the bottom of an earthen pot, sprinkling them over with bay salt and saltpetre, mixed together. Repeat this until your pan is full; then cover them, and bake them gently; when cold, they will be as red as anchovies, and the bones dissolved.

India Pickle, called Picolili. No. 1.

Lay one pound of ginger in salt and water for a whole night; then scrape and cut it in thin slices, and lay them in the sun to dry; put them into a jar till the other ingredients are ready. Peel two pounds of garlic, and cut it in thin slices; cover it with salt for three days; drain it well from the brine, and dry it as above directed. Take young cabbages, cut them in quarters, salt them for three days, and dry them as above; do the same with cauliflowers, celery, and radishes, scraping the latter and leaving the tops of the celery on, French beans, and asparagus, which last two must be salted only two days, and dried in the same manner. Take long pepper and salt it, but do not dry it too much, three ounces of turmeric, and a quarter of a pound of mustard seed finely bruised; put these into a stone jar, and pour on them a gallon of strong vinegar; look at it now and then, and if you see occasion add more vinegar. Proceed in the same manner with plums, peaches, melons, apples, cucumbers; artichoke bottoms must be pared and cut raw; then salt them, and give them just one gentle boil, putting them into the water when hot. Never do red cabbage or walnuts. The more every thing is dried, the plumper it will become in the vinegar. Put in a pound or two of whole garlic prepared as above to act as a pickle. You need never empty the jar, as the pickle keeps; but as things come into season, do them and throw them in, observing that the vinegar always covers them. If the ingredients cannot be conveniently dried by the sun, you may do them by the fire, but the sun is best.

India Pickle. No. 2.

Select the closest and whitest cabbage you can get, take off the outside leaves, quarter and cut them into thin slices, and lay them upon a sieve; salt well between each layer of the cabbage, and let it drain till the next day; then dry it in a cloth, and spread it in dishes before the fire, or the sun, often turning it till dry. Put it in a stone jar, with half a pint of white mustard seed, a little mace and cloves beat to a powder, as much cayenne as will lie on a shilling, a large head of garlic, and one pennyworth of turmeric in powder. Pour on it three quarts of vinegar boiling hot; cover it close with a cloth, and let it stand a fortnight; then turn it all out into a saucepan. Boil it, turning it often, about eight minutes, and put it up in your jar for use. It will be ready in a month. If other things are put in, they should lie in salt three days and then be dried; in this case, it will be necessary to make the pickle stronger, by adding ginger and horseradish, and it must be kept longer before used.

India Pickle. No. 3.

Boil one pound of salt, four ounces of ginger, eight ounces of shalots or garlic, a spoonful of cayenne pepper, two ounces of mustard seed, and six quarts of good vinegar. When cold, you may put in green fruit or any vegetable you choose, fresh as you pick them, only wiping off the dust. Stop your jar close, and put in a little turmeric to colour it.

Lemons. No. 1.

Cut the lemons through the yellow rind only, into eight parts; then put them into a deep pan, a layer of salt and a layer of lemons, so as not to touch one another; set them in the chimney corner, and be sure to turn them every day, and to pack them up in the same manner as before. This you must continue doing fifteen or sixteen days; then take them out of the salt, lay them in a flat pan, and put them in the sun every day for a month; or, if there should be no sun, before the fire; then put them in the pickle; in about six months they will be fit to eat. Make the pickle for them as follows: Take two pounds of peeled garlic, eight pods of India pepper, when it is green; one pound and a half of ginger, one pound and a quarter of mustard seed, half an ounce of turmeric; each clove of the garlic must be split in half; the ginger must be cut in small slices, and, as no green ginger can be had in Europe, you must cover the ginger with salt in a clean earthen vessel, until it is soft, which it will be in about three weeks, or something more, by which means you may cut it as you please; the mustard seed must be reduced, but not to powder, and the turmeric pounded fine: mix them well together, and add three ounces of oil of mustard seed. Put these ingredients into a gallon of the best white wine vinegar boiled; then put the whole upon the lemons in a glazed jar, and tie them up close. They will not be fit in less than six months. When the vinegar is boiled, let it stand to be cold, or rather lukewarm, before you put it to the lemons, and if you use more than a gallon of vinegar, increase the quantity of each ingredient in proportion. Strictly observe the direction first given, to let the lemons lie in salt fifteen or sixteen days, to turn them every day, and to let them be thoroughly dry before you put the pickle to them; it will be a month at least before they are sufficiently dry.

Lemons. No. 2.

Take twelve lemons pared so thin that not the least of the whites is to be seen; slit them across at each end, and work in as much salt as you can, rubbing them very well within and without. Lay them in an earthen pan for three or four days, and strew a good deal of salt over them; then put in twelve cloves of garlic, and a large handful of horseradish; dry the lemons with the salt over them in a very slow oven, till the lemons have no moisture in them, but the garlic and the horseradish must not be dried so much. Then take a gallon of vinegar, cloves, mace, and nutmegs, broken roughly, half an ounce of each, and the like quantity of cayenne pepper. Give them a boil in the vinegar; and, when cold, stir in a quarter of a pound of flour of mustard, and pour it upon the lemons, garlic, &c. Stir them every day, for a week together, or more. When the lemons are used in made dishes, shred them very small; and, when you use the liquor, shake it before you put it to the sauce, or in a cruet. When the lemons are dried, they must be as hard as a crust of bread, but not burned.

Lemons. No. 3.

Take two dozen lemons, cut off about an inch at one end, scoop out all the pulp, fill them with salt, and sew on the tops. Let them continue over the mouth of an oven, or in any slow heat, for about three weeks, till they are quite dried. Take out the salt; lay them in an earthen jar; put to them six quarts of the best vinegar which has been boiled; add some long pepper, mace, ginger, and cinnamon, a few bay-leaves, four cloves of garlic, and six ounces of the best flour of mustard. When quite cold, cover up the jar, and let it stand for three weeks or a month. Then strain off the liquor, and bottle it.

Lemons. No. 4.

Quarter the lemons lengthwise, taking care not to cut them so low as to separate; put a table-spoonful of salt into each. Set them on a pewter dish; dry them very slowly in a cool oven or in the sun; they will take two or three weeks to dry properly. For a dozen large lemons boil three quarts of vinegar, with two dozen peppercorns, two dozen allspices, and four races of ginger sliced. When the vinegar is cold, put it, with the lemons, the ingredients, and all the salt, into a jar; add a quarter of a pound of flour of mustard and two dozen cloves of garlic; the garlic must be peeled and softened in scalding water for a little while, then covered with salt for three days, and dried before it is put into the jar. Let the whole remain for two months closely tied down and stirred every day; then squeeze the lemons well; strain and bottle the liquor.

Lemons. No. 5.

Select small thick-rinded lemons; rub them with a flannel; slit them in four parts, but not through to the pulp; stuff the slits full of salt, and set them upright in a pan. Let them remain thus for five or six days, or longer if the salt should not be melted, turning them three times a day in their own liquor, until they become tender. Then make a pickle of rape, vinegar, and the brine from the lemons, ginger, and Jamaica pepper. Boil and skim it, and when cold put it to the lemons, with three cloves of garlic, and two ounces of mustard seed. This is quite sufficient for six lemons.

Lemons. No. 6.

Boil them in water and afterwards in vinegar and sugar, and then cut them in slices.

Lemons, or Oranges.

Select fruit free from spots; lay them gently in a barrel. Take pure water, and make it so strong with bay-salt as that it would bear an egg; with this brine fill up the barrel, and close it tight.

Mango Cossundria, or Pickle.

Take of green mangoes two pounds, green ginger one pound, yellow mustard seed one pound; half dried chives, garlic, salt, mustard, oil, of each two ounces; fine vinegar, four bottles. Cut the mangoes in slices lengthwise, and place them in the sun till half dried. Slice the ginger also; put the whole in a jar well closed, and set it in the sun for a month. This pickle will keep for years, and improves by age.

Melons.

Scoop your melons clean from the pulp; fill them with scraped horseradish, ginger, nutmeg, sliced garlic, mace, pepper, mustard-seed, and tie them up. Afterwards take the best white wine vinegar, a quartered nutmeg, a handful of salt, whole pepper, cloves, and mace, or a little ginger; let the vinegar and spice boil together, and when boiling hot pour it over the fruit, and tie them down very close for two or three days; but, if you wish to have them green, let them be put over a fire in their pickle in a metal pot, until they are scalding hot and green; then pour them into pots, and stop them close down, and, when cold, cover them with wet bladder and leather.

Melons to imitate Mangoes.

Cut off the tops of the melons, so as that you may take out the seeds with a small spoon; lay them in salt and water, changing it every twenty-four hours for nine successive days: then take them out, wipe them dry, and put into each one clove of garlic or two small shalots, a slice or two of horseradish, a slice of ginger, and a tea-spoonful of mustard seed; this being done, tie up their tops again very fast with packthread, and boil them up in a sufficient quantity of white wine vinegar, bay-salt, and spices, as for cucumbers, skimming the pickle as it rises; put a piece of alum into your pickle, about the size of a walnut; and, after it has boiled a quarter of an hour, pour it, with the fruit, into your jar or pan, and cover it with a cloth. Next day boil your pickle again, and pour it hot upon your melons. After this has been repeated three times, and the pickle and fruit are quite cold, stop them up as directed for mushrooms. These and all other pickles should be set in a dry place, and frequently inspected; and, if they grow mouldy, you must pour off the liquor and boil it up as at first.

Melons or Cucumbers, as Mangoes.

Pour over your melons or other vegetables boiling hot salt and water, and dry them the next day; cut a piece out of the side; scrape away the seed very clean; and fill them with scraped horseradish, garlic, and mustard seed; then put in the piece, and tie it close. Pour boiling hot vinegar over them, and in about three days boil up the vinegar with cloves, pepper, and ginger: then throw in your mangoes, and boil them up quick for a few minutes; put them in jars, which should be of stone, and cover them close.

The melons ought to be small and the cucumbers large. Should they not turn out green enough, the vinegar must be boiled again.

Mushrooms. No. 1.

Gather your mushrooms in August or September, and peel off the uppermost skin; cut the large ones into quarters, and, as you do them, throw them into clear water, but be very careful not to have any worm-eaten ones. You may put the buttons in whole; the white are the best, and look better than the red. Take them out, and wash them in another clear water; then put them into a dry skillet without water; and with a little salt set them on the fire to boil in their own liquor, till half is consumed and they are as tender as you wish them; as the scum rises, take it off. Remove them from the fire: pour them into a colander, and drain off all the water. Have ready pickle, boiled and become cold again, made of the best white wine vinegar; then add a little mace, ginger, cloves, and whole pepper: boil it; put your mushrooms in the pickle when cold, and tie them up close.

Mushrooms. No. 2.

Put your mushrooms into salt and water, and wash them clean with a flannel, throw them into water as you do them; then boil some salt and water: when it boils, put in your mushrooms, and let them boil one minute. Take them out, and smother them between two flannels; when cold, put them into white wine vinegar, with what spice you choose. The vinegar must be boiled and stand till cold. Keep them closely tied down with a bladder. A bit of alum is frequently put to keep them firm.

The white mushrooms are done the same way, using milk and water instead of salt and water, distilled vinegar in the room of white wine vinegar, no spices except mace, and a lump of alum.

Mushrooms. No. 3.

Cut off the stalks of the small hard mushrooms, called buttons, and wash and rub them dry in a clean flannel. Boil some water and salt, and while boiling put in the mushrooms. Let them just boil, and strain them through a cloth. Make a pickle of white wine vinegar, mace, and ginger, and put to them; then put them into pots, with a little oil over them, and stop them close.

Mushrooms. No. 4.

Put young mushrooms into milk and water; take them out, dry them well, and put them into a brine made of salt and spring water. Boil the brine, and put in the mushrooms; boil them up for five minutes; drain them quick, covering them up between two cloths and drying them well. Boil a pickle of double-distilled vinegar and mace; when it is cold, put in the buttons, and pour oil on the top. It is advisable to put them into small glass jars, as they do not keep after being opened. It is an excellent way to boil them in milk.

Mushrooms. No. 5.

Put your mushrooms into water; rub them very clean with a piece of flannel; put them into milk and water, and boil them till they are rather tender. Then pour them into an earthen colander, and pump cold water on them till they are quite cold. Have ready some salt and water; put them into it; let them lie twenty-four hours; then dry them in a cloth. Then put them into a pickle made of the best white wine vinegar, mace, pepper, and nutmeg. If you choose to boil your pickle, it must be quite cold before you put in the mushrooms.

Mushrooms. No. 6.

Peel your mushrooms, and throw them into clean water; wash them in two or three waters, and boil them in a little water, with a bundle of sweet-herbs, a good quantity of salt, a little rosemary, and spice of all sorts. When well boiled, let them remain in the liquor for twenty-four hours; pour the liquor into a hot cloth, smothering them for a night and a day; then put in your pickle, which make of elder and white wine vinegar, with all kinds of spice, horseradish, ginger, and lemon-juice. Put them into pots, cover with oiled paper, and keep them close for use.

Mushrooms. No. 7.

Clean them very well, and take out the gills; boil them tender with a little salt, and dry them with a cloth. Make a strong brine; when it is cold, put in the mushrooms, and in about ten days or a fortnight change the brine, and put them into small bottles, pouring oil on the top.

Brown Mushrooms.

Wipe them very clean, put them into a stewpan with mace, cloves, pepper, and salt, and to every quart of mushrooms put about two large spoonfuls of mushroom ketchup; stew them gently over a slow fire for about half an hour, then let them cool. Put them into bottles. To each quart of mushrooms put a quarter of a pint of white wine vinegar boiled and cooled; stop the bottles close with rosin.

Mushrooms, to dry.

Cut off their stalks, and cut or scrape out the gills, and with a little salt put them into a saucepan. Set them on the fire, and let them stew in their own liquor; then pour them into a sieve to drain. When dry, put them into a slack oven upon tin plates, and, when quite dry, put them into shallow boxes for use.

The liquor will make ketchup.

Mushroom Liquor and Powder.

Take about a peck of mushrooms, wash them, and rub them with a piece of flannel, taking out the gills, but do not peel them. Put to them half an ounce of beaten pepper, four bay-leaves, four cloves, twelve blades of mace, a handful of salt, eight onions, a bit of butter, and half a pint of vinegar; stew all these as quick as possible; keep stirring till the liquor is quite out of the mushrooms; then drain them, and bottle the liquor and spice when cold. Dry the mushrooms in an oven, first on a flat or broad pan, then on sieves, until they can be beaten into powder. This quantity will make about seven ounces. Stop the powder close in widemouthed bottles.

Mustard Pickle.

Cut cabbages, cauliflowers, and onions, in small pieces or slices; salt them together, and let them stand in the salt for a few days. Then take them up in a strainer that the brine may run off; put them in a jar that will hold three quarts;

take enough vinegar to cover them; boil it up, pour it on them, and cover it till next day. Pour the vinegar off, take the same quantity of fresh vinegar, of black pepper, ginger, and Jamaica pepper, each one ounce; boil them up together, let the liquor stand till cold; then mix four tea-spoonfuls of turmeric, and six ounces of flour of mustard, which pour on them cold. Cover the pickle up close; let it stand three weeks; and it will be fit for use. The spices must be put in whole.

Nasturtiums.

The seed must be full grown and gathered on a dry day. Let them lie two or three days in salt and water; take them out, well dry them, and put them into a jar. Take as much white wine vinegar as will cover them, and boil it up with mace, sliced ginger, and a few bay leaves, for a quarter of an hour. Pour the pickle upon the seeds boiling hot. This must be repeated three days, keeping them covered with a folded cloth. After the third time, take care to let them be quite cold before you stop them up, which you must do very close.

Onions. No. 1.

Take your onions when they are dry enough to lay up for winter, the smaller the better they look: put them in a pot, cover them with spring water, with a handful of salt, and let them boil up; then strain them off. Take off three coats; lay them on a cloth, and let two persons take hold of it, one at each end, and rub them backwards and forwards till they are very dry. Then put them in your jars or bottles, with some blades of mace, cloves, and nutmeg, cut into pieces; take some double-distilled white wine vinegar, boil it up with a little salt; let it stand till it is cold, and put it over the onions. Cork them close, and tie a bladder and leather over them.

Onions. No. 2.

Take the smallest onions you can get; peel and put them into spring water and salt made very strong. Shift them daily for six days; then boil them a very little; skim them well, and make a pickle as for cucumbers, only adding a little mustard seed. Let the onions and the pickle both be cold, when you put them together. Keep them stopped very close, or they will spoil.

Onions. No. 3.

Peel some small white onions, and boil them in water with salt; strain them, and let them remain till cool in a cloth. Make the pickle as for mushrooms; when quite cold, put them in and cover them down. Should the onions become mouldy, boil them again, carefully skimming off the impurities; then let them cool, and proceed as at first.

Cauliflowers are excellent done in this way.

Onions. No. 4.

Put your small onions, after peeling them, into salt and water, shifting them once a day for three or four days; set them over the fire in milk and water till ready to boil; dry them; and, when boiled and cold, pour over a pickle made of double-distilled vinegar, a bay-leaf or two, salt, and mace.

Onions. No. 5.

Parboil small white onions, and let them cool. Make a pickle with half vinegar, half wine, into which put some salt, a little ginger, some mace, and sliced nutmeg. Boil all this up together, skimming it well. Let it stand till quite cold; then put in your onions, covering them down. Should they become mouldy, boil the liquor again, but skim it well; let it stand till quite cold before the onions are again put in, and they will keep all the year.

Onions. No. 6.

Take the small white round onions; peel off the brown skin. Have ready a stewpan of boiling water; throw in as many onions as will cover the top. As soon as they look clear on the outside, take them up quickly, lay them on a clean cloth, and cover them close with another cloth.

Spanish Onions, Mango of.

Having peeled your onions, cut out a small piece from the bottom, scoop out a little of the inside, and put them into salt and water for three or four days, changing the brine twice a day. Then drain and stuff them, first putting in flour of mustard, then a little ginger cut small, mace, shalot cut small, then more mustard, and filling up with scraped horseradish. Put on the bottom piece, and tie it on close. Make a strong pickle of white wine vinegar, ginger, mace, sliced horseradish, nutmeg, and salt: put in your mangoes, and boil them up two or three times. Take care not to boil them too much, otherwise they lose their firmness and will not keep. Put them, with the pickle, into a jar. Boil the pickle again next morning, and pour it over them.

Orange and Lemon Peel.

Boil the peels of the fruit in vinegar and sugar, and lay them in the pickle; but be careful to cut them in small long slices, about the length of half the peel of your lemon. It must be boiled in water previously to boiling in sugar and vinegar.

Oysters. No. 1.

Take a quantity of large oysters with their liquor; wash well all the grit from them, and to every three pints of clear water put half an ounce of bruised pepper, some salt, and a quarter of an ounce of mace. Let these boil over a gentle fire, until a fourth part is consumed, skimming it; just scald the oysters, and put them into the liquor; put them into barrels or pots; stop them very close, and they will keep for a year in a cool place.

Oysters. No. 2.

Parboil some large oysters in their own liquor; make pickle of their liquor with vinegar, a pint of white wine, mace, salt and pepper; boil and skim it, and when cold put in the oysters, and keep them.

Oysters. No. 3.

Take whole pepper and mace, of each a quarter of an ounce, and half a pint of white wine vinegar. Set the oysters on the fire, in their own liquor, with a little water, mace, pepper, and half a pound of salt; skim them well as they heat, and only allow them just to boil for fear of hardening them. Take them out to dry, skim the liquor, and then put in the rest of the spice with the vinegar. Should the vinegar be very strong, reduce it a little, and boil it up again for a short time. Let both stand till cold: put your oysters into the pickle: in a day or two, taste your pickle, and, should it not be sharp enough, add a little more vinegar.

Oysters. No. 4.

Take the largest oysters you can get, and just plump them over the fire in their own liquor; then strain it from them, and cover the oysters close in a cloth. Take an equal quantity of white wine and vinegar, and a little of the oyster liquor, with mace, white pepper, and lemon-peel, pared very thin, also salt, the quantity of each according to your judgment and taste, taking care that there be sufficient liquor to cover them. Set it on the fire, and, when it boils, put in the oysters; just give them one boil up; put the pickle in a pot, and the oysters closely covered in a cloth till the pickle is quite cold.

Oysters. No. 5.

Simmer them, till done, in their own liquor; take them out one by one, strain the liquor from them, and boil them with one third of vinegar. Put the oysters in a jar, in layers, with a little mace, whole and white pepper, between the layers; then pour over them the liquor hot.

Oysters. No. 6.

Take whole pepper and mace, of each a quarter of an ounce, and put to them half a pint of white wine vinegar.

Peaches, Mango of.

Take some of the largest peaches, when full grown and just ripening, throw them into salt and water, and add a little bay-salt. Let them lie two or three days, covering them with a board; take them out and dry them, and with a sharp knife cut them open and take out the stone; then cut some garlic very fine, scrape a great deal of horseradish, mix the same quantity of mustard seed, a few bruised cloves, and ginger sliced very thin, and with this fill the hollow of the peaches. Tie them round, and lay them in a jar; throw in some broken cinnamon, cloves, mace, and a small quantity of cochineal, and pour over as much vinegar as will fill the jar. To every quart put a quarter of a pint of the best mustard, well made, some cloves, mace, nutmeg, two or three heads of garlic, and some sliced ginger. Mix the pickle well together; pour it over the peaches, and tie them down close with either leather or a bladder. They will soon be fit for use.

In the same manner you may do white plums.

Purslain, Samphire, Broom Buds, &c.

Pick the dead leaves from the branches of purslain, and lay them in a pan. Make some strong brine; boil and skim it clean, and, when boiled and cold, put in the purslain, and cover it; it will keep all the year. When wanted for use, boil it in fresh water, having the water boiling before you put it in. When boiled and turned green, cool it, take it out afterwards, put it into wide-mouth bottles, with strong white wine vinegar to it, and close it for use.

Quinces.

Cut in pieces half a dozen quinces; put them into an earthen pot, with a gallon of water and two pounds of honey. Mix the whole together, and boil it leisurely in a kettle for half an hour. Strain the liquor into an earthen pot: and, when cold, wipe the quinces clean, and lay them in it. Cover them very close, and they will keep all the year.

Radish Pods.

Make a pickle with cold spring water and bay salt, strong enough to bear an egg; put in your pods; lay a thin board on them to keep them under water, and let them stand ten days. Drain them in a sieve, and lay them on a cloth to dry; then take as much white wine vinegar as you think will cover them, boil and put your pods in a jar, with ginger, mace, cloves, and Jamaica pepper; put your vinegar boiling hot on them; cover them with a coarse cloth three or four times double, that the steam may come through a little, and let them stand two days; repeat this two or three times. When cold, put in a pint of mustard-seed and some horseradish, and cover them close.

Salmon. No. 1.

Cut off the head of the fish, take out the intestines, but do not slit the belly; cut your pieces across, about two or three inches in breadth; take the blood next to the back clean out: wash and scale it; then put salt and water over the fire, and a handful of bay leaves; put in the salmon, and, when it is boiled, take it off and skim it clear. Take out the pieces with a skimmer as whole as you can; lay them on a table to drain; strain a handful of salt slightly over them; when they are cold, stick some cloves on each side of them. Then take a cask, well washed, and seasoned with hot and cold water, three or four days before you use it; put in the pickle you boiled your salmon in hot, some time before you use it; then take broad mace, sliced nutmeg, white pepper, just bruised, and a little black; mix the pepper with salt, sufficient to season the salmon; strew some pepper, salt, and bay-leaves, at the bottom of the cask; then put in a layer of salmon, then spice, salt, bay-leaves, and pepper, as before, until the cask is full. Put on the head, and bore a hole in the top of it; fill up the cask with good white wine vinegar, cork it, and, in two or three days, take out the cork and put more vinegar, and the fat will come out; do so three or four times; then cut off the cork, and pitch it; if it be for present use, put it in a jar, closely covered.

Salmon. No. 2.

Well scrape the salmon, take out the entrails, and well wash and dry it. Cut it in pieces of such size as you think proper; take three parts of common vinegar and one of water, enough to cover the fish. Put in a handful of salt, and stir it till dissolved. Add some mace, whole pepper, cloves, sliced nutmeg, and boil all these till the salmon is sufficiently done. Take it out of the liquor, and let it cool. Put it into a barrel, and over every layer of salmon strew black pepper, mace, cloves, and pounded nutmeg; and, when the barrel is full, pour upon the salmon the liquor in which it was boiled, mixed with vinegar, in which a few bay-leaves have been boiled, and then left till cold. Close up the barrel, and keep it for use.

Salmon. No. 3.

Cut your fish into small slices, and clean them well from the blood, by wiping and pressing them in a dry cloth; afterwards lay it in a kettle of boiling water, taking care not to break it, and, when nearly boiled, make a pickle as follows: two quarts of water, three quarts of rape vinegar; boil it with a little fennel and salt till it tastes strong; then skim it; let it cool; lay the fish in a kettle, and pour the pickle to it pretty warm.

The same process will do for sturgeon, excepting the fennel, and putting a little more salt, or for any other fish.

Salmon, to marinate.

Cut your salmon in round slices about two inches thick, and tie it with matting, like sturgeon; season it with pepper, mace, and salt; then put it into a broad earthen pan, with an equal quantity of port wine and vinegar to cover it, and add three or four bay-leaves. The pickle also must be seasoned with the spices above-mentioned. The pan must be covered with a coarse cloth, and baked with household bread.

Samphire.

Pick and lay it in strong brine, cold; let it remain twenty-four hours, boil the brine once on a quick fire, and pour it immediately on the samphire. After standing twenty-four hours, just boil it again on a quick fire, and stand till cold. Lay it in a pot, let the pickle settle, and cover the samphire with the clear portion of the pickle. Set it in a dry place, and, should the pickle become mothery, boil it once a month, and, when cold, put the samphire into it.

Smelts.

Lay the smelts in a pot in rows, and lay upon them sliced lemon, mace, ginger, nutmeg, pepper, powdered bay-leaves, and salt. Make pickle of red wine vinegar, saltpetre, and bruised cochineal; when cold, pour it on the smelts, and cover the pot close.

Suckers, before the leaves are hard.

Pare off all the hard ends of the leaves and stalks of the suckers, and scald them in salt and water, and, when cold, put them into glass bottles, with three blades of mace, and thin sliced nutmeg; fill them with distilled vinegar.

Vinegar for Pickling. No. 1.

Take the middling sort of beer, but indifferently hopped, let it work as long as possible, and fine it down with isinglass; then draw it from the sediment, and put ten pounds weight of the husks of grapes to every ten gallons. Mash them together, and let them stand in the sun, or, if not in summer, in a close room, heated by fire, and, in about three or four weeks, it will become an excellent vinegar. Should you not have grape husks, you may take the pressing of sour apples, but the vinegar will not prove so good either in taste or body. Cyder will make a decent sort of vinegar, and also unripe grapes, or plums, but foul white Rhenish wines, set in a warm place, will fine, naturally, into good vinegar.

Vinegar. No. 2.

To a pound and a half of the brownest sugar put a gallon of warm water; mix it well together; then spread a hot toast thick with yest, and let it work very well about twenty-four hours. Skim off the toast and the yest, and pour off the clear liquor, and set it out in the sun. The cask must be full, and, if painted and hooped with iron hoops, it will endure the weather better. Lay a tile over the bunghole.

Vinegar. No. 3.

To every gallon of water put three pounds of Malaga raisins; stop it up close, and let it stand in the cellar two years.

Camp Vinegar.

Infuse a quarter of an ounce of cayenne, four heads of garlic, some shalots, half a drachm of cochineal, a quarter of a pint of ketchup, soy, walnut pickle, and an ounce of black, white, and long pepper, allspice, ginger, and nutmeg, all grossly bruised, a little mace, and cloves, in a quart of the best wine vinegar; cork it close, and put a leather and bladder over it. Let it stand before the fire for a month, shaking it frequently. You must let it stand upon the ingredients, and fill up with vinegar as you take any out. This is not only an excellent sauce, but a powerful preservative against infectious disorders.

Another.

Half an ounce of cayenne pepper, a large head of garlic, half a drachm of cochineal, two spoonfuls of soy, the same of walnut pickle, and a pint of vinegar.

Chili Vinegar.

Gather the pods of capsicum when full ripe; put them into a jar with a clove of garlic and a little cayenne pepper; boil the vinegar, and pour it on hot; fill up your jar: let it stand for a fortnight; pour it off clear, and it will be fit for use.

Elder-flower Vinegar. No. 1.

Put two gallons of strong alegar to a peck of the pips of elder-flowers, set it in the sun in a stone jar for a fortnight, and then filter it through a flannel bag; when you draw it off, put it into small bottles, in which it will preserve its flavour better than in larger ones; when you mix the flowers and the alegar together, be careful not to drop any stalks amongst the pips.

Elder-flower Vinegar. No. 2.

Take good vinegar, fill a cask three quarters full, and gather some elder-flowers, nearly or moderately blown, but in a dry day; pick off the small flowers and sprigs from the greater stalks, and air them well in the sun, that they may grow dry, but not so as to break or crumble. To every four gallons of vinegar put a pound of them, sewing them up in a fine rag.

Elder-flower Vinegar. No. 3.

Pick the flowers before they are too much blown from the stalks, and dry them in the sun, but not when it is very hot. Put a handful of them to a quart of the best white wine vinegar, and let it stand a fortnight. Strain and draw it off, and put it into a cask, keeping out about a quart. Make it very hot, and put it into your cask to produce fermentation. Stop it very close, and draw it off when wanted.

Elder-flower Vinegar. No. 4.

Gather the elder-flowers in dry weather, pick them clean from the stalks, and put two pints of them to a gallon of the best white wine vinegar. Let them infuse for ten days, stirring them every day till the last day or two; then strain off the vinegar, and bottle it.

Garlic Vinegar.

Take sixty cloves, two nutmegs sliced, and eight cloves of garlic, to a quart of vinegar.

Gooseberry Vinegar.

To every gallon of water take six pounds of full ripe gooseberries; bruise them, and put them into a vessel, pouring the water cold upon them. Set the vessel in a hot place till the gooseberries come to the top, which they will do in about a fortnight; then draw off the liquor, and, when you have taken the gooseberries out of the vessel, measure the liquor into it again, and to every gallon put a pound of coarse sugar. It will work again, and, when it has done working, stop it down close, set it near the fire or in the sun: it will be fit for use in about six months. If the vessel is not full, it will be ready sooner.

Plague, or Four Thieves' Vinegar.

Take rue, sage, mint, rosemary, wormwood, and lavender, of each a large handful; put them into a stone jar, with a gallon of the best vinegar; tie it down very close, and let it stand a fortnight in the sun, shaking the jar every day. Bottle it, and to every bottle add a quarter of an ounce of camphor, beaten very fine. The best time to make it is in June or July.

Raisin Vinegar.

Put four quarts of spring water to two pounds of Malaga raisins, lay a stone or slate over the bung-hole, and set it in the sun till ready for use. If you put it into a stone jar or bottle, and let it stand in the chimney corner, for a proper time, it will answer the same purpose.

Raspberry Vinegar. No. 1.

Fill a very large jug or jar with raspberries; then pour as much white wine vinegar upon them as it will hold; let it stand four days, stirring it three times every day. Let it stand four days more, covered close up, stirring it once a day. Strain it through a hair sieve, and afterwards through a flannel bag; and to every pint of liquor add one pound of loaf-sugar. Simmer it over the fire, skimming it all the time, till quite clear. As soon as cold, bottle it.

This is very good sauce for a plain batter pudding and pancakes.

Raspberry Vinegar. No. 2.

Take two pounds of sugar; dissolve it in a pint of water; then clarify, and let it boil till it is a thick syrup. Take the same quantity of raspberries, or currants, but not too ripe, and pour over them a quarter of a pint of vinegar, in which they must steep for twenty-four hours. Pour the fruit and vinegar into the syrup, taking care not to bruise the fruit; then give it one boil, strain it, and cork it up close in bottles. The fruit must be carefully picked and cleaned, observing not to use any that is in the least decayed. To the syrup of currants a few raspberries may be added, to heighten the flavour. An earthen pipkin is the best to boil in.

Raspberry Vinegar. No. 3.

Fill a jug with raspberries; add as much of the best vinegar as the jug will hold; let the fruit steep ten or twelve days; then strain the liquor through a fine sieve, without squeezing the raspberries; put three pounds of lump sugar to a quart of juice, and skim it.

Walnuts, black. No. 1.

Take large full grown walnuts before they are hard; lay them in salt and water for two days: then shift them into fresh water, and let them lie two days longer; change them again, and let them lie two days longer; take them out, and put them in your pickle pot; when the pot is half full, put in some shalots, and a head of garlic. To a hundred of walnuts add half an ounce of allspice, half an ounce of black pepper, six bay-leaves, and a stick of horseradish. Then fill your pots, and pour boiling vinegar over them; cover them with a plate, and when cold tie them down.

Before you put the nuts into salt and water, prick them well with a pin.

Walnuts. No. 2.

About midsummer take your walnuts, run a knitting-needle through them, and lay them in vinegar and salt, sufficiently strong to bear an egg. Let them remain in this pickle for three weeks; then make some fresh pickle; shift them into it, and let them lie three weeks longer; take them out, and wipe them with a clean cloth; and tie up every nut in a clean vine-leaf. Put them into fresh vinegar, seasoned with salt, mace, mustard, garlic, and horseradish; and to a hundred nuts put one ounce of ginger, one ounce of pepper, and of cloves and mace a quarter of an ounce each, two small nutmegs, and half a pint of mustard seed. All the pickles to be done in raw vinegar (that is, not boiled). It is always recommended to have the largest double nuts, being the best to pickle.

Walnuts. No. 3.

Take the large French nuts, wipe them clean, and wrap each in a vine-leaf; put them into a weak brine of salt and water for a fortnight, changing it every day, and lay a slate upon them, to keep them always under, or they will turn black. Drain them, and make a stronger brine, that will bear an egg; let them lie in that a fortnight longer; then drain and wipe them very dry, and wrap them in fresh vine-leaves; put them in jars, and pour on them double-distilled vinegar, which must not be boiled. To six or eight hundred nuts put two pounds of shalots, one of garlic, and one of rocambole; a piece of assaf[oe]tida, of the size of a pea, tied up in a bit of muslin, and put into each jar, of white, black, and long pepper, one pound each, half a pound of mace, a quarter of a pound of nutmegs, two ounces of cinnamon, two ounces of cloves, two pounds of allspice, one pound of ginger, two pounds of mustard-seed, some bay-leaves, and horseradish. The mustard-seed and spice must be a little bruised. Mix all these ingredients together, and put in a layer of nuts and then a layer of this mixture; put the assaf[oe]tida in the middle; and as the pickle wastes take care to keep the jar filled up with vinegar.

Walnuts. No. 4.

Take a hundred walnuts, at the beginning of July, before they are shelled; just scald them, that the skin may rub off, then put them into salt and water, for nine or ten days; shift them every day, and keep them covered from the air: dry them; make your pickle of two quarts of white wine vinegar, long pepper, black pepper, and ginger, of each half an ounce; beat the spice; add a large spoonful of mustard-seed; strew this between every layer of nuts. Pour liquor, boiling hot, upon them, three or four times, or more, if required. Be sure to keep them tied down close.

Walnuts. No. 5.

Put into a stone jar one hundred large double nuts. Take one ounce of Jamaica and four ounces of black pepper, two of ginger, one of cloves, and a pint of mustard-seed; bruise these, and boil them, with a head or two of garlic and four handfuls of salt, in a sufficient quantity of vinegar to cover the nuts. When cold, put it to them, and let them stand two days. Then boil up the pickle, pour it over the nuts, and tie them down close. Repeat this process for three days.

Walnuts, green.

Wipe and wrap them one by one in a vine-leaf: boil crab verjuice, and pour it boiling hot over the walnuts, tying them down close for fourteen days; then take them out of the leaves and liquor, wrap them in fresh leaves, and put them in your pots. Over every layer of walnuts, strew pepper, mace, cloves, a little ginger, mustard seed, and garlic. Make the pickle of the best white wine vinegar, boiling in the pickle the same sort of spices, with the addition of horseradish, and pour it boiling hot upon the walnuts. Tie them close down; they will be ready to eat in a month, and will keep for three or four years.

Walnut Ketchup.

To three pints of the best white wine vinegar put nine Seville oranges peeled, and let them remain four months. Pound or bruise two hundred walnuts, just before they are fit for pickling; squeeze out two quarts of juice, and put it to the vinegar. Tie a quarter of a pound of mace, the same of cloves, and a quarter of a pound of shalot, in a muslin rag or bag; put this into the liquor; in about three weeks boil it gently till reduced one half, and when quite cold bottle it.

Another.

Cut in slices about one hundred of the largest walnuts for pickling; cut through the middle a quarter of a pound of shalots, and beat them fine in a mortar, adding a pint and a half of the best vinegar and half a pound of salt. Let them remain a week in an earthen vessel, stirring them every day. Press them through a flannel bag; add a quarter of a pound of anchovies; boil up the liquor, scum it, and run it through a flannel bag. Put into it two sliced nutmegs, whole pepper, and mace, and bottle it when cold.

WINES, CORDIALS, LIQUEURS, &C.

Ale, to drink in a week.

Tun it into a vessel which will hold eight gallons, and, when it has done working and is ready to bottle, put in some ginger sliced, an orange stuck full of cloves, and cut here and there with a knife, and a pound and a half of sugar. With a stick stir it well together, and it will work afresh. When it has done working, bottle it: cork the bottles well; set them bottom upwards; and the ale will be fit to drink in a week.

Very rare Ale.

When your ale is tunned into a vessel that will hold eight or nine gallons, and has done working, and is ready to be stopped up, take a pound and a half of raisins of the best quality, stoned and cut into pieces, and two large oranges. Pulp and pare them. Slice it thin; add the rind of one lemon, a dozen cloves, and one ounce of coriander seeds bruised: put all these in a bag, hang them in the vessel, and stop it up close. Fill the bottles but a little above the neck, to leave room for the liquor to play; and put into every one a large lump of fine sugar. Stop the bottles close, and let the ale stand a month before you drink it.

Orange Ale.

Boil twenty gallons of spring water for a quarter of an hour; when cool, put it into a tub over a bushel of malt, and let it stand one hour. Pour it from the malt, put to it a handful of wheat bran, boil it very fast for another hour; then strain and put it into a clean tub. When cold, pour it off clear from the sediment; put yest to it, and let it work like all other ales. When it has worked enough, put it into the cask. Then take the rind and juice of twenty Seville oranges, but no seeds; cut them thin and small, put them into a mortar, and beat them as fine as possible, with two pounds of fine lump sugar; put them into a ten-gallon cask, with ten gallons of ale. Keep filling up your cask again with ale, till it has done working; then stop it up close. When it has stood eight days, tap it for drink; if you bottle it, let it stand till it is clear before you bottle it, otherwise the bottles may burst.

Aqua Mirabilis, a very fine Cordial.

Three pints of sack, three pints of Madeira, one quart of spirit of wine, one quart of juice of celandine leaves, of melilot flowers, cardamom seeds, cubebs, galingale, nutmeg, cloves, mace, ginger, two drachms of each; bruise them thoroughly in a mortar, and mix them with the wine and spirits. Let it stand all night in the still, closely stopped with rye paste; next morning make a slow fire in the still, and while it is distilling keep a wet cloth about the neck of the still. Put so much white sugar-candy as you think fit into the glass where it drops.

Bitters.

One drachm of cardamom seed, two scruples of saffron, three ounces of green root, two scruples of cochineal, and four ounces of orange-peel. Put these ingredients into a large bottle, and fill it with the very best French brandy, so that they are well covered; after it has stood for three days, take out the liquor, and put it into another large bottle; fill up the first before, and let it stand four or five days; then once more take out the liquor and fill up again, letting it stand ten or twelve days. Then take it out again, put it all together, and it will be fit for use.

Another way.

Ginger and cardamom seed, of each three pennyworth, saffron, orange-peel, and cochineal, of each two pennyworth, put into one gallon of brandy.

Cherry Brandy.

Four pounds of morella cherries, two quarts of brandy, and twelve cloves, to be sweetened with syrup of ginger made in the following manner: one ounce and a half of ginger boiled in a quart of water, till reduced to half a pint; then dissolve in it one pound and a half of sugar, and add it to the brandy. It will be fit for use by Christmas.

After the cordial is made, you can make a most delightful sweetmeat with the cherries, by dipping them into syrup, and drying them in a cool oven.

Cordial Cherry Water.

Nine pounds of the best red cherries, nine pints of claret, eight ounces of cinnamon, three ounces of nutmegs; bruise your spice, stone your cherries, and steep them in the wine; then add to them half a handful of rosemary, half a handful of balm, and one quarter of a handful of sweet marjoram. Let them steep in an earthen pot twenty-four hours, and, as you put them into the alembic to distil them, bruise them with your hands; make a gentle fire under them, and distil by slow degrees. You may mix the waters at your pleasure when you have drawn them all. Sweeten it with loaf sugar; then strain it into another glass vessel, and stop it close that the spirits may not escape.

A very fine Cordial.

One ounce of syrup of gilliflowers, one dram of confection of alkermes, one ounce and a half of borage water, the like of mint water, as much of cinnamon water, well mixed together, bottled and corked. In nine days it will be ready for drinking.

Cup.

Take the juice of three lemons and the peel of one, cut very thin; add a pint, or rather more, of water, and about half a pound of white sugar, and stir the whole well; then add one bottle of sherry, two bottles of cyder, and about a quarter of a nutmeg grated down. Let the cup be well mixed up, and add a few heads of borage, or balm if you have no borage; put in one wine glass of brandy, and then add about another quarter of a nutmeg. Let it stand for about half an hour in ice before it is used.

If you take champagne instead of cyder, so much the better.

Elder-flower Water.

To every gallon of water take four pounds of loaf sugar, boiled and clarified with eggs, according to the quantity, and thrown hot upon the elder-flowers, allowing a quart of flowers to each gallon. They must be gathered when the weather is quite dry, and when they are so ripe as to shake off without any of the green part. When nearly cold, add yest in proportion to the quantity of liquor; strain it in two or three days from the flowers, and put it into a cask, with two or three table-spoonfuls of lemon-juice to every two gallons. Add, if you please, a small quantity of brandy, and, in ten months, bottle it.

Elderberry Syrup.

Pick the elderberries when full ripe; put them into a stone jar, and set them in the oven, or in a kettle of boiling water, till the jar is hot through. Take them out, and strain them through a coarse cloth, wringing the berries. Put them into a clean kettle, with a pound of fine Lisbon sugar to every quart of juice. Let it boil, and skim it well. When clear and fine, put it into a jar. When cold, cover it down close, and, when you make raisin wine, put to every gallon of wine half a pint of elder syrup.

Ginger Beer. No. 1.

Boil six gallons of water and six pounds of loaf sugar for an hour, with three ounces of ginger, bruised, and the juice and rind of two lemons. When almost cold, put in a toast spread with yest; let it ferment three days; then put it in a cask, with half a pint of brandy. When it has stood ten days, bottle it off, and it will be fit to drink in a fortnight, if warm weather.

Ginger Beer. No. 2.

Four ounces of ground ginger, two ounces of cream of tartar, three large lemons, cut in slices and bruised, three pounds of loaf sugar. Pour over them four gallons of boiling water; let it stand till it is milk warm; then add two table-spoonfuls of yest on a toast; let it stand twenty-four hours, strain it through a sieve, bottle it, and it will be fit for use in three days: the corks must be tied or wired, or they will fly.

Ginger Beer. No. 3.

To make ginger beer fit for drinking twenty-four hours after it is bottled, take two ounces of ground ginger, two ounces of cream of tartar, two lemons sliced, one pound and a half of lump sugar; put them into a pan, and pour upon them two gallons of boiling water. When nearly cold, strain it from the lees, add three table-spoonfuls of yest, and let it stand twelve hours. Bottle it in stone bottles, well corked and tied down.

Ginger Beer. No. 4.

Ten gallons of water, twelve pounds of loaf sugar, the whites of four eggs, well beaten; mix them together when cold, and set them on the fire: skim it as it boils. Add half a pound of bruised ginger, and boil the whole together for twenty minutes. Into a pint of the boiling liquor put an ounce of isinglass; when cold, add it to the rest, and put the whole, with two spoonfuls of yest, into a cask: next day, bung it down loosely. In ten days bottle it, and in a week it will be fit for use.

Ginger Beer. No. 5.

One gallon of cold water, one pound of lump sugar, two ounces of bruised ginger, the rind of two large lemons; let these simmer ten minutes. Put in an ounce of cream of tartar the moment it boils, and immediately take it off the fire, stirring it well, and let it stand till cold. Afterwards add the lemon-juice, straining out the pips and pulp, and put it into bottles, tying down the corks fast with string. This will be fit for use in three days.

Imperial. No. 1.

The juice of two large lemons, rather more than an equal quantity of white wine, and an immoderate proportion of sugar, put into a deep round dish. Boil some cream or good milk, and put it into a tea-pot; pour it upon the wine, and the higher you hold the pot the better appearance your imperial will have.

Imperial. No. 2.

Four or five quarts of boiling water poured to two ounces of cream of tartar, and the rinds of two lemons cut very thin, with half a pound of sugar. Well mix the whole together: and, when cold, add the juice of the two lemons.

Imperial. No. 3.

Two ounces of cream of tartar, four ounces of sugar, six quarts of boiling water, poured upon it, the juice and peel of a lemon; to be kept close till cold.

Lemonade. No. 1.

To two quarts of water take one dozen lemons; pare four or six of them very thin, add the juice to the water, and sweeten to your taste with double-refined sugar. Boil a quart of milk and put into it; cover and let it stand all night, and strain it through a jelly-bag till it runs clear. Leave the lemon-pips to go into the bag with the other ingredients.

Lemonade. No. 2.

The peel of five lemons and two Seville oranges pared very thin, so that none of the white is left with it; put them in a basin, with eight ounces of sugar and a quart of boiling water. Let it stand all night, and in the morning squeeze the juice to the peels, and pick out the seeds; then put to it a quarter of a pint of white wine; stir all well together; add half a pint of boiling milk, and pour it on, holding it up high. Let it stand half an hour without touching it; then run it through a jelly-bag.

Lemonade. No. 3.

Three quarts of spring water, the juice of seven lemons peeled very thin, the whites of four eggs well beaten, with as much loaf-sugar as you please: boil all together about half an hour with half the lemon-peel. Pour it through a jelly-bag till clear. The peel of one Seville orange gives it an agreeable colour.

Clarified Lemonade.

Pare the rind of three lemons as thin as you can; put them into a jug, with the juice of six lemons, half a pound of sugar, half a pint of rich white wine, and a quart of boiling water. Let it stand all night. In the morning, add half a pint of boiling milk: then run it through a jelly-bag till quite clear.

Milk Lemonade.

Squeeze the juice of six lemons and two Seville oranges into a pan, and pour over it a quart of boiling milk. Put into another pan the peel of two lemons and one Seville orange, with a pound of sugar; add a pint of boiling water; let it stand a sufficient time to dissolve the sugar; then mix it with the milk, and strain it through a fine jelly-bag. It should be made one day and strained off the next.

Transparent Lemonade.

Take one pound and a half of pounded sugar of the finest quality, and the juice of six lemons and six oranges, over which pour two quarts of boiling water; let it stand twelve hours till cool. Pour on the liquor a quart of boiling milk, and let it stand till it curdles; then run it through a cotton jelly-bag till it is quite clear.

Lemon Water.

Take twelve of the largest lemons; slice and put them into a quart of white wine. Add of cinnamon and galingale, one quarter of an ounce each, of red rose-leaves, borage and bugloss flowers, one handful each, and of yellow sanders one dram. Steep all these together twelve hours; then distil them gently in a glass still. Put into the glass vessel in which it drops three ounces of fine white sugar and one grain of ambergris.

Mead. No. 1.

In six gallons of water dissolve fourteen pounds of honey; then add three or four eggs, with the whites; set it upon the fire, and let it boil half an hour. Put into it balm, sweet marjoram, and sweet briar, of each ten sprigs, half an ounce of cinnamon, the same of mace, twenty cloves, and half a race of ginger sliced very thin: let it boil a quarter of an hour; then take it off the fire, pour it into a tub, and let it remain till nearly cold. Take six ounces of syrup of citron, and one spoonful of ale yest; beat them well together, put it into the liquor, and let it stand till cold. Take a sufficient quantity of coarse bread to cover the barrel, and bake it very hard; then take as much ale yest as will spread it over thin, put it into the liquor, and let it stand till it comes to a head. Strain it out; put the liquor into a cask, and add to it a quart of the best Rhenish wine. When it has done working, stop it up close, and let it stand a month; then draw it out into bottles; tie the corks down close; and let them stand a month.

Mead. No. 2.

Ten quarts of honey boiled one hour with thirty quarts of water; when cold, put it into a cask, and add to it one ounce of cinnamon, one of cloves, two of ginger, and two large nutmegs, to be pounded first, and suspended in a linen bag in the barrel from the bung-hole. The scum must be filtered through a flannel bag.

Mead. No. 3.

Take eight gallons of spring water, twelve pounds of honey, four pounds of powdered sugar; boil them for an hour, keeping it well skimmed. Let it stand all night; the next day, put it into your vessel, keeping back the sediment; hang in your vessel two or three lemon-peels; then stop it up close; in the summer, bottle it in six weeks.

Mithridate Brandy.

Take four gallons of brandy; infuse a bushel of poppies twenty-four hours; then strain it, and put two ounces of nutmegs, the same of liquorice, and of pepper and ginger, and one ounce each of cinnamon, aniseed, juniper-berries, cloves, fennel-seed, and cardamom seed, two drachms of saffron, two pounds of figs sliced, and one pound of the sun raisins stoned. All these must be put into an earthen pot, and set in the sun three weeks; then strain it, and mix with it two ounces of Venice treacle, two ounces of mithridate, and four pounds of sugar. This is an approved remedy for the gout in the stomach.

Nonpareil.

Pare six lemons very thin, put the rinds and juice into two quarts of brandy; let it remain well corked four days. Set on the fire three quarts of spring water and two pounds of sugar, and clarify it with two whites of eggs; let it boil a quarter of an hour; take the scum off, and let it stand till cold. Put it to your brandy; add two quarts of white wine, and strain it through a flannel bag; fill the cask, and it will clarify itself. You may bottle it in a week. Orange-peel greatly improves this liquor.

Noyau.

To one gallon of the best white French brandy, or spirit diluted to the strength of brandy, put two pounds and a half of bitter almonds blanched, two pounds of white sugar-candy, half an ounce of mace, and two large nutmegs. To give it a red colour, add four pounds of black cherries. It must be well shaken every day for a fortnight; then let it stand for six weeks, and bottle it off: it improves much by longer keeping.

Orange Juice.

One pound of fine sugar to a pint of juice; run it through a jelly-bag, and boil it for a quarter of an hour; when cold, skim and bottle it.

Spirit of Oranges or Lemons.

Take the thickest rinded oranges or lemons; pare off the rinds very thin; put into a glass bottle as many of these chips as it will hold, and then as much Malaga sack as it will hold besides. Stop the bottle down close, and, when you use it, take about half a spoonful in a glass of sack. It is a fine spirit to mix in sauces for puddings or other sweet dishes.

Cordial Orange Water.

Take one dozen and a half of the highest coloured and thick-rinded oranges; slice them, and put them into two pints of Malaga sack, and one pint of the best brandy. Take cinnamon, nutmegs, ginger, cloves, and mace, of each one quarter of an ounce bruised, and of spearmint and balm one handful of each; put them into an ordinary still all night, pasted up with rye paste. The next day, draw them with a slow fire, and keep a wet cloth upon the neck of the still; put the loaf sugar into the glass in which it drops.

Orgeat.

Two quarts of new milk, one ounce of sweet almonds and eighteen bitter, a large piece of cinnamon, and fine sugar to your taste. Boil these a quarter of an hour, and then strain. The almonds must be blanched, and then pounded fine with orange-flower water.

Another way.

Four ounces of sweet almonds finely pounded, two ounces of white sugar-candy, dissolved in spring-water, and a quart of cream; mix all together. Put it into a bottle, and give it a gentle shake when going to be used.

Excellent Punch.

Three pints of barley-water and a piece of lemon-peel; let it stand till cold; then add the juice of six lemons and about half a pint of the best brandy, and sweeten it to your taste, and put it in ice for four hours. Put into it a little champagne or Madeira.

Milk Punch.

To twenty quarts of the best rum or brandy put the peels of thirty Seville oranges and thirty lemons, pared as thin as possible. Let them steep twelve hours. Strain the spirit from the rinds, and put to it thirty quarts of water, previously boiled and left to stand till cold. Take fifteen pounds of double-refined sugar, and boil it in a proper proportion of the water to a fine clear syrup. As soon as it boils up, have ready beat to a froth the whites of six or eight eggs, and the shells crumbled fine; mix them with the syrup; let them boil together, and, when a cap of scum rises to the top, take off the pot, and skim it perfectly clear. Then put it on again with some more of the beaten egg, and skim it again as before. Do the same with the remainder of the egg until it is quite free from dirt; let it stand to be cool. Strain it to the juice of the oranges and lemons; put it into a cask with the spirit; add a quart of new milk, made lukewarm; stir the whole well together, and bung up the cask. Let it stand till very fine, which will be in about a month or six weeks—but it is better to stand for six months—then bottle it. The cask should hold fifteen gallons. This punch will keep for many years.

Many persons think this punch made with brandy much finer than that with rum. The best time for making it is in March, when the fruit is in the highest perfection.

Another way.

Take six quarts of good brandy, eight quarts of water, two pounds and a half of lump sugar, eighteen lemons, and one large wine-glassful of ratafia. Mix these well together; then throw in two quarts of boiling skimmed milk; stir it well, and let it stand half an hour; strain it through a very thick flannel bag till quite fine; then bottle it for use. Before you use this punch, soak for a night the rinds of eighteen lemons in some of the spirit; then take it out, and boil it in the milk, together with two large nutmegs sliced.

Norfolk Punch.

Take four gallons of the best rum; pare a dozen lemons and a dozen oranges very thin; let the pulp of both steep in the rum twenty-four hours. Put twelve pounds of double-refined sugar into six gallons of water, with the whites of a dozen eggs beat to a froth; boil and scum it well; when cold, put it into the vessel with the rum, together with six quarts of orange-juice, and that of the dozen of lemons, and two quarts of new milk. Shake the vessel so as to mix it; stop it up very close, and let it stand two months before you bottle it.

This quantity makes twelve gallons of the Duke of Norfolk's punch. It is best made in March, as the fruit is then in the greatest perfection.

Roman Punch.

The juice of ten lemons, and of two sweet oranges, the peel of an orange cut very thin, and two pounds of powdered loaf-sugar, mixed together. Then take the white of ten eggs, beaten into froth. Pass the first mixture through a sieve, and then mix it by degrees, always beating with the froth of the eggs; put the whole into an ice-lead; let it freeze a little; then add to it two bottles of champagne, or rum. Turn it round with a ladle. The above is for twelve persons.

Raspberry Liqueur.

Bruise some raspberries with the back of a spoon, strain them, and fill a bottle with the juice; stop it, but not very close. Add to a pound of fruit nearly a pound of sugar dissolved into a syrup. Let it stand four or five days; pour it from the fruit into a basin; add to it as much rich white wine as you think fit; bottle it, and in a month it will be fit to drink.

Raspberry Vinegar.

Fill a jar with raspberries, gathered dry, and pour over them as much of the best white wine vinegar as will cover them. Let them remain for two or three days, stirring them frequently, to break them; strain the liquor through a sieve, and to every pint of it put a pound and a quarter of double-refined sugar; boil it, and take off the scum as it rises. When cool, bottle and cork it up for use. A spoonful of this liquor is sufficient for a small tumbler of water.

Ratafia Brandy.

Apricot or peach kernels, with four ounces of fine sugar to a quart of brandy. If you cannot get apricot kernels, two ounces of bitter almonds, bruised a little, to the same quantity of spirit, will make good ratafia.

Shrub. No. 1.

To a gallon of rum put three pints of orange-juice and one pound of sugar, dissolving the sugar in the juice. Then put all together in the cask. It will be fine and fit for use in a few weeks. If the rum be very strong, you may add another pint of juice and half a pound of sugar to the above.

Shrub. No. 2.

Take two quarts of the juice of oranges and lemons, and dissolve in it four pounds and a half of sugar. Steep one-fourth part of the oranges and lemons in nine quarts of spirits for one night; after which mix the whole together; strain it off into a jug, which must be shaken two or three times a day for ten days; then let it stand to settle for a fortnight; after which draw it off very carefully, without disturbing the sediment.

Shrub. No. 3.

One gallon of rum, one pound and two ounces of double-refined sugar, one quart of orange-juice, mixed and strained through a sieve.

Currant Shrub.

Pick the currants from the stalks; bruise them in a marble mortar; run the juice through a flannel bag. Then take two quarts of the clear juice; dissolve in it one pound of double-refined sugar, and add one gallon of rum. Filter it through a flannel bag till quite fine.

Spruce Beer.

For one quarter cask of thirty gallons take ten or twelve ounces of essence of spruce and two gallons of the best molasses; mix them well together in five or six gallons of warm water, till it leaves a froth; then pour it into the cask, and fill it up with more water. Add one pint of good yest or porter grounds; shake the cask well, and set it by for twenty-four hours to work. Stop it down close. Next day, draw it off into bottles, which should be closely corked and set by in a cool cellar for ten days, when it will be as fine spruce-beer as ever was drunk. The grounds will serve instead of yest for a second brewing.

In a hot climate, cold water should be used instead of warm.

Bittany Wine.

Take six gallons of water and twelve pounds of sugar; put your sugar and water together. Let it boil two hours; then, after taking it off the fire, put in half a peck of sage, a peck and a half of bittany, and a small bunch of rosemary; cover, and let it remain till almost cold; then put six spoonfuls of ale yest; stir it well together, and let it stand two or three days, stirring two or three times each day. Then put it in your cask, adding a quarter of a pint of lemon-juice; when it has done working, bung it close, and, when fine, bottle it.

Sham Champagne.

To every pound of ripe green gooseberries, when picked and bruised, put one quart of water; let it stand three days, stirring it twice every day. To every gallon of juice, when strained, put three pounds of the finest loaf sugar; put it into a barrel, and, to every twenty quarts of liquor add one quart of brandy and a little isinglass. Let it stand half a year; then bottle it. The brandy and isinglass must be put in six weeks before it is bottled.

Cherry Wine.

Pound morella cherries with the kernels over-night, and set them in a cool place. Squeeze them through canvas, and to each quart of juice put one pound of powdered sugar, half an ounce of coarsely-pounded cinnamon, and half a quarter of an ounce of cloves. Let it stand about a fortnight in the sun, shaking it twice or three times every day.

Another way.

Take twenty-four pounds of cherries, cleared from the stalks, and mash them in an earthen pan; then put the pulp into a flannel bag, and let them remain till the whole of the juice has drained from the pulp. Put a pound of loaf sugar into the pan which receives the juice, and let it remain until the sugar is dissolved. Bottle it, and, when it has done working, you may put into each bottle a small lump of sugar.

Cowslip Wine. No. 1.

To twenty gallons of water, wine measure, put fifty pounds of lump sugar; boil it, and skim it till it is very clear; then put it into a tub to cool, and, when just warm, put to it two tea-spoonfuls of ale yest. Let it work for a short time; then put in fifteen pecks of cut cowslips, and the juice of twenty large lemons, likewise the outward rinds pared off as thin as possible. Keep it in the tub two or three days, stirring it twice each day. Then put it all together in a barrel, cleansed and dried. Continue to stir twice a day for a week or more, till it has done working; then stop it up close for three months, and bottle it off for use.

The cowslips should be gathered in one day, and the wine made as soon as possible after, as the fresh flowers make the wine of a finer colour than when they are withered; but they will not hurt by being kept for a few days if they are spread on a cloth, and moved every day.

Cowslip Wine. No. 2.

To a gallon of water put three pounds of lump sugar; boil them together for an hour, skimming all the while. Pour it upon the cowslips, and, when milk warm, put into it a toast, with yest spread pretty thick upon it; let it stand all night, and then add two lemons and two Seville oranges to each gallon. Stir it well in a tub twice a day for two or three days; then turn it; stir it every day for a fortnight, and bung it up close. It will be fit for bottling in six weeks. To every gallon of water you must take a gallon of cowslips. They must be perfectly dry before they are used, and there should be as many gallons of cowslips as gallons of water; they should be measured as they are picked, and turned into the cask. Dissolve an ounce of isinglass, and put to it when cold. The lemons must be peeled.

Cowslip Wine. No. 3.

Take fourteen gallons of water and twenty-four pounds of sugar; boil the water and sugar one hour; skim it till it is clear. Let it stand till nearly cold; then pour it on three bushels of picked cowslips, and put to it three or four spoonfuls of new yest; let it stand and work in your vessel till the next day; then put in the juice of thirty lemons and the peels of ten, pared thin. Stir them well together; bung up the vessel close for a month; then bottle it.

Currant Wine. No. 1.

Gather the currants dry, without picking them from the stalks; break them with your hands, and strain them. To every quart of juice put two quarts of cold water, and four pounds of loaf sugar to the gallon. It must stand three days, before it is put into the vessel. Stir it every day, and skim it as long as any thing rises. To ten gallons of wine add one gallon of brandy, and one of raspberries, when you put it in the vessel. Let it stand a day or two before you stop it; give it air fourteen days after; and let it stand six weeks before you tap it.

Currant Wine. No. 2.

To every gallon of ripe currants put a gallon of cold water. When well broken with the hands, let it stand twenty-four hours. Then squeeze the currants well out; measure your juice, and to every gallon put four pounds of lump sugar. When the sugar is well melted, put the wine into a cask, stirring it every day, till it has done hissing; then put into it a quart of brandy to every five gallons of wine; close it well up; bottle it in three months.

Currant Wine. No. 3.

Put into a tub a bushel of red currants and a peck of white; squeeze them well, and let them drain through a sieve upon twenty-eight pounds of powdered sugar. When quite dissolved, put into the barrel, and add three pints of raspberries, and a little brandy.

Currant or Elder Wine.

After pressing the fruit with the hand or otherwise, to every gallon of juice add two gallons of water that has been boiled and stood to be cold. To each gallon of this mixture put five pounds of Lisbon sugar. It may be fermented by putting into it a small piece of toasted bread rubbed over with good yest. When put into the cask, it should be left open till the fermentation has nearly subsided.

Black Currant Wine.

Ten pounds of fruit to a gallon of water; let it stand two or three days. When pressed off, put to every gallon of liquor four pounds and a half of sugar.

Red Currant Wine.

Gather the fruit dry; pick the leaves from it, and to every twenty-five pounds of currants put six quarts of water. Break the currants well, before the water is put to them; then let them stand twenty-four hours, and strain the liquor, to every quart of which put a pound of sugar and as many raspberries as you please.

Another way.

Take twenty-four pounds of currants; bruise them, and add to that quantity three gallons of water. Let it stand two days, stirring it twice a day; then strain the liquor from the fruit; and to every quart of liquor put one pound of sugar. Let it stand three days, stirring it twice a day; then put it in your barrel, and put into it six-pennyworth of orris-root well bruised. The above quantities will make five gallons.

Red or White Currant Wine.

Take to every gallon of juice one gallon of water, to every gallon of water three pounds and a half of the best Lisbon sugar. Squeeze the currants through a sieve; let the juice stand till the sugar is dissolved; dip a bit of brown paper in brimstone, and burn in the cask. Then tun the wine, and to every three gallons put a pint of brandy. When it has done hissing, stop it close; it will be fit to drink in six months, but it will be better for keeping ten or twelve.

White Currant Wine.

To each sieve of currants take twenty-five pounds of moist sugar, and to every gallon of juice two gallons of water. Squeeze the fruit well with the hands into an earthen pan; then strain it through a sieve. Throw the pulp into another pan, filling it with water, which must be taken from the quantity of water allowed for the whole, and to every ten gallons of wine put one bottle of brandy. In making the wine, dissolve the sugar in the water above-mentioned, and put it into the cask; then add the remaining juice and water, stirring it well up frequently. Stir it well every morning for ten successive days, and as it works out fill up the cask again until it has done fermenting. Then put in your brandy, and bung it quite close. In about eight months it will be fit to drink; but, if you leave it twelve, it will be better.

Damson Wine.

Take four gallons of water, and put to every gallon four pounds of Malaga raisins and half a peck of damsons. Put the whole into a vessel without cover, having only a linen cloth laid over it. Let them steep six days, stirring twice every day; then let them stand six days without stirring. Draw the juice out of the vessel, and colour it with the infused juice of damsons, sweetened with sugar till it is like claret wine. Put it into a wine vessel for a fortnight; then bottle it up; and it may be drunk in a month.

All made wines are the better for brandy, and will not keep without it. The quantity must be regulated by the degree of strength you wish to give to your wine.

Elder Wine. No. 1.

Take elderberries, when ripe; pick them clean from the stalk; press out the juice through a hair sieve or canvas-bag, and to every gallon of juice put three gallons of water on the husks from which the juice has been pressed. Stir the husks well in the water, and press them over again; then mix the first and second liquor together, and boil it for about an hour, skimming it clean as long as the scum rises. To every gallon of liquor put two pounds of sugar, and skim it again very clean; then put to every gallon a blade of mace and as much lemon-peel, letting it boil an hour. After the sugar is put in, strain it into a tub, and, when quite cold, put it into a cask; bung it close down, and look frequently to see that the bung is not forced up. Should your quantity be twelve gallons or more, you need not bottle it off till about April, but be sure to do so on a clear dry day, and to let your bottles be perfectly dry; but if you have not more than five or six gallons, you may bottle it by Christmas on a clear fine day.

Elder Wine. No. 2.

To a gallon of water put a quarter of a peck of berries, and three pounds and a half of Lisbon sugar. Steep the berries in water forty hours; after boiling a quarter of an hour, strain the liquor from the fruit, and boil it with the sugar till the scum ceases to rise. Work it in a tub like other wines, with a small quantity of yest. After some weeks, add a few raisins, a small quantity of brandy, and some cloves. The above makes a sweet mellow wine, but does not taste strong of the elder.

Elder Wine. No. 3.

Take twenty-four pounds of raisins, of whatever sort you please; pick them clean, chop them small, put them into a tub, and cover them with three gallons of water that has been boiled and become cold. Let it stand ten days, stirring it twice a day. Then strain the liquor through a hair sieve, draining it all from the raisins, and put to it three pints of the juice of elderberries and a pound of loaf-sugar. Put the whole into the cask, and let it stand close stopped, but not in too cold a cellar, for three or four months before you bottle it. The peg-hole must not be stopped till it has done working.

The best way to draw the juice from the berries is to strip them into an earthen pan, and set it in the oven all night.

Elder Wine. No. 4.

Mash eight gallons of picked elderberries to pieces, add as much spring water as will make the whole nine gallons, and boil slowly for three quarters of an hour. Squeeze them through a cloth sieve; add twenty-eight pounds of moist sugar, and boil them together for half an hour. Run the liquor through your cloth sieve again; let it stand till lukewarm; put into it a toast with a little yest upon it, and let it stand for seven or eight days, stirring it every day. Then put it into a close tub, and let it remain without a bung till it has done hissing. Before you bung up close, you may add one pint of brandy at pleasure.

Elder Wine. No. 5.

Half a gallon of ripe berries to a gallon of water; boil it half an hour; strain it through a sieve. To every gallon of liquor put three pounds of sugar; boil them together three quarters of an hour; when cold, put some yest to it; work it a week, and put it in barrel. Let it stand a year. To half a hogshead put one quart of brandy and three pounds of raisins.

Elder-flower Wine.

To six gallons of water put eighteen pounds of lump-sugar; boil it half an hour, skimming it all the time. Put into a cask a quarter of a peck of elder-flowers picked clean from the stalks, the juice and rinds of six lemons pared very thin, and six pounds of raisins. When the water and sugar is about milk warm, pour it into the cask upon these ingredients; spread three or four spoonfuls of yest upon a piece of bread well toasted, and put it into the cask; stir it up for three or four days only; when it has done working, bung it up, and in six or eight months it will be fit for bottling.

Sham Frontiniac.

To three gallons of water put nine pounds of good loaf-sugar; boil it half an hour; when milk-warm, add to it nearly a peck of elder-flowers picked clear from the stalks, the juice and peel of three good-sized lemons, cut very thin, three pounds of stoned raisins, and two or three spoonfuls of yest; stir it often for four or five days. When it has quite done working, bung it up, and it will be fit for bottling in five days.

Mixed Fruit Wine.

Take currants, gooseberries, raspberries, and a few rose-leaves, three pints of fruit, mashed all together, to a quart of cold water. Let it stand twenty-four hours; then drain it through a sieve. To every gallon of juice put three pounds and a half of Lisbon sugar; let it ferment; put it into a cask, but do not bung it up for some time. Put in some brandy, and bottle it for use.

Ginger Wine. No. 1.

With four gallons of water boil twelve pounds of loaf-sugar till it becomes clear. In a separate pan boil nine ounces of ginger, a little bruised, in two quarts of water; pour the whole into an earthen vessel, in which you must have two pounds of raisins shred fine, the juice and rind of ten lemons. When of about the warmth of new milk, put in four spoonfuls of fresh yest; let it ferment two days; then put it into a cask, with all the ginger, lemon-peel, and raisins, and half an ounce of isinglass dissolved in a little of the wine; in two or three days bung it up close. In three months it will be fit to bottle. Put into each bottle a little brandy, and some sugar also, if not sweet enough.

Ginger Wine. No. 2.

Twenty-six quarts of water, eighteen pounds of white Lisbon sugar, six ounces of bruised ginger, the peel of six lemons pared very thin: boil half an hour, and let it stand till no more than blood warm. Put it in your cask, with the juice of six lemons, five spoonfuls of yest, and three pounds of raisins. Stir it six or seven times with a stick through the bung-hole, and put in half an ounce of isinglass and a pint of good brandy. Close the bung, and in about six weeks it will be fit for bottle. Let it stand about six months before you drink it. If you like, it may be drawn from the cask, and it will be fit for use in that way in about two months.

Ginger Wine. No. 3.

To ten gallons of water put eight pounds of loaf-sugar and three ounces of bruised ginger; boil all together for one hour, taking the scum off as it rises; then put it into a pan to cool. When it is cold, put it into a cask, with the rind and juice of ten lemons, one bottle of good brandy, and half a spoonful of yest. Bung it up for a fortnight: then bottle it off, and in three weeks it will be fit to drink. The lemons must be pared very thin, and no part of the white must, on any account, be put in the cask.

Ginger Wine. No. 4.

To every gallon of water put one pound and a half of brown sugar and one ounce of bruised ginger, and to each gallon the white of an egg well beaten. Stir all together, and boil it half an hour; skim it well while any thing rises, and, when milk-warm, stir in a little yest. When cold, to every five gallons, put two sliced lemons. Bottle it in nine days; and it will be fit to drink in a week.

Gooseberry Wine. No. 1.

To every pound of white amber gooseberries, when heads and tails are picked off and well bruised in a mortar, add a quart of spring water, which must be previously boiled. Let it stand till it is cold before it is put to the fruit. Let them steep three days, stirring them twice a day; strain and press them through a sieve into a barrel, and to every gallon of liquor put three pounds of loaf-sugar, and to every five gallons a bottle of brandy. Hang a small bag of isinglass in the barrel; bung it close, and, in six months, if the sweetness is sufficiently gone off, bottle it, and rosin the corks well over the top. The fruit must be fall grown, but quite green.

Gooseberry Wine. No. 2.

To three quarts of full grown gooseberries well crushed put one gallon of water well stirred together for a day or two. Then strain and squeeze the pulp, and put the liquor immediately into the barrel, with three pounds and a half of common loaf-sugar; stir it every day until the fermentation ceases. Reserve two or three gallons of the liquor to fill up the barrel, as it overflows through the fermentation. Put a bottle of brandy into the cask, to season it, before the wine; this quantity will be sufficient for nine or ten gallons. Be careful to let the fermentation cease, before you bung down the barrel.

The plain white gooseberries, taken when not too ripe, but rather the contrary, are the best for this purpose.

Gooseberry Wine. No. 3.

A pound of sugar to a pound of fruit: melt the sugar, and bruise the gooseberries with an apple-beater, but do not beat them too small. Strain them through a hair strainer, and put the juice into an earthen pot; keep it covered four or five days till it is clear: then add half a pint of the best brandy or more, according to the quantity of fruit, and draw it out into another vessel, letting it run into a hair sieve. Stop it close, and let it stand one fortnight longer; then draw it off into quart bottles, and in a month it will be fit for drinking.

Gooseberry Wine. No. 4.

Proceed as directed for white currant wine, but use loaf-sugar. Large pearl gooseberries, not quite ripe, make excellent champagne.

Grape Wine.

Pick and squeeze the grapes; strain them, and to each gallon of juice put two gallons of water. Put the pulp into the measured water; squeeze it, and add three pounds and a half of loaf-sugar, or good West India, to a gallon. Let it stand about six weeks; then add a quart of brandy and two eggs not broken to every ten gallons. Bung it down close.

Lemon Wine.

To every gallon of water put three pounds and a half of loaf-sugar; boil it half an hour, and to every ten gallons, when cold, put a pint of yest. Put it next day into a barrel, with the peels and juice of eight lemons; you must pare them very thin, and run the juice through a jelly-bag. Put the rinds into a net with a stone in it, or it will rise to the top and spoil the wine. To every ten gallons add a pint of brandy. Stop up the barrel, and in three months the wine, if fine, will be fit for bottling. The brandy must be put in when the wine is made.

Sham Madeira.

Take thirty pounds of coarse sugar to ten gallons of water; boil it half an hour; skim it clean, and, when cool, put to every gallon one quart of ale, out of the vat; let it work well in the tub a day or two. Then put it in the barrel, with one pound of sugar-candy, six pounds of raisins, one quart of brandy, and two ounces of isinglass. When it has done fermenting, bung it down close, and let it stand one year.

Orange Wine. No. 1.

Take six gallons of water to twelve pounds of lump-sugar; put four whites of eggs, well beaten, into the sugar and water cold; boil it three quarters of an hour, skim while boiling, and when cold put to it six spoonfuls of yest, and six ounces of syrup of citron, well beaten together, and the juice and rinds of fifty Seville oranges, but none of the white. Let all these stand two days and nights covered close; then add two quarts of Rhenish wine; bung it up close. Twelve days afterwards bottle and cork it well.

Orange Wine. No. 2.

To make ten gallons of wine, pare one hundred oranges very thin, and put the peel into a tub. Put in a copper ten gallons of water, with twenty-eight pounds of common brown sugar, and the whites of six eggs well beaten; boil it for three quarters of an hour; just as it begins to boil, skim it, and continue to do so all the time it is boiling; pour the boiling liquor on the peel: cover it well to keep in the steam, and, two hours afterwards, when blood warm, pour in the juice. Put in a toast well spread with yest to make it work. Stir it well, and, in five or six days, put it in your cask free from the peel; it will then work five or six days longer. Then put in two quarts of brandy, and bung it close. Let it remain twelve or eighteen months, and then bottle it. It will keep many years.

Orange Wine. No. 3.

To a gallon of wine put three pounds of lump sugar; clarify this with the white of an egg to every gallon. Boil it an hour, and when the scum rises take it off; when almost cold, dip a toast into yest, put it into the liquor, and let it stand all night.

Then take out the toast, and put in the juice of twelve oranges to every gallon, adding about half the peel. Run it through a sieve into the cask, and let it stand for several months.

Sham Port Wine.

Cover four bushels of blackberries with boiling hot water, squeeze them, and put them into a vessel to work. After working, draw or pour off the liquor into a cask; add a gallon of brandy and a quart of port wine; let it work again; then bung it up for six months, and bottle it.

Raisin Wine. No. 1.

Take one hundred weight of raisins, of the Smyrna sort, and put them into a tub with fourteen gallons of spring water. Let them stand covered for twenty-one days, stirring them twice every day. Strain the liquor through a hair-bag from the raisins, which must be well pressed to get out the juice; turn it into a vessel, and let it remain four months; then bung it up close, and make a vent-hole, which must be frequently opened, and left so for a day together. When it is of an agreeable sweetness, rack it off into a fresh cask, and put to it one gallon of British brandy, and, if you think it necessary, a little isinglass to fine it. Let it then stand one month, and it will be fit to bottle; but the longer it remains in the cask the better it will be.

Raisin Wine. No. 2.

Take four gallons of water, and boil it till reduced to three, four pounds of raisins of the sun, and four lemons sliced very thin; take off the peel of two of them; put the lemons and raisins into an earthen pot, with a pound of loaf-sugar. Pour in your water very hot; cover it close for a day and a night; strain it through a flannel bag; then bottle it, and tie down the corks. Set it in a cold place, and it will be ready to drink in a month.

Raisin Wine. No. 3.

To one hundred pound of raisins boil eighteen gallons of water, and let it stand till cold, with two ounces of hops. Half chop your raisins; then put your water to them, and stir it up together twice a day for a fortnight. Run it through a hair-sieve; squeeze the raisins well with your hands, and put the liquor into the barrel. Bung it up close; let it stand till it is clear; then bottle it.

Raisin Wine. No. 4.

Take a brandy cask, and to every gallon of water put five pounds of Smyrna raisins with the stalks on, and fill the cask, bunging it close down. Put it in a cool dry cellar; let it stand six months; then tap it with a strainer cock, and bottle it. Add half a pint of brandy to every gallon of wine.

THE END.

Lector House believes that a society develops through a two-fold approach of continuous learning and adaptation, which is derived from the study of classic literary works spread across the historic timeline of literature records. Therefore, we aim at reviving, repairing and redeveloping all those inaccessible or damaged but historically as well as culturally important literature across subjects so that the future generations may have an opportunity to study and learn from past works to embark upon a journey of creating a better future.

This book is a result of an effort made by Lector House towards making a contribution to the preservation and repair of original ancient works which might hold historical significance to the approach of continuous learning across subjects.

HAPPY READING & LEARNING!

LECTOR HOUSE LLP
E-MAIL: lectorpublishing@gmail.com